John

J. Ramsey Michaels

A Good News Commentary

John

Good News Commentaries

John

J. Ramsey Michaels

A GOOD NEWS COMMENTARY

New Testament Editor

W. Ward Gasque

1817

HARPER & ROW, PUBLISHERS, SAN FRANCISCO

Cambridge, Hagerstown, New York, Philadelphia
London, Mexico City, São Paulo, Sydney

To my students in "Gospel and Epistles of John," 1958–81.

John: A Good News Commentary. Copyright © 1984
by J. Ramsey Michaels. All rights reserved. Printed in
the United States of America. No part of this book may
be used or reproduced in any manner whatsoever
without written permission except in the case of brief
quotations embodied in critical articles and reviews.
For information address Harper & Row, Publishers,
Inc., 10 East 53rd Street, New York, NY 10022. Pub-
lished simultaneously in Canada by Fitzhenry &
Whiteside, Limited, Toronto.

FIRST EDITION

Designed by Design Office Bruce Kortebein

**Library of Congress Cataloging in Publication
Data**
Michaels, J. Ramsey
    JOHN.

    (A Good News Commentary)
    Bibliography: p.
    Includes index.
        1. Bible. N.T. John—Commentaries. I. Bible.
N.T. John. English. Today's English. 1983. II. Title.
III. Series.
BS2615.3.M48   1983   226′.5077   83-47729
ISBN 0-06-065575-5

84 85 86 87 88 10 9 8 7 6 5 4 3 2 1

About the Series

This is the first major series to use the popular Good News Bible, which has sold in the millions. Each volume is informed by solid scholarship and the most up-to-date research, yet each is biblically faithful and readily understandable to the general reader. Features include:

Introductory material highlighting authorship, dating, background information, and thematic emphases—plus a map

Full text of each Good News Bible book, with running commentary

Special end notes giving references for key words and concepts and providing suggestions for further reading

Full indexes for Scripture and Subjects/Persons/Places

Series Editor W. Ward Gasque is Vice-Principal and Professor of New Testament at Regent College in Vancouver. A former editor-at-large for *Christianity Today*, he is the author of numerous articles and books and has edited *In God's Community: Studies in the Church and Its Ministry, Handbook of Biblical Prophecy, Apostolic History and the Gospel,* and *Scripture, Tradition, and Interpretation.* Dr. Gasque's major involvement is in the provision of theological resources and education for the laity.

Contents

Foreword

The Good News Bible Commentary Series

Although it does not appear on the standard best-seller lists, the Bible continues to outsell all other books. And in spite of growing secularism ·in the West, there are no signs that interest in its message is abating. Quite to the contrary, more and more men and women are turning to its pages for insight and guidance in the midst of the ever-increasing complexity of modern life.

This renewed interest in Scripture is found outside of, as well as in, the church. It is found among people in Asia and Africa as well as in Europe and North America; indeed, as one moves outside of the traditionally Christian countries, interest in the Bible seems to quicken. Believers associated with the traditional Catholic and Protestant churches manifest the same eagerness for the word that is found in the newer evangelical churches and fellowships.

Millions of individuals read the Bible daily for inspiration. Many of these lay Bible students join with others in small study groups in homes, office buildings, factories, and churches to discuss a passage of Scripture on a weekly basis. This small-group movement is one that seems certain to grow even more in the future, since leadership of nearly all churches is encouraging these groups, and they certainly seem to be filling a significant gap in people's lives. In addition, there is renewed concern for biblical preaching throughout the church. Congregations where systematic Bible teaching ranks high on the agenda seem to have no difficulty filling their pews, and "secular" men and women who have no particular interest in joining a church are often quite willing to join a nonthreatening, informal Bible discussion group in their neighborhood or place of work.

We wish to encourage and, indeed, strengthen this worldwide movement of lay Bible study by offering this new commentary series. Although we hope that pastors and teachers will find these volumes helpful in both understanding and communicating the Word of God, we do not write primarily for them. Our aim is, rather, to provide for the benefit of the ordinary Bible reader reliable guides to the books of the Bible, representing the best of contemporary scholarship presented in a form that does not require formal theological education to understand.

The conviction of editors and authors alike is that the Bible belongs to the people and not merely to the academy. The message of the Bible is too important to be locked up in erudite and esoteric essays and monographs written for the eyes of theological specialists. Although exact scholarship has its place in the service of Christ, those who share in the teaching office of the church have a responsibility to make the results of their research accessible to the Christian community at large. Thus, the Bible scholars who join in the presentation of this series write with these broader concerns in view.

A wide range of modern translations is available to the contemporary Bible student. We have chosen to use the Good News Bible (Today's English Version) as the basis of our series for three reasons. First, it has become the most widely used translation, both geographically and ecclesiastically. It is read wherever English is spoken and is immensely popular with people who speak English as a second language and among people who were not brought up in the church. In addition, it is endorsed by nearly every denominational group.

Second, the Good News Bible seeks to do what we are seeking to do in our comments, namely, translate the teaching of the Bible into terms that can be understood by the person who has not had a strong Christian background or formal theological education. Though its idiomatic and sometimes paraphrastic style has occasionally frustrated the scholar who is concerned with a minute examination of the original Greek and Hebrew words, there can be no question but that this translation makes the Scripture more accessible to the ordinary reader than any other English translation currently available.

Third, we wish to encourage group study of the Bible, particularly by people who have not yet become a part of the church but who are interested in investigating for themselves the claims of Christ. We believe that the Good News Bible is by far the best translation for group discussion. It is both accurate and fresh, free from jargon, and, above all, contemporary. No longer does the Bible seem like an ancient book, belonging more to the museum than to the modern metropolis. Rather, it is as comprehensible and up-to-date as the daily newspaper.

We have decided to print the full text of the Good News Bible—and we are grateful for the kind permission of the United Bible Societies to do this—in our commentary series. This takes up valuable space, but we believe that it will prove to be very convenient for those who make use of the commentary, since it will enable them to read it straight through like an ordinary book as well as use it for reference.

Each volume will contain an introductory chapter detailing the background of the book and its author, important themes, and other helpful information. Then, each section of the book will be expounded as a whole, accompanied by a series of notes on items in the text that need further clarification or more detailed explanation. Appended to the end of each volume will be a bibliographical guide for further study.

Our new series is offered with the prayer that it may be an instrument of authentic renewal and advancement in the worldwide Christian community and a means of commending the faith of the people who lived in biblical times and of those who seek to live by the Bible today.

W. Ward Gasque

Acknowledgments

This volume is a product of the classroom. As I taught John's Gospel year after year, I found that my method gradually changed from a topical or thematic approach to a sequential one. I allowed myself to be guided more and more by the Gospel writer's order of narration, and the course took on more and more of the shape of a commentary coming to realization in dialogue.

The invitation in 1977 to contribute to this series therefore came as a welcome opportunity. It seemed that the volume would practically write itself. In reality, the task has not been that simple. A real commentary, even a nontechnical one, necessitates attention to every verse and to particular details of language and translation to an extent that classroom work seldom requires. Though some earlier translation work I had done on John stood me in good stead, I found myself asking questions I had not asked before and noticing particulars that had previously escaped my attention. The undertaking proved to be more than I had bargained for at the beginning, and I have profited immensely from it.

I would like to thank Ward Gasque for involving me in this worthwhile project, and many of my students over the years, for asking good questions, writing some good papers, and in general sharing my delight in this Gospel. I am grateful as well to the translator and publisher of the *Good News Bible*, for providing (despite legitimate quibbles) a good text from which to work, and to scholars past and present who have enriched my understanding—B. F. Westcott, C. K. Barrett and C. H. Dodd in my early years of teaching, and Raymond Brown more recently.

My personal thanks go to Bill Jackson and my colleague Rod Whitacre, for their helpful comments on the first draft of chapters 1–5, and to Corinne Langeudoc, for her good typing and frequent moral support. Above all, I am grateful to my wife Betty (who is typing this book's index even as I write this) and to our four children. The years in which I have worked on this project have been eventful ones for us all, full of unexpected changes, but I would not have traded them for anything in the world. Without the bonds of family, I would not have produced this book or much else. Many, many thanks to Betty, to Kenneth, to Carolyn and Bill and William, David and Diana, Linda and Michael for helping (more than they know) to bring this modest volume to birth.

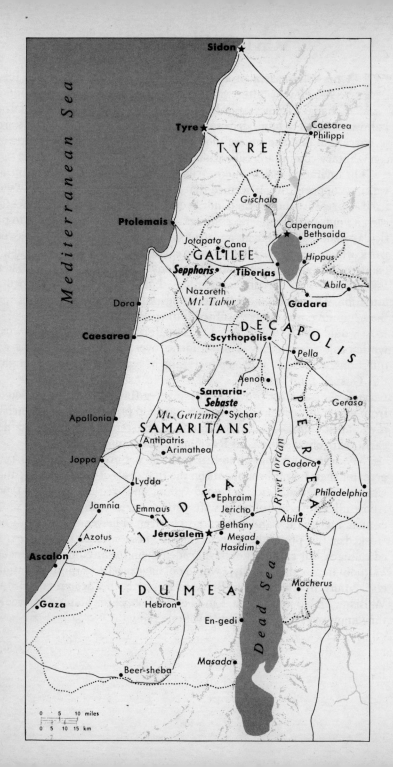

Introduction

The last Gospel in the traditional sequence of four stands somewhat apart from the first three (commonly known as the "Synoptics"). Like theirs, its title, "The Gospel According to John," (or, in some ancient manuscripts, simply "According to John"), was not part of what the author wrote but was prefixed to the text by early Christians when the four Gospels began to circulate as a collection. This Gospel, like the others, is anonymous. But in modern discussions, even those who speak without hesitation of "Matthew," "Mark," and "Luke" (regardless of their views on the authorship of those Gospels!) often use for John the noncommittal term "the fourth Gospel," suggesting that this Gospel is somehow *more* anonymous than the rest. It is not. If anything, it is less anonymous, for at least it bears a kind of signature, "the disciple whom Jesus loved" (21:20–24; cf. 13:23–25; 19:26–27; 20:2–8; 21:7). Who was this disciple? Who was "John"? How did the two come to be identified with each other, and what are the merits of that identification? These are the questions that must be answered about the Gospel's authorship.

The Sons of Zebedee

Besides the brothers Peter and Andrew, the first disciples called to accompany Jesus in his ministry were "James and John, the sons of Zebedee" (Mark 1:19/Matt. 4:21/Luke 5:10). These two are mentioned in the Gospel of John itself only once (21:2), not by name, but simply as "the sons of Zebedee." Almost always in the Gospels, the two brothers are seen together, as, for example, when they asked about a Samaritan village that would not receive Jesus, "Lord, do you want us to call fire down from heaven to destroy them?" (Luke 9:54). Jesus even gave them a name in common: "Boanerges," an Aramaic expression meaning "Men of Thunder" or "Sons of Thunder" (Mark 3:17). On one occasion, they requested of Jesus, "When you sit on your throne in your glorious Kingdom, we want you to let us sit with you, one at your right and one at your left" (Mark 10:37; in Matt. 20:21 it is their mother who makes the request on their behalf). Sometimes the two of them are present along with Peter, as on the mount of transfiguration (Mark 9:1/Matt. 17:1/Luke 9:28) or in Gethsemane (Mark 14:33/Matt. 26:37) or at the raising of Jairus' daughter (Mark 5:37/Luke 8:51); sometimes both sets of brothers—Peter and Andrew, James and John—are on the scene (Mark 1:29; 13:3), just as they were when Jesus called them from their fishing nets. Only once in the entire synoptic tradition does John speak or act alone: "Master," he reported to Jesus, "we saw a man driving out demons in your name, and we told him to stop, because he doesn't belong to our group" (Luke 9:49; cf. Mark 9:38). "Do not try to stop him," was Jesus' reply, "because whoever is not against you is for you" (Luke 9:50; cf. Mark 9:39–40).

•

The Disciple Whom Jesus Loved

How did half of this "brother combination" come to be identified with the so-called disciple whom Jesus loved, and so with the authorship of one of the four Gospels? The logic is simple and appealing. The "disciple whom Jesus loved" must have been one of the twelve Jesus had chosen (6:70–71) to help him and carry on his work, for he was present at the last supper (13:23–25). He was in fact "sitting next to Jesus" (13:23) and "leaned close" to him (21:20). Because in the synoptic Gospels Peter, James, and John (and sometimes Andrew) constitute a kind of "inner circle" who were closest to Jesus at crucial moments in his ministry, it is likely that the beloved disciple is one of these. He is obviously not Peter, for he is distinguished from or contrasted with Peter on four of the five occasions that he appears in the Gospel:

At the last supper, Peter asked him to find out who the predicted betrayer was (13:23–25).

On Easter morning, he and Peter heard the news of the empty tomb; he outran Peter to the tomb, and finally "saw and believed" (20:2–8).

On Lake Tiberias, when a stranger appeared to the disciples as they were fishing, he said to Peter, "It is the Lord" (21:7).

When Jesus predicted Peter's death, Peter turned and looked at this disciple and asked what his fate would be; Jesus replied that it was none of Peter's concern. A concluding note explicitly identifies the beloved disciple as the Gospel's author (21:20–24).

The only incident that does *not* involve Peter is at the crucifixion (after Peter and the others had fled), when Jesus commits his mother into this disciple's care (19:26–27). There are two other occasions where the designation "the disciple whom Jesus loved" does not occur but where this disciple's presence is sometimes assumed: 1:35–41 (where an unnamed disciple is present with Peter's brother Andrew) and 18:15–16 (where an anonymous disciple brings Peter into the High Priest's courtyard). These incidents should probably be left out of consideration, but even when they are, the evidence indicates, if not a rivalry, at least a kind of assertiveness on the beloved disciple's behalf in this Gospel, almost always with Peter on the scene.

Could the beloved disciple be Andrew, Peter's brother? This possibility seems to be excluded by the fact that Andrew is mentioned by name in 1:40, 44; 6:8; 12:22. Why would someone be named freely in certain contexts but in others designated anonymously as "the disciple whom Jesus loved"? The same objection applies to most of the Twelve: Philip (1:43–46; 6:5–7; 12:21–22; 14:8–10), Thomas (11:16; 14:5; 20:24–28; 21:2), and Judah (14:22), as well as Nathanael, who was probably also numbered among the Twelve (1:45–49; 21:2). It applies as well to Lazarus, whom Jesus is said to have "loved" (11:5) and about whom (because of his marvelous resuscitation) the rumor may well have spread that he would never die (21:23). Why would Lazarus be named in chapters 11–12 only to become anonymous in chapters 13–21?

This leaves the sons of Zebedee, who are *not* named in the Gospel, yet who were undoubtedly present at the last supper and on one other occasion in which the beloved disciple played a part (21:2; cf. v. 7). The synoptic account of their bold request to sit immediately on Jesus' right and left when "you sit on your throne in your glorious Kingdom" (Mark 10:37 and parallels) may indicate that those were *already* their customary places when Jesus and his disciples ate together. They may simply have been asking to have the present seating arrangement perpetuated in the eternal Kingdom! There is no ground for certainty about this, because their future hope seems to have focused on thrones and judicial authority (cf. Matt. 19:28) rather than seats at a meal—yet it appears that the two ideas were not far apart (cf. Luke 22:30). In any event, the beloved disciple's seat at the last supper *was* immediately at Jesus' side—whether on the right or left we are not told (13:23). If the identification is narrowed down to James and John the sons of Zebedee, James can be eliminated because of his early martyrdom. His death at the hands of Herod Agrippa I in Acts 12:2 leaves him scant time in which to have written a Gospel, much less for a rumor to have gotten started that he would not die before Christ's Second Coming (John 21:23)! A process of elimination thus leads to Zebedee's other son, the Apostle John.

A few very late testimonies that speak of John as having been martyred appear to be attempts to create for one of Jesus' prophecies a more literal fulfillment than he intended. His warning in Mark 10:39 that the two brothers would "drink the cup I must drink and be baptized in the way I must be baptized" referred in James' case to actual martyrdom, but in John's case may have pointed simply to his exile on the island of Patmos in his later years for "God's word and the truth that Jesus revealed" (Rev. 1:9).[1] At any rate, the identification of the beloved disciple with John the son of Zebedee is almost universally confirmed by early Christian tradition.

John the Apostle

What role did John play in the ancient church? Did he in fact write this Gospel? The second of these questions can only be answered from the testimony of church fathers, but the first can at least begin to be addressed from the New Testament itself. After Jesus' resurrection, John is seen with Peter in Jerusalem at the Beautiful Gate of the Temple (Acts 3:1–11) and before the ruling Council, or Sanhedrin (Acts 4:1–23). Later he and Peter are sent by the Jerusalem church to Samaria to confer the Holy Spirit on those who had believed there and to deal with Simon Magus (Acts 8:14–25). John's association with Peter in the book of Acts recalls the beloved disciple's association with Peter in John's Gospel, as if the one were simply a continuation of the other. They are still together in Paul's letter to the Galatians, where it is agreed that Peter, John, and James (not John's brother, but James the brother of Jesus) would continue their mission to the Jews while Paul and Barnabas worked among the Gentiles (Gal. 2:9).

The author of the book of Revelation (probably written after Peter's death) identifies himself as "John" (Rev. 1:1, 4, 9; 22:8), and the fact that he needs no further introduction suggests that he may be this same John, son of Zebedee and Apostle of Jesus Christ, now a well-known prophet to Christians in Ephesus and other church centers in Asia Minor. Tradition, at any rate, bears out this identification by linking the apostle closely to the church at Ephesus.

Irenaeus, near the end of the second century, wrote of "those who were conversant in Asia with John, the disciple of the Lord, [affirming] that John conveyed to them that information [i.e., about Jesus' age and the length of his ministry]. And he remained among them up to the times of Trajan."[2] Irenaeus added explicitly that "the church in Ephesus, founded by Paul, and having John remaining among them permanently until the times of Trajan [i.e., A.D. 98–117], is a true witness of the tradition of the apostles."[3]

Polycrates, bishop of Ephesus at the end of the second century, wrote to the bishop of Rome: "For great luminaries sleep in Asia, and they will rise again at the last day. . . . And there is also John, who leaned on the Lord's breast, who was a priest wearing the mitre, and martyr and teacher, and he sleeps at Ephesus."[4]

Papias, bishop of Hierapolis in Asia Minor, wrote a generation earlier that "if ever anyone came who had followed the presbyters, I inquired into the words of the presbyters, what Andrew or Peter or Philip or Thomas or James or John or Matthew, or any other of the Lord's disciples, had said, and what Aristion and the presbyter John, the Lord's disciples, were saying. For I did not suppose that information from books would help me so much as the word of a living and surviving voice."[5] Eusebius claimed that Papias referred here to two individuals named John: the first numbered among the "disciples of the Lord," and the second a later "presbyter."[6] But the quotation does not bear out his claim; each time John is mentioned it is as "presbyter" *and* "disciple of the Lord" (it appears in fact that Papias uses the word "presbyter" to mean "apostle," and at one point Eusebius himself follows this practice as well.[7] Papias seems to be referring to John in two ways: first, along with the other apostles, as a guardian of the tradition in the past, and second, as a contemporary figure, the only survivor of the original "apostles" or "presbyters" (cf. the epistles, Second and Third John, sent "From the Elder"—or "presbyter"—2 John 1; 3 John 1).

Polycarp, bishop of Smyrna in Asia Minor about the same time as Papias, is mentioned by Irenaeus as having known John. In a letter to a certain Florinus *On the Sole Sovereignty of God*, Irenaeus wrote: "For I saw you when I was still a boy, in lower Asia with Polycarp. . . . I remember the things of that time better than the things which have happened recently—for the experiences of youth, growing with the soul are united with it—so that I could tell the very place in which the blessed Polycarp sat [and] taught. . . . the addresses which he made to the people, and how he spoke of his association with John and the others who had seen the Lord, and how he remembered their words, and what the things were concerning the Lord which he had heard from them, both concerning His miracles and concerning His teaching"[8]

Early church tradition also links John the Apostle, the son of Zebedee, with the writing of a Gospel, sometimes with direct citation of the Gospel of John as we have it. *Theophilus of Antioch*, late in the second century, wrote: "And hence the holy writings teach us, and all the spirit-bearing [inspired] men, one of whom, John, says, 'In the beginning was the Word, and the Word was with God' ";[9] he continued with a brief exposition of John 1:1–3.

Irenaeus, after recounting the traditions associated with the other Gospels, concluded that "Afterwards, John, the disciple of the Lord, who also had leaned upon His breast, did himself publish a Gospel during his residence at Ephesus in Asia."[10] Later he adds that John wrote his Gospel to refute certain Gnostic heretics who argued that God the Creator and God the Father of Jesus were two different gods, and he quotes extensively from the prologue to prove his point.[11]

Even earlier (about A.D. 130–140) a certain *Ptolemy*, himself one of these Gnostics, attributes to "John, the disciple of the Lord" the words "In the beginning was the Word, and the Word was with God, and the Word was God"[12] and elsewhere attributes to "the apostle" the words that shortly follow, "everything was made through him and apart from him nothing was made."[13]

Such statements show how, in the second century, both orthodoxy and heresy (as they later came to be called) appealed to the Gospel of John and regarded John the Apostle as its author. The testimony to his authorship is early and unanimous, even though some accounts of the circumstances under which it was written appear confused and unreliable. The late second-century Anti-Marcionite prologues (i.e., Gospel headings presumably written to refute the heretic Marcion) have John actually dictating the Gospel to Papias, identified as his disciple. The Muratorian Canon, from about the same period, states that all the disciples fasted together for three days, after which "it was revealed to Andrew. . . . that, with all of them reviewing, John should describe all things in his own name."[14] There could be a kernel of truth in these traditions that John's Gospel embodies the reflections of a whole group of early Christian teachers and prophets associated with the Apostle John and that it is not merely the memoirs of a single individual. If the beloved disciple is indeed John the son of Zebedee, certain factors must have been at work tempering the vengeful zeal of this "man of thunder" (Mark 3:17), and the apocalyptic excitement of the prophet who wrote the book of Revelation. The widely held theory of a Johannine "school," though unproven and probably unprovable, may help to explain both the diversity of the writings attributed to John and the differences in personality between the beloved disciple who appears in the Gospel and the fiery apostle remembered by the church. Who can read and soon forget Clement of Alexandria's vivid narrative of the aged John in Ephesus (after his exile on Patmos) riding boldly on horseback to a robbers' den to reclaim a young convert who had renounced his faith and turned to a life of wickedness?[15] In contrast, the beloved disciple in John's Gospel is often depicted as a meditative, gentle, reflective man in contrast to the hasty and impulsive Peter. Later descriptions of John in his old age sound more like what one might have expected Peter to become! Once, on meeting the heretic Cerinthus at the public bath in Ephesus, John is said to have rushed from the place shouting, "Let us fly, lest even the bath-house fall down, because Cerinthus, the enemy of the truth, is within."[16]

Aside from the question of whether such later stories are reliable, are they necessarily inconsistent with the portrait of the beloved disciple in the fourth Gospel? The traditional image of the beloved disciple as gentle or passive is based more on assumptions than on explicit statements in the text. His personality does not actually emerge in John's Gospel. All that is said is that Jesus loved him and entrusted his own mother to his care (19:26–27), that he sat next to Jesus at table and on one occasion leaned close to ask a question (13:23–25), that he ran faster than Peter to Jesus' tomb and "believed" when he saw the tomb empty (20:2–8), and that he recognized the risen Lord by the sea of Galilee (21:7). None of this characterizes him either as bold and impetuous, on the one hand, or gentle and meditative, on the other. The few glimpses of his behavior in John's Gospel neither strengthen nor weaken the notion that he is John the son of Zebedee, but when all evidence is weighed, the traditional identification remains by far the most convincing yet suggested, and it must be allowed to stand.

The only explicit indication of the involvement of others besides John in the writing of the Gospel is the anonymous "we" in 21:24 who "know that what he said is true." A group of Christians somewhere is vouching for the validity of the beloved disciple's written testimony. The traditions connecting John with Ephesus suggest that "we" refers to the elders of the Ephesian church (and perhaps also that "I" in the following verse is a scribe among them who was responsible for preparing the finished Gospel for publication). But there is no way to be certain of this. What does seem plausible is that the same "we" group had a hand in verse 23 as well, and perhaps in the other cryptic references to the "disciple whom Jesus loved." It is more likely that John's associates would have pointed to him in this way than that he himself would have done so. But the statement in 21:24 that the beloved disciple not only "spoke of these things," but also "wrote them down" sets strict limits to the participation of anyone else in the writing of the Gospel. The most plausible theory is that John, the beloved disciple, put together the Gospel pretty much as we have it but, as narrator, left himself out of the story. His associates in Ephesus (or wherever it might have been), while respecting his anonymity, nevertheless testified in their own way to his personal involvement in the story he told and consequently to the reliability of his Gospel. They did this by weaving into his account several brief glimpses of the disciple himself in action and by adding the explicit postscript at the end.

The fact that John wrote the Gospel that now bears his name does not necessarily mean that he composed it all at once. The end of chapter 20, for example, looks as if it was intended at some point to conclude the entire Gospel. If so, then chapter 21 was added as a kind of appendix, either by the same associates who supplied its final verses or (more likely) by John himself. He is, after all, represented as being present at the scene (21:7), and there is no reason to doubt his responsibility for the substance of the narrative. The repetition of certain themes in Jesus' farewell discourse and especially the apparent termination of the discourse at 14:31 (with the words "come, let us go from this place") suggest that the discourse may have taken shape in two stages, or recensions, consisting of 13:36–14:31 and 15:1–17:26 respectively, unfolding certain key themes that are introduced in 13:31–35 (for further discussion, see the comments on 20:30–31; 13:31–35; 14:31). The prologue (1:1–18), or parts of it, may well have been composed *after* the rest of the Gospel and prefixed to it as a summary of the divine plan of salvation realized through Jesus Christ. But in speaking of recension and rewriting, it is not necessary to imagine other hands modifying the beloved disciple's work. We are dealing in all likelihood with a complex creative process centering on the historical and theological reflections of one man as hammered out in the context of a particular community of faith and in relation to that community's concerns. It is appropriate, therefore, to speak of a Johannine community, even though there is little concrete evidence that John's disciples were formally trained to carry on a certain literary or theological tradition. No religious community can exist without some structure, but John's was a community of the Holy Spirit more than of ecclesiastical structure. Clement of Alexandria perceptively noted in the third century that when John noticed that "the outward facts had been set forth in the Gospels, [he] was urged on by his disciples, and, divinely moved by the Spirit, composed a spiritual Gospel."[17] It is this "spiritual" character of John's Gospel that both undergirds its authority and distinguishes it from Matthew, Mark, and Luke in style and in content.

Authorship and Authority

Despite the considerable evidence that the Apostle John wrote John's Gospel, the Gospel's authority rests on more than simply the identity of the author. Above all, the Gospel's authority rests on its implicit claim to be inspired by the Holy Spirit. In his farewell discourses Jesus is represented as promising his disciples (the beloved disciple included) that he "will ask the Father, and he will give you another Helper [Gr.: *paraklētos*], who will stay with you forever. He is the Spirit, who reveals the truth about God [lit., "the Spirit of truth"]. The world cannot receive him, because it cannot see him or know him. But you know him, because he remains with you and is in you" (14:16–17). The Greek word applied here to the Spirit, *paraklētos* (often simply transliterated into English as "Paraclete"), literally refers to someone "called in" or "called on" to help (hence the translation "Helper"). The word is a noun formed from the verb *parakalein*, to exhort, encourage, or comfort (hence the traditional KJV rendering "Comforter," in the older Latin-derived sense of one who strengthens or encourages). Its meaning therefore is both passive and active: A "Paraclete" is not only one who is called on to help but one who *does* help by actively exhorting, encouraging, or comforting those who are in need. It is a legal term in 1 John 2:1, where Jesus himself is "someone who pleads with the Father in our behalf" (Gr.: *paraklētos*; RSV: "advocate").

The activity of the Spirit as "Paraclete" or "Helper" is spelled out in several other passages in the farewell discourses. The Spirit, Jesus says:

will teach you everything (14:26)

will make you remember all I have told you (14:26)

will speak [lit., "testify"] about me (15:26)

will prove to the people of the world that they are wrong about sin and about what is right and about God's judgment (16:8)

will lead you into all the truth (16:13)

will not speak of his own authority, but he will speak of what he hears (16:13)

will tell you of things to come (16:13)

will give me glory, because he will take what I say and tell it to you (16:14)

The Helper's ministry, like Jesus' own, is a ministry of revelation. He makes things known: by teaching and testimony, by helping the disciples remember what Jesus said, by leading them on in the truth, by revealing things to come, and even by confronting the world and proving that its standards are wrong.

Does the Spirit then bring to the church "new" revelation? Only in the sense that all revelation is by definition "new." More precisely, the Spirit brings out in ever new ways the significance of the once-and-for-all revelation of God in his Son Jesus.

Clearly, the author regards his Gospel as one place—perhaps *the* place—where this is happening. He writes with a consciousness that the Helper is testifying about Jesus Christ through him, and in this very book. He records what Jesus *said*, and what Jesus still *says* to the church and the world following the crucifixion and resurrection. It is no accident that of all the Gospels, John's is the one that often seems to speak most immediately as a word from God to us today. The one who spoke there still speaks after many centuries, inviting all who read to believe in him and receive as the gift of God a new and endless life.

John and the Synoptics

It would be wrong to infer from what has just been said that John's Gospel is more "inspired" than the other three. Clement of Alexandria's sharp distinction between John the "spiritual Gospel" and the Synoptics with their interest in the "outward facts"[18] cannot be allowed to stand without qualification. The Synoptics are also "spiritual," and John's Gospel is vitally interested in "outward facts."

John's distinctiveness lies rather in his *self-consciousness* of the Spirit's inspiration than in the inspiration itself. Inspiration, whether of John or of the synoptic Gospels, has both a "vertical" and a "horizontal" aspect. The vertical aspect is the awareness that God speaks from heaven through the very words of the author and his community. This comes to expression in Jesus' promise that the Paraclete, or Helper, will "teach" the disciples and lead them "into all the truth" (e.g., 14:26; 16:13). The horizontal aspect is the tacit recognition that what is written is based on oral and written traditions about Jesus previously collected in the church and used for instruction and edification of the faithful. This comes to expression in Jesus' promise that the Spirit "will make you remember all that I told you" (14:26) and that because the Spirit "will speak about me," the disciples too must bear their testimony "because you have been with me from the very beginning" (15:26–27). Inspiration does not consist of God dictating a message as to a secretary but is, instead, a complex process realizing itself in the daily life of the church over several decades, that is, between the lifetime of Jesus and the time when the Gospels finally came to be written down.

Although most scholars agree that John's was the last of the four Gospels to be written, it is difficult to decide whether or not he had access to any of the other three. What is certain is that he did not write in a vacuum but had a number of traditions available to him: for example, his own recollections as an eyewitness of much that happened and collections of Jesus' sayings and miracles preserved orally or in writing. Beyond this, some scholars suggest that he used Mark's Gospel (very few would say Matthew or Luke), but the evidence for this is far from conclusive. For the most part, he seems to have written independently of the others, drawing on the same kinds of traditions—in some cases the very same traditions—that they used but putting these traditions to work in his own distinctive way to produce a unique portrait of Jesus.

John's Gospel differs from the Synoptics in two ways: first, in the style of Jesus' teaching (and to some extent the content); and second, in its chronology and way of structuring Jesus' ministry. Whereas the theme of Jesus' proclamation in the Synoptics is the Kingdom of God, in John it is himself and his mission. His revelation turns in upon itself. What he reveals from heaven, over and over again, is simply that he is the Revealer sent from heaven! But in making this known he makes God the Father known, and in his miracles and acts of mercy he reveals God at work. The difference between John and the Synoptics can be summed up by saying that what is implicit in Mark, Matthew, and Luke has become explicit in John. The emphatic yet enigmatic "I" of the Synoptics ("You have heard. . . . but now *I* tell you.") becomes the mysterious and majestic "I Am" of John's Gospel (e.g., 8:58). In proclaiming the kingdom, Jesus makes known—for those who hear in faith—himself as the messenger and God as the Father who sent him. This might be *inferred* from the synoptic Gospels, but only John, through the Spirit's ministry, draws aside the veil to let the reader, after Jesus' resurrection, see the full import of Jesus' words. This is why Jesus' discourses sound so monotonously self-centered to some modern readers of the Gospel; he can only reveal God by revealing himself (14:9). The goal of Jesus' mission to the world is not to reveal a theology (i.e., a body of information *about* God) but to reveal God himself.

This he does by his words and his works, that is, by a series of miracles or symbolic actions combined with sayings and discourses explaining the significance of those acts.

The structure of John's Gospel is largely shaped by this interweaving of word and deed. Unlike the synoptic Gospels, which locate Jesus' ministry in Galilee and conclude it with a journey to Jerusalem and an account of the Passion, John divides the ministry into two parts, both centered mainly in Jerusalem. There are two possible ways of making this division:

1. It is customary to regard chapters 2–12 (or, more precisely, 2:13–12:50) as Jesus' *public ministry* and chapters 13–20 or 13–21 as his *private ministry*, culminating in the account of his death and resurrection. In the first part, his attention is directed toward the "world," that is, toward the crowds and the religious authorities in the synagogue (chap. 6) or in the Temple at the Jewish religious festivals (chaps. 2–3, 5, 7–8, 10, 11–12); the second part consists of two farewell discourses given in private to his disciples and, after the Passion, three resurrection appearances to disciples.

The Passion dominates the entire Gospel. Not only does the private ministry lead up to it, but even the public ministry is set within a Passion framework. The two events that in the Synoptics introduce Passion week—the cleansing of the Temple and the triumphal entry into Jerusalem—are in John separated from each other and used to bracket the whole of the public ministry (2:13–22; 12:12–19). The necessity that Jesus die for the sins of the world is not revealed gradually but is self-evident from the start (cf. 1:29).

2. An alternative way of dividing the Gospel of John is to regard each of the same two well-known events (i.e., the Temple cleansing and the triumphal entry) as introductory to a major section of the Gospel: the book of *judgment* (2:13–11:54) and the book of *glory* (11:55–21:25). The judgment involved in the driving of the merchants from the Temple precincts sets the tone for a series of public discourses that function as John's equivalent of the trial of Jesus before the Sanhedrin, or Jewish ruling council. The secret that the reader understands, but that Jesus' contemporaries do not, is that not Jesus but the Temple itself and the city of Jerusalem, the Jewish religious establishment—and ultimately the world—are on trial in these sharp exchanges. The verdict finally comes down in 11:47–53—Jesus must die—but in condemning him to death, the world is condemning itself.

The "glory" of Jesus' Passion is intimated in the triumphal entry (12:16) and in a series of notices that follow (12:23, 28–30; 13:31–32;

17:1, 5), even while the note of judgment continues (12:31; 16:11). Both judgment and glory come to full realization in Pilate's mock proclamation of Jesus as king in front of the governor's palace (19:14) and in the crucifixion itself (19:17–18).

It is neither possible nor necessary to make a hard and fast choice between 1 and 2, because in either case 11:55–12:50 is somewhat transitional, marking both the end of the public ministry, with its emphasis on judgment, and the beginning of the Passion, with its decisive revelation of Jesus' glory. At the end of this narrative transition stands a shorter, discourse transition (12:37–50), in which Jesus is allowed to summarize the world's response, positively and negatively, to his message. It is the presence of this section that has prompted most commentators to divide the Gospel between chapters 12 and 13, but the matter is somewhat more complicated than that. The striking parallel between 2:13 and 11:55 should not be overlooked:

It was almost time for the Passover Festival, so Jesus went to Jerusalem (2:13).

The time for the Passover Festival was near, and many people went up from the country to Jerusalem (11:55).

The two look almost like alternate beginnings to a Passion story, and their combined effect is to build the whole Gospel around the awareness that Jesus must make his pilgrimage to Jerusalem and die at the Passover Festival.

All that stands outside this Passion framework is the prologue (1:1–18) and a six-day sequence into which the author weaves the ministry of John the Baptist, the call of Jesus' first disciples, and the miracle at the wedding in Cana of Galilee (1:19–2:11). Jesus' entire Galilean ministry as depicted in the synoptic Gospels is symbolized by the Cana miracle (cf. Mark 2:19–20), so that when he comes to Jerusalem to cleanse the Temple, the readers' momentary impression is of stepping suddenly into the last week of the ministry. Clearly, John is handling the familiar synoptic chronology with a certain freedom, a freedom born, it appears, from the author's sense of being led into all truth by the ministry of the Spirit.

At one crucial point, however, John is *not* reshaping an earlier chronology but simply recalling what happened during a period that the synoptic writers have largely overlooked—the period between Jesus' baptism by John the Baptist and the Baptist's imprisonment.[19] According to

Mark, Matthew, and Luke, Jesus' ministry does not begin until John the Baptist's comes to an end (cf., e.g., Mark 1:14), but in the Gospel of John the ministries of the two men overlap. As late as John 3:24, after Jesus has gathered his disciples, performed his first miracle in Galilee, and confronted the religious authorities in Jerusalem, the author reminds his readers that John the Baptist still had not been put in prison. John's Gospel opens up a whole chapter in Jesus' career that the Synoptics have passed over in silence, and it thus supplements their testimony to Jesus in a significant way. It is misleading to characterize the Synoptics as historical and John as theological in interest and intent. Clearly, all four Gospels are historical and all four are theological in their concerns. The different ways in which these interests overlap and limit one another are what give the four their diversity, and especially John its distinctiveness over against the Synoptics.

The Purpose and Date of John's Gospel

The purpose of this Gospel is often said to be stated in 20:31: "But these [acts of the risen Jesus] have been written in order that you may believe that Jesus is the Messiah, the Son of God, and that through your faith in him you may have life." Some have inferred from this that the Gospel was written to unbelievers, to win them over to the Christian faith. This is highly unlikely, because, from beginning to end, John's Gospel presupposes a considerable sophistication and maturity on the part of the readers in understanding Christian symbolism and allusions to practices and beliefs with which only those who were already Christians would ha· · been familiar (e.g., allusions to baptism, the Lord's Supper, or the experience of persecution or martyrdom—from the inside, as it were, rather than from the outside looking in). The main purpose of John's Gospel can probably be identified as the purpose of any Gospel: that is, to make the past career of Jesus Christ a present reality to a later generation, "those who believe without seeing" him (20:29). In the words of another New Testament writing attributed to John: "We write to you about the Word of life. . . . We have heard it, and we have seen it with our eyes; yes we have seen it, and our hands have touched it. . . . What we have seen and heard we announce to you also, so that you will join with us in the fellowship that we have with the Father and with his Son Jesus Christ" (1 John 1:1–3). Whatever other purposes there may have been—the countering of false teaching about the divine or human nature of Jesus Christ, polemic against those who believed John the Baptist was the Messiah, or concern that Jewish Christians break with the synagogue and identify openly with the Christian movement (all of which are frequently suggested as reasons for writing the Gospel)—must be understood as subsidiary to this single and simple primary purpose.

As for the date of John's Gospel, it is more difficult to fix than is commonly assumed. If the author is indeed an eyewitness, the Gospel must be placed within the first Christian century, but since there is no conclusive evidence that John used any of the other Gospels in their finished form, no limit can be fixed to how early it could have been written. Though there is no reason to doubt the commonly accepted notion that John is the latest of the four Gospels, there is no way to prove it either. John's Gospel could have been written any time in the latter half of the first century. Only the reference in 21:23 to a rumor that the beloved disciple would not die suggests that it was probably nearer the end of that period than the beginning.

Notes

1. According to Origen, *Commentary on Matthew* 16.6.

2. Irenaeus, *Against Heresies* 2.22.5; ANF 1.392.

3. Ibid. 3.3.4; ANF 1.416.

4. Eusebius, *Ecclesiastical History* 3.31.3; LCL 1.271.

5. Ibid. 3.39.4; LCL 1.293.

6. Ibid. 3.39.5–7.

7. Ibid. 3.39.7.

8. Ibid. 5.20.4–6; trans. D. J. Theron, *Evidence of Tradition* (Grand Rapids: Baker, 1958), p. 27.

9. Theophilus of Antioch, *To Autolycus* 2.22; ANF 2.103.

10. Irenaeus, *Against Heresies* 3.1.1; ANF 1.414.

11. Ibid. 3.11.1; ANF 1.426.

12. Ptolemy, *Exegesis of John*, in Irenaeus, *Against Heresies* 1.85; ANF 1.328.

13. Ptolemy, *Letter to Flora*, in Epiphanius, *Panarion* 3.33; trans. R. M. Grant, *Gnosticism* (New York: Harper, 1961), p. 184.

14. Theron, *Evidence of Tradition*, pp. 107–109.

15. Clement of Alexandria, *The Rich Man's Salvation* 42; ANF 2.603–604.

16. Irenaeus, *Against Heresies* 3.3.4; ANF 1.416.

17. Clement of Alexandria, *Hypotyposeis*; see Eusebius, *Ecclesiastical History* 6.14.7; LCL 2.49.

18. Ibid.

19. Eusebius, *Ecclesiastical History* 3.24.11–12.

Note: A list of the abbreviations used in the commentary is found at the end of the book (see p. 351). See also For Further Reading (pp. 352–354); full bibliographical references for works referred to in short-form notes within the commentary are supplied there.

The Word of Life

JOHN 1:1–18

Before the world was created, the Word already existed; he was with God, and he was the same as God. [2]From the very beginning the Word was with God. [3]Through him God made all things; not one thing in all creation was made without him. [4]The Word was the source of life,[a] and this life brought light to mankind. [5]The light shines in the darkness, and the darkness has never put it out.

[6]God sent his messenger, a man named John, [7]who came to tell people about the light, so that all should hear the message and believe. [8]He himself was not the light; he came to tell about the light. [9]This was the real light—the light that comes into the world and shines on all mankind. [10]The Word was in the world, and though God made the world through him, yet the world did not recognize him. [11]He came to his own country, but his own people did not receive him. [12]Some, however, did receive him and believed in him; so he gave them the right to become God's children. [13]They did not become God's children by natural means, that is, by being born as the children of a human father; God himself was their Father.

[14]The Word became a human being and, full of grace and truth, lived among us. We saw his glory, the glory which he received as the Father's only Son.

[15]John spoke about him. He cried out, "This is the one I was talking about when I said, 'He comes after me, but he is greater than I am, because he existed before I was born.'"

[16]Out of the fullness of his grace he has blessed us all, giving us one blessing after another. [17]God gave the Law through Moses, but grace and truth came through Jesus Christ. [18]No one has ever seen God. The only Son, who is the same as God and is at the Father's side, he has made him known.

a. *The Word was the source of life; or* What was made had life in union with the Word.

The prologue is set apart from the rest of John's Gospel by its designation of Jesus Christ as **the Word** (Gr.: *logos*, vv. 1, 14) rather than "the Son" or the "only Son." The term **only Son** is introduced, however, in verses 14 and 18 and sets the stage for the Gospel's characteristic emphasis on the Father-Son relationship between God and Jesus.

The prologue also stands somewhat apart from the rest of the Gospel stylistically. The repetition and linking of certain key words lend a special dignity and solemnity to the first twelve verses or so. For example (following the vocabulary and word order of the original Greek), in verse 1:

"Word . . . Word . . . God . . . God . . . Word"; in verses 4–5: "life . . . life . . . light . . . light . . . darkness . . . darkness"; in verses 7–9: "for a testimony . . . to testify about the light . . . not the light . . . to testify about the light . . . the real light . . . the light that comes into the world"; in verses 10–12: "the world . . . the world . . . the world . . . his own . . . his own . . . receive . . . receive." In the middle of verse 12 the chainlike repetitions abruptly come to an end. The effect is a marked increase in pace and intensity, building to a small crescendo at the end of verse 13. The reader's eye rushes through the phrases describing what believers are *not* (NIV: "children born not of natural descent, nor of human decision or a husband's will") to settle triumphantly on what they *are* ("born of God").

Verse 14 brings a subtle change. The writer pauses to reflect on the impact of what he has just said. The message of the first thirteen verses is that **the Word became a human being**. At the same time the writer injects himself and his community into the story of the Word becoming human. The Word **lived among** *us.* *We* **saw his glory. . . . Out of the fullness of his grace he has blessed** *us all***, giving** *us* **one blessing after another** (vv. 14, 16). The prologue can thus be divided into two parts: first, a capsule summary of the Gospel story, beginning in eternity and reaching as far as the present experience of Christian believers (vv. 1–13), and second, the confessional response of these believers to this revelation in history (vv. 14–18).

The distinct style and vocabulary of the prologue has led many scholars to the conclusion that the writer has incorporated into his Gospel, right at the beginning, an early Christian (or pre-Christian) hymn. Pliny, the Roman governor of Asia Minor early in the second century, wrote to the emperor Trajan that Christians "were in the habit of meeting on a certain fixed day before it was light, when they sang in alternate verses a hymn to Christ, as to a god" (*Epistles* 10.96; trans. D. J. Theron, *Evidence of Tradition* [Grand Rapids: Baker, 1958], p. 15). Possible fragments of hymns that fit this description are known within the New Testament itself (e.g., Phil. 2:6–11; Col. 1:15–20), and it is also possible (though it cannot be proven) that parts of John 1:1–18 first took shape in the context of Christian worship. But there is no agreement among scholars as to which verses of the prologue belonged to this supposed hymn. Some have attempted to separate poetry from prose, so that when certain prose "insertions" about John the Baptist (vv. 6–8, 15) are removed the remainder can be regarded as the original hymn or poem. Others have proposed even subtler and more complex reconstructions. But the chainlike word repetitions that give the first part of the prologue its stylistic flavor run through the first so-called prose section (vv. 6–8) as well as through the supposed poetry. Though the prologue of John's Gospel is haunting and in its way poetic, the GNB (like most English versions) prints all of it as prose. If there is an underlying hymn, no sure way has been found of reconstructing it. Whatever its sources, the prologue in its present form is just what it appears to be—the literary introduction to John's Gospel.

If the introduction had begun at verse 6, there would have been no mistaking the story it intended to tell. Verse 6 begins where Mark's Gospel begins (and where the narrative portion of John's Gospel itself gets under way), with John the Baptist (cf. Mark 1:2–5; John 1:19–28). In the written Gospels and in early Christian preaching, his ministry serves to introduce the ministry of Jesus (cf. Acts 10:37; 13:24–25). But the first five verses of the Gospel of John reach back to an earlier beginning, the same "beginning" spoken of in Genesis 1:1, when "God created the heavens and the earth" (NIV). The refrain of Genesis ("And God *said* . . . and God *said* . . .") finds its equivalent in the prologue's designation, **the Word** (cf. Ps. 33:6: "By the word of the Lord were the heavens made, their starry host by the breath of his mouth").

The purpose of the Gospel writer is to place the story of Jesus in a cosmic perspective. The light that came into the world in Jesus Christ is the same light that illumined every human creature from the beginning. The word that created all things, as well as the life that it created, now finds expression in a particular person and a particular life lived **among us**. The first few verses of John's Gospel lay claim to the past, briefly and decisively, on behalf of Jesus Christ. He is here the personification of God's creative word, just as he will later be seen as the personification of things that the word called into being—light, truth, life and resurrection, bread from heaven, and the vine that God planted. The one who gives life *is* the Life; the one who speaks truth *is* the Truth. Above all, Jesus is introduced in the prologue as the Revealer, the one through whom God spoke in the beginning and through whom he continues to speak. Elsewhere in John's Gospel, Jesus *speaks* the word, but in the prologue he *is* the Word, the personal embodiment of all that he proclaims.

The Epistle to the Hebrews introduces Jesus in a remarkably similar way: "In the past God spoke to our ancestors many times and in many ways through the prophets, but in these last days he has spoken to us through his Son. He is the one through whom God created the universe, the one whom God has chosen to possess all things at the end" (Heb. 1:1–2). But if John's Gospel lays claim to the past in much the same way as

Hebrews, its center of interest from the prologue on is almost entirely the present and future, not the past. Whatever their wider implications, the immediate function of the opening verses is simply to lay a basis for the irony of the Word's subsequent rejection in the world: "He was in the world, and *though the world was made through him,* the world did not recognize him" (v. 10, NIV). The past is not an end in itself. The main purpose of the opening paragraph about God's creative work through the Word is to lead up to an affirmation about the present: **The light shines in the darkness, and the darkness has never put it out** (v. 5). The writer boldly passes over the entire Old Testament period in silence. In one breath he speaks of light and life coming into existence at the creation, and in the next he proclaims that same light shining today, unquenched by the darkness around it. The rest of the Gospel makes clear that the reference is to the life and death of Jesus, who came into the world as a light (3:19; 8:12; 12:46) and confronted darkness in the hour of his death (9:4–5; 11:9–10; 12:35–36; 13:30). **The light shines in the darkness** *now*, because of Jesus and what he has done.

In verses 6–13 the writer goes back and describes in rapid summary fashion how this light came to shine so triumphantly in a dark world. The story begins in the customary way, with John the Baptist; what is unusual is the insistence that John the Baptist **was not the light** but merely **came to tell about the light** (v. 8). Like Jesus Christ he was **sent** as God's messenger, but the similarity, says the Gospel writer, ends there. Why was such an explanation thought necessary? The most likely reason is that the writer knew of individuals or groups who actually believed that John, and not Jesus, was **the light**, that is, the decisive revealer of God. Such beliefs are known to have existed by the third century A.D. (see note on 1:8) and John's Gospel gives evidence of countering them here and elsewhere (cf. 1:20–21; 3:27–30). But though John the Baptist's role was simply **to tell about the light**, even as he spoke, **the real light** was coming into the world (v. 9). It was **in the world** in the person of Jesus during John the Baptist's ministry, even though John was at first unaware of it (cf. 1:31, 33).

If Jesus in the prologue is the personification of the Word, he is no less the personification of the light that the Word produces. The question whether the implied subject of verses 10–12 is the Word or the light is secondary to the observation that in either case it is Jesus. Whatever distinction can be made between the Word and the light has been transcended in him. *He* (not "it") was in the world; the world was made through *him*; the world did not know *him*. The Gospel writer is not here

4

recounting a myth or an allegory, in which abstract ideas take on a life of their own, but genuine history, telescoped into a sentence or two but waiting to be developed and expanded in the remainder of the Gospel.

Jesus **came to his own country, but his own people did not receive him** (v. 11). In the immediate sense **his own country** was Israel and **his own people** the Jews. Israel and Judaism were the stage on which the drama of his public ministry was played out. Yet the prologue has just mentioned **the world** three times within two lines. The context strongly suggests that in a wider sense Jesus' **own country** is the world to which he was sent and **his own people** are human beings of every race or nation, all those on whom God's light shines (cf. vv. 4, 9). These wider implications will become apparent when Jesus comes to Jerusalem for the last time (cf. 12:19, 32) and when he confronts Pilate and the authority of Rome.

The story of the coming of the light ends with an account of the experience of the writer's own community. They have done what the rest of Jesus' **own people** have not done. They have received him as God's messenger and put their faith in him. They have been given the status of God's children not by creation or natural descent but by a new and divine begetting. In the words of Jesus to Nicodemus, they have been "born again" (cf. 3:3).

It is from this vantage point that the writer can say, **The light shines in the darkness, and the darkness has never put it out** (v. 5), and from this perspective as well that he reviews how the light came to shine on him and his community. So it was that the Word **became a human being and . . . lived among us** (v. 14a). The writer's community comes alive and begins to speak for itself: **We saw his glory, the glory which he received as the Father's only Son**. Like Isaiah in the Temple (cf. 12:41) or like the three disciples at the Transfiguration (cf. Luke 9:32), they had seen the glory of God displayed in Jesus Christ. Yet it was not a matter of a particular incident or a single vision. They had seen Jesus' glory in a whole series of events, from his baptism and the wedding at Cana (cf. 2:11) to his death and resurrection.

The first to see it was John the Baptist, now introduced as the spokesman for the whole Christian community. First, John is identified by means of a quotation of what he once said about Jesus: **He comes after me, but he is greater than I am, because he existed before I was born** (v. 15). Although these words reinforce the prologue's opening verses on the pre-existence of Jesus, their purpose in their immediate context is to introduce a *new* testimony from John the Baptist's lips, that is, that "from

5

his fullness have we all received, grace upon grace," v. 16 RSV). Here John speaks no longer as a solitary prophet but as part of the Christian community. He is numbered among those who have "received" Jesus (cf. v. 12). As the messenger through whom others will come to faith (cf. v. 7), he is the appropriate spokesman for them all. Verse 16 is therefore not a testimony that John uttered for himself on one particular occasion but a testimony common to all believers in Jesus. The **fullness** of Jesus Christ is an expression based on the conviction that Jesus himself was a man **full of grace and truth** (v. 14), a phrase recalling the description of Stephen in Acts 6:8 ("full of grace and power," RSV) and the more common expression "full of the Holy Spirit" (Acts 6:3, 5; cf. Luke 4:1; John 3:34). If the Spirit in Luke-Acts means "power" (Luke 24:49; Acts 1:8), the Spirit in the Johannine writings means "truth" (John 4:23–24; 14:17; 15:26; 16:13; 1 John 5:6). **Grace and truth** is therefore a circumlocution for the Holy Spirit. The Spirit that rested on Jesus after his baptism now belongs to all his followers, for Jesus is "the one who baptizes with the Holy Spirit" (1:33).

The confession of the believing community probably does not extend beyond verse 16. The tone of verses 17–18 is again didactic and impersonal, like that of verses 1–13, as the writer undertakes to explain concretely the puzzling phrase "grace upon grace" (RSV). God's gift of the Jewish Law, he says, makes way for **grace and truth**, the gift of the Spirit through Jesus Christ. The distinction is not between law and grace as contrasting ways of salvation, but between *two* gifts of grace: the Law and the Spirit (cf. Paul in 2 Cor. 3:7–18). When the writer adds that **no one has ever seen God**, he apparently has in mind Moses in particular, who was not allowed to see God's face (Exod. 33:20–23). In Jesus, the limitation imposed on Moses and the Israelites has been taken away (cf. 2 Cor. 3:18). To see his glory is to see God's glory, for he is **the Father's only Son** (v. 14). To see him is to see God (cf. 14:9), for he is **the same as God** (cf. v. 1).

The theme of the prologue has been revelation. Only God can reveal God, whether he is called **the Word** (v. 1) or **the only Son** (v. 18). The deity of Jesus Christ is presupposed throughout, yet the message is not simply that Jesus is God. The message is that because he is God his ministry on earth has made God known to us, and that now **at the Father's side** he continues to make God known through the Spirit (cf. 17:26). Throughout this Gospel, we see and hear him doing just that.

6

Additional Notes

1:1 / **Was the same as God**: lit., "was God." The absence in Greek of the definite article with "God" has led some to assume it to be used as an adjective ("the Word was divine") or even to supply, with polytheistic implications, an indefinite article ("the Word was a god," The New World Translation of the Jehovah's Witnesses, 1961). But there are two reasons why **Word** has the definite article in Greek and **God** does not: (1) to indicate that **Word** is the subject of the clause, even though in Greek it follows the verb "to be" (i.e., "the word was God" and not "God was the Word") and (2) to indicate that **Word** and **God** are not totally interchangeable terms. Though the Word is God, God is more than just the Word; God is also "the Father," while the Word is identified in v. 14 not as the Father but as the Father's "only Son." In the terms of later debates about Christ, the Word has the very nature of God, but the Word and the Father are not the same person.

1:4 / **The source of life**: There is a question of punctuation in the Greek text: Do the words *ho gegonen* (lit., "that which has been made") conclude the thought of v. 3, or begin v. 4? See B. M. Metzger, *A Textual Commentary on the Greek New Testament* (London and New York: United Bible Societies, 1971), pp. 195–96. The GNB, like most English versions, appears to presuppose the former by including in v. 3 the words "in all creation" (lit., "not one thing that has been made was made without him"). Yet the GNB wording in v. 4. (**the word was the source of life**) looks like an attempt to do justice to *ho gegonen* at the start of v. 4 as well (lit., "what had been made in him was life")! The latter is in any case the intent of the margin reading for v. 4: **What was made had life in union with the Word**. But a choice has to be made, and the overwhelming evidence of ancient manuscripts and church fathers is that in the early centuries *ho gegonen* was read as the beginning of v. 4, not the conclusion of v. 3. The point is not that in the Word there was life, but that through the Word life came into being. The GNB translation is therefore satisfactory if one assumes that the phrase, "in all creation" in v. 3 is merely a paraphrastic expansion and not an attempt to translate *ho gegonen* redundantly in the wrong place. Nothing essential would be lost if this phrase were simply omitted in v. 3, for *ho gegonen* has been acceptably, though freely, rendered in v. 4.

1:8 / **He himself was not the light**. Such a disclaimer about John the Baptist would have an especially pointed meaning over against the belief mentioned in the third-century Pseudo-Clementine *Recognitions* I, 54: "Some even of the disciples of John [the Baptist], who seemed to be great ones, separated themselves from the people, and proclaimed their own master as the Christ" (ANF 8.92).

1:9 / **That comes into the world**: The phrase in Greek can go either with **all mankind** or with **the light**. The context strongly favors the latter. To speak of every human being who **comes into the world** is wordy and out of keeping with

7

the prologue's economy of language. To speak of the light coming into the world lays an intelligible basis for the statement in the next verse that Jesus "was in the world." If the second alternative is correct, it may be construed either as GNB has done or (perhaps better) as a periphrastic construction, joining the verb "was" to the participle "coming": "The real light—the light that shines on all mankind—was coming into the world."

1:13 / **Not ... by natural means, that is, by being born as the children of a human father**: lit., "not of bloods, nor of the will of the flesh, nor of the will of the male"; i.e., not by ordinary sexual intercourse initiated by a husband's desire. They *are*, of course, born physically by those means, but this is not the birth referred to here.

1:14 / **Full of grace and truth**: Earlier editions of GNB ("We saw his glory, full of grace and truth") have been changed so as to connect the phrase **full of grace and truth** with Jesus personally, rather than with his glory. The ambiguity arises because the Greek word for **full** *(plērēs)* is here indeclinable, so that what it modifies must be determined from the context. It is difficult to know what "glory, full of grace and truth" might mean. The phrase is more intelligible as a decription of a person (cf. Acts 6:3, 5, 8; 7:55; 11:24). The change in the fourth edition of GNB therefore appears justified.

The Father's only Son: The phrase has metaphorical overtones. Jesus is to God as an only son is to a loving father. Yet here the metaphor has become reality, a serious confession of faith. Jesus does not receive glory *as if* God were his Father and he an only Son, but because that is in fact the case. The language is reminiscent of the baptism of Jesus. The term **only son** *(monogenēs)* focuses not on birth (as the KJV translation, "only-begotten," suggests) but on being uniquely the object of a father's love. It is used in much the same way as "beloved" *(agapētos)* in the synoptic accounts of the voice from heaven at Jesus' baptism (Mark 1:11; Matt. 3:17; Luke 3:22). The author of John's Gospel speaks as if he and his community, like John the Baptist, were eyewitnesses to the baptism of Jesus (cf. "we saw" in v. 14 with "I saw" in v. 32).

1:15 / **This is the one I was talking about**. An ancient text known to Origen in the third century (and probably to his Gnostic opponents even earlier) makes most of v. 15 a parenthesis identifying John the Baptist: "This was *the one who said*, 'He comes after me, but he is greater than I am, because he existed before I was born.' " The effect of this reading is to make v. 16 the actual message that John "speaks" and "has cried out" as a present testimony to the readers of the Gospel. (The tenses of GNB, **spoke** and **cried out**, are inexact and misleading in v. 15.) John the Baptist who once *said*, **He comes after me**, *etc.*, now *says*, **Out of the fullness of his grace he has blessed us all**, *etc.* This variant reading was adopted by Westcott and Hort in their Greek New Testament of 1881 (New York: Harper & Brothers) but by no other Greek edition (cf., however, the New World Translation of 1961 [Brooklyn: Watchtower and Tract Society], and the

8

1979 translation by Richmond Lattimore, *The Four Gospels and the Revelation* [New York: Farrar Straus Giroux]). For a defense of this reading and the above translation of it, see J. R. Michaels, "Origen and the Text of John 1:15," *New Testament Textual Criticism: Its Significance for Exegesis. Essays in Honour of Bruce M. Metzger* (Oxford: At the Clarendon Press, 1981), pp. 87–104.

1:18 / **Who is the same as God**: Some ancient manuscripts lack the identification of the **only Son** as **God** (*monogenēs theos* in Greek) using *monogenēs* instead as an adjective to reinforce *huios*, the more common Greek word for "son") i.e., *ho monogenēs huios*, "the unique Son," cf. 3:16; 1 John 4:9). But the reading presupposed by GNB is supported by better manuscripts and in all likelihood is correct. It is very improbable that scribes would have changed such a familiar Johannine expression as "the unique Son" to something so unusual and unfamiliar as *monogenēs theos*.

2

The First Two Days:
John the Baptist's Message

JOHN 1:19–34

The Jewish authorities in Jerusalem sent some priests and Levites to John to ask him, "Who are you?"

²⁰John did not refuse to answer, but spoke out openly and clearly, saying; "I am not the Messiah."

²¹"Who are you,then?" they asked. "Are you Elijah?"

"No, I am not," John answered.

"Are you the Prophet?"ᵇ they asked.

"No," he replied.

²²"Then tell us who you are," they said. "We have to take an answer back to those who sent us. What do you say about yourself?"

²³John answered by quoting the prophet Isaiah:

" 'I am the voice of someone
    shouting in the desert:
    make a straight path for the
    Lord to travel!' "

²⁴The messengers, who had been sent by the Pharisees, ²⁵thenᶜ asked John, "If you are not the Messiah nor Elijah nor the Prophet, why do you baptize?"

²⁶John answered, "I baptize with water, but among you stands the one you do not know. ²⁷He is coming after me, but I am not good enough even to untie his sandals."

²⁸All this happened in Bethany on the east side of the Jordan River, where John was baptizing.

²⁹The next day John saw Jesus coming to him, and said, "There is the Lamb of God, who takes away the sin of the world! ³⁰This is the one I was talking about when I said, 'A man is coming after me, but he is greater than I am, because he existed before I was born.' ³¹I did not know who he would be, but I came baptizing with water in order to make him known to the people of Israel."

³²And John gave this testimony: "I saw the Spirit come down like a dove from heaven and stay on him. ³³I still did not know that he was the one, but God, who sent me to baptize with water, had said to me, 'You will see the Spirit come down and stay on a man; he is the one who baptizes with the Holy Spirit.' ³⁴I have seen it," said John, "and I tell you that he is the Son of God."

b. THE PROPHET: *The one who was expected to appear and announce the coming of the Messiah.* c. The messengers, who had been sent by the Pharisees, then; *or* Those who had been sent were Pharisees; they.

The narrative portion of John's Gospel begins by referring yet a third time to the message of John the Baptist (cf. vv. 6–8, 15–16). The difference between this section and the references in the prologue is that attention now focuses on a *particular* testimony of John the Baptist given on a particular occasion when the Jewish authorities, later designated more precisely as **Pharisees** (v. 24), sent a delegation of priests and Levites from Jerusalem to question him. This occasion stretches out to at least a week. By the use of the phrase, **the next day** (vv. 29, 35, 43), and "two days later" (2:1), the writer presents a six-day sequence followed by an indefinite "few days" (2:12). The purpose is to highlight a memorable period at the beginning of Jesus' ministry. Day One consists of John the Baptist's negative testimony: He tells what he himself is *not* (vv. 19-28). Day Two consists of John's positive testimony: He proclaims Jesus and tells the people who Jesus is (vv. 29-34). The rest of the week consists of stories of how people came to faith, directly or indirectly as a result of John's testimony (1:35-2:11). C. H. Dodd has noticed how 1:6-8 serves as an appropriate outline for what follows: John was not the light (1:19-28) but came to testify about the light (1:29-34), so that through him everyone might believe (1:35-37; cf. 10:42). (*Historical Tradition in the Fourth Gospel* [Cambridge: Cambridge University Press, 1963], pp. 248-49.)

The questioning of John the Baptist on the first day recalls the popular response to his ministry according to Luke's Gospel: "People's hopes began to rise, and they began to wonder whether John perhaps might be the Messiah" (Luke 3:15). The difference in John's Gospel is a tone of implied hostility, rather than hopefulness. Both Luke and John presuppose considerable prior activity by John the Baptist. He must have attracted considerable attention in order to prompt such questions as **Who are you? Are you Elijah? Are you the Prophet?** It appears that the reader is being introduced to him rather well along in his ministry, perhaps even toward its end. According to the Book of Acts, it is "as John was about to finish his mission" that he "said to the people, 'Who do you think I am? I am not the one you are waiting for. But listen! He is coming after me' " (Acts 13:25).

The Baptizer knows what his questioners have in mind. They have not mentioned the Messiah explicitly, but he states without hesitation, **I am not the Messiah.** The Messiah, or anointed one, was viewed in several ways by the Jews of Jesus' time. Most often he was expected as a mighty king from the line of David (cf. "King of Israel," v. 49), but sometimes he was pictured as a great priest like Aaron or Melchizedek or a great teacher or prophet like Moses. When the messengers from Jerusalem ask **Are you Elijah?** and **Are you the Prophet?** they are still pressing the question of messiahship. John the Baptist's **no** to each of these titles sounds like a simple denial, but the Gospel writer insists that "he con-

11

fessed, he did not deny, but confessed" (v. 20, RSV) when he said **I am not the Messiah**. John the Baptist's disclaimer is actually a confession because of its implication to the reader that what John is not, Jesus is. Clearly, Jesus is the Messiah (cf. 1:41; 20:31), but he is also Elijah, and he is the Prophet. These are not titles John the Baptist will use in formulating his own positive testimony to Jesus (vv. 29, 34), but they are applicable nonetheless. The narrator has an interest throughout this chapter in collecting titles by which Jesus can be named and known. All are legitimate and appropriate, and some will prove more important than others, but in the Gospel as a whole the reality of who Jesus is will exceed any one title or even a collection of every possible title.

The prophecy of Malachi ends with God's promise that "before the great and terrible day of the Lord comes, I will send you the prophet Elijah. He will bring fathers and children together again; otherwise I would have to come and destroy your country" (Mal. 4:5–6). Christian tradition has regarded Elijah as a forerunner of the Messiah, but here he is seen as the forerunner of God himself and therefore a messianic figure in his own right. His mission is one of reconciliation, and his message one of repentance, the last chance for repentance before the dreaded "day of the Lord." This understanding of Elijah is apparently what lies behind the question addressed to John the Baptist. John's call to repentance and his baptizing ministry based on people's response to that call (cf. Mark 1:4–5) certainly raised the question, **Who are you?** and may well have prompted the conjecture that John was Elijah.

The question **Are you the Prophet?** also rests on a specific biblical text, in which Moses tells the Israelites that the Lord "will send you a prophet like me from among your own people, and you are to obey him. On the day that you were gathered at Mount Sinai, you begged not to hear the Lord speak again or to see his fiery presence any more, because you were afraid you would die. So the Lord said to me, 'They have made a wise request. I will send them a prophet like you from among their own people; I will tell him what to say, and he will tell the people everything I command. He will speak in my name, and I will punish anyone who refuses to obey him'" (Deut. 18:15–19). As far as this Gospel is concerned, the Prophet is Jesus just as surely as the Messiah is Jesus (cf. 6:15). Jesus is "the one whom Moses wrote about in the book of the Law" (1:45; cf. 5:46), and even when he is designated in other ways (e.g., as the Son), the repeated insistence in this Gospel is that he speaks only the words that the Father has given him. He is the Revealer, and thus the Prophet par excellence (cf. once more Heb. 1:1–2).

On the other hand, Jesus is nowhere in the New Testament explicitly identified as Elijah or said to fulfill Elijah's messianic role. Though analogies exist between Jesus' ministry and that of the historical Elijah (e.g., Luke 4:25–26; 7:11–17), and though some saw Jesus in this way (Mark 6:15; 8:28), Jesus himself is said to have reinterpreted Elijah's role in prophecy as preliminary rather than final and assigned that role to none other than John the Baptist! (e.g., Matt. 11:14; 17:10–13). But this was something new. John the Baptist himself still saw Elijah as a messianic figure and so shrank from identification with him. Implicit in his denial is the assumption that the One coming after him is Elijah, as well as the Prophet and the Messiah. This may account, as Raymond Brown suggests (*The Gospel According to John*, AB I [New York: Doubleday, 1966], p. 64) for John's remarkable pronouncement that the Coming One **existed before I was born** (v. 30). Elijah, like the Messiah and the Prophet, turns out by implication to be Jesus but there the Gospel writer lets it rest. The term "Messiah" will emphasize Jesus' kingship, and "Prophet" will call attention to the revelation that he brings; but an identification of Jesus as "Elijah" would only have complicated the picture without adding a useful dimension of its own. So the Gospel writer allows it to remain a merely negative and indirect testimony to Jesus Christ.

When the delegation from Jerusalem kept pressing the question of John's identity, he claimed (in the words of Isaiah) to be only **the voice of someone shouting in the desert: "Make a straight path for the Lord to travel!"** (v. 23; cf. Isa. 40:3). From the narrator's standpoint this meant that John the Baptist would prepare the way for Jesus (cf. 3:28), but from the standpoint of John's questioners, it was merely another evasion. If he is not a messianic figure, they asked, why does he baptize? (v. 25). John's baptizing ministry had attracted the authorities' attention, but is is not clear why they thought the practice had messianic implications. There is no evidence in ancient sources that baptism was considered part of the Messiah's (or the Prophet's) work. What concerned the messengers, therefore, was probably not the baptizing activity as such but the call to repentance that they knew it signified. How could a man who claimed for himself no messianic role summon the Jews of his day to such a decisive turning?

Yet even though the Gospel writer presupposes earlier traditions about John the Baptist's repentance preaching (cf. Mark 1:4, 15; Matt. 3:2, 7–10; Luke 3:2–3, 7–14), his own interest centers on the act of baptism itself. When asked **Why do you baptize?** John never mentions repentance in his answer. For the moment, in fact, he does not answer the question at all but defers the answer until Day Two. John the Baptist's crucial pronouncement is actually begun on one day and completed on the next. Someone familiar with the earlier traditions would expect him to say, "I baptize in water, but the One coming after me will baptize in the Holy Spirit" (cf. Mark 1:8). Instead, he pauses to emphasize the greatness of the Coming One (v. 27) and postpones the mention of Spirit baptism until Day Two (v. 33), *after* the Coming One has been identified. And even the completed pronouncement about water and Spirit leaves unanswered the question of *why* John baptizes. That too is left for Day Two. It is sufficient for the moment to make two points: first, that the identity of the Coming One is still unknown, but second, that he is incomparably greater than John himself.

The account of Day Two begins with John the Baptist's explicit identification of the Coming One as Jesus (vv. 29–30), an identification only hinted at in the other Gospels (e.g., Matt 11:3/Luke 7:20; Matt 3:14). John here carries out the role assigned to him in the prologue. He speaks for the entire Christian community in confessing Jesus to be both **Lamb of God** (v. 29) and **Son of God** (v. 34). Only now does he answer the question "Why do you baptize?" His baptism is for the sake of Jesus, "that he might be revealed to Israel" (v. 31, NIV). The **Israel** to whom Jesus is revealed is not the whole nation but a small circle of disciples, a group of "real Israelites" (cf. 1:47) who become the nucleus of a new community and to whom Jesus is later said to have "revealed his glory" (2:11, NIV) at Cana in Galilee.

Jesus is first identified as **the Lamb of God who takes away the sin of the world** (v. 29). The apparent reference to his sacrificial death comes unexpectedly at this point and (except for v. 36) has no known parallel in John the Baptist's teaching. Yet even in the Synoptics, John's baptism is said to be "for the forgiveness of sins" (Mark 1:4; Luke 3:3, NIV). The Coming One that he proclaims "will clear his threshing floor, gathering the wheat into his barn and burning up the chaff with unquenchable fire" (Matt. 3:12, NIV; cf. Luke 3:17). God's world is to be purified; all sin will be purged from the earth, and everything evil will be destroyed. **Lamb of God** by itself suggests a quite different image, the blood sacrifice of an innocent victim, but the point of the saying is not so much that the Lamb bears the *guilt* of the world's sin as that the Lamb quite literally *takes sin away*. The focus is on the result of the Lamb's work, not on the means of reaching that result.

The best commentary on this passage is 1 John 3:5, in which the language of John the Baptist lives on: "You know that Christ appeared in order to take away sins, and that there is no sin in him." "Appeared" is the same verb translated in the present passage as "revealed" or "made known," and though the title **Lamb** is missing in First John the mention of Jesus' sinlessness recalls the sacrificial lamb "without defect" pre-scribed in Old Testament Law (e.g., Exod. 12:15; Lev. 22:18–25; cf. 1 Pet. 1:19–20). "Taking away sins" is then equated, in a parallel formation in the context, with destroying the Devil's works: "The Son of God appeared for this very reason, to destroy what the Devil had done" (1 John 3:8). This, according to John's Gospel, is exactly what Jesus' death accom-plished: "Now is the time for this world to be judged; now the ruler of this world will be overthrown" (John 12:31; cf. 16:8–11). John the Baptist's message involves *both* salvation and judgment. Though he sees Jesus as a lamb, the work of this lamb is as many-sided as that of the messianic Lamb in the book of Revelation (e.g., Rev. 5:6–14). He is not simply a victim, but the world's Savior (cf. John 4:42) and its Judge. The future of the world, and of everyone in it, is in his hands.

John the Baptist immediately explains that it was indeed Jesus, the Lamb of God, that he was announcing earlier when he spoke somewhat indefinitely about the Coming One. At that time he did not know who the Coming One would be (v. 31), but now he does. Before the identity of the Coming One could be "revealed to Israel," it had to be revealed to John himself, and John proceeds to tell how that revelation came about. God gave him a signal: When he saw the Spirit come down from the sky and rest on a certain person, he would know that that person was the Coming One, who (just as John had promised) would baptize in the Holy Spirit (v. 33). At some point (presumably the baptism of Jesus), John the Baptist saw exactly that. The Spirit came down **like a dove** out of the sky and rested on Jesus, signifying to John that Jesus was **the Son of God** (vv. 32, 34). John the Baptist here becomes a participant in the supernatural events attending Jesus' baptism. The voice from heaven ("You are my own dear Son," Mark 1:11) goes unmentioned, but its place is taken by **Son of God** in John's testimony.

The baptism of Jesus is recounted only indirectly and in retrospect. It is not really part of the narrator's six-day sequence. Already on the first day, John the Baptist had told the delegation from Jerusalem that **among you stands the one you do not know** (1:26). The implication is that by this time John himself *does* know him, for he adds **I am not good enough even to untie his sandals** (1:27). The events recalled in verses 32–34 are already in the past, and Jesus is in Bethany (**among you,** 1:26), probably

15

in the company of John's followers. Therefore, when John sees **Jesus coming to him** (v. 29) it is not for baptism but is simply the narrator's way of bringing Jesus dramatically on the scene. There is no way to be sure how long before the six days Jesus' baptism is supposed to have taken place or how long Jesus' association with John is thought to have lasted. The references to the Spirit not only "coming down" on Jesus but "staying" on him (vv. 32, 33) suggest that John the Baptist may have had weeks or even months to get to know Jesus as a man full of the Spirit (cf. 1:16; 3:34) before publicly revealing him to **Israel**. Whether this means that Jesus was himself one of John's disciples is a question of interest to historians, but apparently not to the Gospel writer. Looking back on the association two chapters later, John's disciples refer to Jesus vaguely as "the man who was with you on the east side of the Jordan" (3:26), and the author is content to leave the matter there.

Additional Notes

1:23 / **John answered by quoting**. Only in this Gospel does the quotation of Isa. 40:3 appear on the lips of John the Baptist himself. In the other Gospels it is part of the comment of the Gospel writer (Mark 1:3; Luke 3:4; Matt. 3:3). In Matthew, however, it is closely joined to John's own words and may have been adapted from them with only slight changes ("This is [rather than "I am"] he who was spoken of through the prophet Isaiah," NIV). If Isa. 40:3 helped shape the consciousness of the Essene community of Qumran in going out to the Judean desert to study the Law (1 QS viii 13–16), there is no reason why it could not have influenced John the Baptist as well.

1:24 / **Who had been sent by the Pharisees**: The parenthetical remark that the delegation was from the Pharisees reiterates v. 19 and thus (by appearing to make a fresh start) sets off the last and most crucial question (**Why do you baptize?**) from the series of preliminary questions that led up to it.

Another possible translation is, "Some Pharisees also were sent," but it is highly unlikely that the writer would either introduce a new delegation at this point or belatedly add **Pharisees** to "priests and Levites" in the same delegation!

1:25 / **If you are not . . . Elijah**: The only hint of a Jewish belief that Elijah was expected to baptize comes from a Christian document a half century later than the Gospel of John. Justin Martyr, in his *Dialogue with Trypho* 8.4, represents Trypho the Jew as claiming that the Messiah is unknown "until Elijah comes to anoint him and make him manifest to all" (see ANF 1.199). It should be noted, first, that even here the word **baptize** is not used, and second, that in other respects the passage appears to have been shaped by the Gospel's account of what John the Baptist actually did for Jesus (cf. John 1:31). It therefore testifies more faithfully to Christian than to Jewish traditions.

1:28 / **In Bethany on the east side of the Jordan River**: The place is otherwise unknown. It was a mystery even to Origen in the third century, who adopted instead the reading "Bethabara" (*Commentary on John* 6.40), a town east of the Jordan mentioned in other ancient sources. Pierson Parker (" 'Bethany beyond Jordan,' " *JBL* 74 [1955], p. 258) identified this Bethany with the Bethany just outside Jerusalem by translating the location as "across from where John had baptized in Jordan." But elsewhere in John's Gospel (i.e., 3:26; 10:40) the phrase "beyond the Jordan" clearly refers to the east bank (i.e., the present Kingdom of Jordan), and there is no reason to understand it differently here. It is in any case unlikely that the writer would identify the well-known Bethany of Martha, Mary, and Lazarus in such a strange manner (contrast 11:1, 18). So the location of this other Bethany east of the Jordan remains undetermined.

Two features of the narrative deserve mention: (1) Aside from the quotation of Isa. 40:3, no particular emphasis is placed on John's ministry being "in the desert." Bethany to the east of the Jordan is presumably a village, like "Aenon, not far from Salim" on the Judean side (cf. 3:23). The ensuing narrative suggests that Jesus had a place to live there (1:39), and that fig trees grew in the vicinity (1:48). (2) The text does not say in so many words that John the Baptist was baptizing in the Jordan River. Though the synoptic Gospels make it clear that he did baptize in the Jordan (Mark 1:5; Matt. 3:6), John's Gospel indicates greater mobility on his part. He baptized at Aenon because "there was plenty of water" there (i.e., probably natural springs and pools), and the same may have been true at Bethany.

1:29 / **Lamb of God**: C. H. Dodd (*The Interpretation of the Fourth Gospel* [Cambridge: University Press, 1958], pp. 230–38) argued for a Jewish background to the title from apocalyptic references to the Messiah as a powerful young ram who defends the flock of God against its adversaries and puts them to flight. This is an appealing suggestion and one that may well be correct, but the evidence is meager (only *Enoch* 90.38 and *Testament of Joseph* 19.8, the latter of which may actually be a Christian interpretation of John 1:29 rather than the source of it). As Dodd himself seemed to recognize (pp. 236–38), the more significant evidence is the Lamb in the book of Revelation, together with 1 John 3:5 and the undeniable fact that making an end of sin was one of the functions of the Jewish Messiah.

Other suggestions (for example, that **Lamb of God** recalls the Passover Lamb, or the Servant described in Isaiah 53, or Abraham's sacrifice of Isaac in Genesis 22) fall short, first, because they weaken the credibility of this verse as a pronouncement of John the Baptist in particular, and second, because even for the Gospel writer these themes are peripheral rather than central to the understanding of Jesus' redemptive death (though see 8:56; 19:14, 36).

1:30 / **A man is coming after me**. It is necessary to keep in mind the time frame of this verse. The announcement that **a man is coming after me, but he is greater than I am, because he existed before I was born** was made earlier than

17

the events described in this Gospel, earlier even than Jesus' baptism. Back at that time, John says, **I did not know who he would be** (v. 31). John was still speaking of an indefinite Coming One, not of Jesus in particular, for he had not yet seen the sign of the dove that identified the Coming One as Jesus. Therefore, when he says, **a man is coming after me**, he must be referring to real temporal succession ("a man will come along later") and not, as some have suggested, to discipleship ("a man now following me as my disciple has taken precedence over me"). To "come after" can indeed be an expression for discipleship (cf. Mark 8:34), but John's statement here cannot be used as proof that Jesus was John's disciple.

The same is probably true of 1:27, even though this verse is spoken at a later time when John the Baptist knows that the Coming One is now present (v. 26). The statement that "he is the one who comes after me" (v. 27, NIV) is probably another reference back to the same earlier saying quoted in v. 30, *not* an intimation that Jesus is John's disciple. This saying is quoted *only* in retrospect in the Gospel (1:15, 30), and the brief allusion to it in 1:27 appears to be no exception.

1:33 / **I still did not know**. The translation is confusing. John has just said that he saw the Spirit come down on Jesus, so that according to v. 33 he now should know that Jesus is the one. More commonly, these words are given the same time reference as in v. 31: At first John *had not known* who the Coming One was. It is also possible grammatically to read the sentence as conditional: "I would not have known . . . *except that* God said to me . . ." (see *BDF* par. 360, 448[8]).

1:34 / **Son of God**: Some important ancient manuscripts read, instead, "the Chosen One (Gr.: *eklektos*) of God." A strong case can be made for this variant. It is easy to see how a copyist might have changed "Chosen One of God" to the better-known **Son of God**, and difficult to imagine a change in the opposite direction. Also the titles given to Jesus in this chapter are, as a rule, not duplicated, and **Son of God** does appear later in 1:49. Yet the manuscript evidence for **Son of God** is very strong. That the copyists of the most ancient manuscripts were quite willing to let an unusual or unfamiliar title for Christ stand if they judged it authentic is shown by the well-attested "Holy One of God" in 6:69. Here **Son of God** is probably what the author wrote, but "Chosen One of God" was also clearly remembered and firmly fixed in some of the earliest traditions about John the Baptist (whether written or oral), so that it persisted in the manuscript tradition. **Son** possibly represents the Gospel writer's interpretation of John the Baptist's own term "Chosen One" (c.f., e.g., the use of "Son of God" in connection with a reference to Jesus' baptism in 1 John 5:5).

3

The Next Two Days:
The Call of the Disciples

JOHN 1:35–51

The next day John was standing there again with two of his disciples, ³⁶when he saw Jesus walking by. "There is the Lamb of God!" he said.

³⁷The two disciples heard him say this and went with Jesus. ³⁸Jesus turned, saw them following him, and asked, "What are you looking for?"

They answered, "Where do you live, Rabbi?" (This word means "Teacher.")

³⁹"Come and see," he answered. (It was then about four o'clock in the afternoon.) So they went with him and saw where he lived, and spent the rest of that day with him.

⁴⁰One of them was Andrew, Simon Peter's brother. ⁴¹At once he found his brother Simon and told him, "We have found the Messiah." (This word means "Christ.") ⁴²Then he took Simon to Jesus.

Jesus looked at him and said, "Your name is Simon son of John, but you will be called Cephas." (This is the same as Peter and means "a rock.")

⁴³The next day Jesus decided to go to Galilee. He found Philip and said to him, "Come with me!" (⁴⁴Philip was from Bethsaida, the town where Andrew and Peter lived.) ⁴⁵Philip found Nathanael and told him, "We have found the one whom Moses wrote about in the book of the Law and whom the prophets also wrote about. He is Jesus son of Joseph, from Nazareth."

⁴⁶"Can anything good come from Nazareth?" Nathanael asked.

"Come and see," answered Philip.

⁴⁷When Jesus saw Nathanael coming to him, he said about him, "Here is a real Israelite; there is nothing false in him!"

⁴⁸Nathanael asked him, "How do you know me?"

Jesus answered, "I saw you when you were under the fig tree before Philip called you."

⁴⁹"Teacher," answered Nathanael, "you are the Son of God! You are the King of Israel!"

⁵⁰Jesus said, "Do you believe just because I told you I saw you when you were under the fig tree? You will see much greater things than this!"

⁵¹And he said to them, "I am telling you the truth: you will see heaven open and God's angels going up and coming down on the Son of Man."

John the Baptist repeats his testimony to Jesus as **Lamb of God** in the presence of two of his disciples (v. 36). This is how he makes Jesus known to "Israel." In effect, he delivers his own disciples over to Jesus. One of the two is said to be Andrew (v. 40), but the other is not identified. It is widely assumed that the second disciple is the Gospel writer himself, the "beloved disciple" mentioned five times in the latter half of the Gospel. But not all anonymous disciples have to be the same. More likely, the second disciple is Philip (cf. 1:43), who appears alongside Andrew on two other occasions (6:5–9; 12:21–22) and who, like Andrew, brings someone else to Jesus (1:43–51). The two disciples in verses 35–39 thus anticipate verses 40–42 and 43–51 respectively: Jesus calls Andrew and Philip; Andrew brings his brother Simon to Jesus, while Philip brings Nathanael.

The story of the call is classically simple. The two disciples hear John's proclamation and follow Jesus. The act of **following**, however, which connotes discipleship, is not the end of the story but its beginning. Jesus asks them what they are looking for, and their request is to see where he lives. So they visit his quarters in Bethany and spend the day with him. In the interest of accuracy, the narrator adds the qualification that they actually spent only part of a day, because it was already **about four o'clock in the afternoon** (v. 39) and the day ended at sundown. What mattered most was not how long they stayed, but simply the fact that they spent time with Jesus. He became their rabbi, or teacher (v. 38; cf. 13:13). Discipleship in this Gospel means not only following Jesus but remaining with him. From time to time Jesus will be seen spending time privately with disciples or would-be disciples between public confrontations with the authorities in Jerusalem (e.g., 2:12; 3:22; 4:40; 6:3; 10:40–42; 11:54; 18:2). Before his departure from the world, Jesus tells his disciples to "remain" united to him by remaining in his love and obeying his commands (15:1–10). Discipleship begins with leaving one's past life to "follow" Jesus (cf. Mark 1:16–20) and comes to completion either in "following" him at last to a martyr's death or "remaining" faithful to him in a life of loving obedience (cf. John 21:19–23).

Because the two disciples spend the rest of Day Three with Jesus, the events of verses 40–42 must take place on Day Four. The **at once** of verse 41 apparently means "at the first opportunity." But if the call of Simon belongs to Day Four, why has the narrator not put it there? A possible explanation is that he does not want it to detract from the more extended account of the call of Nathanael, which is where his chief interest lies. The call of Simon is part of his tradition and he has no desire to leave it out, but strictly speaking it has no day of its own assigned to it in the six-day sequence. It is simply an appendix to Day Three, included for the sake of completeness and to prepare for the events of Day Four. Andrew finds Simon and says, **We have found the Messiah** (v. 41); Philip finds Nathanael and says, **We have found the one whom Moses wrote about**

(1:45); Jesus calls Simon **a rock** (**Cephas** or **Peter**, v. 42), and Nathanael, **a real Israelite** (1:47). But here the parallels stop. Jesus' interview with Simon Peter ends as abruptly as it began, whereas Nathanael goes on to confess his faith and receive a promise on behalf of all the disciples (1:49–51).

If we had only this introductory narrative we would conclude that Simon Peter was a minor figure in John's Gospel and Nathanael a major one, but as it turns out, the reverse is true. Simon Peter's confession is not omitted, only deferred (6:68–69), and the reader will learn more about him than about any other disciple (e.g., 13:36–38; 18:15–18, 25–27; 21:15–19). But little is made of Simon's new name. There is no equivalent to the Matthean promise to Peter that "on this rock I will build my church" (Matt. 16:18, NIV). Though this disciple is commonly known as "Peter" or "Simon Peter," Jesus can still address him as late as 21:15–17 as "Simon son of John." The tradition of Peter the Rock is preserved and affirmed, but more important to the Gospel writer is Simon the Shepherd (again cf. 21:15–17).

Philip's "call" is different from the call described in verses 35–39. Jesus **found** Philip (v. 43) just as Andrew "found" Simon (v. 41) and just as Philip himself **found** Nathanael a short time later (v. 45). In the other two cases, "finding" implies the seeking out of a particular person: Andrew looked for his brother, and Philip looked for his Galilean friend. It is likely that Jesus, too, did not just run into Philip by chance but knew him and sought him out deliberately.

This makes sense if Philip is indeed the unnamed disciple of the previous day. When Jesus says to Philip, **Come with me** (v. 43), it is therefore *not* the initial call to discipleship but an invitation to accompany Jesus to Galilee. The point of the parenthetical note that Philip, as well as Andrew and Peter, were Galileans from Bethsaida is to show the appropriateness of such an invitation. But what were all these Galileans doing in Bethany, on the east side of the Jordan, with John the Baptist? Even Nathanael turns out to be from Cana in Galilee (21:1). Galilee and the region beyond the Jordan were both under the rule of Herod Antipas the Tetrarch, whose marital adventures John denounced and who finally imprisoned John and put him to death (Mark 6:17–29; cf. Josephus, *Antiquities* 18.116–19). John the Baptist obviously attracted considerable attention in Galilee, a center for messianic expectations, and it is not surprising that he is represented here as having gained a Galilean following.

Now the group of Galileans is going home. Their journey to attend

21

the wedding at Cana (2:1–11) and to spend a few days at Capernaum (2:12) is under way. Only Jesus and Philip are mentioned at first, but the assumption in chapter 2 is that all of Jesus' disciples (at least four in number) are present. The group forms when Philip tells his fellow Galilean Nathanael a startling bit of news: The Messiah has appeared and is himself a Galilean, **Jesus son of Joseph, from Nazareth** (v. 45). Nathanael's answer reflects a kind of provincialism in reverse that refuses to see glory or greatness in anything familiar or close to home. When he asks, **Can anything good come from Nazareth?** (v. 46), it is not a matter of small town rivalries but of that human blindness described in Francis Thompson's *In No Strange Land:*

Not where the wheeling systems darken,
And our benumbed conceiving soars!
The drift of pinions, would we hearken,
Beats at our own clay-shuttered doors.

The angels keep their ancient places;
Turn but a stone, and start a wing!
'Tis ye, 'tis your estrangèd faces,
That miss the many-splendored thing.

Nathanael's attitude parallels that of the people in the synagogues at Capernaum (6:42) and at Nazareth itself (Mark 6:1–6; cf. Luke 4:16–30). Because Jesus' antecedents are local, and known locally, he cannot be anyone special. He certainly cannot be **the one whom Moses wrote about in the book of the Law and whom the prophets also wrote about** (v. 45). As some said later in Jerusalem, "when the Messiah comes, no one will know where he is from. And we all know where this man comes from" (7:27). In particular, the Messiah was not supposed to come from Galilee (7:40). Though Nathanael's skepticism was probably based as much on feeling as on doctrine, the narrator has made him the spokesman for all such biases. Probably, when the Gospel was written, Jews were saying of the Christians (or Nazarenes), "Can anything good come from Nazareth?" (cf. Acts 24:5). Nathanael's conversion therefore typifies the conversion of any Jew who overcomes such prejudices against Christianity and believes in Jesus. Nathanael, Jesus declares, is **a real Israelite; there is nothing false in him** (v. 47).

Jesus shows here, even more clearly than in his renaming of Simon, a supernatural insight into people's character (cf. 2:25). He is apparently referring to the patriarch Jacob, who practiced deception until he met God in the person of an angel and had his name changed to "Israel" (Gen. 32:28). Nathanael is an **Israelite** worthy of that name. Jesus is not so much praising Nathanael's candor in giving voice to his skepticism (v. 46) as simply doing what he did for Simon: looking at him and seeing not what he is but what he will become. Nor does Nathanael's reply (v. 48a) mean that he immodestly considers himself "a real Israelite." He merely expresses surprise that Jesus speaks as if they had met before. Jesus' strange allusion to seeing him **under the fig tree** (v. 48b) strikes a responsive chord and becomes for him a sign of Jesus' supernatural knowledge.

One can only speculate about what Jesus meant by **under the fig tree**. Was he referring to an incident in Bethany just before Philip brought Nathanael to him, or to something in Galilee in the more distant past? Why was the fig tree so significant to Nathanael? Because there are no answers to these questions, it is possible that the story has a symbolic side to it. If Nathanael is a **real Israelite** representing the "Israel" to whom Jesus must be revealed (cf. 1:31), then the saying recalls Hosea 9:10: "When I found Israel, it was like finding grapes in the desert; when I saw your fathers, it was like seeing the early fruit on the fig tree" (NIV). The point is perhaps that Jesus finds the new Israel in the same way that God his Father found the old. Jesus spoke elsewhere of the delight of uncovering an unexpected treasure in a field or of selling everything to acquire a magnificent pearl (Matt. 13:44–45), or of finding a lost coin or a lost sheep (Luke 15:1–10). Hosea's image of discovering fruit in a barren land was well suited to make a similar point. Jesus' disciples are indeed a precious find, a gift from the Father (cf. 6:37; 17:6), but because it is too early in the Gospel for such a disclosure, the pronouncement remains something of an enigma.

Nathanael, like the Samaritan woman after him, hears Jesus' words as the pronouncement of One "who told me everything I have ever done" (cf. 4:29). But while the Samaritan woman merely raised the possibility that Jesus might be the Messiah, Nathanael announces boldly and without question that **you are the Son of God! You are the King of Israel!** (v. 49).

The two titles, virtually synonymous in this context, are alternate ways of saying that Jesus is the Messiah (cf. vv. 41, 45). The designation of Israel's anointed king as God's son goes back to Psalm 2:6–7. The Gospel writer knows that Jesus is the Son of God in a more profound sense than Nathanael could have understood (cf. 1:14, 18), yet he allows Nathanael (like John the Baptist) to speak for the Christian community.

23

Nathanael's **Son of God** and **King of Israel** anticipate the Gospel writer's hope that all his readers "may believe that Jesus is the Messiah, the Son of God" and so have life (20:31). Within Nathanael's limitations, **King of Israel** (i.e., Messiah) defines what **Son of God** means, but for the writer and his readers **Son of God** (i.e., the divine eternal Son) defines what "Messiah" or **King of Israel** means. The Gospel of John is the story of the crowning of the Son of God as King, paradoxically, in his death (cf. 12:13, 15; 19:14, 19).

Nathanael has prophesied the end from the beginning, yet his confession is not quite adequate. The words are right, but they rest on an insufficient foundation. Nathanael believed because he was impressed with Jesus' supernatural knowledge. Jesus promises him, and the other disciples, **much greater things than this** (v. 50). They will see **heaven open and God's angels going up and coming down on the Son of Man** (v. 51). The promised vision is like that of Jacob, who "dreamed that he saw a stairway reaching from earth to heaven, with angels going up and coming down on it" (Gen. 28:12). In the place of Jacob is the **Son of Man**, Jesus himself. The vision is his, but the disciples, like John the Baptist at Jesus' baptism (1:32–34), will share in that vision. They will begin to see "his glory, the glory which he received as the Father's only Son" (1:14).

The events of four days have been leading up to this pronouncement. All the varied titles for Jesus—"Messiah," "Lamb of God," "Son of God," "King of Israel"—find their answer in the self-designation **Son of Man**. In all the Gospels, this is Jesus' most characteristic and distinctive term for himself. The promise of a vision of the Son of Man recalls his statement in Mark 14:62 at his trial that "you will all see the Son of Man seated at the right side of the Almighty and coming with the clouds of heaven" (cf. Matt. 26:64). The difference is that in our passage the Son of Man is *on earth*. Like Jacob, he is at the *bottom* of the stairway, the recipient of divine revelation and the focus of that revelation in the world. Nathanael and the other disciples will see the truth, not in the far-off heavens or a distant future, and not in the messianic doctrines of the rabbis, but right now before their very eyes, in Jesus himself (cf. Rom. 10:6–8). Nathanael is promised a vision that will overcome his disdain for the familiar and the commonplace. He will learn what it means that "the Word became a human being . . . and lived among us" (1:14). His vision of glory (even from Nazareth!) lives on in the next stanza of Francis Thompson's poem:

But (when so sad thou canst not sadder)
Cry, and upon thy so sore loss
Shall shine the traffic of Jacob's ladder
Pitched between heaven and Charing Cross!

The question remains of when and how the vision came to pass. Did Nathanael and the others actually see **angels going up and coming down on the Son of Man**? John the Baptist's promised vision of the descending Spirit came to pass at Jesus' baptism, but there is no comparable event with which to connect this promise. There is no definite time at which the disciples literally *saw* Jesus re-enacting the dream of Jacob, any more than there is a definite time at which the Jewish High Priest *saw* Jesus "seated at the right side of the Almighty and coming with the clouds of heaven" (Mark 14:62). Nor do angels play any significant role in the fourth Gospel (cf. only 12:29; 20:12). Yet **angels going up and down on the Son of Man** is just as much a reality as Jesus seated at God's right hand and coming to earth again. It is the same reality witnessed by John the Baptist, the reality that Jesus Christ *even in his humanity* is united to heaven and enjoys perfect communion with God his Father (cf. 8:29; 11:41–42). The disciples will **see** this reality not in a particular vision of angels, but in Jesus' ministry as a whole, beginning with the wedding at Cana.

Additional Notes

1:39 / **About four o'clock in the afternoon**: lit., "the tenth hour." The Jews reckoned the daylight hours from 6:00 A.M. Some have argued that John's Gospel follows instead a Roman-Egyptian system similar to ours, in which the day begins at midnight. This would mean that the two disciples joined Jesus at 10:00 A.M. The reckoning of hours becomes an issue in fixing the exact time of Jesus' death (cf. 19:14), but the burden of proof is on those who deny that the writer is following the common Jewish practice.

1:51 / **I am telling you the truth**: lit., "Amen, amen, I say to you." This formula is used twenty-four times in John's Gospel with sayings of special importance either to the Gospel writer himself or those from whom he received his traditions. It is a solemn attestation of the truth of the saying to follow, a rhetorical form that originated with Jesus. "Amen" was customarily used to conclude a statement or a prayer, but Jesus used it instead as an introduction. The doubled "amen" occurs only (and always) in the fourth Gospel, but appears to have the same meaning as the single "amen" of the Synoptics.

On the Son of Man: In the Greek translation of Gen. 28:12, Jacob saw the angels going up and down "on it" (i.e., on the ladder or stairway), but the original Hebrew is ambiguous and some of the rabbis read the text as "on him" (i.e., on Jacob). The phrase in John's Gospel uses the Greek preposition *epi* with the accusative case to denote motion toward an object. The one preposition actually does service for two; the meaning is that angels ascend *from* and descend *to* the Son of Man. The Son of Man does not correspond to the stairway in Jacob's vision, but to Jacob himself at the bottom. Jesus enters into the vision of the patriarch, imaginatively makes it his own, and by his word, shares it in turn with his disciples.

The Last Two Days:
A Wedding in Galilee

JOHN 2:1–12

Two days later there was a wedding in the town of Cana in Galilee. Jesus' mother was there, [2]and Jesus and his disciples had also been invited to the wedding. [3]When the wine had given out, Jesus' mother said to him, "They are out of wine."

[4]"You must not tell me what to do," Jesus replied. "My time has not yet come."

[5]Jesus' mother then told the servants, "Do whatever he tells you."

[6]The Jews have rules about ritual washing, and for this purpose six stone water jars were there, each one large enough to hold between twenty and thirty gallons. [7]Jesus said to the servant, "Fill these jars with water." They filled them to the brim, [8]and then he told them, "Now draw some water out and take it to the man in charge of the feast." They took him the water, [9]which now had turned into wine, and he tasted it. He did not know where this wine had come from (but, of course, the servants who had drawn out the water knew); so he called the bridegroom [10]and said to him, "Everyone else serves the best wine first, and after the guests have drunk a lot, he serves the ordinary wine. But you have kept the best wine until now!"

[11]Jesus performed this first miracle in Cana in Galilee; there he revealed his glory, and his disciples believed in him.

[12]After this, Jesus and his mother, brothers, and disciples went to Capernaum and stayed there a few days.

The journey home to Galilee is not described. The writer focuses instead on a single incident that took place after the group arrived. Debates about whether one could reach Galilee from Bethany in two days are pointless, first, because the exact location of Bethany is unknown (see note on 1:28), and second, because the phrase **two days later** (lit., "on the third day") could sometimes be used to express a short indefinite period of time (like "a couple of days" in colloquial English). Strictly speaking, the phrase means "the day after tomorrow" (cf. Luke 13:32), that is, the third day after Jesus met Nathanael. This would be Day Six. But the Gospel writer may not be speaking strictly, and in any case, the number he has assigned to this day is not six but three! He is surely more precise here than in verse 12 ("a few days"), and there is nothing wrong in counting a six-day sequence. But the emphasis is on the *sequence*, not on the total of six. If there were more days, or fewer, the point would be much the same. Interpretations that speak of the sequence as "six days of the new creation" corresponding to the six-day week of Genesis 1 are questionable. Nor is it likely that the sequence is intended to correspond to the "six days before the Passover" near the end of Jesus' ministry (cf. 12:1) or the six days prior to his transfiguration (cf. Mark 9:2; Matt. 17:1). More to the point is the observation that "the third day" recalls language used of Jesus' resurrection from the dead (e.g., Matt. 16:21; Luke 24:7, 21; 1 Cor. 15:4), as the miracle at Cana anticipates the glory of that event. Yet even this is speculative at best; "the third day" is not used explicitly of Jesus' resurrection in John's Gospel (though cf. "three days" in 2:19). To expect it to carry that connotation here, where it is part of a larger sequence, probably attributes too much ingenuity to the writer and too much sophistication to his readers.

The story unfolds quickly. A marriage took place in Cana. Jesus' mother, Mary (who is not named in this Gospel), was among the invited guests, and probably because of her, Jesus and his disciples were invited as well. The Gospel writer assumes that she attributes to Jesus supernatural power, for when the wine gives out she speaks to him as if he can do something about it (v. 3). His answer confirms the notion that her remark was actually an implied request: **"You must not tell me what to do,"** **Jesus replied. "My time has not yet come."** (v. 4). Undeterred by his apparent refusal, Mary takes him at his word and leaves the matter in his hands (v. 5). Jesus proceeds to have six huge ceremonial jars filled with water (well over a hundred gallons in all), and when the water is drawn out it is found to have been changed to wine (vv. 6–9)! The actual transformation is hardly mentioned at all, being relegated to a participle in Greek, a subordinate clause in English (v. 9). But the greatness of the miracle is attested (unwittingly!) by a humorous comment of the man in charge of the feast. **Everyone else serves the best wine first, and after** **the guests have drunk a lot, he serves the ordinary wine. But you** **have kept the best wine until now!** (v. 10).

The incident can be viewed either in itself or as part of the Gospel as a whole. In itself, it is a curious account of a rather extravagant miracle performed not to meet a desperate human need but simply to avert a social disaster. It is told soberly and simply, as a true incident, yet it has richly symbolic overtones that probably account for its inclusion here. Though the story proper is framed by references to Jesus' disciples (vv. 2, 11), the disciples have no role in the actual account of the miracle. They serve instead to fix the story in its present context in John's Gospel. The disciples' response is what gives the story significance within that larger context: **Jesus performed this first miracle in Cana in Galilee; there he revealed his glory, and his disciples believed in him** (v. 11). For the narrator, their place within the story proper is taken by the **servants** to whom Mary said, **"Do whatever he tells you"** (v. 5), and who alone, we are told, knew where the good wine had come from (v. 9). In a sense these servants represent not only the first four disciples but everyone who knows where Jesus comes from and does what he commands. As soon as the miracle story has been told, attention centers on the disciples and their response. The purpose of the miracle is to reveal Jesus' glory to them, the new Israel (cf. 1:31), and so bring to realization the vision promised to Nathanael. The explicit statement that they believed in Jesus (v. 11) completes their call and marks an auspicious beginning to his Galilean ministry.

After the single miracle at Cana and a short stay at Capernaum, Jesus will go to Jerusalem at the season of Passover and drive the money-changers from the Temple (cf. 2:13–22). To a reader familiar with the other Gospels, it appears that Jesus' Passion is already under way (cf. Mark 11:15–18). The impression given is that the Gospel of John is to be a short Gospel indeed! The impression is, of course, misleading, because Jesus' activities continue, with several journeys back and forth between Jerusalem and Galilee. Not until chapter 12 does he come to Jerusalem for the last time, and not until chapter 18 is he placed under arrest. In chapter 2, as he tells his mother, his **time has not yet come** (v. 4). Yet the early placement of the Temple cleansing is deliberate, and its effect is twofold. First, it puts everything that follows under the shadow of Jesus' impending Passion and gives his dialogues with the Jews the character of a trial. Second, it makes the story of the Cana wedding a kind of epitome or scale model of Jesus' entire Galilean ministry, in which he turns the water of traditional ritual cleansing (v. 6) into the wine of a new and joyous messianic age.

Jesus' ministry is seen in much the same way here as in certain synoptic parables. When asked why his disciples did not fast, he once asked in return, "Do you expect the guests at a wedding party to go without food? Of course not! As long as the bridegroom is with them, they will not do that" (Mark 2:19). Jesus was not, of course, the bridegroom at the Cana wedding, yet in the imaginative world of his parables he saw himself as a bridegroom and his time on earth as a joyful wedding celebration. He also spoke significantly of "new wine," which he said "must be poured into new wineskins" (Mark 2:22). It was probably imagery of this kind, traceable to Jesus himself, that led the writer of John's Gospel to use a wine miracle at a wedding feast as an appropriate symbol for all that preceded the Passion.

A sense of "already, but not yet" pervades the narrative. Jesus displays his glory and his disciples come to faith, but only after a clear signal to the reader that this revelation is provisional and not final (v. 4). The proper time for Jesus' "glorification" is at his death (cf. 12:23; 13:31; 17:1, 5), and that time has not yet come. The miracle at Cana is a display of glory ahead of time, a display that typifies his Galilean ministry as a whole and specifically fulfills his promise to Nathanael. The juxtaposition of 1:19–51 and 2:1–11 in the text of John's Gospel allows each to interpret the other. Jesus is now "revealed to Israel" (1:31, NIV). But if the Cana narrative is the end of something—that is, the six-day sequence with its promise of glory—it is also a beginning. **First miracle** (v. 11) indicates that more will follow. More miracles do follow, but the Gospel writer has in mind one in particular, the healing of a government official's son at that same Cana in Galilee (see 4:54). Much has been written about a miracle or signs source used by the author of this Gospel, but the numbering of Jesus' miracles stops at two. The two Cana miracles form a pair distinct from all the rest. Neither of them gives rise to discourse or controversy. Both do exactly what the Gospel writer wants miracles to do: They lead people to believe in Jesus and through faith in him to gain life (see 20:31).

The length of Jesus' stay in Capernaum with his mother and brothers and his disciples cannot be determined from the text. The vagueness of **a few days** stands in marked contrast to the deliberate sequence of days extending from 1:19 to 2:11. Verse 12 represents a momentary pause, a brief respite in the action before Jesus' first confrontation with Jerusalem and the Temple. Other such pauses take place in Bethany, east of the Jordan (10:40–42), and in a town called Ephraim, near the desert (11:54). Jesus has said to his mother, **My time has not yet come** (v. 4), and now, it appears, they are simply waiting.

Additional Notes

2:4 / **You must not tell me what to do**: lit., "what to me and to you?" A slightly more literal translation suitable to the present context is "What has that to do with me?" The idiom is used both in Hebrew and Greek literature to dissociate the speaker from the listener (cf., e.g., the demons crying out at Jesus in Mark

1:24 and 5:7). The GNB translation is interpretive but accurate: Jesus is insisting that if he acts, it must be on his own initiative in obedience to God his Father. His hand will not be forced, even by a close relative (cf. 7:6–10).

In the Greek he addresses his mother as "woman," a term which carries no disrespect (cf. 19:26), but which similarly dissociates Jesus from the traditional mother-son relationship and places him solely under God's directive.

2:6 / Between twenty and thirty gallons: lit., "two or three measures." A "measure" was about nine gallons, yielding an approximation of 20 or 25 gallons for each jar.

2:8 / Now draw some water out. B. F. Westcott suggested that Jesus is commanding more water to be drawn *from the well* from which the jars had been filled, not from the jars themselves (*The Gospel According to St. John* [Grand Rapids: Eerdmans, 1950; reprint of 1881 edition], pp. 37–38). This would avoid the assumption that Jesus produced such a huge quantity of wine, and it is true that the same verb is used in 4:7, 15 for drawing water from a well. But there has been no explicit mention of the water source (as, e.g., 4:6 and 9:7), only of the jars, their purpose, and their capacity. Why are these details included if the miracle affects only a small quantity of water taken directly from a well? As for the extravagance of 120–150 gallons of **the best wine**, it hardly exceeds that of "a whole pint of a very expensive perfume" poured out on Jesus' feet (12:3) or the seventy-five pounds of spices "used to embalm his body" (19:39). Abundant wine was part of Jewish and Jewish-Christian apocalyptic hopes, and the six jars at Cana were modest compared to the fantastic bounty expected in the days of the Messiah (cf. *Enoch* 10.19, *2 Baruch* 29.5). Papias, a second-century bishop from Asia Minor, attributed to Jesus and to "John the Lord's disciple" a prophecy of "vineyards . . . with 10,000 vines, and on one vine 10,000 branches, and on one branch 10,000 shoots, and on every shoot 10,000 clusters, and in every cluster 10,000 grapes, and pressed from every grape 25 measures of wine" (Irenaeus, *Against Heresies* 5.33.3). The "extravagance" of the canonical Gospel of John seems tame by comparison, for it has, after all, a basis in history. Yet it makes the point that when Jesus gives life, he gives it abundantly (cf. 10:10). There is more than enough for everyone in need (cf. 6:13).

2:11 / This first miracle: lit., "this beginning of the signs." The word for "miracles" or "signs" (Gr.: *sēmeia*) emphasizes the symbolic character of these acts. They are important not simply because they are miraculous but because they convey a meaning or message.

5

The First Passover

JOHN 2:13–25

It was almost time for the Passover Festival, so Jesus went to Jerusalem. [14]There in the Temple he found men selling cattle, sheep, and pigeons, and also the moneychangers sitting at their tables. [15]So he made a whip from cords and drove all the animals out of the Temple, both the sheep and the cattle; he overturned the tables of the moneychangers and scattered their coins; [16]and he ordered the men who sold the pigeons, "Take them out of here! Stop making my Father's house a marketplace!" [17]His disciples remembered that the scripture says, "My devotion to your house, O God, burns in me like a fire."

[18]The Jewish authorities came back at him with a question, "What miracle can you perform to show us that you have the right to do this?"

[19]Jesus answered, "Tear down this Temple, and in three days I will build it again."

[20]"Are you going to build it again in three days?" they asked him. "It has taken forty-six years to build this Temple!"

[21]But the temple Jesus was speaking about was his body. [22]So when he was raised from death, his disciples remembered that he had said this, and they believed the scripture and what Jesus had said.

[23]While Jesus was in Jerusalem during the Passover Festival, many believed in him as they saw the miracles he performed. [24]But Jesus did not trust himself to them, because he knew them all. [25]There was no need for anyone to tell him about them, because he himself knew what was in their hearts.

Jesus' first visit to Jerusalem, like each of his subsequent visits, takes place in connection with one of the Jewish feasts. He comes as a pilgrim, to keep the Passover Festival. In particular, the wording of verse 13 corresponds closely to that of 11:55, which signals the last Passover and the beginning of Jesus' Passion. When the notice here in chapter 2 is followed by an account of the Temple cleansing, an event associated in the other Gospels with the Passion week, it appears that this first Passover is indeed the last and that the events of Jesus' Passion are about to start. The impression has been created because the Gospel writer has transferred the Temple cleansing almost to the beginning of Jesus' ministry. This is more likely than supposing that Jesus actually cleansed the Temple twice. John's Gospel has taken the symbolic acts with which Passion week begins in the synoptic Gospels (i.e., the triumphal entry and the Temple cleansing) and separated them, so that each serves as a heading for its own version of the Passion drama: the book of Judgment (2:13–11:54) and the book of Glory (11:55–21:25; see Introduction).

The note of judgment is struck almost immediately in the Temple cleansing. Fashioning a cat-o'-nine-tails out of cords, Jesus drove from the Temple area all the sacrificial animals—sheep and oxen—that he found being sold for profit. He scattered the coins of the moneychangers and overturned their tables. Though he did not release the pigeons (the sacrifices of the poor), he commanded those selling them, "Get these out of here! How dare you turn my Father's house into a market!" (v. 16, NIV). At the historical level, this "attack" of Jesus on the Temple has essentially the same meaning as in the synoptic Gospels. It is an act of radical reform. The changing of money and the selling of animals "on the spot" for sacrificial use were apparently a way of making Temple sacrifice more convenient for worshipers, while at the same time enriching the Temple treasury. In the spirit of an Amos or a Jeremiah, Jesus brought this practice to an abrupt (if temporary) end. But the Gospel writer is less interested in Jesus' reforms than in what these reforms would cost him, and what his future would be. The Jewish leaders immediately demanded from him a sign from heaven as evidence of his messianic authority (v. 18). His answer is a riddle: **Tear down this Temple, and in three days I will build it again** (v. 19). It is a riddle they cannot solve. How can a magnificent structure that has taken forty-six years to build be rebuilt in three days? Why should it be destroyed in the first place?

Here, as in the Cana story, the disciples are the vehicle for the concerns of the Gospel writer. The things they "remember" punctuate the narrative as a kind of chorus (vv. 17, 22). In connection with the driving out of the moneychangers, they remembered a verse of scripture: "Zeal for your house will consume me" (v. 17, NIV; cf. Ps. 69:9). In connection with the ensuing dispute with the Jewish authorities, they remembered his riddle about the Temple and realized that he meant his own body (vv. 21–22). The narrator then links the two notices by commenting that the disciples "believed the Scripture and the words that Jesus had spoken" (v. 22, NIV). The same emphasis on the postresurrection faith of the disciples reappears in the account of the triumphal entry: "His disciples did not understand this at the time, but when Jesus had been raised to glory, they remembered that the scripture had said this about him and that they had done this for him" (12:16). In 2:22, the reference to the disciples' faith becomes a sequel to 2:11: they "believed in him" at Cana, but they believed and understood more deeply "after he was raised from the dead" (NIV). The faith of 2:11 is preparatory to the postresurrection faith of

33

2:22, the faith of the Gospel writer and his readers. Christian belief is incomplete until it fixes itself on the death and resurrection of Jesus.

The link between verses 17 and 22 suggests that the remembering of the passage in Psalm 69, no less than the remembering of Jesus' riddle, is postresurrection and has in view Jesus' Passion. The GNB translation of verse 17 misses the future tense of the verb: Zeal for the house of God "will consume" Jesus (NIV), that is, it will bring about his death at the hands of the Temple authorities. Only after his Passion could his disciples "remember" the passage in this way. Similarly, the riddle about the Temple can only be solved by one who knows that "the Son of Man . . . must be killed, and after three days rise again" (cf. Mark 8:31, NIV). That such knowledge was "after the fact" is stated explicitly in verse 22. Before the fact, there seemed to be no alternative to taking the prophecy literally, and the Temple authorities did just that (v. 20). The charge that Jesus was actually planning to destroy the Temple comes to the surface in the synoptic accounts of his trial (Mark 14:58; Matt. 26:64), based apparently on a garbled version of this Johannine utterance. For the writer of the fourth Gospel, misunderstanding serves as a foil for correct understanding, in this case the postresurrection knowledge shared by author and readers that **the temple Jesus was speaking about was his body** (v. 21).

The fact that **temple** and **body** are both New Testament metaphors for the church has led some commentators to find corporate implications here: The body-temple that Jesus will raise up is the Christian church (cf. Matt. 16:18). But though it is true that the church is built on Jesus' resurrection (cf. Eph. 1:20–23), there is no evidence that the Gospel writer has more in mind here than the raising of one man from the dead after three days. It is the resurrection of Jesus, and of him alone, that gives him authority over the Temple and his disciples a sure foundation for their faith.

The account of Jesus' first Passover continues. Even though the Temple cleansing itself took place at the end of his ministry, there is no reason to doubt that he did pay an early visit to Jerusalem and to the Temple. Such a visit (involving a demand for a sign!) is mentioned in Luke 4:9–13. John's Gospel speaks generally of **the miracles he performed** at the Passover (v. 23), but these are not enumerated. When challenged to give a miraculous sign (2:18), Jesus had granted the Jewish authorities only a riddle, yet the writer assumes that some miracles (probably akin to those described later in the Gospel) did take place. Nicodemus mentions these signs in 3:2, and the Galileans who welcomed Jesus back from Samaria

(4:45) are said to have "seen everything that he had done during the [Passover] festival."

On the basis of these miracles **many believed in him** (v. 23). The situation seems, on the face of it, closely parallel to 2:11: More and more disciples are coming to faith. But the parallel is a false one. Something is wrong with the faith of those who "believed" in Jesus at this Passover feast. Playing on the word for "believe" or "trust" (Gr.: *pisteuein*), the narrator remarks that even though these people "trusted" in Jesus, he did not trust himself to them. He did not accept their faith as genuine. What is not clear is the ground for his suspicion. Did he disclaim their belief because it rested on a mere fascination with the miraculous for its own sake (cf. 4:48)? Or was it because he knew that out of fear they would fail to confess him publicly and put their faith into action (cf. 12:42)? Did he know that in their hearts they "loved the approval of men rather than the approval of God" (12:43)?

The fact that the Gospel writer has no problem in 2:11 with a faith based on miracles suggests that this in itself is not the problem in verse 24. The problem is, rather, one of cowardice. Those who believe but hide their faith from the world have not believed at all. They do not stand in the tradition of John the Baptist or of Nathanael. Jesus knows such people's hearts just as surely as he knew that Simon would be a "rock" or that Nathanael was a "real Israelite." He unmasks their unbelief in a later confrontation: "I am not looking for human praise. . . . I know what kind of people you are, and I know that you have no love for God in your hearts" (5:41, 42). Jesus knew that the "faith" of many at this first Passover in Jerusalem was mere "human praise" and not faith that gains eternal life.

Additional Notes

2:15 / **Drove all the animals out**: The Greek is not totally clear as to whether Jesus used the whip only on the animals or on the moneychangers as well. According to Raymond Brown (*The Gospel According to John*, AB I [New York: Doubleday, 1966], p. 114), Jesus "drove the whole pack of them out of the temple area with their sheep and oxen." But there is a reluctance among translators to suppose that Jesus used physical violence on human beings. The way in which he speaks to the sellers of pigeons (v. 16) suggests that they at least are still on the scene and that he has not used the whip on them. Jesus probably improvised the cat-o'-nine-tails to move the livestock out of the Temple, knowing that the owners would be close behind to protect their investments.

2:18 / **What miracle**: The word is "sign" (Gr.: *sēmeion*), the same word used in 2:11 but with a different meaning. The reference is to a spectacular demonstration of power, or a sign from heaven (cf. 6:30). A close synoptic parallel is Matt. 12:38, in which the Pharisees ask for such a sign and Jesus similarly answers with a veiled prediction of his resurrection (the "sign of the prophet Jonah," 12:39–40).

2:19 / **Tear down this temple**. The meaning of the imperative is "if you tear down this temple, I will rebuild it in three days." As the authorities' response indicates, the emphasis is on the rebuilding rather than on the tearing down. Nevertheless, the form of the verb probably reflects the notion that the Jewish authorities are the ones who will destroy **this temple** (i.e., will execute Jesus; cf. 8:28; 19:16). The effect of the imperative is to challenge the authorities right at the outset to do their worst and see what happens.

I will build it again. The word translated "build again" here and in the following verse literally means "raise." Although it can refer to building a temple, it is one of the New Testament words characteristically used for resurrection of the dead. It is the same word use in v. 22 ("when he was raised from death"). The distinction between Jesus raising himself (v. 19) and being raised (i.e., by the Father, v. 22) is not of interest to the Gospel writer.

2:20 / **Forty-six years**: The Second Temple, begun by Herod the Great about 20 B.C. (Josephus, *Antiquities* 15.390), was not completed until 63 A.D. (*Antiquities* 20.219). The past tense here indicates that the Temple has been under construction for forty-six years but not necessarily that it is complete (for a similar usage, cf. Ezra 5:16). Because the reference is clearly to the Jerusalem Temple not metaphorically to Jesus' body, it affords no clue to Jesus' age.

2:22 / **Remembered that he had said this**: Remembrance in this passage means remembrance with understanding. The disciples probably recalled the words Jesus had used from the time he spoke them, but only after the resurrection did they realize what those words meant.

2:23 / **Many believed in him**: lit., "believed in his name" (cf. 1:12). "Believe in him" and "believe in his name" appear to be used interchangeably in John's Gospel. The similarity of the grammatical constructions in Greek suggests that the one is simply an abbreviated form of the other, based on the assumption that the name represents the person.

2:25 / **There was no need for anyone to tell him**. For this idiom, expressing the idea of complete knowledge, cf. 16:30; 1 John 2:27; 1 Thess. 4:9; 5:1.

6

Jesus and Nicodemus

JOHN 3:1–21

There was a Jewish leader named Nicodemus, who belonged to the party of the Pharisees. [2]One night he went to Jesus and said to him, "Rabbi, we know that you are a teacher sent by God. No one could perform the miracles you are doing unless God were with him."

[3]Jesus answered, "I am telling you the truth: no one can see the Kingdom of God unless he is born again."[d.]

[4]"How can a grown man be born again?" Nicodemus asked. "He certainly cannot enter his mother's womb and be born a second time!"

[5]"I am telling you the truth," replied Jesus, "that no one can enter the Kingdom of God unless he is born of water and the Spirit. [6]A person is born physically of human parents, but he is born spiritually of the Spirit. [7]Do not be surprised because I tell you that you must all be born again.[e] [8]The wind blows wherever it wishes; you hear the sound it makes, but you do not know where it comes from or where it is going. It is like that with everyone who is born of the Spirit."

[9]"How can this be?" asked Nicodemus.

[10]Jesus answered, "You are a great teacher in Israel, and you don't know this? [11]I am telling you the truth: we speak of what we know and report what we have seen, yet none of you is willing to accept our message. [12]You do not believe me when I tell you about the things of this world; how will you ever believe me, then, when I tell you about the things of heaven? [13]And no one has ever gone up to heaven except the Son of Man, who came down from heaven."

[14]As Moses lifted up the bronze snake on a pole in the desert, in the same way the Son of Man must be lifted up, [15]so that everyone who believes in him may have eternal life. [16]For God loved the world so much that he gave his only Son, so that everyone who believes in him may not die but have eternal life. [17] For God did not send his Son into the world to be its judge, but to be its savior.

[18]Whoever believes in the Son is not judged; but whoever does not believe has already been judged, because he has not believed in God's only Son. [19]This is how the judgment works: the light has come into the world, but people love the darkness rather than the light, because their deeds are evil. [20]Anyone who does evil things hates the light and will not come to the light, because he does not want his evil deeds to be shown up. [21]But whoever does what is true comes to the light in order that the light may show that what he did was in obedience to God.

d. again; or from above. e. again; or from above.

Nicodemus is introduced as a particular example of the "believers" mentioned in 2:23–25. As a **"Jewish leader"** and **"great teacher in Israel"** (vv. 1, 10), he is perhaps not wholly typical of the group, though later indications are that leaders of the people were indeed conspicuous among these so-called believers (12:42). It is probably out of fear that Nicodemus comes to Jesus at night. Speaking perhaps for the larger group, he makes a confession that puts the narrator's summary (2:23) into his own words: **Rabbi, we know that you are a teacher sent from God. No one could perform the miracles you are doing unless God were with him.** (v. 2).

Jesus brings Nicodemus up short with a solemn declaration that **no one can see the Kingdom of God unless he is born again** (v. 3). The image is a heightened form of Jesus' use elsewhere of children as a metaphor of discipleship: "I assure you that unless you change and become like children, you will never enter the Kingdom of heaven" (Matt. 18:3). The extreme example of becoming a child is, as Nicodemus put it, to go back to one's mother's womb and be born a second time (v. 4). Jesus explains that **born again** actually means **born of water and the Spirit** (v. 5), a phrase intended to clarify but one that has for some modern readers just the opposite effect. Verse 6 uses **born . . . of the Spirit** by itself, while a similar expression, "born of God," has appeared already in the prologue (1:13, NIV; cf. also 1 John 2:29; 3:9; 4:7; 5:1, 4, 18).

Only here is water mentioned in connection with this new birth. To be **born again** or "born of the Spirit" is to have one's life radically transformed by the power of God. It is like beginning life over again, with new perceptions and new relationships. But what has water to do with it? Are **water and the Spirit** two distinct elements, or one? Is Jesus saying that a person must be "born of water" (whatever that means) and *also* "born of the Spirit"? Or does he intend water as a metaphor for the Spirit (i.e., that one must be "born of water, even the Holy Spirit")? If water simply represents the Spirit (as, e.g., in 7:39), why is water mentioned at all? The metaphor is pointless unless the phrase "born of water" by itself has a definite meaning on which a metaphor can be based. Some have suggested that it refers to physical birth. **Water** in Jewish writings can be a euphemism for the male sperm (e.g., the Qumran *Hymns* speak of humanity as dust or clay "kneaded with water" (1 QH 1.21, 3.24, 12.25, 13.15). Metaphorically, **born of water and the Spirit** would then mean born of a seed or sperm that is spiritual and not physical (H. Odeberg, *The Fourth Gospel* [Amsterdam: B. R. Grüner, 1968; reprint of 1929 edition], pp. 63–64). This would yield a masculine metaphor of God as Father in the sense of male procreator (cf. 1 John 3:9). The problem with this view (aside from the heaping of metaphor on metaphor!) is that **water** is not among the expressions for physical birth listed in 1:13. And when Jesus proceeds to mention physical birth to Nicodemus in verse 6, the phrase is "born of the flesh" (RSV), not "born of water."

If water and Spirit are two distinct elements, then it is all the more true that the phrase **born of water** must be assigned a meaning of its own. Again, there are those who connect it with physical birth: A person must be born both physically and spiritually. In popular discussions of this passage, **water** is sometimes understood in connection with birth itself rather than procreation, that is, with the breaking of the water bag in the mother's womb at the onset of labor. But the difficulties inherent in the "spiritual seed" interpretation are present here as well and are compounded by the redundancy of saying that one must be born physically in order to enter the Kingdom. The whole point of verse 6 is that the new birth itself is *not* physical but spiritual.

It is more likely that **born of water and the Spirit** is a metaphor for baptism in water and in the Holy Spirit. The two elements were joined earlier in John the Baptist's testimony about baptism: John baptizes in water, but Jesus is the one who will baptize in the Holy Spirit (1:26, 33). The pairing of the two elements involves both contrast and continuity. John's baptism is incomplete without the Spirit, yet there is no evidence that water baptism came to an end when John passed from the scene. Baptism in water and the Spirit (in that order) becomes in the book of Acts the normative way of initiation into the Christian community. "Repent and be baptized, every one of you," said Peter on the day of Pentecost, "so that your sins may be forgiven. And you will receive the gift of the Holy Spirit" (Acts 2:38, NIV). In a similar way, Jesus is telling Nicodemus that he cannot enter the Kingdom of God unless he takes the step of initiation into the new community of faith forming itself around Jesus. He must leave the group he is in and join a new group by being baptized in water and in the Holy Spirit. The metaphor of becoming a child is combined with the language of Christian initiation. Nicodemus is being addressed as a representative of those who believed in Jesus but were afraid to confess him (2:23–25, 12:42). Unless such people risk persecution by publicly identifying themselves as Christians, their faith is declared invalid. In the first century, this public identification consisted of water baptism and the experience of receiving the Spirit. The point is not that baptism is always and everywhere necessary for salvation, or that a person is born again simply by being baptized. The point is that a faith that risks nothing is no faith at all and brings no one into the Kingdom of God.

Jesus' meeting with Nicodemus is more than an exchange between two individuals. The plurals in verse 7 (**you must all be born again**) and verse 11 (**none of you is willing to accept our message**) make it clear that two communities confront each other here: the Christian followers of Jesus and the Jewish community represented by **a great teacher in Israel** (v. 10). The thrust of the interview is negative: The community of Nicodemus can no more understand the community of Jesus than one can understand where the wind comes from or where it goes. The lives of those who are born again are an utter mystery to those who are not (v. 8). The conversation between Jesus and Nicodemus centers around the impossible. Jesus' miracles are impossible without the help of God (v. 2). No one can see or enter the Kingdom of God without a new birth (vv. 3, 5), and no one can go through the process of birth a second time (v. 4). There are two spheres of existence, the physical and the spiritual, with no natural access from the one to the other (vv. 6–8). **How can this be?** asks Nicodemus, not realizing that he is the living proof of it. He is Israel's great teacher, yet even he cannot understand (v. 10). There is nothing in the world (or in Judaism in particular) that offers genuine access to God or his Kingdom. Only by accepting the testimony of Jesus and his followers (v. 11) and becoming part of the Christian community can a person enter the realm of the Spirit. This is what Nicodemus and his community have (so far) failed to do.

After a brief transition, the positive Christian testimony is set forth in verses 14–17. The **things of this world** (v. 12) are the impossibilities of the preceding section, while the **things of heaven** represent the good news of eternal life through the gift of God's Son. The note of impossibility continues in the pronouncement that **no one has ever gone up to heaven** (v. 13a), but a crucial exception marks a change of tone: **except the Son of Man, who came down from heaven** (v. 13b). The time perspective of this verse and the verses that follow is postresurrection, as if Jesus, the Son of Man, has *already* gone up into heaven (cf. 6:62; 20:17), or as if the writer is looking *back* on God's gift of his Son (v. 16). The third-person, almost detached, way of summarizing the gospel story is reminiscent of the first half of the prologue.

It is difficult to tell where Jesus' words spoken during his earthly ministry end and these postresurrection words begin. Jesus' speech to Nicodemus and the reflections of the narrator under the inspiration of the Spirit are so closely intertwined that it is neither possible nor necessary to distinguish them. Together they comprise the **things of heaven** uniquely known and made known by the ascended Son of Man. Verse 14 appears to be a kind of riddle addressed by Jesus to his opponents (or to Nicodemus in particular) in the manner of 2:19, a riddle solved for Christian readers by the reflection on Jesus' redemptive death in verse 16. Formally, the pattern, **as Moses . . . in the same way the Son of Man**, recalls a synoptic saying about Jonah: "In the same way that Jonah . . . so will the Son of Man" (Matt. 12:40): cf. Luke 11:30. In each case a biblical incident is made the point of comparison for a veiled reference to Jesus' death or resurrection. Here the bronze snake raised on a pole in the desert to bring healing from a plague of snakes (Num. 21:8–9) becomes a grotesque intimation of Jesus nailed high on a cross (cf. 12:33; 18:32). But instead of mere physical healing, Jesus brings eternal life (vv. 15–16) or salvation (v. 17).

God's intent is a saving intent, and the scope of his salvation is worldwide. His love for the whole human race expresses itself in the giving of his only Son to die on the cross (v. 16). This "giving" is more specific than "sending" (v. 17). God "sent" his Son into the world (the Incarnation), but he **gave** his Son in death (the Passion) so that the world might be saved and not condemned (v. 17). The universality is qualified, however, by the phrase **everyone who believes** in verses 15 and 16. To gain eternal life, a person must believe, just as the Israelites had to look at the bronze snake in order to be healed (Num. 21:8–9). **Eternal life** is this Gospel's equivalent of the **Kingdom of God**, about which Jesus had spoken to Nicodemus (vv. 3, 5). It is not simply endless life; nor is it a life that begins after death. It is a new *kind* of life, a new order of existence that characterizes even now the person who believes in Jesus and is born again.

In verses 18–21, the alternatives of faith and unbelief are examined. Even though salvation and not judgment is God's prime intent, judgment is inevitable on those who do not believe. Judgment, like salvation, is a present reality. Unbelievers are condemned **already** (v. 18). The verdict is that they "loved darkness instead of light because their deeds were evil" (v. 19, NIV). Once again it appears that the Gospel writer is looking back at Jesus' teaching from a later vantage point, as if the issue of belief and unbelief were already settled. He writes in anticipation of a later verdict on those who "loved the approval of men rather than the approval of God" (12:43). It is likely that the same group is in view in both instances, that is, the so-called believers of 2:23–25 and 12:42.

True belief is understood in verses 20–21 as coming **to the light**. The light that has entered the world is Jesus (cf. 1:5–10), and to come to the light is to come to Jesus, publicly and not in secret, for baptism and discipleship. Genuine faith requires open participation in a community of faith. The indictment of Nicodemus and his friends is that they have not taken this step. A person's failure to come to the light is attributed to fear that his or her "deeds will be exposed" (v. 20, NIV). It is a sign that that person is an evildoer. The one who comes to the light is a person who "lives by the truth" (v. 21, NIV) and demonstrates by coming that his or her deeds have been done "through God" (NIV). Coming to Jesus proves that God has *already* been at work in one's life. In a curious reversal of later Christian theology, Jesus makes the point that people prove their good works by their faith!

Behind this surprising logic is not the notion that salvation is earned by good works but rather a strong doctrine of divine election. From a human perspective the new birth is a conversion, but from God's perspective "conversion" simply brings out in the open the true nature of those whom God has chosen to be his children. No one can come to Jesus unless God draws that person to him (6:44). The one who comes is the one who has first listened to God and been instructed (6:45). Only the person "willing to do what God wants" will understand the message of Jesus (7:17). All people will one day be divided into "those who have done good" and "those who have done evil" and judged accordingly (5:29). But the test of whether one has done good or evil is whether or not one **comes to the light.** The dualism of John's Gospel has been called a "dualism of decision" (R. Bultmann, *Theology of the New Testament*, vol. 2 [New York: Scribners, 1955], p. 21). Back of it is the dualism implicit in God's sovereign choice, and after it comes the dualism of the last judgment, but the one is an eternal mystery and the other a ratification of something already decided. What matters in history is whether a person decides to remain in darkness or to come to the light that has dawned in Jesus Christ. This is the main theological issue arising out of Jesus' first visit to Jerusalem.

Additional Notes

3:1 / **Who belonged to the party of the Pharisees**: lit., "a man of the Pharisees." The repetition of the word "man" (*anthrōpos*) after two occurrences of the same word in 2:25 links Nicodemus closely to the group described in the preceding section.

3:3, 5 / **I am telling you the truth**: lit., "Amen, amen" or "Truly, truly." The introductory formula calls attention to the importance of the sayings and possibly to their derivation from a particular tradition (cf. 1:51).

3:3, 7 / **Born again**: The word for **again** (Gr. *anōthen*) could also be translated "from above" (cf. 3:31). The rebirth of which Jesus speaks is in fact a birth from God (1:13) or from the realm of the Spirit, and in that sense "from above," but Nicodemus' answer focuses simply on the fact that it is a second birth. Its divine character remains to be spelled out in vv. 5–8.

3:5 / **Water and the Spirit**: It is impossible to tell grammatically whether **water** and **Spirit** are two distinct elements or one. The fact that both are governed by a single preposition in Greek suggests that they are one. Yet in 1 John 5:6 the same sort of construction ("by water and blood," NIV) is immediately followed by a singling out of each element with its own preposition and definite article (lit., "not with the water alone, but with the water and with the blood"). The decision must therefore be made on other than grammatical grounds.

3:6 / The NIV rendering is better: "Flesh gives birth to flesh, but the Spirit gives birth to spirit." Jesus is not summarizing the life of a Christian (first physical birth and then spiritual birth) but distinguishing between two realms of existence that must not be confused (cf. 3:31; 8:23).

3:8 / **The wind blows**. The Greek word *pneuma* (the word for **Spirit** in this context and throughout the NT) can also mean "wind." Its use here with the cognate verb *pnei* ("blows") indicates that **wind** is the intended meaning (cf. only Heb. 1:7 in the NT). The choice of *pneuma* rather than another word for **wind** (e.g., *pnoe*, Acts 2:2) enables the writer to make a play on words. The term used as a *metaphor* for the Spirit is the same as the word for **Spirit** itself! No one knows where the wind comes from or goes, and the same is true of those born of the "wind" (i.e., **of the Spirit** of God).

3:10 / **You are a great teacher in Israel, and you don't know this?** The logic of the dialogue suggests that these words should be taken as a statement rather than a question. Those who say that Jesus is asking in surprise why Nicodemus did not know about baptism or the new birth are then compelled to seek intimations of these things in the Old Testament (e.g., Jer. 31:33 or Ezek. 36:25–27). But the OT plays no part in the discussion at this point, and there is no way Nicodemus can be expected to understand Jesus' new teaching. Far from being a surprise to Jesus, his ignorance proves Jesus' point: that spiritual things can only be grasped by those born of the Spirit (cf. Paul in 1 Cor. 2:11–14).

3:13 / **Except the Son of Man, who came down from heaven**: Some ancient manuscripts have a longer reading: "except him who came down from heaven, even the Son of Man who is in heaven." This variant makes explicit the notion implied by the better-attested shorter reading that the Son of Man has already ascended.

3:15 / **Believes in him**: Only here in John's Gospel is the Greek preposition *en* used with the verb *pisteuein*, "to believe." Everywhere else the preposition *eis* ("into") or a dative without a preposition is used. It is therefore likely that "in" goes with the expression "to have life" rather than with "believe": "so that everyone who believes may have eternal life in him." The case for the GNB rendering rests largely on the parallelism with v. 16, where *pisteuein* is used in the normal Johannine way, with *eis*.

3:19 / **People love the darkness . . . their deeds are evil**. The past tenses of the Greek verbs are obscured in GNB. From the Gospel writer's standpoint, the decisions have been made and the verdict is in: People *loved* darkness, and their deeds *were* evil (cf. NIV). It is possible that **people** (Gr.: *anthrōpoi*) is intended to recall the thrice-repeated *anthrōpos* of 2:25 and 3:1.

3:21 / **Does what is true** (or "lives by the truth," NIV): lit., "does the truth." The phrase "to do the truth" occurs in the Qumran literature as an expression for faithful participation in the elect desert community. See, e.g., 1QS 1.5, 5.3, 8.2, 9. In early Christian Gnosticism (Ptolemy, *Letter to Flora* 6.5), a similar expression can mean to live according to the Reality that has come in Christ (i.e., to obey the Law of God spiritually and not literally). Such terminology suggests that the sharp distinction between faith and works that characterizes later Christian theology is not always helpful in understanding Jewish and (aside from Paul) early Christian literature.

Jesus and John the Baptist

JOHN 3:22–30

After this, Jesus and his disciples went to the province of Judea, where he spent some time with them and baptized. [23]John also was baptizing in Aenon, not far from Salim, because there was plenty of water in that place. People were going to him, and he was baptizing them. ([24]This was before John had been put in prison.) [25]Some of John's disciples began arguing with a Jew[f] about the matter of ritual washing. [26]So they went to John and told him, "Teacher, you remember the man who was with you on the east side of the Jordan, the one you spoke about? Well, he is baptizing now, and everyone is going to him!"

[27]John answered, "No one can have anything unless God gives it to him. [28]You yourselves are my witnesses that I said, 'I am not the Messiah, but I have been sent ahead of him.' [29]The bridegroom is the one to whom the bride belongs; but the bridegroom's friend, who stands by and listens, is glad when he hears the bridegroom's voice. This is how my own happiness is made complete. [30]He must become more important while I become less important."

f. a Jew; *some manuscripts have* some Jews.

Jesus' interest in "water and the Spirit" (3:5) as the way of initiation into his new community is now explained. As soon as he leaves Jerusalem, Jesus himself takes up a baptizing ministry in Judea. Verse 22, along with 4:1–3, has the appearance of a transitional passage summarizing a stay in Judea of indefinite length (cf. the brief stay at Capernaum in 2:12). But certain details in the summary require further explanation. For example, did Jesus actually baptize people? No, but his disciples did (4:2). Also, the reason for terminating this Judean ministry is said to have been the Pharisees' perception of a possible rivalry between John the Baptist and Jesus (4:1). Was there any truth to this perception? Verses 23–30 (and indirectly vv. 31–36 as well) represent the Gospel writer's answer to this second question. The brief summary is thereby expanded into a significant historical and theological reflection on the relationship between Jesus and John the Baptist.

John's baptizing activity is located quite specifically at **Aenon, not far from Salim** (v. 23). The fact that a definite location is assigned to John but not to Jesus suggests that verses 23–30 may come from early material preserved within the community of John's followers (cf. the reference to Bethany in 1:28). Aenon (like Bethany) cannot be located with certainty today, but the Gospel writer (or his source) assumes some familiarity with these place-names—probably more with Salim than with Aenon, or else why would Salim have been mentioned at all? Verse 23 confirms the evidence of 1:28 that John did not limit his baptizing ministry to the Jordan River. Aenon was chosen for its ample water supply, probably from natural springs. Whatever its exact location, Aenon was on the west side of the Jordan, for John's earlier ministry at Bethany is said to have been "on the other side" (v. 26, NIV).

The parenthetical note that **this was before John had been put in prison** (v. 24) is redundant in its present position. If John was baptizing, then he was obviously not in prison! The comment is a storyteller's aside that belongs logically *before* verse 23 as an explanation of how John can be in the story at all. It comes where it does as an afterthought, but a wholly natural one. The Gospel writer assumes a knowledge of John's imprisonment, but refers to it only in this indirect way. John the Baptist is not forcibly removed from the scene but allowed to make his own exit and to say his farewell with dignity (vv. 27–30).

John's final testimony is introduced by a remark of his disciples (v. 26) arising out of a dispute they had had with an anonymous Jew about **ritual washing** (including, presumably, baptism). The nature of the dispute is unclear, but the disciples' remark perhaps echoes something the Jew had said about the apparent success of Jesus' ministry of baptism. If so, the scene aptly illustrates the situation referred to in 4:1: Jesus and John are seen as rivals, and Jesus appears to be the more successful of the two. Even while recalling John's earlier testimony to Jesus in 1:19–34, John's disciples seem surprised and puzzled by Jesus' growing popularity (v. 26).

The unity of the chapter is maintained in the linking of baptism with coming to Jesus (v. 26; cf. v. 21) and in John's reply to his disciples (vv. 27–30). John speaks, as Jesus did to Nicodemus, of what is humanly impossible: "No one can have anything unless God gives it to him" (v. 27; cf. vv. 2, 3, 5). In particular, John bears witness to his own limitations, citing part of the very testimony to which his disciples have just referred (v. 28). John is not the Messiah, but only a messenger sent on ahead to prepare for the Messiah's coming (cf. 1:20, 23). In his imagination, John sees the present time as a wedding (cf. 2:1–12; Mark 2:19–20; Matt. 22:1–14; 25:1–13), but he himself is not the bridegroom. Jesus is the bridegroom in John's parable, and John is merely the trusted friend who rejoices when the bridegroom summons him to the festivities (v. 29). As he completes the role of forerunner, John takes on the more modest role of confessor and disciple of Jesus. He becomes a kind of ideal disciple who hears Jesus' voice (cf. 10:3, 27) and finds his joy made complete (cf. 15:11; 16:24).

The real answer to the implied question of John's disciples comes in verse 30. What they see happening in Judea is historically inevitable: Jesus' stature will grow, while John's will diminish. But at the same time, it is what John wants, for his parting words are those of any disciple willing to become small like a child in order to gain the Kingdom (cf. Matt. 18:3–4; 23:12; John 3:5). They are intended as words to repeat and to make one's own.

Additional Notes

3:23 / Aenon, not far from Salim: The sixth-century mosaic map from Madeba in Jordan shows two Aenons, one east of the Jordan near where John was baptizing before ("Aenon there now Sapsaphas") and the other west of the river and further north. The latter is specifically connected with our passage by being labeled "Aenon near Salim," and agrees with the location eight miles south of Beth-shan assigned in a fourth-century gazetteer of biblical place-names, the *Onomasticon* of Eusebius (cf. also the fourth-century travel diary of the European pilgrim Egeria). Modern attempts to locate Aenon in Samaria, where there is today a Salim southeast of Nablus and an Ainun nearby, are unconvincing because of John 4:1–4. The narrative hardly makes sense if John was already baptizing in Samaria! Such names would have been common in any case: **Aenon** comes from the Aramaic word for "springs," while **Salim**, like Salem or Jerusalem, is from a Semitic root meaning "peace." The location assigned by Eusebius and the Madeba map appears not to rest simply on inferences from John's Gospel and may therefore be regarded as an independent—and plausible—tradition. See J. Finegan, *The Archaeology of the New Testament* (Princeton: Princeton University Press, 1969), pp. 12–13.

3:25 / A Jew: Some important ancient manuscripts read **some Jews** (GNB margin). This could be correct if the variant rests on a copyist's mistake. But if a deliberate alteration was made, it is more likely that an original singular was changed to a plural ("Jews" frequently being the disputants in this Gospel) than that a plural was changed to a singular (raising the question What Jew? What was his name?). The absence of the article with either form also suggests that the singular is original, for Jews everywhere else in John's Gospel are "the Jews" and comprise a well-defined group, while an individual Jew (unless named) would almost inevitably be designated as such without the article.

3:28 / I am not the Messiah. The first half of John's self-quotation refers clearly to 1:20, but the second half is not a word-for-word quote of anything that has appeared earlier (though cf. Mark 1:2; Luke 7:27). John is designated in the prologue as having been "sent" (1:6), whereas the idea that he was sent **ahead of**

the Messiah may be an inference from statements that the Messiah would come "after" him (1:15, 27, 30). The matter is complicated by the assertion in 1:15, 30 that the Messiah is "ahead of" John in quite a different sense, referring to status or dignity rather than time. Alternatively, it is possible that John is quoting verbatim a form of the tradition that did not find its way into chapter 1.

8

He Who Comes from Heaven

JOHN 3:31–36

He who comes from above is greater than all. He who is from the earth belongs to the earth and speaks about earthly matters, but he who comes from heaven is above all. [32]He tells what he has seen and heard, yet no one accepts his message. [33]But whoever accepts his message confirms by this that God is truthful. [34]The one whom God has sent speaks God's words, because God gives him the fullness of his Spirit. [35]The Father loves his Son and has put everything in his power. [36]Whoever believes in the Son has eternal life; whoever disobeys the Son will not have life, but will remain under God's punishment.

T he Gospel writer adds a theological reflection to John the Baptist's farewell, just as he did to John's testimony in the prologue (1:17–18) and to Jesus' conversation with Nicodemus at Jerusalem (3:13–21). Playing on John's characteristic phrase, "the Coming One" (cf. 1:15, 27; Matt. 3:11; Matt. 11:3; Luke 7:20), he designates Jesus as the one who **comes from above** or **comes from heaven** (v. 31). Accordingly, **he who is from the earth** and speaks out of human limitations is probably John the Baptist himself. Verse 31 is built on John's own recognition of those limitations in verse 27: he can "receive only what is given him from heaven" (NIV).

Verse 33 indicates definitely that he has received it. The "man who has accepted" Jesus' testimony from heaven and "certified that God is truthful" (v. 33, NIV) is not just anyone, it refers first of all to John the Baptist as portrayed in this Gospel. Nicodemus and his community have rejected Jesus' testimony (v. 32; cf. v. 11), but John and those like him have accepted it as a message from God himself. John the Baptist is the prototype of all who endorse God's truthfulness by recognizing Jesus as his unique messenger. In that sense, John is the first Christian. Jesus' words are to him the words of God because God has given Jesus the Spirit "without limit" (v. 34, NIV). At his baptism the Holy Spirit came down on Jesus to "stay" (1:32, 33), and John testified, and continues to testify, that this was the case.

The last two verses of the chapter are a brief meditation on Jesus' baptism. The statement that **the Father loves his Son and has put everything in his power** (v. 35) echoes the synoptic tradition of the voice from heaven: "You are my Son, whom I love" (Mark 1:11, NIV; cf. the use of *monogenēs* or "only Son" in John 1:14, 18; 3:16, 18). Also, the picture of God's wrath "remaining" on those who reject the Son (v. 36) stands as a grim counterpart to the Spirit "remaining" on Jesus (1:32–33, NIV).

In the present context, the reflection on the baptism serves two purposes: It summarizes the main theological theme of the chapter (i.e., the alternatives of faith or unbelief), and it anticipates the Christology of the rest of the Gospel. The Father's love for the Son and delegation to him of all authority becomes the theme of Jesus' first major discourse at Jerusalem (5:19–29) and the presupposition of all his discourses to follow (cf., e.g., 13:3; 17:2). The last verse of the chapter brings the reader back to the point reached in verses 18–21 and gives unity to the chapter as a whole. John's testimony reinforces the testimony of Jesus that believing in him makes all the difference between salvation and the judgment of God.

Additional Notes

3:33 / **But whoever accepts his message**: There is a formal similarity between vv. 32–33 and 1:11–12. A general statement about nonacceptance of Jesus is followed by a crucial exception: People for the most part did not receive him, but some (or someone) did. V. 33, however, is not general but specific. Not **whoever accepts** (GNB) but "the man who has accepted" (NIV) Jesus' testimony. The verb "accept" or "receive" recalls John the Baptist's own language in 1:16 and 3:27. The most likely reference is to him in particular, not just any hearer. The verse is therefore a statement of what in fact has happened, not (as in GNB) a relative conditional sentence (i.e., *If* someone accepts, he or she confirms God's truthfulness).

Confirms (Gr.: *esphragisen*, lit., "affixed a seal") apparently means that John by his testimony (in chapter 1 and in 3:27–30) formally certified the truth of Jesus' witness, perhaps on the principle that the testimony of two witnesses was considered valid (cf. 8:17; Deut. 19:15). Though Jesus attaches some importance to this attestation of his ministry (cf. 5:33–35), he makes it clear that his real attestation is from God (cf. 5:34, 36–39; 8:16–18; and especially the use of the verb *esphragisen* in 6:27: "God the Father has put his mark of approval on him").

9

Jesus and the Samaritan Woman

JOHN 4:1–42

The Pharisees heard that Jesus was winning and baptizing more disciples than John. ([2]Actually, Jesus himself did not baptize anyone; only his disciples did.) [3]So when Jesus heard what was being said, he left Judea and went back to Galilee; [4]on his way there he had to go through Samaria.

[5]In Samaria he came to a town named Sychar, which was not far from the field that Jacob had given to his son Joseph. [6]Jacob's well was there, and Jesus, tired out by the trip, sat down by the well. It was about noon.

[7]A Samaritan woman came to draw some water, and Jesus said to her, "Give me a drink of water." ([8]His disciples had gone into town to buy food.)

[9]The woman answered, "You are a Jew, and I am a Samaritan—so how can you ask me for a drink?" (Jews will not use the same cups and bowls that Samaritans use.)[g]

[10]Jesus answered, "If you only knew what God gives and who it is that is asking you for a drink, you would ask him, and he would give you life-giving water."

[11]"Sir," the woman said, "you don't have a bucket, and the well is deep. Where would you get that life-giving water? [12]It was our ancestor Jacob who gave us this well; he and his sons and his flocks all drank from it. You don't claim to be greater than Jacob, do you?"

[13]Jesus answered, "Whoever drinks this water will get thirsty again, [14]but whoever drinks the water that I will give him will never be thirsty again. The water that I will give him will become in him a spring which will provide him with lifegiving water and give him eternal life."

[15]"Sir," the woman said, "give me that water! Then I will never be thirsty again, nor will I have to come here to draw water."

[16]"Go and call your husband," Jesus told her, "and come back."

[17]"I don't have a husband," she answered.

Jesus replied, "You are right when you say you don't have a husband. [18]You have been married to five men, and the man you live with now is not really your husband. You have told me the truth."

[19]"I see you are a prophet, sir," the woman said. [20]"My Samaritan ancestors worshiped God on this mountain, but you Jews say that Jerusalem is the place where we should worship God."

[21]Jesus said to her, "Believe me, woman, the time will come when people will not worship the Father either on this mountain or in Jerusalem. [22]You Samaritans do not really know whom you worship; but

we Jews know whom we worship, because it is from the Jews that salvation comes. [23]But the time is coming and is already here, when by the power of God's Spirit people will worship the Father as he really is, offering him the true worship that he wants. [24]God is Spirit, and only by the power of his Spirit can people worship him as he really is."

[25]The woman said to him, "I know that the Messiah will come, and when he comes, he will tell us everything."

[26]Jesus answered, "I am he, I who am talking with you."

[27]At that moment Jesus' disciples returned, and they were greatly surprised to find him talking with a woman. But none of them said to her, "What do you want?" or asked him, "Why are you talking with her?"

[28]Then the woman left her water jar, went back to the town, and said to the people there, [29]"Come and see the man who told me everything I have ever done. Could he be the Messiah?" [30]So they left the town and went to Jesus.

[31]In the meantime the disciples were begging Jesus, "Teacher, have something to eat!"

[32]But he answered, "I have food to eat that you know nothing about."

[33]So the disciples started asking among themselves, "Could somebody have brought him food?"

[34]"My food," Jesus said to them, "is to obey the will of the one who sent me and to finish the work he gave me to do. [35]You have a saying, 'Four more months and then the harvest.' But I tell you, take a good look at the fields; the crops are now ripe and ready to be harvested! [36]The man who reaps the harvest is being paid and gathers the crops for eternal life; so the man who plants and the man who reaps will be glad together. [37]For the saying is true, 'One man plants, another man reaps.' [38]I have sent you to reap a harvest in a field where you did not work; others worked there, and you profit from their work."

[39]Many of the Samaritans in that town believed in Jesus because the woman had said, "He told me everything I have ever done." [40]So when the Samaritans came to him, they begged him to stay with them, and Jesus stayed there two days.

[41]Many more believed because of his message, [42]and they told the woman, "We believe now, not because of what you said, but because we ourselves have heard him, and we know that he really is the Savior of the world."

g. Jews will not use the same cups and bowls that Samaritans use; or Jews will have nothing to do with Samaritans.

The transition begun in 3:22 is continued in 4:1–4. Jesus moves from Jerusalem to the Judean countryside and from there to Galilee by way of Samaria. The intervening material (3:23–36) enables the reader to make sense of this cumbersome introduction to chapter 4. That Jesus **was winning and baptizing more disciples than John** (v. 1) has already been intimated in 3:26. That the Pharisees noticed this is suggested by the fact that John's disciples seem to have been re-minded of it by a Jew (3:25). What has not been told is Jesus' response to these developments. The purpose of verses 1–3 is to explain Jesus' actions by his knowledge. The parenthetical comment recalls other instances in which the narrator attributes things that Jesus said or did to supernatural knowledge that he possessed (cf., e.g., 2:24–25; 6:6, 64; 13:1, 3, 11; 18:4). In this case, however, the knowledge is gained through normal channels. When Jesus got word that the Pharisees were beginning to perceive him and John as rivals, he decided to leave the area (v. 3).

The writer takes a moment in passing to correct a possible false impression given by 3:22 and 4:1 (as well as 3:26). Jesus was not personally baptizing anyone. Baptisms were taking place in Judea as a result of his ministry and under his jurisdiction, but the actual baptizers were his disciples. The intent is to assure the reader that the Pharisees' perception was incorrect. Jesus and John were not rivals and could not have been, for their roles were different and they moved in different spheres (cf. 3:27–36). Theologically, the notion that Jesus, who was supposed to baptize in the Holy Spirit (1:33), also baptized in water as John did is surprising and without parallel in the other Gospels. To the writer of this Gospel, it appears to have been a firmly fixed tradition that he felt compelled to acknowledge but to which he added his own qualifying explanation. Almost in spite of himself, he furnishes strong evidence that Jesus did for a time supervise a baptizing ministry in Judea that invited comparison with John's and appeared, to some at least, to be a rival movement.

The account of Jesus' itinerary provides a reason for almost every step. If verses 1–3 tell why Jesus returned to Galilee, verse 4 adds that he **had to** go by way of Samaria, thus introducing the incident of Jesus and the Samaritan woman. The necessity to go through Samaria was not geographical but theological. There was work to be done. Samaria was a mission field **ripe and ready to be harvested** (v. 35), and Jesus' intent was **to obey the will of the one who sent me and to finish the work he gave me to do** (v. 34). Jesus' movements are dictated not by circumstances but by his divine calling.

Jesus' visit to Samaria has two parts: first, his interview with a Samaritan woman at the well of Jacob (vv. 5–26) and, second, an alternating series of glimpses of Jesus and his disciples, on the one hand, and the woman and the Samaritan townspeople, on the other (vv. 27–42). Jesus' conversation with the woman centers on the theme of holy places, specifically a field and a well traditionally associated with Jacob (vv. 5–15), and the Samaritan temple on Mount Gerizim (vv. 19–26). Jesus promises the woman the Holy Spirit, who transcends these holy places and makes devotion to them obsolete (vv. 13–14, 23–24). Between the discussion of the well and the discussion of the holy mountain comes an abrupt glance at the woman's personal history (vv. 16–18), which lays a basis for her testimony that Jesus had told her **everything I have ever done** (vv. 29, 39).

How are these segments of Jesus' interview with the Samaritan woman related to each other? The woman serves to represent three "oppressed groups" in which Jesus, according to the synoptic Gospels, showed a marked interest. Simply the fact that she is a woman elicits surprise from his disciples that he would talk with her (v. 27). Though not a prostitute, she is sexually immoral (v. 18). By race and religion she is from the Jewish standpoint an outsider, a hated Samaritan. Jews and Samaritans, the writer explains, will not even touch the same utensils (v. 9). In reaching out to her, Jesus in this narrative is recognizably the Jesus of the Synoptics (cf., e.g., Mark 7:24–30; Luke 7:36–50; 10:25–37), the one who came to show mercy to tax collectors, prostitutes, and all such outcasts of Jewish society.

The encounter begins surprisingly, not with Jesus granting mercy to the woman, but with him *asking* mercy from her. He is placed in the curious position of needing help (a drink of water, cf. Mark 9:41) from someone his culture would have him hate. But his thirst provides the occasion for him suddenly to reverse roles and offer **life-giving water** (v. 10) to the woman. Whether she actually gave Jesus a drink before this turn of events we are not told. But what began with Jesus asking water from her (v. 7) concludes with the woman asking him for the never-ending supply of water he claimed to be able to give (v. 15).

The reversal of roles is made possible by Jesus' use of water as a metaphor for the Holy Spirit (vv. 10, 13–14). What he promises is nothing less than baptism in the Spirit (cf. 1:33). The identification of the **life-giving water** as the Spirit is not explicit here, as it is in 7:38–39 but is valid nonetheless. The "gift of God" (v. 10, NIV) is an expression used of the Spirit in Acts 8:20 (cf. Acts 2:38; 10:45; 11:17), and the Spirit becomes unmistakably the theme of the latter part of Jesus' self-disclosure to the woman (vv. 21–24). The only other possibility is that the water represents **eternal life** (v. 14), but the point of Jesus' pronouncement is that this water provides or sustains eternal life (just as physical water sustains physical life), not that water is itself the metaphor for life. The Spirit is a "life-giving Spirit" (6:63; cf. 1 Cor. 15:45). Spirit baptism is an impartation of life, the beginning of a new creation (20:22; cf. Gen. 2:7). Jesus' ministry is more than merely a continuation of John's. Whatever baptizing activity Jesus may have carried on in Judea is of secondary importance and is now behind him. His real work is not to baptize in water but to do what John had predicted he would do: baptize in the Holy Spirit. The metaphor of water is used here not in the sense of washing or being immersed, but of *drinking* (cf. Paul in 1 Cor. 12:13: "In the same way, all of us . . . have been baptized into the one body by the same Spirit, and we have all been given the one Spirit to drink"). The Spirit quenches thirst, not in the sense of removing a person's desire for the presence of God, but in the sense of continually satisfying that desire. The Holy Spirit will be like an eternal self-replenishing spring within the believer "welling up to everlasting life" (v. 14, NIV).

The Samaritan woman takes the metaphor literally. The only life-giving water she knows is the water in the well, which belongs to her and her people already (vv. 11–12). Jesus' promise of the Spirit and eternal life means only that she will never have to come back to this well to draw water! (v. 15). The sequence ends in misunderstanding, yet the woman's remark is curiously apt, for when the Spirit comes, such holy places as the well of Jacob will in fact lose their significance. Religious or ethnic identities based on control of these sites will give way to a new identity in the Spirit (cf. vv. 21, 23).

Jesus' reply to the woman signals a turn in the narrative. Instead of correcting her misunderstanding, he tells her that she must come back to the well at least once more, with her husband (v. 16). It appears that Jesus' mission to Samaria will begin with the conversion of a whole family. Such things occur in the book of Acts (16:15, 33–34; 18:8; cf. 11:14) and at the end of this very journey in John's Gospel when Jesus reaches Galilee (4:53), but in Samaria it is not to be. Perhaps in the hope of receiving the life-giving water immediately, the woman tells Jesus that she has no husband. Jesus ironically commends her for telling the truth (vv. 17, 18) and so exposes her adultery (cf. Mark 10:12). The change of subject is not so abrupt as it appears. The narrative assumes a close connection between baptism in the Spirit and the forgiveness of sins (cf. Mark 1:4–8; Acts 2:38). Jesus, who will baptize in the Spirit, is "the Lamb of God, who takes away the sin of the world" (1:29). When the Spirit is given (20:22), Jesus will say to his disciples, "If you forgive people's sins, they are forgiven; if you do not forgive them, they are not forgiven" (20:23). Sin, to be forgiven, must first be exposed, and it is, but the woman's adultery is not the center of interest in this chapter. The movement of the narrative is not from the woman to her present husband (or lover) but from the woman directly to the rest of the townspeople (vv. 28–30). Whatever feelings of guilt she may have had go unmentioned.

Instead of guilt, her reaction to Jesus' supernatural insight into her life is one of amazement (vv. 29, 39). He immediate conclusion is that he is a prophet (v. 19). Because he is a Jew and a prophet, she seizes the opportunity to start a discussion with him about the respective claims of the Jewish and Samaritan places of worship—the temple mountain in Jerusalem and Mount Gerizim near Shechem (v. 20), the latter probably visible from where they were standing. It is useless to speculate whether or not she was trying to divert attention from her personal morality. To the Gospel writer, at least, her remark is not a diversion but carries forward the main thrust of the story.

Jesus tells her that the crucial question is not *where* but *how* to worship God. Soon the alternatives of Jerusalem or Mount Gerizim will lose their significance. The "true worshippers" (i.e., the Christians) will worship God as their Father "in spirit and truth" (v. 23, NIV), that is, **by the power of God's Spirit** (GNB) as a result of the promised baptism. In the words of later Christian writers, they are a "new race" (*Epistle to Diogenetus 1*) or a "third race" ("For what has reference to the Greeks and Jews is old. But we are Christians, who as a third race worship him in a new way"; *Preaching of Peter*, cited in Clement of Alexandria, *Stromateis* VI, 5.39–41, translated in Hennecke-Schneemelcher, *New Testament Apocrypha II* [Philadelphia: Westminster, 1964], p. 100). Playing on the woman's reference to her fathers, or Samaritan ancestors who worshiped on Gerizim (v. 20), Jesus subtly introduces the title **Father** in connection with the worship of God (vv. 21, 23), making the point that only in the Spirit (i.e., in the new Christian community) is it possible to worship God as Father (cf. Paul in Rom. 8:15–16; Gal. 4:6). Because he is Father, this is how he wants to be worshiped, and Christians are the kind of worshipers he seeks (v. 23).

Jesus speaks in verse 22 as a Jew, for it is as a Jew that the Samaritan woman has addressed him. Yet he speaks not for Judaism as a whole but for the small community of faith that has formed itself around him (cf. 3:11). When his Jewish opponents in a later confrontation (8:41) claim to know God as Father, Jesus denies their claim (8:42). The only advantage of Jew over Samaritan is that **it is from the Jews that salvation comes** (v. 22b), that is, Jesus himself has come from among the Jews, bringing "grace and truth" and the knowledge of God to the whole world (cf. 1:17–18). This knowledge makes it possible, first for Jesus' Jewish disciples and then for Samaritans and Gentiles, to know whom they worship (v. 22) or to **worship the Father as he really is** (vv. 23–24). If **God is Spirit** (v. 24), then only the coming of the Spirit makes his true character known.

The woman responds to Jesus' teaching in the only terms she knows, the Samaritan expectation of a **Messiah** who **will come** and **tell us everything** (v. 25). The Gospel writer has borrowed the Jewish term **Messiah** (i.e., "Anointed One") to designate the figure of whom the woman speaks.

The Samaritans' own term was "Taheb" (or "Restorer"). The Taheb, whose functions corresponded generally to those of the Jewish Messiah, was a figure modeled after Moses, in line with the biblical expectation of a prophet like Moses who would come and tell the people everything that God commanded (Deut. 18:18). Such an expectation was alive in Judaism as well (cf. 1:21) but played a larger role among the Samaritans. Significantly, it is here in a Samaritan context, and only here, that Jesus acknowledges his messiahship clearly and without hesitation (v. 26). Six chapters later, the people of Jerusalem will still be asking, "How long are you going to keep us in suspense? Tell us the plain truth: are you the Messiah?" (10:24). Yet long before, in a small Samaritan village, the secret is already out! Jesus' acceptance of this woman's version of messiahship is probably to be explained by the prophetic or teaching role she assigns to her **Messiah**. The statement that **when he comes, he will tell us everything** (v. 25) anticipates the language of Jesus' promise of the Spirit to his disciples in the farewell discourse (cf. 16:13–15). The Spirit's work is an extension of the work of Jesus. It is a work of revelation, and when the Samaritan woman thinks of revelation she thinks of the Taheb. Reaching beyond her recognition of him as a prophet (v. 19), Jesus finally makes himself known to her as the Prophet-Messiah for whom she and her people have been waiting (v. 26). The basis on which he said **the time will come** (v. 21), and quickly added **the time is coming and is already here** (v. 23) is now made clear. Jesus' interview with the woman (vv. 5–26) has achieved its purpose. A revelation has taken place, and the woman's hope has become reality.

The disciples, who have been mentioned only parenthetically in verse 8, come on the scene at this point (v. 27). Surprised that he would even talk with a woman (a Samaritan woman at that!), they seem for the moment too much in awe of Jesus to ask why. Even though the disciples were not present at his self-revelation to the woman, they are left speechless in its wake (cf. their hesitation to ask him questions in 16:5, 19 and 21:12). As soon as the disciples arrive from the town, the woman returns to town, and the narrative divides itself into two scenes centering on two sets of characters: the woman and the townspeople (vv. 28–30, 39–42), and the disciples and Jesus (vv. 31–38).

When the disciples offer Jesus some of the food they have bought in Sychar (see v. 8), Jesus tells them he has food of his own that they know nothing about (v. 32). For the moment, these "true worshipers" who will one day supersede both Jew and Samaritan, are as ignorant as the Samaritan woman (cf. v. 22). They are not yet ready to worship God in the

Spirit. The Spirit rests on Jesus, and on him alone (cf. 3:34). The **food** of which he speaks is obedience to God (cf. Matt. 4:4) and the completion of the task God sent him to do (v. 34).

This task ultimately spans the whole of the fourth Gospel (cf. 17:4; 19:30) but is defined in the immediate setting (with a change of metaphor) as a **harvest** (i.e., an ingathering of new believers) among the Samaritans. We may contrast the situation with that described in Matt. 9:36–10:6, where the "harvest" includes only the "lost sheep, the people of Israel" and specifically excludes "any Samaritan towns." Jesus' horizons are wider (or at least are widened sooner) in John's Gospel than in the Synoptics. He who "takes away the sin of the world" (1:29) is about to be acknowledged by an alien people as the world's Savior (v. 42). It is no ordinary harvest. To show its uniqueness, Jesus makes use of two familiar proverbs (vv. 35, 37):

1. **Four more months and then the harvest**. Conventional wisdom dictated four months between planting and reaping (v. 35), but Jesus speaks of messianic abundance like that foreseen by Amos the prophet, in which "the reaper will be overtaken by the plowman and the planter by the one treading grapes" (Amos 9:13, NIV; cf. the abundance of wine at the Cana wedding). Verses 35–36 repeat in metaphorical language Jesus' assurance to the Samaritan women that **the time is coming and is already here** (v. 23). A bountiful harvest of **eternal life** (cf. v. 14) is about to begin. For sower and reaper alike, it is a moment of joy (v. 36).

2. **One man plants, another man reaps**. Jesus transforms a traditional saying on the inequity and futility of human life (cf. Eccles. 2:18–21) into a word of promise to the disciples: They are to benefit from the labor of **others** for they are sent to reap a harvest they have not planted (v. 38). But in Jesus' application of these proverbs who is the sower and who is the reaper? And who are the **others** mentioned in verse 38?

Verse 34 suggests that God is the sower, for Jesus' task is to **finish the work** God gave him to do. And in verses 39–42 it is Jesus alone who actually carries out the **harvest** among the Samaritan townspeople. Yet in verse 35 he summons his disciples to the ripe harvest fields, and they are the ones who in verse 38 are to reap a harvest for which **others** have worked. The roles in this drama are not fixed. Jesus is not speaking in allegories or riddles but using a simple metaphor capable of several applications. A transition of sorts can be detected at verse 37. If the controlling thought of verses 34–36 was "as the Father sent me," the controlling thought of verses 37–38 is "so I send you" (cf. 20:21; also 17:18). But the fact that the disciples play no part whatever in the ensuing mission among the Samaritans suggests that verses 37–38 are intended as a momentary glimpse beyond the immediate situation to the narrator's own time. Those who proclaim the Christian message, whether to the Samaritans (e.g., Acts 8:4–25) or to the whole world (cf. 20:21) should not be discouraged but remember that Jesus and **others** (e.g., the woman and the converts of Sychar) have been there already to prepare the way. Even though Samaria may have been off his "beaten track" (cf. Matt. 10:5), Jesus had passed through it on occasion (cf. Luke 9:51–56) and carried on a teaching mission in at least one Samaritan town.

The distinction between sowing and reaping is perhaps echoed in the two stages of the Samaritans' faith in verses 39–42. Their faith had begun with the hesitant testimony of the woman about what Jesus had told her (vv. 29, 39), but when they met Jesus and heard his message for themselves, many more believed. Their "secondhand" faith (as they regarded it) had given way to a personal knowledge and deep conviction that Jesus was truly **the Savior of the world** (v. 42). These words make it clear at last that, for the Gospel writer, the Samaritans stand as representatives of all the peoples of the world. In passing, by divine necessity, through one Samaritan town and talking with one sinful woman, Jesus both reaps a harvest and anticipates a greater harvest to come, the church's mission to the Gentiles.

Additional Notes

4:4 / **He had to go through Samaria.** If the traditional location of Aenon is correct (see note on 3:23), and if Jesus' baptizing activity was near there, it is all the more clear that the necessity was not a geographical one. Samaria, in fact, would represent a detour if one's destination were Galilee.

4:5 / **Sychar**: The place is shown on the sixth-century Madeba map as "Sychar which is now Sychora." This probably corresponds to the present-day Arab village of Askar on the slope of Mount Ebal a mile east of Nablus. 'Askar has a spring that may correspond to the "spring of Sychar" (En Soker) mentioned in the Mishnah (*Menachoth* 10.2), but a very deep well fitting the description of the one where Jesus stopped is found one kilometer further south, at the village of Balatah on the site of ancient Shechem (destroyed by the Jewish king John Hyrcanus before 100 B.C.). Some have suggested that **Sychar** in John 4:5 is a mistake for "Shechem" (two Syriac manuscripts actually read "Shechem"), but it is not even certain that a town existed on the site of Shechem in Jesus' time.

The movements in the story back and forth between the well and the town make more sense if the distance is one kilometer than if it is only the 250 feet or so that today separate the Well of Jacob (as it is still known) from Tell Balatah (the excavations of Shechem by Ernst Sellin and, later, G. Ernest Wright). The woman may have traveled the extra distance from Sychar to this well either for religious reasons or because her neighbors made her unwelcome at her own town's spring (see J. Finegan, *Archaeology of the New Testament* [Princeton: Princeton University Press, 1969], pp. 3–38).

4:6 / **Sat down by the well**: In Greek the adverb *houtōs* ("thus") adds a vivid storyteller's touch to the account, which is lost in most translations (including GNB): Jesus "sat down, thus" or "sat right down" beside the well. The adverb is used similarly in 13:25.

About noon: lit., "the sixth hour." See note on 1:39.

4:9 / **Jews will not use the same cups and bowls that Samaritans use**. A few ancient manuscripts omit this parenthetical remark, but such explanatory asides are entirely characteristic of the narrator's style. The words belong in the text.

4:16 / **Come back**: or "come back here." The repetition in Greek of the adverb *enthade* ("here") in vv. 15 ("come here to draw water") and 16 ("come back here") somewhat lessens the abruptness of Jesus' request in v. 16 and helps to link two stages of the conversation.

4:23 / **The time is coming and is already here**. The new worship had already begun (among the followers of Jesus) even though the end of temple worship at Jerusalem and on Mt. Gerizim was still future ("the time will come," v. 21); for the expression, cf. 5:25, 16:31.

By the power of God's Spirit people will worship the Father as he really is. The subject of the clause is definite rather than indefinite: not **people** but "the true worshippers" (cf. NIV). They will worship (lit.) "in Spirit and in truth." The Holy Spirit is called "the Spirit of truth" in 14:16; 15:26; 16:13. "Spirit" and "truth" are equated in 1 John 5:6, while "truth" (2 John 2; 3 John 12), or "grace and truth" (John 1:14, 17) can be used as designations for the Holy Spirit. To worship God as Father in the new age of the Spirit is to worship him **as he really is**. The relationship to him as **Father** is a new relationship made possible by the coming of Jesus Christ into the world.

4:26 / **I am he**: lit., "I am" (Gr.: *egō eimi*). Formally, these words correspond to the formula by which Jesus later reveals himself as God (8:58). But here they simply identify him as the Messiah (v. 25).

10

Jesus and the Official's Son

After spending two days there, Jesus left and went to Galilee. ⁴⁴For he himself had said, "A prophet is not respected in his own country."
⁴⁵When he arrived in Galilee, the people there welcomed him, because they had gone to the Passover Festival in Jerusalem and had seen everything that he had done during the festival.
⁴⁶Then Jesus went back to Cana in Galilee, where he had turned the water into wine. A government official was there whose son was sick in Capernaum. ⁴⁷When he heard that Jesus had come from Judea to Galilee, he went to him and asked him to go to Capernaum and heal his son, who was about to die. ⁴⁸Jesus said to him, "None of you will ever believe unless you see miracles and wonders."

⁴⁹"Sir," replied the official, "come with me before my child dies."
⁵⁰Jesus said to him, "Go; your son will live!"
The man believed Jesus' words and went. ⁵¹On his way home his servants met him with the news, "Your boy is going to live!"
⁵²He asked them what time it was when his son got better, and they answered, "It was one o'clock yesterday afternoon when the fever left him." ⁵³Then the father remembered that it was at that very hour when Jesus had told him, "Your son will live." So he and all his family believed.
⁵⁴This was the second miracle that Jesus performed after coming from Judea to Galilee.

Once again the narrator provides an explanation for Jesus' itinerary. After two days at Sychar (cf v. 40), Jesus leaves Samaria and continues his journey to Galilee (v. 43; cf. vv. 3–4). The reason given is Jesus' own remark (probably made on a different occasion), **A prophet is not respected in his own country.** A great deal of speculation has centered on whether Jesus' **own country** (Gr: *patris*) refers to Galilee or Judea. If it refers to Galilee, the principle seems to be contradicted right away by the welcome Jesus receives there (v. 45), even though he is suspicious of the Galileans' motives (v. 48). But if it refers to Judea or Jerusalem, why was the saying not quoted earlier, when Jesus "did not trust himself" to people in Jerusalem (2:24) or when he decided to leave Judea (4:3)? Curiously, it is quoted in connection with his departure from *Samaria* after a two-day visit. Is Samaria then Jesus' *patris*? Obviously not. Even though his enemies will later denounce him as a Samaritan

(8:48), the clear assumption of his encounter with the woman is that she is a Samaritan and he is a Jew (4:9, 19, 22).

That none of the proposed identifications of the *patris* makes sense suggests that the point of the saying does not depend on such an identification. The purpose of the statement is simply to explain why Jesus left Sychar after only two days. The principle corresponds to that of the "ordinance of the gospel" laid down in the second-century church manual known as the *Didache*: "Let every apostle who comes to you be received as the Lord, but he shall stay only one day or if necessary a second as well; but if he stays three days, he is a false prophet" (11:4–5). This is part of what the writer calls the "behavior of the Lord" (11:8) and is probably based on Jesus' own practice. Certainly Jesus' ministry was an itinerant one (cf. Matt. 8:20/Luke 9:58), and the point of verse 44 is that he must not wear out his welcome by remaining too long at Sychar. To stay in a place more than two days is to make it his *patris* and to have no honor there. His *patris* in this sense turns out finally to be Jerusalem, the place where prophets traditionally are dishonored and killed (cf. Luke 13:33!), but this application is outside the scope of the present passage.

In Galilee, Jesus is welcomed by people who had seen the things he had done in Jerusalem at the Passover feast (v. 45; cf. 2:23; 3:2). The apparent reason for mentioning this is to help explain Jesus' abrupt reply to the government official's plea in verse 48: **None of you will ever believe unless you see miracles and wonders**. The reply puts the Galileans in the same class with those in Jerusalem who had challenged Jesus to prove his authority by performing a miracle (2:18) or with those who "believed" on the basis of his miracles but whose faith he would not accept as genuine (2:23–25). The narrator implies at the outset that because these Galileans had actually been present on the earlier occasion, Jesus' suspicions of them were well founded. Yet the story that unfolds (vv. 46–54) has to do with a Galilean who did *not* fit this stereotype or fall under this indictment.

It is uncertain whether the **government official** (Gr.: *basilikos*, lit., "royal" or "a royal official") was a Gentile or a Jew. The theme of healing at a distance (therefore without physical contact) recalls two synoptic narratives in which Jesus, as an observant Jew, heals Gentiles without touching them or going to their homes (i.e., the daughter of the Syro-Phoenician woman, Mark 7:24–30/Matt. 15:21–28; the Roman centurion's servant, Matt. 8:5–13/Luke 7:1–10). But in each of these cases, part of the point of the story is that the victim is a non-Jew, whereas in the Johannine account nothing is made of whether he is or not. Jesus' apparent reluctance to repond to the official's plea (v. 48) has nothing to do with the man's race or with the laws of uncleanness that separated Jew from Gentile (cf. 4:9) but is based on a general suspicion of those who either request or delight in miracles. The similarity with the two synoptic incidents makes it likely that the official was in fact a Gentile, but the Gospel writer has already established the universal scope of Jesus' ministry in 4:1–42 (esp. v. 42) and now moves on to other (though not unrelated) concerns.

The story of the healing is framed by references linking it to the story of the wedding at Cana (2:1–12). Jesus meets the government official and performs the healing at the same village of Cana (v. 46) even though the official's son lies sick at nearby Capernaum. When the story is over and the miracle has been verified, the narrator calls it Jesus' **second miracle** (v. 54), corresponding to the "first" that took place at Cana (2:11). What do these two miracles have in common that allows the Gospel writer simply to pass over others that are assumed to have taken place in Jerusalem at the Passover? (cf. 2:23; 3:2). And why does the enumerated sequence stop at two, even though five more miracles (two of them in Galilee) are recorded during Jesus' public ministry, and one other (also in Galilee) after his resurrection?

Clearly, more is involved here than simply a pious geographical interest in Cana as a place of miracles. The two stories have in common a direct connection between a miracle and a decisive act of faith. When Jesus "revealed his glory" by turning a great amount of water into wine, "his disciples believed in him" (2:11). After his resurrection, their faith was deepened and perfected as "they believed the Scripture and the words that Jesus had spoken" (2:22, NIV). In the case of the government official, the two stages merge into one. As soon as Jesus told him his son would live, he **believed Jesus' words and went** (v. 50). Right from the beginning he demonstrated faith in the *words* of Jesus, a faith that is attributed to the disciples only *after* Jesus' words are verified by his resurrection (2:22). If the disciples typify those who believed because of what they saw, the government official typifies "those who have not seen and yet have believed" (20:29, NIV). He is therefore a figure with whom the readers of this Gospel can identify, for they too have "believed the word" without seeing. He functions in the narrative as a postresurrection, or even second-generation, Christian portrayed in advance, like those mentioned in Jesus' last prayer who would come to believe in him through the message proclaimed by the original disciples (17:20). Just as there was a miracle for those first disciples (2:11), so there is one for this later group as well

(4:54). The distinction is not between Jew and Gentile but is simply a distinction of time and circumstances.

For the most part, the distinction is not pressed in the ensuing narratives. The disciples as a group are the ones with whom the readers are expected to identify. They too (even before the resurrection) come to believe Jesus' words (e.g., 6:68–69; 15:3, 7; 17:8, 14), and what Jesus says to them is obviously intended for the readers of the Gospel as well. The point is not that the government official's faith is "superior" to that of the first disciples but only that his story defines more concisely than theirs what faith entails: a total, unqualified trust in Jesus and in all that he promises. To believe is to take him at his word, regardless of how much or how little of his "glory" (2:11) one has been privileged to see.

The story is not quite over. The faith of the government official must yet become sight. He who demanded no verification is given verification nonetheless (vv. 51–53). On his way back to Capernaum, his servants come out to meet him with the good news that his child will live. On inquiring at what time the fever had broken, he learns it was at the very time when Jesus said to him, "Your son will live." The repetition of these exact words in verses 50 and 53 (cf. also v. 51) both verifies the miracle and makes the point that Jesus' words are life-giving words. The restoration of the physical life and health of the government official's son illustrates and reinforces Jesus' promises made earlier at Jerusalem (3:15–16) and in Samaria (4:14, 36). To some degree it also anticipates his self-revelation as giver of life in the following chapter (5:19–29).

For the moment, these deeper implications are left unexplored. The government official, his faith confirmed, becomes a convert. Like several converts in the book of Acts, **he and all his family believed** (cf. Acts 11:14; 16:15, 31–33; 18:8). Once more the reader is reminded that Jesus is on a mission (from Judea through Samaria to Galilee). Like the townspeople of Sychar, the government official and his family (including at least his son and his servants) are part of the "harvest" from that mission.

The first cycle of Jesus' ministry is now complete. He has established a new "Israel" at Cana and completed a circle back to Cana again. The converts of Sychar and Capernaum represent both a widening and a deepening of the first disciples' faith. Their stories mark a modest beginning to that universal mission which, for the Gospel writer, is still going on. They typify the people to whom the disciples will be sent (cf. 17:18; 20:21) and to whom the Gospel itself is written (20:30–31).

Additional Notes

4:44 / A prophet is not respected in his own country. Slightly different forms of this proverbial saying are found in Mark 6:4/Matt. 13:57 and in Luke 4:24. In each case the reference is to Jesus' hometown of Nazareth rather than to a whole region such as Galilee or Samaria. Because of this and because of the difference in context, these passages should not be allowed to determine the meaning here.

4:46 / A government official was there whose son was sick. The story that follows cannot be identified (as some have tried to do) with the synoptic account of the healing of a Roman centurion's servant (Matt. 8:5–13/Luke 7:1–10). *Basilikos* is not a term normally applied to Roman soldiers, and in our passage it is the man's son who is ill, not a servant (it is definitely a servant in Luke, and probably so in Matthew). The major similarity is that in each case the healing is accomplished from a distance, but this is a feature also shared with the story of the Syro-Phoenician woman and her daughter (Mark 7:24–30/Matt. 15:21–28). The latter story is actually more similar to the story in John's Gospel, in that the woman, like the government official, overcomes an initial hesitation on Jesus' part and, by her persistent faith, gains deliverance for her loved one. (The same is not true of the centurion *unless* Matt. 8:7 is taken as a question: "Am *I* to come and make him well?") The parallels among the three stories suggest, not that they are all based on the same incident, but that they reflect a characteristic way of describing Jesus' encounters with Gentiles. This remains true even though the writer of John's Gospel no longer has any particular interest in whether the government official was a Gentile or a Jew.

4:50, 53 / Your son will live is lit., "Your son lives." The point, of course, was not that the son still held on to life as to a slender thread, but that he would recover—and was even then recovering—from his illness. Death, which had seemed inevitable (v. 47), was now turned away. The present tense also conveys the notion that Jesus gives eternal life *now*, and not just at the last day (cf. 5:24–25).

4:52 / One o'clock yesterday afternoon is lit., "Yesterday at the seventh hour." See note on 1:39. The official may have begun the seventeen-mile trip from Cana to Capernaum immediately and stopped overnight on the way, perhaps at Magdala. The servants would probably not have gone out with the good news until the next day, when the boy was safely out of danger.

4:54 / Second miracle: This reference, along with 2:11, has been made the basis of theories that John's Gospel drew on a "signs source," a collection of miracle stories told to bring people to faith in Christ. It is argued that at one time 20:30–31 or 12:37 (or both) belonged to this source. Later, 20:30–31 was used as an epilogue to the finished Gospel, whereas 12:37 served to summarize the first half of it. Such theories are not impossible, but they fail to explain on what basis the miracles in chapters 5–11 can legitimately be incorporated into the sequence.

None of these is referred to *individually* as "miracle" or "sign." Moreover, the general references in this Gospel to signs or miracles (2:18, 23; 3:2; 4:48; 6:2, 30) display a considerable variety of meaning, so there is no real basis for assuming that the general references in 12:37 and 20:30–31 have in mind a particular set of miracle stories.

11

The Healing at the Pool

JOHN 5:1–18

After this, Jesus went to Jerusalem for a religious festival. [2]Near the Sheep Gate in Jerusalem there is a pool[h] with five porches; in Hebrew it is called Bethzatha.[i] [3]A large crowd of sick people were lying on the porches—the blind, the lame, and the paralyzed.[j] [5]A man was there who had been sick for thirty-eight years. [6]Jesus saw him lying there, and he knew that the man had been sick for such a long time; so he asked him, "Do you want to get well?"

[7]The sick man answered, "Sir, I don't have anyone here to put me in the pool when the water is stirred up; while I am trying to get in, somebody else gets there first."

[8]Jesus said to him, "Get up, pick up your mat, and walk." [9]Immediately the man got well; he picked up his mat and started walking.

The day this happened was a Sabbath, [10]so the Jewish authorities told the man who had been healed, "This is a Sabbath, and it is against our Law for you to carry your mat."

[11]He answered, "The man who made me well told me to pick up my mat and walk."

[12]They asked him, "Who is the man who told you to do this?"

[13]But the man who had been healed did not know who Jesus was, for there was a crowd in that place, and Jesus had slipped away.

[14]Afterward, Jesus found him in the Temple and said, "Listen, you are well now; so stop sinning or something worse may happen to you."

[15]Then the man left and told the Jewish authorities that it was Jesus who had healed him. [16]So they began to persecute Jesus, because he had done this healing on a Sabbath.

[17]Jesus answered them, "My Father is always working, and I too must work."

[18]This saying made the Jewish authorities all the more determined to kill him; not only had he broken the Sabbath law, but he had said that God was his own Father and in this way he made himself equal with God.

h. Near the Sheep Gate . . . a pool; or Near the Sheep Pool . . . a place. i. Bethzatha; *some manuscripts have* Bethesda. j. *Some manuscripts add verses 3b-4:* They were waiting for the water to move, *because every now and then an angel of the Lord went down into the pool and stirred up the water. The first sick person to go into the pool after the water was stirred up was healed from whatever disease he had.*

A t this point the narrator's interest in Jesus' itinerary begins to wane. The events of chapters 5, 6, and 7 are introduced by the vague connective phrase, **after this** (5:1; 6:1; 7:1). The transition from chapter 4 to chapter 5 is a natural one in that a person appropriately goes to Jerusalem from Galilee for a **religious festival** (v. 1), but the transition between chapters 5 and 6 is more awkward. Jesus is assumed to be still in Jerusalem at the end of chapter 5, but the beginning of chapter 6 finds him about to cross from one side of Lake Galilee to the other (6:1). For this reason, some scholars have proposed that the order of chapters 5 and 6 be reversed: Jesus is in Galilee at the end of chapter 4, continues there in chapter 6, and finally returns to Jerusalem in chapter 5! But this proposal leaves unexplained the beginning of chapter 7, which does not say that Jesus returned to Galilee but implies that he was already there, traveling from town to town (7:1). The rearrangement of chapters creates as many problems as it solves. Its fallacy lies in the attempt to make the Gospel more chronological than it actually intends to be. The phrase **after this** at the beginning of each of these chapters appears to mean no more than "the next thing I would like to tell is . . ." Having brought Jesus from Cana to Jerusalem and back to Cana again, the author now turns to other, more overtly theological concerns.

In view of this Gospel's interest in the Jewish religious festivals (e.g., "Passover" in 2:13; 6:4; 11:55; 12:1; 13:1; "Shelters," or Sukkoth, in 7:2; "Dedication," or Hanukkah, in 10:22), it is surprising that the festival mentioned in verse 1 is not named. On the assumption that Passover is meant, some have assumed that Jesus was in Jerusalem for three Passovers (chaps. 2, 5, and 12–19) and spent one other in Galilee (chap. 6). Others have suggested the Festival of Shelters, or the Festival of Weeks (i.e., Pentecost). But the author has left the festival anonymous, either deliberately or because the story was handed down to him without an exact temporal setting. If it was left anonymous deliberately, it may have been to conceal a departure from chronological order. It may be that the story of the healing at the pool was originally preserved as a sample of the (otherwise unspecified) miracles performed at Jesus' *first* Passover in Jerusalem (2:23; 3:2). Once the story of the Temple cleansing had been transferred to that early Passover visit (2:13–22), the tendency would have been for it to overshadow other miracles associated with that visit. The account found in 5:1–18 is perhaps one of those miracle stories "rescued" from its original setting, given a new literary setting of its own, and made the basis both of Jesus' ongoing controversy with the Jewish authorities and of his self-revelation as the giver of life.

In any case, this was the miracle that Jesus later singled out as a focus of opposition to him (7:21–23), even though he was known to have performed others as well (7:31; cf. 6:2). It is presented as a sample of the kind of action that from an early point in his ministry produced conflict over Sabbath observance and over Jesus' personal claims (vv. 16, 18).

The scene is described carefully (vv. 2–5). The healing occurs at a place where healings were expected. **Bethzatha** was apparently a healing shrine consisting of a pool with an intermittent spring popularly believed to have healing properties. Jesus surveys a scene in which a large number of the sick and the disabled have gathered for healing. Attention is focused on one man in particular who had been **sick for thirty-eight years** (v. 5). Though it is often assumed that he was a paralytic (cf. Mark 2:1–12), the text does not say so. Like the government official's son at Capernaum, he is diagnosed only as being **sick** (cf. 4:46). The narrator's interest is not in the medical particulars of the case (except for the duration of the man's condition) but in the cure—and, even more, its consequences.

The irony of the cure is that Jesus bypasses the healing sanctuary that has just been so carefully described and heals the sick man (just as he did the government official's son) with a spoken word: **Get up, pick up your mat, and walk** (v. 8; cf. Mark 2:9, 11). The form of this command is what determines the consequences. The sick man is immediately healed and does exactly what Jesus tells him. At this point the narrator pauses to supply a necessary bit of information: It was the Sabbath (v. 9b; cf. 9:14). The man had broken the Sabbath law, not by being healed, but by carrying his mat (v. 10). Instead of accepting responsibility for his actions, he blames **the man who made me well** (v. 11), but Jesus' identity is still unknown to him, and Jesus has slipped away in the crowd (v. 13). Neither the man nor the Jewish authorities "find " Jesus. It is Jesus who "finds" the man nearby in the Temple area and questions him (v. 14a). The initiative throughout belongs to Jesus. His identity, his goings and comings, are known only to those to whom he discloses himself (cf. 9:35–37). Yet he knows the character and circumstances of the man he has just healed. Echoing the synoptic story of the paralytic, in which healing and the forgiveness of sins are virtually equated (Mark 2:5–11), Jesus warns the man to **stop sinning or something worse may happen to you** (v. 14b; cf. Jesus' warning to the adulterous woman in 8:11, at the end of a passage inserted into John's Gospel by later copyists: "Go, but do not sin again"). The question of whether the man's sickness was a punishment for his sins is not addressed directly in this story, as it is in the subsequent account of the healing of the man born blind (cf. 9:1–3), nor are the two situations identical. The sick man of Bethzatha ignores Jesus' warning as if he had not heard. His encounter with Jesus at the Temple means only that he can now identify Jesus to the Jewish authorities as the one responsible for his violation of the Sabbath (v. 15). At this point he disappears from the narrative, and the reader never learns if **something worse** happened to him or not. His main function has been to precipitate a conflict between Jesus and the Jewish authorities that will continue to the end of this Gospel.

The conflict develops in two stages. The first stage centers on the issue at hand, the law of the Sabbath (v. 16). Jesus speaks to this issue concisely and dramatically (v. 17), but his reply forces the conflict into a second stage, centering on Jesus' claim to be God's son and thus **equal with God** (v. 18). Jesus' response to this charge is dramatic but hardly concise, for it extends all the way to the end of the chapter (vv. 19–47). Verses 16 and 18 have in common an introductory form that highlights these two stages:

And *this was why the Jews* persecuted Jesus . . . (v. 16, RSV)
This was why the Jews sought all the more to kill him . . . (v. 18, RSV)

The alternating verses, accordingly, also begin with a common form,

Jesus answered them (*apekrinato*, vv. 17, 19)

In the Gospels Jesus is represented as replying in several ways to the charge that he or his disciples are guilty of breaking the Sabbath. Most of his answers are based on logic or on practical considerations (e.g., John 7:22–23; Mark 2:25–27; 3:4; Matt. 12:3–7, 11–12; Luke 13:15-16; 14:5), but at least one focuses on the person of Jesus himself: "So the Son of Man is Lord even of the Sabbath" (Mark 2:28 and parallels). His answer in John 5:17 belongs in the latter category: **My Father is always working, and I too must work.** The background of this pronouncement lies in certain debates among Jewish rabbis and philosophers over the meaning of the biblical statements that God rested on the seventh day (Gen. 2:2–3; cf. Exod. 20:11). Their conclusion was that God did not actually stop working after six days, for if he had, the world would have ceased to exist. Instead, he simply ended his work of creation and began his work of sustaining and watching over the world (see. e.g., Philo, *Allegory of the Laws* I, 5f.). In this sense, God himself breaks the Sabbath. Building on this conclusion, Jesus argues that if God (whom he calls his Father) is still at work, it is appropriate and necessary that he also should work, even on the Sabbath. Jesus' assumption is that his works are the works of God (cf. 4:34).

The Jewish authorities take offense, not at Jesus' reference to the traditional discussion of God and the Sabbath, but at the phrase, **my Father,** with its implied claim that Jesus was God's son in a unique sense (v. 18). To them it sounded as if he was making himself **equal with God** (something Jesus is said in Phil. 2:6 to have deliberately chosen *not* to do). The charge will be repeated in 10:33: "You are only a man, but you are trying to make yourself God." To any Jew familiar with the Old Testament, such a claim was equivalent to blasphemy (10:33; cf. Exod. 20:3; Deut. 6:4, 13–14). Only once before in the Gospel has Jesus spoken so openly of God as **my Father** (2:16), and the full extent of the hostility provoked by such language is only now becoming clear.

Additional Notes

5:1 / **A religious festival**: The Greek has the additional words "of the Jews," as a reminder to Gentile readers of the historical situation. Some manuscripts have the definite article ("*the* religious festival of the Jews"), which could mean either Shelters (Sukkoth) or Passover. Although this reading is incorrect, it may preserve a memory that the events about to be recorded did in fact take place at one of Jesus' Passover visits to Jerusalem.

5:2 / **Near the Sheep Gate in Jerusalem there is a pool with five porches**. The description is probably intended for readers unfamiliar with the city. Another possible translation is that of the GNB margin: **Near the Sheep Pool in Jerusalem there is a place with five porches**. The text has supplied the word **Gate**, because the Greek word *probatikē* is simply an adjective meaning "of sheep." The margin has instead connected this adjective with **pool**, requiring that the indefinite word **place** be supplied as the subject of the English sentence (cf. v. 13). But when the Gospel writer wants to designate a location as being **called** something, he normally uses either the actual word "place" (as in 19:13, 17) or a more specific word, such as "town" (4:5, 11:54). In this case he is describing a pool, and it is on the pool that he wants to focus attention (cf. v. 7). If the **Sheep Gate** was a well-known location in Jerusalem (cf. Neh. 3:1; 12:39), it is natural that the pool in question would be located in relation to it. The translation in the text is therefore the more probable one.

5:2 / **Bethzatha**: Some ancient manuscripts read **Bethesda,** meaning "house of mercy" (see GNB margin). The Copper Scroll found at Qumran (3Q15 xi 12) alludes to twin pools ("Bethesdatain": a type of Hebrew plural indicating duality). **Bethzatha** may represent an effort (whether by the Gospel writer or a later copyist) to transcribe in Greek the corresponding Aramaic plural, "Bethesdatha." Archaeology, as well as later testimony of geographers and pilgrims, confirms the notion that the pool was double. See J. Finegan, *Archeology of the New Testament* (Princeton: Princeton University Press, 1969), pp. 142–47; J. Wilkinson, *Jerusalem as Jesus Knew It* (London: Thames & Hudson, 1978), pp. 95–104.

5:3 / At the end of this verse, a number of manuscripts add the words **they were waiting for the water to move**. Of these, these are some that continue with the words **because every now and then an angel of the Lord went down into the pool and stirred up the water. The first sick person to go into the pool after**

the water was stirred up was healed from whatever disease he had (GNB margin). These additions were made by scribes attempting to explain the sick man's statement in v. 7. Probably the shorter addition was made first, as a point of reference for the clause "when the water is stirred up" in v. 7. The longer addition was then attached as an explanation (based on popular legend) of why the waters became agitated from time to time. The truth in the legend is perhaps that the pool contained an intermittent spring that was thought to have healing properties. There is archaeological evidence that after A.D. 135 the pool was used by the Roman official cults as a pagan healing sanctuary sacred to the god Asclepius, and it is likely that already in Jesus' time the place and its traditions were frowned on by orthodox Jews even while it was being frequented by Jews and pagans alike. See R. M. Mackowski, *Jerusalem City of Jesus* (Grand Rapids: Eerdmans, 1980), pp. 79–83.

5:6 / **And he knew**: There is no reason to think that Jesus' knowledge at this point was supernatural (as, e.g., in 2:24–25). The meaning is rather that Jesus *found out* how long the man had been sick, presumably by being told.

5:10 / **It is against our Law for you to carry your mat**. Ironically, it would *not* have been against the Sabbath law for someone to carry the man on his mat or couch (cf. Mark 2:3). See Mishnah *Shabbath* 10:5. It was the carrying of the couch purposefully as an end in itself that was forbidden.

5:16 / **Because he had done this healing**: lit., "because he was doing these things." The imperfect tense, used consistently in this verse and in v. 18, suggests that the healing (and the authorities' response to it) was typical of many incidents that could have been cited from the early days of Jesus' ministry. The idea is that the authorities began persecuting him because this was the kind of thing he used to do even on the Sabbath. In the same way, the claim that God was "his own Father" (v. 18) is understood to have been made repeatedly.

5:17 / **Jesus answered them**. The aorist middle form of the verb (*apekrinato*), instead of the passive used as a middle (*apekrithē*), occurs in John's Gospel only here and in v. 19 out of more than seventy occurrences in all. Though it is the usual form in the writings of the Jewish historian Josephus, it is found only seven times in the New Testament and seems to be reserved for "solemn . . . or legal . . . utterance" (W. Bauer, *A Greek-English Lexicon of the New Testament*, 2d ed., rev. W. F. Arndt, F. W. Gingrich, and F. W. Danker [Chicago: University of Chicago Press, 1979], p. 93). A good analogy to John 5:17, 19 is Luke 3:16, where John the Baptist makes a solemn declaration in response to no particular question he has been asked but simply to the hopes and thoughts of the people. So here, Jesus is not "answering" a specific question raised on a specific occasion but making a formal (and typical) defense of his behavior. His responses in v. 17 and in vv. 19–47 are therefore to be regarded as only loosely tied to their narrative context.

12

The Father
and the Son

JOHN 5:19–29

So Jesus answered them, "I tell you the truth: the Son can do nothing on his own; he does only what he sees his Father doing. What the Father does, the Son also does. ²⁰For the Father loves the Son and shows him all that he himself is doing. He will show him even greater things to do than this, and you will all be amazed. ²¹Just as the Father raises the dead and gives them life, in the same way the Son gives life to those he wants to. ²²Nor does the Father himself judge anyone. He has given his Son the full right to judge, ²³so that all will honor the Son in the same way as they honor the Father. Whoever does not honor the Son does not honor the Father who sent him.

²⁴"I am telling you the truth: whoever hears my words and believes in him who sent me has eternal life. He will not be judged, but has already passed from death to life. ²⁵ I am telling you the truth: the time is coming—the time has already come—when the dead will hear the voice of the Son of God, and those who hear it will come to life. ²⁶Just as the Father is himself the source of life, in the same way he has made his Son to be the source of life. ²⁷And he has given the Son the right to judge, because he is the Son of Man. ²⁸Do not be surprised at this; the time is coming when all the dead will hear his voice ²⁹and come out of their graves: those who have done good will rise and live, and those who have done evil will rise and be condemned.

Jesus responds to the second charge brought against him by the authorities with a long discourse (vv. 19–47) introduced by the solemn formula, **I tell you the truth** (v. 19; cf. also vv. 24, 25). He begins by appearing to set limits to his authority as God's unique son: **The Son can do nothing on his own; he does only what he sees his Father doing** (v. 19). But Jesus is not backing down, for his words reiterate the claim of verse 17 that the works he performs are the very works of God (v. 19). His language is like that of a parable; he is like a son apprenticed to a human father, learning by example and imitation (v. 20). His authority is absolute, not in spite of the fact that he does **nothing on his own**, but because of it. His authority is a derived authority. In all that he does he is subject to his Father and totally dependent on his Father's power and love.

In his response, Jesus begins speaking mysteriously of himself in the third person **the Son**, in much the same way that he speaks of himself in all the Gospels as **the Son of Man**. **Son** and **Son of Man**, in fact, are used almost interchangeably in verses 26–27. Some have argued that terms such as **the Son** and **the Father** represent the confessional language of the Gospel writer (as perhaps they do in 3:16–18, 35–36). But the kinship of **Son** with **Son of Man** and the firm testimony of John's Gospel that Jesus was actually accused of claiming divine sonship (5:18; 10:33–36) make it more likely that language of this kind goes back to Jesus (cf. Matt. 11:27/ Luke 10:22; also, the voice at Jesus' baptism in the Synoptics and Jesus' address to God in prayer as "Abba," or "Father").

Jesus' authority as **the Son** comes to expression in his deeds or "works" (v. 20, RSV). The works of the Father carried out by the Son are two: the giving of life and the executing of judgment. Jesus refers to this twofold work in verses 21–23 and again in verses 26–27, each time introducing the pronouncement with the same words:

Just as the Father . . . in the same way the Son (v. 21).
Just as the Father . . . in the same way . . . his Son (v. 26).

If a distinction can be made between these two cycles, it is that the emphasis of the first is on the Son's actual performance of the works (e.g., the healing of the sick man at the pool), while the second cycle looks rather at the underlying authority by which the Son gives life and carries out the judgment of God.

Interlocked with the two cycles are three pronouncements clarifying the time frame of the works of the Son (vv. 24, 25, 28–29). A distinction between present and future works was already hinted at in verse 20: "For the Father loves the Son, and shows him all that he himself is doing: and greater works than these will he show him, that you may marvel" (RSV). The tenses of the verbs suggest that the "greater works" are future. These are clearly set forth in verses 28–29: At the end of the age there will be a resurrection of all who have ever died, either to life with God, or to judgment (i.e., condemnation).

Even though this twofold resurrection was a common Jewish hope (at least among the Pharisees, Acts 23:6; 24:15), Jesus suggests that it will be a cause for amazement (vv. 20, 28) because God will accomplish these "greater works" through his Son, who is also **Son of Man** (v. 27). But if the God of creation is *still* at work in Jesus (v. 17), his power to bring consummation is *already* at work in Jesus (vv. 24, 25). In such miracles as the healing at Bethzatha the long-expected resurrection to life comes to realization in advance. The "greater works" are yet future, but Jesus' emphasis (indicated by the twice-repeated **I am telling you the truth** in vv. 24–25) is on what is already happening in his ministry. Eternal life is available *now*. Those who hear Jesus' message and believe in the Father who sent him will never face judgment or condemnation. They have **already passed from death to life** (v. 24; cf. 3:18). The next verse makes the same point in language more closely conformed to that of verses 28–29. A comparison can be made as follows:

Verse 25	Verses 28–29
the time is coming—the time has already come—	**the time is coming**
when the dead will hear the voice of the Son of God	**when all the dead will hear his voice**
and those who hear it will come to life	**and come out of their graves**

The differences in wording show that verses 28–29 refer to a literal, general resurrection at the end of the age, while verse 25 (like v. 24) refers to something that Jesus considered a present experience. In his ministry the sick were being healed, and those who were spiritually dead were coming alive at the message he was bringing from the Father.

If verses 28–29 represent conventional eschatology (i.e., theological teaching about the future and the end of this age), verses 24–25 represent what C. H. Dodd and others have call realized eschatology. What is supposed to happen at the end is already happening now—in a sense. It is not the Gospel writer's purpose (any more than it was Jesus' purpose) to deny the traditional future hope. The future events, after all, are the **greater things** that will amaze the hearers. The purpose is rather to use this future hope to help explain what Jesus has been doing and what he will be doing in the chapters that follow. He is giving life, both physically and spiritually, even now; he is also executing judgment, for as people accept or reject the message he proclaims, they are even now condemned or vindicated (see, e.g., 3:18–19; 5:30–47; 9:39–41).

The goal of Jesus' twofold work is **that all will honor the Son in the same way as they honor the Father** (v. 23). Because Jesus' work and the work of the Father are the same (cf. vv. 19–20), a person's response to Jesus is by definition that person's response to God as well. Jesus is God's agent or representative, with power to act on the Father's behalf. Later he will extend this principle to his disciples acting on his behalf (13:20; cf. Matt. 10:40; Luke 10:16). His intent **that all will honor the Son** is universal in scope, like John the Baptist's intent "that all might believe through him" (1:7, RSV). But the appended warning, **Whoever does not honor the Son does not honor the Father who sent him** (v. 23b), strikes a more negative note, anticipating both the outcome of Jesus' public ministry in general (e.g., 8:42, 49; 12:37, 43, 48) and of this confrontation in particular (5:37–44).

Additional Notes

5:22 / **Nor does the Father himself judge anyone**. It should be noticed that the parallel between life-giving and judgment in vv. 21–22 is not perfect. The Father raises the dead and so does the Son, but the Father does *not* judge, having delegated all judgment to the Son. This distinction, however, is perhaps more apparent than real. Elsewhere Jesus denies that he came to judge the world (3:17) or that he judges those who reject his message (12:47; cf. 8:15), but he makes these disclaimers simply to emphasize that his intent is a saving intent. They do not exclude the fact that judgment does proceed from his ministry (cf. 3:18–19; 8:16; 12:48). In a similar way the disclaimer here about the Father does not exclude the fact that the Father does judge (with and through the Son).

5:26 / **The source of life**: lit. "to have life in himself." The same Greek construction is translated in 6:53 as "have life in yourselves." The idea that the Son "has life in himself" is understood within the framework of his dependence on the Father for his life. To "have life in oneself" apparently means to have God's life as a secure possession that cannot be taken away. In itself, the phrase does not include the notion that one has the power to confer that life on others, but such translations as **source of life** (both GNB and Jerusalem Bible) can be defended on the basis of the context, especially the parallelism with v. 21.

5:27 / **The Son of Man**: Although the expression **Son of Man** in Greek lacks the definite article (the only place in the Gospels where this is so), it is still to be taken as a title. The absence of the article is normal in Greek when a predicate noun precedes the verb "to be" (as here) even if the noun is understood as definite. It is also true that "Son of Man" lacks the definite article in the LXX Greek translation of Dan. 7:13 (cf. Rev. 1:13; 14:14), but this is not a good parallel because the phrase there is a simile, not a title: i.e., "one like a son of man" (RSV) or "what looked like a human being" (GNB).

5:28 / **Do not be surprised at this**, i.e., do not be surprised at the present authority of the Son to give life and to judge, for he will carry out even greater resurrection and judgment at the last day (cf. v. 20).

5:29 / **Those who have done good** . . . **those who have done evil**: A final judgment on the basis of works (with the appropriate rewards and punishment) was an integral part of the Jewish expectation of the end. Jesus is represented here as endorsing that expectation, but in the context of John's Gospel v. 28 should be understood in relation to 3:20–21: **those who have done good** are those who "come to the light," while **those who have done evil** are those who refuse to come. In the immediate context, v. 24 makes this unmistakably clear.

13

Witnesses to Jesus

JOHN 5:30–47

I can do nothing on my own authority; I judge only as God tells me, so my judgment is right, because I am not trying to do what I want, but only what he who sent me wants. [31]"If I testify on my own behalf, what I say is not to be accepted as real proof. [32]But there is someone else who testifies on my behalf, and I know that what he says about me is true. [33]John is the one to whom you sent your messengers, and he spoke on behalf of the truth. [34]It is not that I must have a man's witness; I say this only in order that you may be saved. [35]John was like a lamp, burning and shining, and you were willing for a while to enjoy his light. [36]But I have a witness on my behalf which is even greater than the witness that John gave: what I do, that is, the deeds my Father gave me to do, these speak on my behalf and show that the Father has sent me. [37]And the Father, who sent me, also testifies on my behalf. You have never heard his voice or seen his face, [38]and you do not keep his message in your hearts, for you do not believe in the one whom he sent.

[39]You study the Scriptures, because you think that in them you will find eternal life. And these very Scriptures speak about me! [40]Yet you are not willing to come to me in order to have life.

[41]"I am not looking for human praise. [42]But I know what kind of people you are, and I know that you have no love for God in your hearts. [43]I have come with my Father's authority, but you have not received me; when, however, someone comes with his own authority, you will receive him. [44]You like to receive praise from one another, but you do not try to win praise from the one who alone is God; how, then, can you believe me? [45]Do not think, however, that I am the one who will accuse you to my Father. Moses, in whom you have put your hope, is the very one who will accuse you. [46]If you had really believed Moses, you would have believed me, because he wrote about me. [47]But since you do not believe what he wrote, how can you believe what I say?"

The discourse of verses 19–47 can be divided into two parts on the basis of a change from the third to the first person at verse 30. Instead of referring to himself as "the Son," Jesus now uses the emphatic pronoun I (vv. 30, 31, 34, 36, 43). But part two of the discourse begins like part one with the insistence that Jesus' authority is a derived authority. He does nothing on his own but acts entirely on his Father's instructions (v. 30; cf. v. 19). If he does what he *sees* his Father do (vv. 19–20), he also judges according to what he *hears* God telling him (v. 30, NIV).

Possibly the reference at the end of verse 29 to "the resurrection of judgment" (RSV) provided a natural transition to part two of the discourse. The twofold work of life giving and judgment is still in view, but attention for the moment centers on Jesus' role as judge. His decisions are just, and not arbitrary or based on personal whim: **I am not trying to do what I want, but only what he who sent me wants** (v. 30). The atmosphere is that of a courtroom. From the standpoint of the Jewish authorities (cf. v. 18), Jesus is on trial, but from the Gospel writer's standpoint they themselves are on trial, and Jesus is the prosecuting attorney. His case is built on the scriptural principle that at least two witnesses are necessary to make a charge stand up in court (8:17; cf. Deut. 19:15). One person's testimony—even the testimony of Jesus—is insufficient by itself (v. 31). He therefore begins calling his witnesses: John the Baptist (vv. 33–35); the works of Jesus (v. 36); the Father himself (vv. 37–38); and the Scriptures (v. 39; cf. vv. 45–47). But the list is not a random one. Jesus begins by speaking in the singular of **someone else** (v. 32), a particular witness who testifies on his behalf. Though he mentions John the Baptist in passing, he makes it clear that John is *not* this witness (v. 36). John's testimony to the Jewish authorities (cf. 1:19–28) had its own value, and Jesus reminds them of it in the hope that they still might believe it and be saved. Yet it is only a human testimony (vv. 33–34). Jesus has in mind someone far greater than John, and a testimony far more decisive.

Clearly, the **someone else** who testifies is the Father (v. 37). Jesus' works are mentioned not for their own sake but as pointers to the Father. They are **deeds my Father gave me to do** and they **show that the Father has sent me** (v. 36). Are the works then the Father's testimony on Jesus' behalf (v. 37), or is something more specific in mind? The thought of the Father testifying *directly* on the Son's behalf recalls the synoptic accounts of the divine voice at Jesus' baptism, and especially the transfiguration ("This is my own dear Son, with whom I am pleased—listen to him!" Matt. 17:5; cf. also 1 John 5:9). But the primary point of reference (and one to which the transfiguration account may itself be alluding) is God's promise to Moses to send Israel "a prophet like you from among their own people; I will tell him what to say, and he will tell the people everything I command" (Deut. 18:18; cf. John 1:21). The context of this promise was a request by the people "not to hear the Lord speak again" as he spoke from Mount Sinai "or to see his fiery presence anymore" for fear they would die (Deut. 18:16). Because it is easier to listen to the voice of a man than to the voice of God, a prophet is announced as a kind of substitute for the terrifying Sinai revelation. When Jesus reminds his hearers that they have **never heard** [the Father's] **voice or seen his face** (v. 37), his point is not merely that they were not present at Sinai, nor that their experience suffers from the same limitations as that of Moses and the people of Israel, who were not allowed to see God's face (e.g., Exod. 33:20–22; Deut. 4:12). His point is that they have rejected the promised messenger. They **do not believe in the one whom** [the Father] **sent**, and because they do not, God's message has no place in their hearts (v. 38). If they believed, they would hear God's voice, and even see his face–in the person of Jesus (cf. 1:18; 14:9).

The implied reference to the prophet like Moses mentioned in Deuteronomy 18 leads Jesus to discuss more generally the Father's testimony on his behalf in the Scriptures (vv. 39–47). At the heart of the issue was a tragic irony. If there was one testimony that should have counted with the Jewish authorities it was that of the Scriptures. They studied the Scriptures earnestly in the hope of gaining eternal life, yet when the Scriptures pointed them to Jesus as the way to life (as in Deut. 18:15–18), they were unwilling to come (vv. 39–40). Jesus returns to this point in verses 45–47: If they really believed Moses (i.e., the Scriptures that he wrote), they would have believed what he said about Jesus. It is because they do *not* believe Moses' writings that they cannot accept Jesus and his claims (vv. 46–47). In this sense Moses is their accuser (v. 45), but to believe Jesus is to believe Moses as well; to reject what he says is to reject Moses and the Scriptures. In the end, Jesus is the touchstone determining whether a person lives or dies.

It turns out, therefore, that the two witnesses necessary to make a charge stand up in court are *both* embodied in the testimony of Jesus. The **someone else** who testifies on his behalf (i.e., the Father) speaks most decisively, not apart from Jesus, but in and through his very words. In a later discourse, where this inseparable bond between Jesus and the Father is assumed, Jesus can say: "No . . . even though I do testify on my own behalf, what I say is true, because I know where I came from and where I am going. . . . I pass judgment on no one. But if I were to do so, my judgment would be true, because I am not alone in this; the Father who sent me is with me" (8:14, 16; contrast 5:31). Jesus' words are self-authenticating precisely because they are not his own. They are words that the Father commanded him to speak (cf. Deut. 18:18).

Sandwiched between Jesus' final references to the testimony of the Scriptures (vv. 39–40, 45–47) is a brief section in which he contrasts his own attitude toward praise or glory with that of his hearers (vv. 41–44). Jesus' goal is not human praise but **praise from the one who alone is**

God (vv. 41, 44). They, on the other hand, **like to receive praise from one another** (v. 44). Even those among them who are later said to have believed in Jesus "did not talk about it openly, so as not to be expelled from the synagogue. They loved the approval of men rather than the approval of God" (12:42–43). Jesus' estimate of them parallels and helps to explain his unwillingness to trust himself to those who "believed in him" at his first Passover visit to Jerusalem (2:23–24). There the narrator explains that Jesus "knew them all. There was no need for anyone to tell him about them, because he himself knew what was in their hearts" (2:24–25). But here Jesus speaks for himself: **I know what kind of people you are, and I know that you have no love for God in your hearts** (v. 42).

The similarity in thought tends to confirm the suggestion that chapter 5 is actually a collection of material preserved in connection with that early Passover visit, not all of it directly related to the controversy over the Sabbath and over Jesus' authority as the Son. It is entirely possible that traditions of Jesus defending his authority against bitter opponents were remembered and handed down alongside traditions in which he unmasked the pretensions of some who aspired to be his disciples. Verses 41–44 show traces of belonging to the second category, but in the present form of the Gospel, the two "audiences" have merged. Jesus is represented as addressing the Jewish authorities in the same way whether they oppose him and seek his life or whether they privately believe in him but refuse to break with the religious establishment (cf. 8:30–59; 12:37–43).

Jesus' second answer to challenges leveled against him by the Jewish authorities thus ends appropriately, with an implicit (vv. 36–38) and an explicit (vv. 39–47) appeal to the Jewish Scriptures. Verses 19–47 can now be seen as a long and illuminating sequel to the terse claim of verse 17, "My Father is always working, and I too must work." They unfold for the reader the nature of Jesus' divine work (exemplified in the healings that precede and follow), and they establish the continuity of Jesus' words and deeds with the Father's self-revelation in the past to Moses and, through Moses' writings, to the Jewish authorities themselves. The authorities' unwillingness to acknowledge Jesus' claims calls into question their commitment to Scripture, the very heart of their faith and basis of their hope of life.

Additional Notes

5:31 / **If I testify on my own behalf**: The principle stated in this verse appears in the Mishnah as well: "But none may be believed when he testifies of himself" (*Ketuboth* 2.9).

5:39 / **You study the Scriptures**. The Greek could also be read as an imperative ("Study the Scriptures"), but the context supports the indicative rendering. The Jewish authorities *already* study the Scriptures because they themselves **think** that in these writings they will find life. Jesus' point is that their rejection of him contradicts their own aspirations and makes their diligent study worthless.

5:39, 45 / The possibility that vv. 41–44 interrupt a unified section dealing with the testimony of the Jewish Scriptures (vv. 39–40, 45–47) is supported by a noncanonical Gospel fragment dating from the second century (*Papyrus Egerton* 2), part of which can be reconstructed as follows: "You search the Scriptures, in which you think you will find life; these very Scriptures speak about me! Do not think that I have come to accuse you to my Father. Moses, in whom you have put your hope, is the very one who will accuse you." (cf. vv. 39, 45; the fragment continues with a saying parallel to John 9:29). See E. Hennecke and W. Schnee-melcher, *New Testament Apocrypha I* (Philadelphia: Westminster, 1964), pp. 94–97.

5:43 / **When, however, someone comes with his own authority, you will receive him**. The **someone** (Gr.: *allos*: lit., "another") is not definite like the "someone else" (*allos*) of v. 32. There is no reference here to antichrists (cf. 1 John 2:22; 4:3; 2 John 7) or (as some have suggested) to particular Jewish messianic claimants (e.g., Simon Bar Cochba, the leader of the last Jewish revolt against Rome about A.D. 135). Jesus is instead referring to *anyone* who might come promoting himself and "looking for human praise" (v. 41). Because the character of such a person would correspond so closely to their own (v. 44) the authorities would quickly give him the allegiance they withheld from Jesus.

5:44 / **Praise from the one who alone is God**: lit., "the glory that is from the only God" (in contrast to "glory from one another," cf. 12:43). The word translated **praise** (*doxa*) is the same word translated "glory" in 2:11. The contrast here is between human praise or approval (cf. v. 41) and God's approval, but the choice of the word *doxa* suggests that the "glory" of God is being revealed in Jesus' words (vv. 43, 47) no less than in his miracles (2:11), and that in rejecting him, his hearers are rejecting this "glory."

14

The Feeding of the Five Thousand

JOHN 6:1–15

After this, Jesus went across Lake Galilee (or, Lake Tiberias, as it is also called). ²A large crowd followed him, because they had seen his miracles of healing the sick. ³Jesus went up a hill and sat down with his disciples. ⁴The time for the Passover Festival was near. ⁵Jesus looked around and saw that a large crowd was coming to him, so he asked Philip, "Where can we buy enough food to feed all these people?" (⁶He said this to test Philip; actually he already knew what he would do.)

⁷Philip answered, "For everyone to have even a little, it would take more than two hundred silver coins^k to buy enough bread."

⁸Another one of his disciples, Andrew, who was Simon Peter's brother, said, ⁹"There is a boy here who has five loaves of barley bread and two fish. But they will certainly not be enough for all these people."

¹⁰"Make the people sit down," Jesus told them. (There was a lot of grass there.) So all the people sat down; there were about five thousand men. ¹¹Jesus took the bread, gave thanks to God, and distributed it to the people who were sitting there. He did the same with the fish, and they all had as much as they wanted. ¹²When they were all full, he said to his disciples, "Gather the pieces left over; let us not waste a bit." ¹³So they gathered them all and filled twelve baskets with the pieces left over from the five barley loaves which the people had eaten.

¹⁴Seeing this miracle that Jesus had performed, the people there said, "Surely this is the Prophet^l who was to come into the world!" ¹⁵Jesus knew that they were about to come and seize him in order to make him king by force; so he went off again to the hills by himself.

k. SILVER COINS: *A silver coin was the daily wage of a rural worker (see Mt 20.2).* l. THE PROPHET: See 1.21.

T he indefinite connecting phrase **after this** (v. 1; cf. 5:1) introduces a narrative that abruptly locates Jesus in Galilee, crossing from one side of Lake Galilee to the other.

Such a beginning suggests that the Gospel writer is picking up a narrative source in the middle of things. The only real link to the two preceding incidents in John is the mention in verse 2 of **his miracles of healing the sick** (cf. 4:43–54; 5:1–18). There is no way to be sure how much time has elapsed since the miracle and controversy of the previous chapter. If the "religious festival" of 5:1 was the Passover, then at least a year has gone by, for it is again the Passover season (v. 4). The author's interest at this point is not in chronology but in providing a sample glimpse of Jesus' Galilean ministry (in addition to 2:1–12 and 4:43–54), and particularly of his Galilean synagogue teaching (cf. 6:59).

The story of the feeding of the five thousand is found in all four Gospels (cf. Mark 6:32–44; Matt. 14:13–21; Luke 9:10b–17), while the account of Jesus walking on the water is paralleled in Mark (6:45–52) and Matthew (14:22–33). The theme by which John's Gospel draws this material together is the familiar synoptic theme of the pursuit of Jesus by large and persistent crowds (vv. 2–5, 14–15, 22–24; cf., e.g., Mark 1:35–37; Matt. 4:25–5:1). This pursuit becomes the occasion for Jesus to teach the crowds what "following" or **coming to him** (vv. 2, 5) actually entails (6:26–59). Many turn back when they learn discipleship's cost, but "the Twelve" (with Simon Peter as their spokesman) affirm their faith and are established as Jesus' helpers and companions (6:60–71).

The reference to the Passover (v. 4) is in keeping with the author's tendency to place Jesus' deeds and discourses in the context of Judaism's major religious festivals (cf. 2:13; 5:1; 7:2; 10:22; 11:55), but this is the only instance in which Jesus is not in Jerusalem for the occasion. Why is the season mentioned in a context that otherwise shows little interest in chronology? Is the reference intended to characterize the feeding of the five thousand as a kind of Christian Passover anticipating the Lord's Supper? Does it set the stage for the subsequent controversy over Moses and the manna in the desert (6:30–32; cf. Exod. 16:4, 15)? The feeding of the crowd is indeed described in terms reminiscent of the institution of the Lord's Supper: **Jesus *took the bread, gave thanks* to God, and *distributed it* to the people who were sitting there. He did *the same* with the fish, and they all had as much as they wanted** (v. 11; cf., e.g., 1 Cor. 11:23–25). Moreover, the synagogue address on "Jesus the Bread of Life" (vv. 26–59) concludes with what many regard as a meditation explicitly on the Lord's Supper as a Christian sacrament (6:52–58). Yet *in itself*, the mention of Passover in verse 4 carries no hint that the emphasis of the narrative is to be on the Passover meal as such or any adaptation of it. In the two other places where the Passover is said to be **near** (i.e., 2:13; 11:55; cf. 12:1; 13:1), the statement introduces material that in some way points forward to Jesus' death at the last Passover in Jerusalem (i.e., 2:14–22; 12:1–36). In the present passage the effect is similarly to introduce a reflection on Jesus' death, but this time with particular focus on its implications for discipleship. The chapter as a whole functions in much the same way as Jesus' first

84

Passion prediction in the synoptic Gospels, with its accompanying call to discipleship (cf. Mark 8:31–9:1 and parallels).

John's account of the multiplication of the loaves and fishes begins with the approach of a **large crowd** that had seen Jesus' healings and with Jesus' consequent withdrawal to a hill where he sat down, probably to teach his disciples (vv. 2–3; cf. Matt. 5:1–2). It ends with his solitary retreat to the same hill to escape the crowd's attempt to make him king by force (vv. 14–15). Between the two withdrawals, Jesus encounters the crowd and ministers to its needs. As he looks out over the crowd (v. 5), Jesus looks at the same time into the future (cf. 4:35). He has already formed a plan (v. 6) in anticipation of a problem that in the other Gospels arises only later: How will the crowd be fed? (cf. Mark 6:35–36 and parallels). He elicits from Philip and Andrew, two of his first disciples (cf. 1:40–44), that it would be virtually impossible to provide food for so many (vv. 7, 9b). Andrew mentions in passing, however, a boy who has brought five barley loaves and two fish (v. 9a), and with these Jesus feeds the whole crowd (vv. 10–13). All the Gospels are specific about the five loaves and two fish, but only John tells the story of the anonymous youth who brought them. The human interest touch is most easily explained as an actual recollection of what happened. Though certain aspects of the narrative are reminiscent of the story of Elisha and twenty loaves of barley bread in 2 Kings 4:42–44 (e.g., the emphasis on what is left over), the OT incident is not a sufficient model to explain either Jesus' actions or the Gospel writer's account of them.

The story is recognizably the same in John's Gospel as in the Synoptics. Jesus makes the crowd of five thousand recline on the grass and distributes bread and fish to them until they are all satisfied. The distinctive feature of John's account is that Jesus distributes the food to the crowd directly, not through the hands of his disciples (v. 11; contrast Mark 6:41). The disciples do, however, gather the pieces of bread that are left over, twelve baskets full, "that nothing may be lost" (v. 12, RSV). The effect of the shift in the disciples' role is to enhance the symbolism, already present in the Synoptics, of the twelve baskets of surplus bread (cf. Mark 6:43). The abundance of bread points to the abundance of life that Jesus supplies, but the detail that none of it is lost or wasted anticipates the symbolism of the eucharistic prayer found in the *Didache*, a second-century manual of church order. The prayer appears to be based on this very passage in John or on the incident it describes: "As this broken bread was scattered upon the mountains, but was brought together and became one, so let your church be gathered together from the ends of the earth into your kingdom" (*Didache* 9.4). The twelve baskets of bread left over are here understood to represent the Christian church kept safe in the world by the power of God. As the bread is gathered in twelve baskets, so the church is personified in twelve apostles (cf. 6:70; 17:12; 18:9). As none of the bread is lost or wasted, so none of those who believe in Jesus will be left to wander from his saving care (cf. 6:39; 10:28).

Yet it is an oversimplification to say that the feeding of the five thousand symbolizes the Christian Eucharist. Though the distribution of the food is described in eucharistic terms (v. 11), the miracle points beyond the Eucharist to that which the Eucharist itself represents: the unity and security of Jesus' followers as his body in the world. In his own way, Paul too sees the bread of the Lord's Supper as the church: "Because there is the one loaf of bread, all of us, though many, are one body, for we all share the same loaf" (1 Cor. 10:17). The fact that Paul emphasizes the "oneness" of the bread while John emphasizes its "twelveness" should not obscure the similarity in what the two are saying. At most, however, the mention of the twelve baskets of leftover barley bread furnishes only a hint of the narrator's intended meaning. The real theological interpretation of the feeding of the crowd comes in the synagogue discourse of verses 26–59 and in the concluding exchange between Jesus and his disciples (and would-be disciples) in verses 60–71. The unstated link between the twelve baskets of bread and the church kept safe in the world is the person of Jesus himself (cf. 6:35, 48). That the miracle says something about Jesus even the crowd could perceive (v. 14), but on its own terms. He must be the expected Prophet like Moses because, like Moses, he had miraculously fed those who followed him (cf. 6:30–31). The custom of messianic pretenders in Jesus' time was to seek credibility by either re-enacting or matching famous OT miracles (see, e.g., Josephus, *Antiquities* 20.97, 167–70). The men in the crowd saw in Jesus just such a potential messiah, one who fulfilled their political hopes and whom they thought they could use for their own political ends. Their intent was a violent one, perhaps nothing short of kidnapping Jesus to make him a puppet pretender to the long-vacant throne of David. But he knew their intent (cf. 2:24) and returned alone to the hill. For the time being, his manifestation to the Galilean crowd was at an end.

Additional Notes

6:1 / **Or, Lake Tiberias**: The double name is striking. **Tiberias** appears to be the name preferred by the writer of this Gospel (cf. 21:1), while the more familiar **Galilee** has been retained alongside it from an oral or written source similar to the synoptic accounts.

6:5 / **Where can we buy**: Philip's answer indicates that Jesus' meaning is

"How can we buy enough food? Where would we get the money?" The notion that they were in the desert, with no markets nearby, seems not to be an issue here.

6:6 / To test Philip: Test is not used here in an ethical sense but means simply to elicit a response. Jesus wants to draw from the disciples a clear expression of the human impossibility of providing food for so many people. The purpose of the parenthetical remark is to make clear that Jesus' question to Philip did not imply any uncertainty on his part about the outcome.

6:8 / Another one of his disciples: Unlike Philip, Andrew is introduced here as if he has not been mentioned before, yet cf. 1:40. In both passages he is identified as **Simon Peter's brother**. Either (a) the terminology is that of John's narrative source (which may not have included an account of Andrew's call) or (b) the phrase should be translated, "the first of his disciples," referring *explicitly* to the call mentioned in 1:40. The Greek word *heis*, translated as **one**, is occasionally used for the ordinal number "first" and it is perhaps noteworthy that some ancient manuscripts refer to Andrew as the "first" (*prōtos*) among Jesus' disciples in 1:41. The former alternative, however, is the more likely.

6:9 / boy: The Greek word *paidarion* means a child, a youth, or a young slave, and can refer to either a male or a female. A masculine relative pronoun makes it clear that in this instance a boy is in view.

6:10 / People . . . people . . . men. The GNB preserves a distinction between a generic word for people (Gr.: *anthrōpoi*) and a word that usually (though not always) refers to adult males in particular (*andres*). This presupposes a situation described explicitly only in Matthew: "The number of men who ate was about five thousand, not counting the women and children" (Matt. 14:21; cf. 15:38). The group is thus assumed to be a mixed group, considerably larger than five thousand (even the boy who furnished the food was probably not counted among the five thousand!). The "people" in v. 14 who acclaim Jesus as the coming Prophet are the whole crowd: The impression was a universal one among those who were fed. But the indefinite "they" (v. 15) who were "about to come and seize him" probably refers to an unspecified faction (presumably of "men") within the larger crowd.

6:11 / Gave thanks to God: Gr.: *eucharistēsas* (cf. 6:23). The parallel passages (Mark 6:41; Matt. 14:19; Luke 9:16) use a different verb *eulogein* (lit., "bless," but in GNB consistently translated "give thanks to God," as here). The verb in John corresponds to the verb used in the *second* feeding (i.e., of the four thousand) in Mark (8:6) and Matthew (15:36). The giving of thanks plays a crucial part in the working of a miracle again in John 11:41. Thanksgiving becomes Jesus' way of calling on the Father to display his power.

Jesus Walks on the Water

JOHN 6:16–25

When evening came, Jesus' disciples went down to the lake, [17]got into a boat, and went back across the lake toward Capernaum. Night came on, and Jesus still had not come to them. [18]By then a strong wind was blowing and stirring up the water. [19]The disciples had rowed about three or four miles when they saw Jesus walking on the water, coming near the boat, and they were terrified. [20]"Don't be afraid," Jesus told them, "it is I!" [21]Then they willingly took him into the boat, and immediately the boat reached land at the place they were heading for.

[22]Next day the crowd which had stayed on the other side of the lake realized that there had been only one boat there. They knew that Jesus had not gone in it with his disciples, but that they had left without him. [23]Other boats, which were from Tiberias, came to shore near the place where the crowd had eaten the bread after the Lord had given thanks. [24]When the crowd saw that Jesus was not there, nor his disciples, they got into those boats and went to Capernaum, looking for him.

[25]When the people found Jesus on the other side of the lake, they said to him, "Teacher, when did you get here?"

Jesus' solitary escape from those who would make him king provides an additional reason for a detail in the synoptic Gospels that is only partially explained. After the feeding "Jesus made his disciples get into the boat and go ahead of him to Bethsaida, on the other side of the lake, while he sent the crowd away. After saying good-bye to the people, he went away to the hill to pray" (Mark 6:45–46; cf. Matt. 14:22–23). John's Gospel suggests that he also "went away to the hill" to prevent a kidnap attempt!

In similar fashion, Mark and Matthew supply a reason for something John leaves unexplained. Why did Jesus' disciples (v. 16) abruptly return to Capernaum in the boat without him? The synoptic answer is that they embarked because Jesus made them do so. Behind both accounts is the assumption that Jesus was in control of the situation and planned his moves carefully. The action is divided into two days, the **evening** of the (indefinite) day on which the miracle took place (v. 16) and the **next day** (v. 22). The reference to the next day is not intended to begin another sequence like that of 1:19–2:11 but is simply necessitated by the mention of evening and of **night** (lit., "darkness," v. 17).

The approach of night lends a dramatic note to the readers' awareness that **Jesus still had not come to them** (v. 17). The narrator and the readers both know the story of Jesus rejoining his disciples by walking on the water, but the participants in the drama do not. When he appears, they are surprised and terrified (v. 19). Their perspective and the literary perspective of the author and his readers merge into one. The readers share the terror of the disciples in the boat in verse 19, but already in verse 17 the disciples have been made dramatic sharers in the readers' anticipation of Jesus' appearance on the lake. In the actual incident, it is doubtful that the disciples were expecting to meet Jesus, whether miraculously walking on the water or at some prearranged point on the shore.

Far from calming anxieties they may have had about the rising storm (v. 18), the visitation itself produced among the disciples immediate fear (v. 19). The synoptic account explains that they thought they had seen a ghost (Gr.: *phantasma*: Mark 6:49; Matt. 14:26). When Jesus assures them, **Don't be afraid . . . it is I** (Gr.: *egō eimi*, v. 20; cf. Mark 6:50; Matt. 14:27), his intent is simply self-identification. He is not a ghost, but the one who that very day had fed the crowd, escaped to the hill, and sent them back across the lake to Capernaum. Here is where the disciples and the readers part company. To the disciples, Jesus reveals himself as a human being, their teacher and friend. But to the readers his use of the formula *egō eimi* suggests something more. He is nothing less than God himself, the I Am, the self-revealing God of the Hebrew Scriptures (cf., e.g., Isa. 43:25; 45:18; 51:12; 52:6) who existed before Abraham (cf. 8:58) and whose power was displayed over the waters (e.g., Ps. 77:16–20) as well as the dry land. In Psalm 107, after reflecting on God's care for his people "in the trackless desert" and how he satisfied their hunger and thirst and set them free (107:4–22), the psalmist writes:

Some sailed over the ocean in ships,
  earning their living on the seas.
They saw what the Lord can do,
  his wonderful acts on the seas.
He commanded, and a mighty wind began to blow
  and stirred up the waves.
The ships were lifted high in the air
  and plunged down into the depths.
In such danger the men lost their courage;

they stumbled and staggered like drunks—
    all their skill was useless.
Then in their trouble they called to the Lord,
    and he saved them from their distress.
He calmed the raging storm,
    and the waves became quiet.
They were glad because of the calm,
    and he brought them safe to the port they wanted.
(Ps. 107:23–30)

The last lines in particular are dramatized in the strange statement of verse 21 that when the disciples tried to take Jesus aboard, **immediately the boat reached land at the place they were heading for**. The whole scene has a supernatural quality about it, like a resurrection appearance (more even than chap. 21). Jesus assures the disciples that he really is the person they have known all along, yet his presence—and, for a moment, theirs—is elusive, transcending time and space. He does not so much enter their world—the boat and the storm on the lake—as give them a glimpse and a taste, however fleeting, of his world. The disciples' reaction is not expressed (contrast Mark 6:51–52; Matt. 14:32–33). As soon as they reach shore, they drop out of the story until at least verse 60 (possibly, vv. 66 or 67). It is left to the reader to sense the mystery of what has happened and to wait for the explanation that only Jesus' words (and they only in part) will later provide.

The next day's events are told from the standpoint of the crowd left behind at the place of the miraculous feeding, still looking for Jesus (cf. v. 15). When they saw no boats, they realized that there had only been one to begin with, and that Jesus' disciples (whose departure they apparently had witnessed) had taken it (vv. 22, 24). They knew Jesus had not left with his disciples in the boat, but having looked for him in vain in the hill country, they could only conclude that somehow he was on his way to rejoin the disciples at Capernaum. Not only had they failed to find their Prophet-king, but they were stranded on the opposite shore. Other boats from Tiberias, however, arrived just in time to allow them to resume their search (vv. 23–25). The purpose of the abrupt mention of these other boats is simply to explain how the crowd (or rather that portion of the crowd that was pursuing Jesus) got across the lake, and thus to set the stage for the long discourse of 6:26–59. The theme of this section is the search for Jesus. Those who searched found him on the other side of the lake, but how he got there remained a mystery to them. If his comings and goings are beyond the understanding even of his true disciples (vv. 16–21), how much more are they beyond the reach of those who seek him for their own purposes? Those who pursue him in unbelief will never find him (cf. 7:34; 8:21). There is a right way and a wrong way to come to Jesus or to follow him, and the purpose of the ensuing discourse will be to set forth the right way.

Verse 25 is more appropriately included with this section than with the discourse that follows, because it allows the crowd to give voice to the question implicit in the section as a whole: How did Jesus get across the lake? (i.e., Where did he come from? Where does he go?).

Additional Notes

6:17 / **And Jesus still had not come to them**: In addition to those who suggest that Jesus and the disciples had prearranged a meeting somewhere along the shore, some scholars maintain that the time reference of this statement is *before* the disciples got into the boat. In that case, the purpose of the statement would be to explain why they finally left without him. But such assumptions are unnecessary if the statement is intended simply for the readers of the Gospel and not understood as reflecting the subjective impressions of the disciples, in or out of the boat.

6:19 / **About three or four miles**: lit., "about twenty-five or thirty stadia." A "stadium" or "stade" was the length of a Roman stadium (i.e., about 607 feet or 185 meters).

6:19 / **Walking on the water**, or "on the lake." Some scholars have argued from the use of the genitive case (rather than the accusative) with the Greek preposition *epi* that what is meant is that Jesus was walking "along" the shore of the lake, not **on** the lake itself (cf. the same construction in 21:1). This would make the story not only nonmiraculous but pointless as well. It would leave unexplained both the disciples' fear and the impression given by vv. 22–24 that Jesus crossed the lake by supernatural means. The reference to Jesus **coming near the boat** is also difficult to reconcile with the picture of him merely walking along the shore. For a good example of the same phrase, **on the water** (or "on the sea") used in connection with the expression "on the land" (as two clearly differentiated spheres), cf. Rev. 10:2, 5.

6:21 / **They willingly took him into the boat**: lit., "they wanted to take him into the boat." When the verb is used in the aorist tense in John (i.e., 1:43; 5:35), it refers to an intention that is realized. When it is used (as here) in the imperfect tense (cf. 7:44; 16:19), it refers to an unrealized intention. The likely meaning is that the disciples wanted to take Jesus into the boat, but before they had a chance, they found themselves suddenly at their destination. It is worth noting that in Mark, on this same occasion (6:48), the same verb in the same tense is used of *Jesus'* unrealized intention. It is possible that the two Gospel writers are drawing on a common oral or written source in the telling of this story.

6:23 / **Which were from Tiberias**: The text is ambiguous. It can mean either that the boats came from the city of Tiberias to the (undefined) place where the crowd had been fed, or that Tiberias itself was **near the place where the crowd had eaten the bread**. The ambiguity could stem from the fact that both things are true and both intended. That boats should have come from Tiberias was natural if Tiberias was the nearest significant port. Luke, however, seems to locate the feeding with reference to Bethsaida on the other side of the lake (9:10). Geographers have been unable to agree on the actual site. The spot honored by tradition (i.e., et-Tabgha, Gr.: *heptapegon*, a place identified by seven springs) is actually closer to Capernaum than to Tiberias or Bethsaida and seems to have been chosen more for the convenience of pilgrims than for its authenticity.

6:25 / **When did you get here**? i.e., under what circumstance? how? They are not so much asking for information as expressing amazement.

16

Jesus the Bread of Life

JOHN 6:26–59

Jesus answered, "I am telling you the truth: you are looking for me because you ate the bread and had all you wanted, not because you understood my miracles. ²⁷Do not work for food that spoils; instead, work for the food that lasts for eternal life. This is the food which the Son of Man will give you, because God, the Father, has put his mark of approval on him."

²⁸So they asked him, "What can we do in order to do what God wants us to do?"

²⁹Jesus answered, "What God wants you to do is to believe in the one he sent."

³⁰They replied, "What miracle will you perform so that we may see it and believe you? What will you do? ³¹Our ancestors ate manna in the desert, just as the scripture says, 'He gave them bread from heaven to eat.' "

³²"I am telling you the truth," Jesus said. "What Moses gave you was not^m the bread from heaven; it is my Father who gives you the real bread from heaven. ³³For the bread that God gives is he who comes down from heaven and gives life to the world."

³⁴ "Sir," they asked him, "give us this bread always."

³⁵ "I am the bread of life," Jesus told them. "He who comes to me will never be hungry; he who believes in me will never be thirsty. ³⁶Now, I told you that you have seen me but will not believe. ³⁷Everyone whom my Father gives me will come to me. I will never turn away anyone who comes to me, ³⁸because I have come down from heaven to do not my own will but the will of him who sent me. ³⁹And it is the will of him who sent me that I should not lose any of all those he has given me, but that I should raise them all to life on the last day. ⁴⁰For what my Father wants is that all who see the Son and believe in him should have eternal life. And I will raise them to life on the last day."

⁴¹The people started grumbling about him, because he said, "I am the bread that came down from heaven." ⁴²So they said, "This man is Jesus son of Joseph, isn't he? We know his father and mother. How, then, does he now say he came down from heaven?"

⁴³Jesus answered, "Stop grumbling among yourselves. ⁴⁴No one can come to me unless the Father who sent me draws him to me; and I will raise him to life on the last day. ⁴⁵The prophets wrote, 'Everyone will be taught by God.' Anyone who hears the Father and learns from him comes to me. ⁴⁶This does not mean that anyone has seen the Father; he who is from God is the only one who has seen the Father. ⁴⁷ I am telling you the truth: he who believes has eternal life. ⁴⁸I am the bread of life. ⁴⁹Your ancestors ate manna in the desert, but they died. ⁵⁰But the bread that comes down from heaven is of such a kind that whoever eats it will not die. ⁵¹I am the living bread that came down from heaven. If anyone eats this bread, he

will live forever. The bread that I will give him is my flesh, which I give so that the world may live."

⁵²This started an angry argument among them. "How can this man give us his flesh to eat?" they asked.

⁵³Jesus said to them, "I am telling you the truth: if you do not eat the flesh of the Son of Man and drink his blood, you will not have life in yourselves. ⁵⁴Whoever eats my flesh and drinks my blood has eternal life, and I will raise him to life on the last day.

⁵⁵For my flesh is the real food; my blood is the real drink. ⁵⁶Whoever eats my flesh and drinks my blood lives in me, and I live in him. ⁵⁷The living Father sent me, and because of him I live also. In the same way whoever eats me will live because of me. ⁵⁸This, then, is the bread that came down from heaven; it is not like the bread that your ancestors ate, but then later died. The one who eats this bread will live forever."

⁵⁹Jesus said this as he taught in the synagogue in Capernaum.

m. What Moses gave you was not; *or* it was not Moses who gave you.

T he discourse begins as a dialogue between Jesus and the crowd, and becomes more and more of a monologue as it goes on. The crowd had begun following him because of the miracles he had done (cf. 6:2), but since the multiplication of the loaves, they have been pursuing him as one who can satisfy their physical hunger and (they hope) their political ambitions as well (cf. 6:15). They think they have found him, but they have not. They have been fed, yet they have not begun to receive what Jesus has to give. Their search must therefore continue (cf. Luke 11:9–10). What they do not yet realize is that food is a metaphor. Like Jesus himself, whose food was "to obey the will of the one who sent me and to finish the work he gave me to do" (4:34), they must **work for the food that lasts for eternal life . . . the food which the Son of Man will give you** (v. 27; cf. the "water" Jesus offered to the Samaritan woman, 4:14). This "work of God" is "to believe in the one he sent" (v. 29, NIV).

The mention of "believing" (rather than merely seeking or pursuing) draws from the crowd a demand for another miracle or sign comparable to that of the manna that Moses provided for the Israelites in the desert (vv. 30–31). The incident is recounted fully in Exodus 16, but Jesus' questioners cite merely the psalmist's summary of it: **He gave them bread from heaven to eat** (v. 31; cf. Ps. 78:24). The request is strange, coming so soon after a miracle that itself invites comparison with Moses and the manna. Why would those whom Jesus had miraculously fed only the day before ask for **bread from heaven**? It appears that the controlling term is not **bread** but the phrase **from heaven**. The scene recalls an argument between Jesus and the Pharisees just after the *second* feeding of a crowd in Mark and Matthew: "To test him, they asked him for a sign from heaven. He sighed deeply and said, 'Why does this generation ask for a miraculous sign? I tell you the truth, no sign will be given to it' " (Mark 8:11–12, NIV). In Matthew (16:4, NIV) there is one exception: "the sign of Jonah" (i.e., the resurrection of Jesus, cf. 12:39–41). Whether or not the occasion is the same in John 6, the apparent nature of the request is similar in the two instances. Nor is the incident unique within John's Gospel. Jesus had been challenged in much the same way when he first visited Jerusalem (2:18) and had replied (as in Matthew) with a veiled reference to his resurrection (2:19). Here his answer is much more elaborate. He begins by adding certain interpretive comments to the psalm just quoted (v. 32):

Not ...	But ...
Moses	God (Jesus' Father)
gave	gives
bread	real bread

The **real bread** is immediately defined as **he who comes down from heaven and gives life to the world** (v. 33). The terms of the discussion are almost totally changed. It is not a question of what Moses did in the time of the Exodus but of what God is doing right now. It is not a question of manna from the sky but of a flesh-and-blood person who stands before them—**Jesus son of Joseph** (cf. v. 42). Jesus does not merely *give* bread (or a miraculous sign) from heaven. He *is* that bread; in all that he says and does, he *is* God's miraculous sign. The crowd, not ready to grasp this distinction, still asks him to **give us this bread always** (v. 34). Their plea recalls that of the Samaritan woman (4:15), yet their situation is not the same as hers. Their hunger for food is satisfied, but not their hunger for miracles. These Jews who "want miracles for proof" (1 Cor. 1:22) have not yet understood that to which Jesus' miracles are pointing. They know that his miracles give life (v. 33) but not that life means believing in him (cf. 5:39–40).

At verse 35 the dialogue becomes a monologue with interruptions (i.e. vv. 41–42, 52). These interruptions by the crowd, now called "the Jews" (vv. 41, 52, NIV) can be used to divide the discourse into three sections: verses 35–40, 41–51, and 52–58. An alternative structure is in two sections (vv. 35–47 and 48–58), each introduced by the identical pronouncement, **I am the bread of life** (vv. 35, 48), and each subdivided by a dispute among "the Jews." In either case the discourse as a whole is designated a synagogue discourse given (presumably on a Sabbath) in the synagogue at Capernaum (v. 59). At some point (perhaps v. 35?), the scene has shifted from the lakeshore to the synagogue, and the discussion has taken on a somewhat more formal character.

Many scholars prefer the threefold division of the discourse because of the definite breaks at verses 41 and 52 and because the last section is regarded by some as the work of a later editor, but if *content* is the prime consideration, the twofold division is more appropriate. Verses 35–47 unfold further the meaning of the phrase **bread from heaven** in the preceding Scripture quotation (v. 31), whereas verses 48–58 expand on the words **to eat** in the same quotation. Psalm 78:24 is the text, and verses 35–47 and 48–58 comprise a two-part synagogue sermon based on it. In the middle of each section, the hearers take offense at the claim Jesus is making—in verses 41–42 the claim to have come down from heaven, and in verse 52, the claim to be able to give them his flesh to eat.

Part One: The Bread from Heaven (vv. 35–47). The theme of the first section was anticipated in verse 33: The bread from heaven is Jesus. In verse 35, Jesus repeats the claim in the form of an "I am" pronouncement, the first of seven such pronouncements found throughout this Gospel:

I am the bread of life (6:35, 48; cf. vv. 41, 51).

I am the light of the world (8:12; cf. 9:5).

I am the gate for the sheep (10:7; cf. v. 9).

I am the good shepherd (10:11, 14).

I am the resurrection and the life (11:25).

I am the way, the truth, and the life (14:6).

I am the real vine (15:1; cf. v. 5).

Of these, all but the fifth and sixth occur twice. The repetition allows Jesus to use the metaphors in different ways. In some instances the first use of the metaphor introduces Jesus in his uniqueness or in contrast to others who might claim a similar designation, and the second explores a particular aspect or implication of the metaphor. Here, the context suggests that Jesus is the **real** bread (v. 32) in contrast to the manna, just as he is the "real" vine (15:1), or the "good" shepherd in contrast to hirelings (10:11–13), or the sheep gate in contrast to thieves (10:7–8). Yet what dominates part one of the discourse is not the metaphor of bread but the personality of Jesus. Aside from a passing reference to hunger in verse 35, the metaphor lies mostly dormant until part two. In verses 35–47, Jesus speaks as **the Son** (v. 40) more than as **bread of life**. If he is bread, he is **bread *from heaven*** (vv. 38, 41–42; cf. v. 33), and it is on his divine origin and mission that the main emphasis falls. Though in his coming he satisfies hunger and thirst (v. 35), he is not "eaten" as bread. Those to whom he ministers **see** him (vv. 36, 40), **come** to him (vv. 35, 37, 45) and **believe** in him as the Son (vv. 35–36, 40, 47; cf. v. 29). The metaphor of eating is in the background (cf. v. 27), but Jesus prefers to speak in straightforward language. It is necessary to define for the crowd all that it means to come to him and follow him (cf. vv. 2, 5, 22–25), not so they will do it (for they will not), but for the sake of a "hidden" audience—the disciples (vv. 60–71) and, ultimately, the readers of the Gospel. The conclusion of part one is that in the fullest sense "coming to Jesus" means believing in him and receiving eternal life (vv. 40, 47). This is the food that never spoils (cf. vv. 27, 29) and that satisfies the deepest hunger. It is food this crowd will not taste (v. 36).

Implanted in the metaphor of bread from heaven is a sketch of the whole plan of salvation as seen in John's Gospel (vv. 37–40). Jesus came down from heaven **to do not my own will but the will of him who sent me** (v. 38; cf. 4:34). God's will for Jesus is then spelled out twice, in parallel fashion:

. . . **that I should not lose any of all those he has given me, but that I should raise them all to life on the last day** (v. 39).

. . . **that all who see the Son and believe in him should have eternal life. And I will raise them to life on the last day** (v. 40).

The Father's intent, realized through the Son, is a saving intent. Those who come to Jesus, those who see and believe, are those the Father has given him. The Father will see to it that they are kept safe; he will grant them new life as a present possession and raise them from the dead **on the last day** (cf. 5:24–25, 28). They are the Father's gift to Jesus his Son.

Even as Jesus explains the plan of salvation to the crowd, he makes clear what the reader of the Gospel must already suspect, that the crowd itself is not a part of it: **Now, I told you that you have seen me but will not believe** (v. 36). The crowd's reaction to his words (vv. 41–42) is therefore no surprise. Verse 44 is the negative complement to verse 37: All whom the Father gives Jesus will come to him, and no one can come unless "drawn" to Jesus by the Father. A person is drawn by hearing the Father's voice and learning from him. Though this "educational" process has deep roots in divine election and in the individual conscience (cf. 3:20–21), only the free outward act of coming to Jesus in faith proves that a person has been thus **taught by God** (v. 45). As far as human experience is concerned, to hear and learn from the Father means hearing and believing the message of Jesus, for only Jesus (having come from heaven) has seen the Father (v. 46; cf. 5:19; 8:38) and only he can interpret the Father to the world (cf. 1:18). In Jesus, the Father speaks (cf. 5:37–38).

Verse 47 summarizes the discourse thus far and reduces the divine message to its simplest terms: **I am telling you the truth: he who believes has eternal life.**

Part Two: Eating the Bread (vv. 48–58). With the second occurrence of **I am the bread of life** (v. 48), the bread metaphor begins to come into its own, giving a new shape to the argument and a new dimension to the simple need of believing in order to gain life.

Attention centers on the phrase, **to eat,** in the Psalm 78 text. Jesus virtually repeats the word uttered earlier by his questioners, **Your ancestors ate manna in the desert** (v. 49; cf. v. 31), adding significantly, **but they died.** The manna is then contrasted with **the bread that comes down from heaven** (v. 50; cf. v. 33). Whoever eats this bread will not die, but live forever. Once more Jesus identifies himself with this bread. Specifically, he calls it **my flesh, which I give so that the world may live** (v. 51). Here for the first time he connects the metaphor of bread with the prospect of his own death. His language recalls words attributed to him in the earliest account of the institution of the Lord's Supper: "This is my body which is for you" (1 Cor. 11:24; cf. Luke 22:19). His **flesh** or his "body" means the giving up of his body in death, just as Christ's **blood** frequently refers in the New Testament to the shedding of his blood on the cross. Paul uses "body" in this way when he says that Christians have "died to the law through the body of Christ" (Rom. 7:4, NIV), and "flesh" when he declares that "in his flesh" (Eph. 2:14, NIV) Christ destroyed the enmity between Jew and Gentile.

Near the beginning and at the end of part two of the discourse, Jesus speaks of eating the bread that is his flesh (vv. 50–52, 57–58):

98

whoever eats it (v. 50)

if anyone eats this bread (v. 51)

the bread . . . is my flesh (v. 51)

how can this man give us his flesh to eat? (v. 52)

whoever eats me (v. 57)

the one who eats this bread (v. 58)

Verses 53–56 present a different phenomenon. Four times in rapid succession Jesus speaks of the twofold necessity of eating his flesh and drinking his blood. Nothing in the bread metaphor prepares the reader for the mention of drinking blood, so abhorrent to the Jewish mind (e.g., Lev. 17:10–14). Just when the Jews take offense at the notion of eating his flesh (v. 52), Jesus multiplies the offense many times over. Instead of explaining the statement away, he tells them they must drink his blood as well! The metaphor of eating flesh and drinking blood was used in the Old Testament for slaughter and utter desolation (e.g., Ezek. 39:17–20). Israel's oppressors would be made to eat their own flesh and drink their own blood (Isa. 49:26: cf. Zech. 11:9).

Because such a meaning seems impossible in the present context, many scholars find in Jesus' shocking language a symbolic allusion to the two elements of bread and wine in the Christian sacrament of the Lord's Supper. If that is the meaning, it is argued, the passage (usually defined as vv. 51c–58, starting with the words, **The bread that I will give him is my flesh**) must have been added to John's Gospel by a later editor. Neither Jesus nor the Gospel writer would have spoken so directly of the Lord's Supper or made participation in it a condition of salvation (v. 53). If it is early tradition at all, it must have originated in the context of the last supper, as a variant form of the words of institution ("This is my body. . . . This is my blood"), not in Galilee at the height of Jesus' ministry. But these conclusions are all based on the assumption that verses 51c–58 present a different teaching than the rest of the discourse. Is this the case? The only new factor introduced in verse 51 is the allusion to Jesus' death (**my flesh which I give so that the world may live**). Even the Synoptics represent Jesus as predicting his death while still in Galilee (e.g., Mark 8:31; 9:31), and there is no reason why John's Gospel might not do so as well. The statement in verse 33 that Jesus **gives life to the world** surely hints at the notion that he gives his flesh **so that the world may live.** He has **come down from heaven to do not my own will but the will of him who sent me** (v. 38). It is only a small step from speaking of Jesus' mission, or his obedience to the Father, to speaking of his death on the cross. In Gethsemane he will pray "not what I will, but what you will" (Mark 14:36).

Before discussing whether or not the references to eating Jesus' flesh and drinking his blood are sacramental, it is well to notice something closer at hand, the fact that they presuppose his violent death. Their effect is to intensify what is already implied by **flesh** alone in verse 51. The mention of **blood** adds no distinct theological dimension of its own but simply makes more vivid and shocking the notion that Jesus will give his life, his very flesh, for the sake of the world. The references to **flesh** and **blood** together stand within the framework of references simply to eating the bread that is Jesus (i.e., vv. 50–52, 57–58) and must be interpreted in light of these. The **bread** or **flesh** references, in turn, stand within the framework of Jesus' mission. Only the truth (established in part one of the discourse) that he is **the living bread that came down from heaven** (v. 51) makes it possible to **eat** his flesh.

In verse 57 he bases the "eating" even more explicitly on his own mission and his relationship to the Father: **The living Father sent me, and because of him I live also. In the same way whoever eats me will live because of me.** What is this "eating"? Whatever the metaphor means concretely, it expresses a relationship to Jesus corresponding to Jesus' own relationship to God the Father. As Jesus depends on the Father for his very life, so the person who **eats** Jesus depends on him for life. Though Jesus' dependence on the Father is not explicitly described here in terms of eating, he had said earlier: "My food is to obey the will of the one who sent me and to finish the work he gave me to do" (4:34). As the Father sent Jesus, Jesus will send out disciples (4:38; 17:18, 20:21). As his food is to obey the Father and complete the Father's work, their food is to obey him and complete his work. This divine work was earlier defined as believing in Jesus (vv. 27, 29), with the promise that **he who believes has eternal life** (v. 47). But now faith is shown to involve discipleship. As Jesus obeyed the Father and completed the Father's work by giving his life (cf. 17:4; 19:30), a disciple of Jesus will obey him and follow him even to death.

The language of violent death—eating Jesus' flesh and drinking his blood—points to the necessity, not merely to accept the reality of Jesus' death for the life of the world, but to follow him in the way of the cross. In the Synoptics, when Jesus began to predict his Passion he added, "If anyone wants to come with me, he must forget himself, carry his cross, and follow me. For whoever wants to save his own life will lose it; but whoever loses his life for me and for the gospel will save it" (Mark 8:34–35). Later in John's Gospel, Jesus will speak simultaneously of his own death and of what it means to be his disciple; "I am telling you the truth: a grain of wheat remains no more than a single grain unless it is dropped into the ground and dies. If it does die, then it produces many grains. Whoever loves his own life will lose it; whoever hates his own life in this world will keep it for life eternal. Whoever wants to serve me must follow me, so that my servant will be with me where I am. And my Father will honor anyone who serves me" (12:24–26). The metaphors vary, but the point is much the same. To **eat the flesh of the Son of Man and drink his blood** (v. 53) is not merely to partake of the benefits of Jesus' death but to participate in *the death itself* by becoming his servant and disciple. It is to follow him and (in one's own way) to share his mission and destiny. The point is not that actual martyrdom is inevitable but that if a person is faithful it is always a distinct possibility (e.g., 13:36; 15:18–16:4; 21:18–19).

Ignatius, bishop of Antioch in the early second century, seems to have understood the metaphor along similar lines. As he sailed toward Rome, and martyrdom, he wrote: "I want the bread of God, which is the flesh of Jesus Christ, who was of the seed of David, and for drink I want his blood, which is uncorruptible love" (*To the Romans* 7.3). The emphasis on discipleship or martyrdom does not, of course, rule out a connection with the Lord's Supper. It is likely that Ignatius saw the two aspects as interrelated and inseparable, and if Ignatius did so, the possibility must be allowed that John's Gospel as well viewed the Lord's Supper as a key expression and example of the Christian community taking up its cross to follow Jesus.

The promise of life in this chapter unfolds against a backdrop of death, not only Jesus' death, but (potentially at least) the death of those called to follow him. It is the prospect of actual death that gives special poignancy to the recurring refrain **I will raise them to life at the last day** (vv. 39, 40, 44, 54), and to the concluding assurances that those who eat **will live forever** (vv. 51, 58). Part two of the discourse ends where it began, with the ancestors in the desert who died and stayed dead even though they received the manna (v. 58; cf. v. 49). Jesus promises something far greater than manna in the desert: Life with him now and victory over death at the last day.

Additional Notes

6:27 / Because God, the Father, has put his mark of approval on him: Like 3:35–36, this brief explanatory clause is best understood as the Gospel writer's reflection on the baptism of Jesus. There are several other such possible asides in this chapter that either carry the argument along (vv. 33, 50, 58) or add a necessary qualification (v. 46).

6:33 / For the bread that God gives is he who comes down from heaven. The abrupt use of the third person again suggests a parenthetical comment merging Jesus' words with the words of the narrator in the manner of 3:13–21 or 3:31–36. The identification of Jesus with the bread from heaven in this verse seems to get ahead of the story, for such an identification does not become explicit on Jesus' lips until v. 35. Also, v. 33 appears to be ignored in this immediate context. The crowd's request in v. 34 to **give us this bread always** is most easily understood as a reply, not to v. 33, but to Jesus' initial reference to **the real bread from heaven** in v. 32.

On the other hand, a serious attempt to give v. 33 a place in the give-and-take of an actual conversation would require that it be translated differently: "For the bread that God gives is *that which* comes down from heaven and gives life to the world." Such a rendering is grammatically possible because the Greek word for **bread** is masculine (like the pronoun **he**). It avoids explicitly identifying Jesus with the bread (leaving that until v. 35) and makes the statement more at home in its immediate context. Either translation is legitimate, and it may be that the Gospel writer is being deliberately ambiguous. From the crowd's standpoint the bread is "that which" comes from heaven (like the manna), yet the GNB translation is the appropriate one for the *reader* of the Gospel, who knows from the outset that the Bread is a person.

6:35 / Will never be thirsty: It is important not to read back into this pronouncement the references in vv. 53–56 to drinking Jesus' blood. Jesus is here presented simply as the giver of the *water* of life as in 4:14 and 7:37–38. The pronouncement is only loosely connected to the bread metaphor and the exposition of Psalm 78:24, for the verbs used are not "eat" and "drink" but "come" and "believe."

6:36 / Now, I told you that you have seen me but will not believe. When did he tell them this? The most plausible answer is 5:38: "for you do not believe in the one whom he sent" (cf. 5:40, 43, 46–47). When Jesus' discourses take on a formal character, there is a sense in which his opponents are always the same people (i.e., "the Jews" 5:18; 6:41, NIV), whether he is in Galilee or Jerusalem and regardless of the occasion.

He did not tell them in so many words that they had **seen** him. The association of seeing with believing arises, rather, out of the *present* context. They ask to see a sign in order to believe (v. 30), but Jesus tells them that *he* is the sign (v.

102

35). Verse 36 could be paraphrased "But I told you that you do not believe—and you don't, even though you have seen me" (contrast v. 40: "that all who see the Son and believe in him should have eternal life").

6:37 / **I will never turn away anyone who comes**. Unlike the coming of the crowd in 6:5, the "coming to Jesus" referred to in vv. 35 and 37 is synonymous with "believing."

6:39 / **That I should not lose any ... but ... raise them all**: The relevant Greek pronouns in this verse are neuter and singular: lit. "that of everything he has given me I should not lose any of it, but raise it at the last day"; cf. v. 37a (lit., "everything that the Father gives me"). This grammatical feature suggests that Jesus views the redeemed corporately, as a single entity. In contrast, the pronouns in v. 40 are masculine singular, implying that the same promises are also held out to Christian believers as individuals.

6:41 / **The people**: lit., "the Jews," as in NIV. Similarly, "among them" in 6:52 is "among the Jews." John's Gospel often designates Jesus' opponents as "the Jews" because in the writer's day the Jews and the Jewish synagogue stood as a threat against the Christian community (cf. 16:1–2). Sometimes the term refers particularly to the religious authorities (e.g., 5:15–18), but here it becomes a designation for the crowd as it begins to grumble to itself about Jesus. The word **grumbling** recalls the behavior of the Israelites in the desert in the time of Moses (cf. Exod. 16:2, 7, 8). Ironically, it was in response to their grumbling that God gave them the manna.

6:46 / This time the narrator's aside adds a qualification: "hearing" and "learning" from the Father is not the same as seeing him. Neither those who follow Moses nor those who claim secret divine revelations have genuine access to such a vision. The thought is the same here as in the prologue. God reveals himself only in his Word (cf. 1:1, 18).

6:50 / **But the bread that comes down from heaven is of such a kind**: lit., "this is the bread that comes down from heaven." Once more the use of the third person suggests that the narrator is rephrasing Jesus' claims from the perspective of a confessing Christian (cf. vv. 27b, 33). An alternation is thus created between "I" or "I am" pronouncements (vv. 48–49, 51), and confessional statements beginning with "this" or "this is" (v. 50, and "this bread" in v. 51). As elsewhere in John's Gospel, the words of Jesus and the words of the believing community are regarded as almost interchangeable (cf. also v. 58).

6:54 / **Eats**: Here and in vv. 56–58 a Greek word is used that normally means to "feed on" something as an animal feeds. Some say John has chosen this crude term deliberately to lend realism to the idea of eating Jesus' flesh. But in the present tense he uses *only* this word for "eat" (cf. 13:18), and it is therefore best regarded simply as a peculiar feature of his style.

6:56 / **Lives in me, and I live in him**: This word for **live** (Gr.: *menein*), which is not used elsewhere in the chapter, means to "dwell" or "remain." It is used most conspicuously in Jesus' farewell discourses (e.g., 15:4–10).

6:57 / **Because of him I live also . . . will live because of me**: The meaning suggested by the context is that Jesus lives his life on earth from day to day in dependence on the Father, while the disciple in turn lives in daily dependence on Jesus. In 14:19, however, Jesus uses similar language to refer to his resurrection. It is possible that both aspects are in view here. Jesus lives because of the Father *both* in his life on earth and in resurrection from the dead, while the disciple lives because of Jesus in both senses as well. There is little doubt, however, that the emphasis in each case is on the present aspect, that is, from day to day.

6:58 / **This, then, is the bread that came down from heaven** . . . The last of the asides by the Gospel writer virtually repeats v. 50, gathering into the pronouncement the phraseology of vv. 49–51 with which part two of the discourse began. This summary gives unity and cohesion to vv. 48–58 and makes it difficult to sever (as many have tried to do) vv. 51c–58 from the rest.

17

The Words of Eternal Life

JOHN 6:60-71

Many of his followers heard this and said, "This teaching is too hard. Who can listen to it?" [61]Without being told, Jesus knew that they were grumbling about this, so he said to them, "Does this make you want to give up? [62]Suppose, then, that you should see the Son of Man go back up to the place where he was before? [63]What gives life is God's Spirit; man's power is of no use at all. The words I have spoken to you bring God's life-giving Spirit. [64]Yet some of you do not believe." (Jesus knew from the very beginning who were the ones that would not believe and which one would betray him.) [65]And he added, "This is the very reason I told you that no one can come to me unless the Father makes it possible for him to do so."

[66]Because of this, many of Jesus' followers turned back and would not go with him any more. [67]So he asked the twelve disciples, "And you— would you also like to leave?"

[68]Simon Peter answered him, "Lord, to whom would we go? You have the words that give eternal life. [69]And now we believe and know that you are the Holy One who has come from God."

[70]Jesus replied, "I chose the twelve of you, didn't I? Yet one of you is a devil!" [71]He was talking about Judas, the son of Simon Iscariot. For Judas, even though he was one of the twelve disciples, was going to betray him.

If the real theme of the bread of life discourse is discipleship, it is not surprising that the real (though hidden) audience turns out to be Jesus' disciples (GNB: **followers**), unmentioned since 6:22. What is surprising is that their reaction to the discourse corresponds closely to that of "the Jews" who grumbled about Jesus (v. 41) and argued among themselves over his claims (v. 52). It is not self-evident that Jesus' disciples in this passage are a well-defined group firmly committed to following him—except for the Twelve, who emerge as a distinct entity in verses 67–71. The term "disciples" or **followers** is perhaps used loosely to refer to all who traveled with Jesus (for however short a period) and listened to his teaching. When questioned later about "his disciples and about his teaching," Jesus emphasized that he always taught publicly "in the synagogues and in the Temple, where all the people come together." His teaching was not esoteric and his disciples were not a secret or subversive group (18:19–21). Here in Capernaum in chapter 6, the Gospel writer has just furnished a lengthy example of Jesus' public synagogue teaching (cf. v. 59), and "disciples" seems to have become a general term for *all* who listened to his teaching—both the group of committed adherents whom he encountered on the lake (6:16–21) and the crowd that followed the next day (6:22–25). This would help to explain how "the Jews" (who "will not believe," 6:36) and "the disciples" (who are at least potential believers) can function in the narrative in such similar ways.

The point of the "disciples'" complaint that Jesus' teaching is **too hard** (v. 60), is probably not that it is difficult to understand (because of its literal implication of cannibalism!) but that it is difficult to put into practice. Jesus' meaning was no longer obscure to them, but all too clear. To follow the Son of Man to a violent death was hard teaching indeed! Yet their **grumbling** (v. 61) recalls that of "the people" (lit., "the Jews," v. 41), and Jesus' answer suggests that what scandalized them were the same two questions that had caused controversy earlier. First, how could Jesus, a mere Galilean like themselves, say that he had come down from heaven? (v. 42). Second, how could he give them "his flesh to eat?" (v. 52); that is, how could he demand that they follow him and become sharers in his violent death?

Jesus replies to the two objections together in verses 62–63. First, what if they were to **see the Son of Man go back up to the place where he was before**? (v. 62). Would that not convince them that he came down from heaven in the first place? To the hearers, such a notion was pure theory and imagination. Yet the *readers* of the Gospel would know and believe that the Son of Man did exactly that. "Do not hold on to me," Jesus would later say to Mary Magdalene, "because I have not yet gone back up to the Father. But go to my brothers and tell them that I am returning to him who is my Father and their Father, my God and their God" (20:17).

Second, Jesus reminds his reluctant "disciples" that "the Spirit gives life; the flesh counts for nothing" (v. 63, NIV). Ascension and the Spirit go together, whether in the theology of John's Gospel in particular (cf. 7:39; 20:22) or of the New Testament generally (e.g., Acts 2:33). But what kind of distinction is Jesus making here between Spirit and flesh? How can he insist in one breath on the absolute necessity of "eating his flesh" and admit in the next that "the flesh counts for nothing"? Some have argued that the preceding synagogue discourse is no longer in mind, but that Jesus is reverting to the distinction made to Nicodemus between that which comes from God and that which is of merely human origin (cf. 3:6). Others interpret verse 63 as qualifying the sacramentalist tendencies of verses 53–58: Partaking of the Lord's Supper is crucial to a person's

Christian life as long as one partakes "spiritually" (i.e., in accord with the sacrament's true meaning).

It is more likely that "flesh" has the same meaning here as in its first occurrence in the discourse, that is, in verse 51. "Flesh" there referred to Jesus' death for the world, and if the word is given a similar sense in verse 63, the assertion is that death by itself is worthless. **Spirit** functions here as a life-giving spirit, the means of resurrection (cf. 1 Cor. 15:45; Rom. 8:11). Without the hope of resurrection, death even for a noble cause "counts for nothing," and death *so that the world may live* (v. 5) is an impossibility. Verse 63 thus accents the repeated promise of the preceding discourse that "I will raise them to life at the last day" (6:39, 40, 44, 54). To the hesitant "disciples" of verse 60 Jesus' words seemed hard, for their theme was "flesh" and "death," but because of the promise of resurrection Jesus can characterize them instead as "Spirit" and "life" (v. 63, NIV).

Despite his explanation, however, many **turned back and would not go with him any more** (v. 66). Without minimizing this crisis in Jesus' ministry, the narrator emphasizes that he was not taken by surprise. He knew of the discontent **without being told** (v. 61) and was quick to conclude, even after making his case, that **some of you do not believe** (v. 64). The narrator uses this statement (along with the reference to Judas Iscariot in v. 70) as evidence that Jesus knew all along which of his followers would turn their backs on him and which one would betray him. Jesus himself points to his earlier warning that **no one can come to me unless the Father makes it possible** (v. 65; cf. v. 44) as further evidence of the same supernatural knowledge.

In contrast to the indefinite **many** of verses 60–66, **the twelve** (vv. 67, 70) are assumed to be a fixed group already called and chosen (cf. Mark 3:13–19 and parallels). In John's Gospel the call of at least four of them has been recorded (1:35–51), but their existence as a group is made explicit only here (cf., however, the twelve baskets gathered by Jesus' disciples in v. 13). Simon Peter, whose role was a relatively minor one in the narrative of their call (1:42), now appears as the group's spokesman. He acknowledges Jesus' words as **words that give eternal life** and Jesus as God's **Holy One**. The faith of the Twelve thus established will serve as a basis for the instructions Jesus will give them in his farewell discourses.

Even from this group one will still turn away. **Judas, the son of Simon Iscariot**, anonymously mentioned already as Jesus' betrayer (v. 64), is named for the first time. He is a **devil** because through him finally the devil will seek Jesus' life (cf. 13:2, 27). But this is a momentary glimpse of the future; the immediate threat that hangs over Jesus' head is from the "Jewish authorities" in Judea (7:1).

Additional Notes

6:61 / **Does this make you want to give up?**: lit., "Does this scandalize you?" The GNB translation has the advantage of suggesting that what is at stake is discipleship, yet "scandalize" has a stronger meaning than making someone give up. It refers to a shock or a personal offense leading to a defection.

6:63 / **Man's power**: lit., "the flesh." The GNB translation conceals the use of the same word as in vv. 51–58 and takes the reader back to the contrast in 3:5–8 between "flesh" as human power and "Spirit" as the power or life of God. This is perhaps supported by the emphasis in v. 65 on what is humanly impossible (cf. the phrase "no one can" in 3:3, 5, 27).

If this is the meaning, then Jesus is not explaining anything to the grumblers but simply reminding them of the limitations of their knowledge. The statement that God's Spirit **gives life**, however, seems to refer, not to illumination or revelation, but to actual resurrection from the dead (cf. 5:21). It is more likely, therefore, that v. 63 is addressing substantively the same life and death issues raised in vv. 48–58.

6:69 / **The Holy One who has come from God**: lit., "the Holy One of God." According to 10:36, the Father "consecrated" (RSV) the Son as holy on sending him into the world. Some ancient manuscripts read "the Messiah, the Son of the living God" (harmonizing the text with Matt. 16:16) but "Holy One of God" is clearly to be preferred. In Mark and Luke, ironically, a *demon* addressed Jesus in this same Capernaum synagogue with exactly the same title (Mark 1:24/Luke 4:34)!

6:71 / **Judas, the son of Simon Iscariot**: Only John's Gospel mentions that Judas' father was named Simon (cf. 13:2, 26). **Iscariot** probably means "a man from Kerioth," an understanding reflected in variant readings in some of the manuscripts. Kerioth could be one of two towns on either side of the Dead Sea, one in Moab and one in southern Judea.

18

Jesus and His Brothers

JOHN 7:1–13

After this, Jesus traveled in Galilee; he did not want to travel in Judea, because the Jewish authorities there were wanting to kill him. ²The time for the Festival of Shelters was near, ³so Jesus' brothers said to him, "Leave this place and go to Judea, so that your followers will see the things that you are doing. ⁴No one hides what he is doing if he wants to be well known. Since you are doing these things, let the whole world know about you!" (⁵Not even his brothers believed in him.)

⁶Jesus said to them, "The right time for me has not yet come. Any time is right for you. ⁷The world cannot hate you, but it hates me, because I keep telling it that its ways are bad. ⁸You go on to the festival. I am not going[n] to this festival, because the right time has not come for me." ⁹He said this and then stayed on in Galilee.

¹⁰After his brothers had gone to the festival, Jesus also went; however, he did not go openly, but secretly. ¹¹The Jewish authorities were looking for him at the festival. "Where is he?" they asked.

¹²There was much whispering about him in the crowd. "He is a good man," some people said. "No," others said, "he fools the people." ¹³But no one talked about him openly, because they were afraid of the Jewish authorities.

n. I am not going; *some manuscripts have* I am not yet going.

For the third time (cf. 5:1; 6:1) a narrative begins vaguely with the words **after this**. The remark that **Jesus traveled in Galilee** (v. 1) is probably intended as a summary or a general characterization of his ministry, acknowledging the truth of the synoptic witness that Galilee was indeed the location of most of Jesus' teaching and healing activities. The narrator probably assumes that Jesus lived in Capernaum with his mother, brothers, and disciples (2:12; cf. 6:59), using that town as the base for his Galilean travels.

Yet, ironically, Jesus is never in Galilee again from verse 10 of this chapter until after his resurrection (chap. 21). John's Gospel is less interested in where Jesus traveled and lived most of his life than in his visits to Jerusalem. These visits are always occasioned by one of the Jewish festivals (cf. 2:13; 5:1), but now the question arises of whether Jesus will go to Jerusalem or not. The question is raised first in Galilee (vv. 2–10: Will he *go* to the Festival of Shelters?) and then in Jerusalem itself (vv. 11–13: Will he *come* to the festival?)

The uncertainty exists because Jesus is wanted by **the Jewish authorities** (v. 1; cf. 5:18). Despite the danger, his brothers urge him to go to Judea **so that your followers will see the things that you are doing** (v. 3). It is unclear what they have in mind. Does their proposal assume the existence of a definite group of Jerusalem disciples with whom Jesus has been out of touch for a while? Are they urging him to take steps to regain the followers who had recently (6:66) turned away from him? Against both of these possibilities is the fact that Jesus' brothers seem to speak of **your followers** (v. 3) and **the whole world** (v. 4) almost interchangeably. They are asking of Jesus nothing less than a public display of his miracles. It is likely that they are using the term **followers** (or "disciples") to refer generally to *any* in Jerusalem who might see his miracles and come to faith. Jesus' audience is indeed the whole world, for he teaches "in the synagogues and in the Temple, where all the people come together" (18:20). Specifically, his brothers are calling him to a Temple ministry. He has taught already in the synagogue at Capernaum (6:59), and now it is time to reveal himself publicly at the Festival of Shelters in Jerusalem.

What his brothers urge is what Jesus in fact will do in chapters 7 and 8. Yet the narrator is careful to point out that their counsel is a counsel of unbelief. They do not believe in him, nor are they heard from again in this Gospel. Their place is taken by his true "brothers," the disciples (20:17–18), one of whom is pronounced the son of Jesus' mother (19:26–27). Jesus' natural brothers are described in precisely the opposite manner from the believing disciples, as friends of the world (v. 7; contrast 15:19). Because their times are not in God's hands but in their own, it makes no difference whether they go to the festival or stay home (v. 6). But for Jesus the time must be right because his life and his plans are at God's direction.

The exchange between Jesus and his brothers recalls his conversation with his mother in chapter 2. In both cases a request, implicit or explicit, from within Jesus' family is met with an initial refusal (2:4; 7:6–9), after which Jesus proceeds to grant the request on his own terms (2:6–10; 7:10). The reason for the refusal is the same in each instance: Jesus' "hour" or **time** has not yet come (2:4; 7:6). To the narrator, Jesus' **time** refers to the final display of his glory when he will be crucified and raised from the dead in Jerusalem (cf. 12:23; 13:1). Only when Jesus has made it very clear that what he is about to undertake is *not* that final self-disclosure but a preliminary one is he free to go ahead and undertake it. His hand will not be forced by anyone, not even his own relatives. No one directs his movements but the Father, and when the time comes, "No one," he says, "takes my life away from me. I give it up of my own free will" (10:18). It makes little difference whether the request is a gentle mention of a need by an (apparently) believing loved one (2:3) or a cynical and faithless challenge to give the public what it wants (7:4). In either case the request introduces a course of action already decided in God's sovereign freedom. Jesus will go to Jerusalem for the Festival of Shelters, but not with his brothers and not at their prodding. He will make himself known to the world in his own way in Jerusalem, but the world will not set his agenda.

These concerns help explain the seeming duplicity of Jesus' behavior in verses 8–10. He waits until his brothers have left for the festival and then makes his journey not **openly, but secretly** (v. 10). Whether the secrecy consists merely in the avoidance of normal travel routes or of the company of his brothers en route—or whether something deeper is involved—is not explained at this point. There is undeniably a movement in chapters 7–8 from secrecy (7:10) to public discourse (7:26) and back to secrecy once more (8:59). The purpose of Jesus' visit to the Festival of Shelters is revelation. He intends to do just what his brothers have suggested: **let the whole world know** about himself (v. 4). His self-revelation has a beginning, a certain duration, and a definite end. When it is finished, those who have heard his words will be divided, like his followers in chapter 6, into believers and unbelievers.

The basic division exists already. Even *before* Jesus arrives, some in the city are defending him as a **good man** while others denounce him as a deceiver of the people (v. 12; for similar disputes about Jesus, cf. 7:40–43; 9:16; 10:19–21). Jesus comes not only for self-disclosure but to make known as well "the thoughts of many hearts" (Luke 2:35 NIV; cf. John 3:19–21). The remainder of chapters 7–8 should be regarded as a continuous series of discourses by which a decisive judgment on the **world**—represented by Jerusalem and its Temple—is accomplished.

Additional Notes

7:1 / **Jesus traveled**. The word **traveled** links the narrative to its preceding context (cf. 6:66) and recalls the synoptic testimony that Jesus' ministry in Galilee was an itinerant one, though with Capernaum as a base (cf., e.g., Matt. 8:20/ Luke 9:58).

7:2 / **Festival of Shelters**: The origin of this festival (Hebrew: *Sukkoth*, traditionally translated into English as "Tabernacles" or "Booths") is sketched in Lev. 23:33–43 (cf. Deut. 16:13–17). The observance of the festival in Jesus' time and later, as well as various traditions connected with it, is described in detail in the tractate *Sukkah* in the Mishnah and the Talmud. It is significant at this point in the narrative because it was one of only three occasions (along with Passover and the Harvest Festival, or Pentecost) at which all the people of Israel were expected "to come to worship the Lord . . . at the one place of worship" (Deut. 16:16).

7:8 / **I am not going**. Some ancient manuscripts read, "I am not yet going," probably to take account of the fact that two verses later Jesus goes to the festival after all. But the more definite—and more difficult—reading is undoubtedly the correct one. Jesus is represented as clearly refusing his brothers' proposal. He will not go to this festival at their request or initiative but only as his Father directs.

Going in Greek is lit. "going up" (*anabainō*). The usage is idiomatic. Because Jerusalem was the center of Israel—and of the world—for the observant Jew, one always "went up" to Jerusalem, no matter from what direction one was coming. It is therefore far-fetched to see in this word a subtle hint that Jesus will later "go up" to the cross or to heaven (cf. 3:13; 6:62; 20:17).

Because the right time has not come for me: lit., "my time is not yet fulfilled," or (v. 6) "my time is not yet here." The **right time** (both here and in v. 6) could refer to the moment that came in v. 10 when Jesus actually went to this festival, but other passages in this Gospel (e.g., 2:4; 12:23; 13:1; 17:1) suggest instead that the **right time** (elsewhere, lit., "hour") refers to Jesus' *final* visit to Jerusalem, when he was crucified and rose from the dead. Thus, even though Jesus goes to the Festival of Shelters in v. 10, his **right time** has still not come (cf. 7:30, 39; 8:20).

19

Jesus at the Festival of Shelters

The festival was nearly half over when Jesus went to the Temple and began teaching. ¹⁵The Jewish authorities were greatly surprised and said, "How does this man know so much when he has never been to school?"

¹⁶Jesus answered, "What I teach is not my own teaching, but it comes from God, who sent me. ¹⁷Whoever is willing to do what God wants will know whether what I teach comes from God or whether I speak on my own authority. ¹⁸A person who speaks on his own authority is trying to gain glory for himself. But he who wants glory for the one who sent him is honest, and there is nothing false in him. ¹⁹Moses gave you the Law, didn't he? But not one of you obeys the Law. Why are you trying to kill me?"

²⁰"You have a demon in you!" the crowd answered. "Who is trying to kill you?"

²¹Jesus answered, "I performed one miracle, and you were all surprised. ²²Moses ordered you to circumcise your sons (although it was not Moses but your ancestors who started it), and so you circumcise a boy on the Sabbath. ²³If a boy is circumcised on the Sabbath so that Moses' Law is not broken, why are you angry with me because I made a man completely well on the Sabbath? ²⁴Stop judging by external standards, and judge by true standards."

²⁵Some of the people of Jerusalem said, "Isn't this the man the authorities are trying to kill? ²⁶Look! He is talking in public, and they say nothing against him! Can it be that they really know that he is the Messiah? ²⁷But when the Messiah comes, no one will know where he is from. And we all know where this man comes from."

The unity of 7:14–8:59 becomes apparent once it is recognized that 8:1–11 is the record of a separate incident, and not an original part of John's Gospel. Only by ignoring these verses and moving from 7:52 to 8:12 without a break can the reader sense how closely chapters 7 and 8 go together. Jesus' Temple ministry is presented in the form of one long discourse, even though it is probably assumed to have been given over a period of several days during the Festival of Shelters, and even though the material comprising it may well have been gathered from collections of sayings associated with many different occasions. It is Jesus' Temple discourse par excellence, standing as a sequel to the synagogue discourse of chapter 6. If the theme of the latter was redemption through Jesus' death, the theme of this discourse is to be judgment on Jerusalem and on the world. (For further discussion see J. R. Michaels, "The Temple Discourse in John," *New Dimensions in New Testament Study*, ed. R. N. Longenecker and M. C. Tenney [Grand Rapids: Zondervan, 1974], pp. 200–213).

If the public ministry in John's Gospel is viewed as an anticipation of Jesus' Passion (see Introduction) this discourse corresponds to the summary found in Luke 21:37–38: "Jesus spent those days teaching in the Temple, and when evening came, he would go out and spend the night on the Mount of Olives. Early each morning all the people went to the Temple to listen to him." Such, at any rate, is the pattern presupposed by whoever was responsible for using 8:1–11 to split the discourse in two: **Then everyone went home, but Jesus went to the Mount of Olives. Early the next morning he went back to the Temple** (8:1–2a). Instead of connecting the theme of Jesus teaching in the Temple with Passion week in particular, as the Synoptics have done, John has used it as a conspicuous feature of Jesus' ministry prior to the Passion. This is perhaps a natural corollary of the fact that in John's Gospel Jesus visits Jerusalem several times. Teaching publicly in the Temple is not an occasional thing for him, nor limited to one period in his life, but (like teaching in synagogues) his customary practice (cf. 18:20). The formal Temple discourse of chapters 7–8, like the synagogue discourse of chapter 6, is presented as a sample.

Again and again the reader is reminded that the Temple is the setting, and the Festival of Shelters the occasion, for all that Jesus says:

The festival was nearly half over when Jesus went to the Temple and began teaching (v. 14).

As Jesus taught in the Temple, he said in a loud voice . . . (v. 28).

On the last and most important day of the festival Jesus stood up and said in a loud voice . . . (v. 37).

Jesus said all this as he taught in the Temple, in the room where the offering boxes were placed. (8:20).

Then they picked up stones to throw at him, but Jesus hid himself and left the temple (8:59).

The first three of these references introduce major divisions of the discourse: 7:14-27, 7:28-36, and 7:37-8:20. The fourth terminates the discourse proper in much the same way that 6:59 terminated the synagogue discourse. The last concludes a long postscript (8:21-59) that develops some of the issues raised previously, building to the sharpest of confrontations and bringing Jesus' self-disclosure to an end.

Because he delays his journey until after the departure of his brothers, Jesus arrives at the festival late (v. 14). He begins immediately to teach in the Temple, and immediately his teaching attracts the attention of the religious authorities. How, they ask, can a person without formal rabbinic training speak so ably and wisely? The content of the **teaching** that impressed them is not given as a part of the narrative. The narrator probably has in mind expositions of the Hebrew Scriptures, but the center of interest lies rather in Jesus' reply to the authorities' question. But just as their question had been directed not to him but to each other, so his answer (vv. 16-18) is intended not for them but for the readers of the Gospel. The reason he can teach so well without formal education is that he himself is "taught of God" (cf. 6:45). Those who choose to obey God are those who will recognize that God speaks through Jesus. They will know that Jesus is God's true messenger, desiring glory for God and not himself. The reverse is equally true: Those who do not see Jesus in this way show by their rejection of him their disobedience to God.

Focusing his attention on the religious authorities, Jesus puts them in the second category. They are disobedient to God and to God's Law because they are seeking to kill Jesus (v. 19). Because the Law of God for them means the Law of Moses, Jesus takes the opportunity to vindicate his own actions (and condemn theirs) in terms of what the Mosaic Law stipulates. When the law of circumcision (i.e., that a male child should be circumcised when he was eight days old) came into potential conflict with the law of the Sabbath, it was agreed that the Sabbath law should give way (e.g., Mishnah *Shabbat* 18.3-19.2); the boy should receive circumcision even on the Sabbath. Arguing from the lesser to the greater, Jesus concludes that he too was in agreement with the Law when he **made a man completely well on the Sabbath** (v. 23), that is, when he healed the sick man at the pool of Bethzatha (cf. 5:1-9). This was the **one miracle** (v. 21) that had amazed them all (cf. 5:20, 28). The rational defense he makes here provides a belated postscript to his enigmatic remark two chapters earlier, "My Father is always working, and I too must work" (5:17).

Jesus' argument makes sense because of an assumption among Jewish teachers that circumcision accomplished the perfection of man (e.g., Mishnah *Nedarim* 3.11: Abraham was not called perfect until he was circumcised). They too argued from the lesser to the greater that if circumcision "which attaches to only one of the 248 members of the human body, suspends the Sabbath, how much more shall [the saving of] the whole body suspend the Sabbath" (Babylonian Talmud, *Yoma* 85b). The difference is that the rabbis confined the principle to immediately life-threatening situations, while Jesus applied it on behalf of anyone in need of help or healing (cf., e.g., Matt. 12:1-8, 9-14; Luke 13:10-17; 14:1-6).

The implication of all this for the hearers is inescapable. If Jesus is in the right as far as the Law is concerned, they are wrong to be angry with him and to seek his life. They are in fact disobedient to the very Law they claim to uphold (v. 19). The real shock for them comes not in the logic of the argument, however, but in Jesus' remark, almost in passing, that they are trying to kill him (v. 19b). Indignantly they deny any such intent (v. 20). Their seeming lack of awareness of what the narrator and the readers have known all along is puzzling and incongruous. As early as 5:18 the religious authorities in Jerusalem had made up their minds to kill Jesus. This was why he remained in Galilee as long as he did (7:1). When he finally decided to go to Jerusalem, the authorities were still "looking for him at the festival" (7:11), apparently with hostile intent. Even the crowds knew that Jesus was a wanted man, though "no one talked about him openly, because they were afraid of the Jewish authorities" (7:13). Why then the surprise at Jesus' blunt charge in verse 19 that his hearers wanted to kill him? Are they hiding their true intentions? Or is a distinction to be made between **the Jewish authorities** in verses 15-19 and **the crowd** in verse 20? Is the crowd feigning ignorance of the whole matter out of the same fear mentioned in verse 13?

Neither of these suggestions is particularly convincing. A better explanation is that the crowd's disclaimer in verse 20 is an honest one. They really do not understand why Jesus thinks someone is out to kill him. *This is possible only if Jesus' identity is unknown* to them, that is, if they do not realize that Jesus is the notorious healer of Bethzatha wanted by the authorities. A few verses later, in an apparent reversal, some in the crowd will say, **Isn't this the man the authorities are trying to kill?** (v. 25).

The contrast between this statement and the disclaimer in verse 20 indicates that their question is not merely rhetorical. Verse 25 is, rather, a genuine moment of recognition, a breakthrough in the crowd's perception of Jesus. *Now* they realize that he is indeed the man wanted by the authorities for the Bethzatha healing.

The interpretation of the Law or of the Hebrew Scriptures is the theme of Jesus' teaching only formally. The real point at issue is his own identity. He comes to reveal *himself*, not the meaning of this or that text. But the self-revelation occurs against a background of concealment. The exchange recorded in verses 14–24 is best explained on the assumption that Jesus is at the Temple incognito. This, it appears, is what was meant by the statement that when Jesus went to the festival "he did not go openly, but secretly" (v. 10).

Whether Jesus concealed his identity supernaturally (cf. 20:14–15) or by an actual disguise is not indicated. Possibly the "disguise" consisted simply of avoiding the distinctive dress or appearance of a rabbi (see, e.g., Matt. 23:5). This would explain why one who elsewhere in this Gospel is addressed as "Rabbi" (e.g., 1:38; 3:2; 6:25) or "Teacher" (13:13) is here described as unschooled (v. 15). It is unlikely that this conclusion was based on any direct knowledge of Jesus' personal history. The judgment of the religious authorities that Jesus had **never been to school** (v. 15) was probably made on the basis of his *appearance*. As far as they could tell by looking at him he was one of the uneducated "people of the land" (Hebrew: *Am ha-àretz*) who knew nothing of the Law of Moses (cf. 7:49). Yet his words belied any such conclusion. To those willing to obey God they were recognizable as God's own words (vv. 16—17).

Finally, after dropping the hint that he is a wanted man, and the somewhat broader hint that he has performed a miracle, Jesus invites his hearers to penetrate the disguise and discern his true identity: "Stop judging by mere appearance, and make a right judgment" (v. 24, NIV). This is exactly what happens in verses 25–27, where the question of Jesus' identity moves immediately into a new phase. The conclusion that the stranger who appeared suddenly at the Festival of Shelters is indeed Jesus, the Bethzatha miracle worker, is preliminary to the question, Who then *is* Jesus? The first answer to come to mind is that he is the Messiah (v. 26), but Jesus (now that he has been identified as Jesus!) is known to be a Galilean from Nazareth (cf. 1:45; 6:42; 7:1, 40), while the Messiah is believed to be of unknown and mysterious origin. The persistent question Who is Jesus? is not yet settled but will dominate the Temple discourse to the very end, as Jesus' self-disclosure runs its course.

Additional Notes

7:15 / **Know so much** is lit. "know letters." Though the phrase can refer to literacy, the reference here is to Jesus' knowledge and understanding of the Scriptures. This terminology is used because in Judaism a child customarily learned to read by reading the Scriptures. The word "letters" or "writing" is also used to refer to the Hebrew Scriptures in 5:46.

7:16 / **Jesus answered**. Here, as in 5:17, 19, Jesus is not answering a specific question directed at him but initiating a discourse. The middle form of the verb (*apekrinatō*) used in the earlier passage would have been appropriate here as well, but the narrator has chosen instead the more common passive (*apekrithē*), possibly because of v. 21, where the dialogue has become a realistic one and *apekrithē* is used in direct answer to the crowd's question.

7:19 / **Moses gave you the Law, didn't he**? It is possible to read these words as a negative statement rather than a question: "It was not Moses who gave you the Law." This would correspond in syntax to 6:32 ("It was not Moses who gave you the bread from heaven," GNB margin) and would anticipate the qualification made in v. 22 that the law of circumcision began with the patriarchs rather than Moses. But this would lose the irony intended in v. 19: They acknowledged that the Law came from Moses, yet they disobeyed it. It must be remembered, moreover, that the qualification in v. 22 is a mere afterthought. Jesus begins the sentence by explicitly attributing circumcision to Moses, and it is virtually certain that v. 19 is intended the same way.

7:20 / **You have a demon in you**! This statement is not to be taken as a serious charge of demon possession. It is closer to the colloquial expression "You're crazy" and is strictly preliminary to the incredulous question, **Who is trying to kill you**?

7:24 / **External standards ... true standards**: It is not primarily a question of the **standards** by which a judgment is made. The distinction is rather between drawing one's conclusions about Jesus on the basis of "sight" or "outward appearance" and being "willing to do what God wants" so as to know whether or not his teaching is from God (v. 17).

7:27 / **No one will know where he is from**. In the context of the chapter, this belief about the Messiah seems to contradict the belief referred to in v. 40 (i.e., that he will come from Bethlehem). The narrator wants to underscore the confusing diversity of Jewish messianic expectations, while at the same time affirming that Jesus (in his own way) fulfills *all* these varied expectations. The Jewish expectation of a Messiah who is hidden or whose origin is unknown is attested in apocalyptic literature (e.g., 1 Enoch 48.6; 4 Ezra 13.51–52) and (perhaps) in Justin Martyr's *Dialogue with Trypho* 8.4 (though see note on 1:25). Possibly the roots of this notion are tied in with the roots of the title "Son of Man" and the association of that title with the Jewish Messiah.

20

"I Come from Him and He Sent Me"

JOHN 7:28–36

As Jesus taught in the Temple, he said in a loud voice, "Do you really know me and know where I am from? I have not come on my own authority. He who sent me, however, is truthful. You do not know him, ²⁹but I know him, because I come from him and he sent me."

³⁰Then they tried to seize him, but no one laid a hand on him, because his hour had not yet come. ³¹But many in the crowd believed in him and said, "When the Messiah comes, will he perform more miracles than this man has?"

³²The Pharisees heard the crowd whispering these things about Jesus, so they and the chief priests sent some guards to arrest him. ³³Jesus said, "I shall be with you a little while longer, and then I shall go away to him who sent me. ³⁴You will look for me, but you will not find me, because you cannot go where I will be."

³⁵The Jewish authorities said among themselves, "Where is he about to go so that we shall not find him? Will he go to the Greek cities where our people live, and teach the Greeks? ³⁶He says that we will look for him but will not find him, and that we cannot go where he will be. What does he mean?"

The Temple discourse begins anew with Jesus speaking **in a loud voice.** This second announcement (vv. 28–29), like the first (vv. 16–19), initiates an encounter with the crowd, yet itself comes as a response to something already expressed. As verses 16–19 addressed the question that perplexed the religious authorities in verse 15, so verses 28–29 address the debate among the people of Jerusalem in verses 25–27.

Specifically, they address the objection that Jesus cannot be the Messiah because everyone knows where he comes from. It is true; they know where he is from, geographically. But Jesus' real origin is not a place but a person, **he who sent me,** a Person known to Jesus but unknown to them. In this sense Jesus fits the profile of a Messiah of whom it is said "no one will know where he is from." Jesus knows where he comes from, and the readers of the Gospel know (cf. 1:1–18), but to the religious authorities and the crowds in Jerusalem his origin remains a mystery.

Up to this point in the discourse, **he who sent me** has not been explicitly identified. It is possible to infer from verse 16 (as the GNB translators have done) that the term refers to God, because Jesus clearly indicates that his *teaching* comes from God. But Jesus avoids the designation Father, which played such a major part in the discourse in chapter 5, and instead expresses himself vaguely and indirectly. The fact that Jesus' hearers do not know his Father (i.e., where Jesus comes from) is dramatized by the fact that the word is not even used. Later, when he begins to speak openly about his Father (8:16–18), the term provokes an immediate controversy that dominates the remainder of the discourse.

The stage for that final controversy is being set already in chapter 7. Jesus' words consistently divide his hearers into two groups. To some he is a "good man"; to others a deceiver (v. 12). Some believe in him as a genuine miracle-worker and a possible Messiah (v. 31), but others are ready to turn him over to the authorities. The statement that **they tried to seize him, but no one laid a hand on him, because his hour had not yet come** (v. 30) is illustrated by the failure of the Pharisees and chief priests in verses 32–36. When the guards are sent to arrest him, Jesus turns them back with his mysterious words (vv. 33–34). If Jesus' origin is unknown to the crowds and the religious authorities, so too is his destination. If he comes from God, it follows that he will go to God again, but the mention of his going is as much an enigma as the reference to his coming. Though he says he will **go away to him who sent me** (v. 33), the messengers of the priests and Pharisees hear nothing in this of going to be with God. All they hear is **you will not find me, because you cannot go where I will be** (v. 34), and all they can conclude from this is that perhaps Jesus will **go to the Greek cities where our people live, and teach the Greeks** (v. 35). The suggestion displays their ignorance. They no more understand where he is going than where he came from, and their very failure to arrest him (cf. vv. 45–46) fulfills his prediction that they will look for him but will not find him. There is a touch of irony in the remark about teaching the Greeks, for the narrator and his readers know that Jesus' departure (i.e., his death and resurrection) will indeed spread his teaching throughout the Greek-speaking world. This second exchange between Jesus and the Jerusalem authorities ends, like the first, on a note of mystery and misunderstanding.

Additional Notes

7:28 / **Said in a loud voice** is lit. "cried out." The use of this verb suggests a solemn and decisive utterance, comparable to John the Baptist's testimony in 1:15–16 (cf. also 7:37 and 12:44).

7:28 / **Do you really know me and know where I am from?** These words are more naturally read as a statement: "Yes, you do know me and you know where I am from." This sentence in Greek is connected to what follows by **and** (Gr.: *kai*), which, because it introduces a qualification, should be translated "and yet." They do know where he comes from geographically, but this knowledge means little because he did not come on his own authority and they do *not* know the one from whom he came.

7:31 / **When the Messiah comes, will he perform more miracles?** The question assumes that the Messiah is to perform miracles when he comes (cf. 2:18; 6:30; Mark 13:22), and that the sheer number or frequency of his miracles testifies to his identity. These notions, while not widely attested in Jewish sources, are assumed to be part of the Jewish expectation in 20:30, 31 as well: Jesus' miracles bear witness that he is the Messiah, and the ones written about are but a sampling from a much larger number. In the immediate context at the Festival of Shelters, however, Jesus himself has referred only to "one miracle" (v. 21). The crowd's reaction in v. 31 is apparently based on his reputation, now that they know who he is (cf. 3:2; 6:2).

7:35 / **The Jewish authorities**: lit., "the Jews," a term that in this Gospel does frequently refer to the religious authorities (cf., e.g., 7:15), but which in the immediate context seems to refer instead to the guards sent by the authorities to arrest Jesus. Their reaction is described further in v. 46: "Nobody has ever talked the way this man does." Since they are messengers of the Pharisees and chief priests, however, it is possible that the misunderstanding attributed to them in v. 35 is regarded as characteristic of the religious authorities as well (cf. 8:22).

To the Greek cities where our people live: lit., "to the diaspora of the Greeks." Cities are not mentioned explicitly. The Greek word *diaspora* was used to refer to non-Palestinian Jews (and later to Christians, 1 Peter 1:1) as the people of God scattered throughout the Greek world. The "diaspora of the Greeks" must therefore mean the diaspora of the Jews *among* the Greeks. The supposition is that Jesus will go and teach not the diaspora Jews, however, but **the Greeks** (i.e., Gentiles). What is presented here as a crude misunderstanding becomes in later chapters of this Gospel, on the basis of Jesus' death, a realistic hope (cf. 10:16; 11:52; 12:20–24).

21

The Last Day of the Festival

JOHN 7:37–8:20

On the last and most important day of the festival Jesus stood up and said in a loud voice, "Whoever is thirsty should come to me and drink. [38]As the scripture says, 'Whoever believes in me, streams of lifegiving water will pour out from his heart.' "[o] [39]Jesus said this about the Spirit, which those who believed in him were going to receive. At that time the Spirit had not yet been given, because Jesus had not been raised to glory.

[40]Some of the people in the crowd heard him say this and said, "This man is really the Prophet!"[p]

[41]Others said, "He is the Messiah!"

But others said, "The Messiah will not come from Galilee! [42]The scripture says that the Messiah will be a descendant of King David and will be born in Bethlehem, the town where David lived." [43]So there was a division in the crowd because of Jesus. [44]Some wanted to seize him, but no one laid a hand on him.

[45]When the guards went back, the chief priests and Pharisees asked them, "Why did you not bring him?"

[46]The guards answered, "Nobody has ever talked the way this man does!"

[47]"Did he fool you, too?" the Pharisees asked them. [48]"Have you ever known one of the authorities or one Pharisee to believe in him? [49]This crowd does not know the Law of Moses, so they are under God's curse!"

[50]One of the Pharisees there was Nicodemus, the man who had gone to see Jesus before. He said to the others, [51]"According to our Law we cannot condemn a man before hearing him and finding out what he has done."

[52]"Well," they answered, "are you also from Galilee? Study the Scriptures and you will learn that no prophet ever comes[q] from Galilee."

[1][Then everyone went home, but Jesus went to the Mount of Olives. [2]Early the next morning he went back to the Temple. All the people gathered around him, and he sat down and began to teach them. [3]The teachers of the Law and the Pharisees brought in a woman who had been caught committing adultery, and they made her stand before them all. [4]"Teacher," they said to Jesus, "this woman was caught in the very act of committing adultery. [5]In our Law Moses commanded that such a woman must be stoned to death. Now, what do you say?" [6]They said this to trap Jesus, so that they could accuse him. But he bent over and wrote on the ground with his finger. [7]As they stood there asking him questions, he straightened up and said to them, "Whichever one of you has committed no sin may throw the first stone at her." [8]Then he bent over again and wrote on the ground. [9]When they heard this, they all left one by one, the older ones first. Jesus was left alone, with the woman still standing there. [10]He straightened up and said to her, "Where are they? Is there no one left to condemn you?"

[11]"No one, sir," she answered.

"Well, then," Jesus said, "I do not condemn you either. Go, but do not sin again."ʳ

[12]Jesus spoke to the Pharisees again. "I am the light of the world," he said. "Whoever follows me will have the light of life and will never walk in darkness."

[13]The Pharisees said to him, "Now you are testifying on your own behalf; what you say proves nothing."

[14]"No," Jesus answered, "even though I do testify on my own behalf, what I say is true, because I know where I came from and where I am going. You do not know where I came from or where I am going. [15]You make judgments in a purely human way; I pass judgment on no one. [16]But if I were to do so, my judgment would be true, because I am not alone in this; the Father who sent me is with me.

[17]It is written in your Law that when two witnesses agree, what they say is true. [18]I testify on my own behalf, and the Father who sent me also testifies on my behalf."

[19]"Where is your father?" they asked him.

"You know neither me nor my Father," Jesus answered. "If you knew me, you would know my Father also."

[20]Jesus said all this as he taught in the Temple, in the room where the offering boxes were placed. And no one arrested him, because his hour had not come.

o. *Jesus' words in verses 37-38 may be translated:* "Whoever is thirsty should come to me, and whoever believes in me should drink. p. THE PROPHET: See 1.21. q. no prophet ever comes; *one manuscript has* the Prophet will not come. r. *Many manuscripts and early translations do not have this passage* (8.1-11); *others have it after Jn 21.24; others have it after Lk 21.38; one manuscript has it after Jn 7.36.*

J esus' third public announcement at the Festival of Shelters took place **on the last and most important day of the festival** (v. 37). It is perhaps the most remembered and certainly the most widely discussed saying in Jesus' Temple discourse, if not in the entire Gospel. Of the nineteen articles on John 7 listed in the bibliography of Raymond Brown's major commentary, seventeen deal with verses 37–39! (*The Gospel According to John*, ABI [New York: Doubleday, 1966], p.331). This is attributable both to the intrinsic appeal of Jesus' words and to the unique combination of difficulties in knowing how they should be heard or read. Verses 37–39 might be plausibly understood in any of at least four ways (italics indicate words attributed to Jesus):

1. Jesus . . . said . . . *Whoever is thirsty should come to me and drink. As the scripture says "Whoever believes in me, streams of life-giving water will pour out from his heart."* Jesus said this about the Spirit . . . (GNB).

2. Jesus . . . said . . . *Whoever is thirsty should come to me and drink. The scripture has said of anyone who believes in me, "Streams of life-giving water will pour from his heart."* Jesus said this about the Spirit . . .

3. Jesus . . . said . . . *Whoever is thirsty should come to me, and whoever believes in me should drink. As the scripture says, "Streams of life-*

giving water will pour out from his heart." Jesus said this about the Spirit . . . (GNB margin).

4. Jesus . . . said . . . *Whoever is thirsty should come to me, and whoever believes in me should drink.* [It was] as the scripture said, "Streams of life-giving water will pour out from his heart." But it said this about the Spirit . . .

In the interpretation of this text two issues present themselves: the issue of punctuation and the issue of whether Jesus, or the narrator, is represented as introducing the scripture quotation of uncertain origin. The first two renderings connect the phrase, **whoever believes in me,** with the scripture quotation so that the believer (any believer) is the one from whom the **streams of life-giving water** are to come. The only difference between them is that version 1 actually places the reference to the believer *within* the scripture quotation, whereas version 2 (more plausibly) assigns it to Jesus' interpretation of his text. In both of them, and in version 3 as well, it is *his* text and not the narrator's. But in version 3 the punctuation is different: The phrase **whoever believes in me** is made to stand parallel with **whoever is thirsty,** and the scripture quotation follows as Jesus' comment on the whole preceding sentence. But as soon as the scripture quotation is set apart from the phrase **whoever believes in me,** it is no longer obvious that the quotation is being attributed to Jesus. The third rendering still assumes that it is, but the fourth attributes it instead to the narrator.

The effect of this shift is significant. According to version 4, Jesus extends an invitation to the spiritually thirsty to come and drink, but without an explicit promise attached. The Gospel writer takes the opportunity to state that this appeal by Jesus fulfills a particular text of scripture. The one from whose heart the **life-giving water** flows is now Jesus himself, not the believer. This rendering of the passage has certain considerations in its favor. It is more natural to think of Jesus than of individual Christian believers as the source or wellspring of the life-giving Spirit of God. Verse 39 mentions the Spirit that believers in Jesus were later to *receive* (not dispense to others). It is Jesus who dispenses the Holy Spirit as the very breath of his mouth (20:22). At his crucifixion, in a scene rich with symbolism, water as well as blood flows from his pierced side (19:34).

The real choice in the interpretation of verses 37–39 is not between versions 1 and 3 (i.e., the GNB text and the GNB margin), but between versions 2 and 4. In support of version 2, it can be said that Jesus is freely represented as quoting scripture in this Gospel, and there are hints, as we have seen, that the exposition of scripture may have played a larger part in the Temple discourse than first appears (cf. vv. 15, 22–23). Verse 39 is a comment of the narrator in any case, and such a comment makes good sense on the assumption that Jesus himself is still the speaker in verse 38.

If, on the other hand (as in version 4), the narrator is already responsible for verse 38, then in verse 39 he is commenting on *his own* appended words (i.e., the scripture quotation), not the words of Jesus. This means that in number 4 the subject of verse 39 (unexpressed in Greek) is not Jesus (as assumed in versions 1, 2, and 3) but the scripture. The scripture is virtually personified in verse 38 ("the scripture said"—like a person speaking in the past; cf. Gal. 3:8), and the same verb in verse 39 suggests that the personification continues: "But it said this about the Spirit . . ." (cf., perhaps, the scripture quotations presented in 12:38, 39, and 41 as what Isaiah "said" long ago).

It is difficult to decide between version 2 and 4 and the modern reader is perhaps inclined to ask how *necessary* it is to decide. The weight of tradition favors version 2, and the burden of proof still rests with those who would depart from that rendering, yet an appreciation of version 4 sheds its own light on the text's meaning. Here, as elsewhere (e.g., 3:11–21), Jesus' words have merged so closely with those of the narrator that the two renderings of the passage convey broadly similar meanings. In both, Jesus invites the thirsty hearer to **come** and **drink** from the **water** he has to give. Both attach to the invitation a promise (i.e., of **life-giving water**) whether explicit (2) or implicit (4). Both interpret the water as the Spirit, and both add the qualification that this gift of the Spirit was something believers **were going to receive** *later*, that is, that the invitation and the promise were actually future from the standpoint of the events just recorded at the Festival of Shelters. The Spirit, after all, **had not yet been given, because Jesus had not been raised to glory** (v. 39). Verses 37–39 belong with those references within and just before the Temple discourse that keep emphasizing that the time for Jesus' decisive and final self-revelation is **not yet** (i.e., 7:6, 30; 8:20, 28). Jesus' announcement **on the last and most important day of the festival** is an invitation to faith and a promise of life, embedded within a discourse focused primarily on unbelief and judgment. It is a joyful announcement whose time has not yet come. Yet for the narrator and his readers the time *has* come: Jesus has been raised to glory and the Spirit has been given. The invitation and the promise are now in effect.

These features that the two renderings have in common far outweigh the points on which they differ. The principal difference is simply that version 4 makes Jesus the sole source of the life-giving Spirit, whereas version 2 assigns this role—at least derivatively—to the believer as well. But in neither case is the believer viewed as a source of life, or of the Spirit, *to others*. The image of streams of water from the believer's heart (if that is intended) is akin rather to 4:14, where Jesus promises to whoever drinks of the water he gives "a spring which will provide him with life-giving water and give him eternal life." That the believer in Jesus will become a channel of God's life to others is implicit in the total message of John's Gospel, but is not the point of either 4:14 or 7:37–38 in particular. The accent is on the rich abundance of the Spirit's life and power in the heart of the believer, like a self-replenishing and overflowing stream. The source of the stream is Jesus, no less in version 2 than in 4, for he alone can say **come to me and drink**.

Most of the "I am" statements in John's Gospel are accompanied by a corollary of some kind—an invitation or a promise or both (e.g., 6:35: "I am the bread of life. . . . He who comes to me will never be hungry; he who believes in me will never be thirsty"; cf. 8:12; 10:9; 11:25–26; 14:6; 15:5, etc.). This passage has the appearance of one of these statements in which the "I am" saying proper has been omitted, and only its corollary remains—as if Jesus had said, "I am the fountain of life; whoever is thirsty, come to me and drink" (cf. Rev. 21:6).

Whether this is the case or not, the passage invites comparison with 8:12, in which Jesus' self-disclosure and confrontation with the religious authority continues: **I am the light of the world. . . . Whoever follows me will have the light of life and will never walk in darkness**. Each of these pronouncements takes on special meaning against the background of a daily ritual at the Festival of Shelters—the pouring of water from the pool of Siloam into a bowl beside the altar in the Temple and the lighting of giant candles in the Court of the Women, respectively (cf. the Mishnah, *Sukkah* 4:9–5:4). On the last day, when these rituals had ceased, Jesus proclaims himself the true source of water and of light—for Jerusalem and for all the world. In 8:12 he again extends an invitation and a promise, but again the note of hope is submerged in a context of rejection and judgment (8:12–20).

The parallelism between 7:37–38 and 8:12 suggests that the scene of the action has not changed. The smaller units comprising 7:37–8:20, loose-knit though they may be, are legitimately treated as one unfolding drama in the Temple on the **last and most important day of the festival**. Jesus' self-revelation in 7:37–39 provokes a division in the crowd (vv. 40–

43) or, rather, brings to a head the division that has existed all along (cf. v. 12). The events of verses 30–31 seem to be happening again, but with more intensity. This time, some actually confess Jesus as **the Prophet** or **the Messiah** (vv. 40–41), but others raise theological objections: Jesus the Galilean cannot be the Messiah because the Messiah must come from Bethlehem in Judea (cf. Micah 5:2). An attempt is made to arrest Jesus, **but no one laid a hand on him** (v. 44; cf. v. 30). The narrator might have added, "because his hour had not yet come," but there was no need to labor the point.

Instead of describing in detail the second unsuccessful effort to arrest Jesus, the narrator simply chooses this as the place to give the outcome of the *first* attempt. Verses 45–52 are the sequel to verses 32–36. The **guards** who are abruptly mentioned as returning to the **chief priests and Pharisees** in verse 45 are the same guards sent out in verse 32. Their testimony to the power of Jesus' speech and presence (v. 46) refers to his baffling pronouncement in verses 33–34. The guards can only carry their bafflement back to the religious authorities who sent them.

From verse 47 at least through 8:20, the Pharisees move center stage. Jesus will confront them directly, but first their attitudes and their character will be demonstrated. It is probably to be assumed that they speak for the chief priests as well as themselves. They are intensely conscious of their own status, in contrast to that of the crowd, which **does not know the Law of Moses, so they are under God's curse** (v. 49). The Pharisees' implication is that Jesus and his followers fit this description as well. It was probably common knowledge that Jesus' disciples came mostly from the social class known as the *Am ha-àretz*, or "people of the land." Because they had neither studied the Law systematically nor been brought up to obey it in anything but a very general way, they were regarded by some of the pious as cursed of God (For illustrations of this rabbinic literature, see the Mishnah, *Aboth* 2.6; 3.11). The authorities' first impression of Jesus when he appeared at the festival was that he was unschooled in the Law (cf. v. 15), and despite all that had transpired since then the Pharisees persisted in keeping this impression alive. Their scornful question in verse 48 implies that none of their number has believed in Jesus, and that no one who truly knows the Law would ever do so.

Out of nowhere, and as if in reply to this claim, Nicodemus (who has not been heard from since chap. 3) speaks up. Introduced as a "Jewish leader" and a Pharisee (3:1), Nicodemus had functioned as an individual example of those in Jerusalem who had "believed" in Jesus but whose faith Jesus did not accept as genuine (2:23–25). Formally, at least, he is a living refutation of the sweeping judgment the Pharisees have just made on Jesus and his followers (cf. also 12:42). Yet the genuineness of his faith remains in doubt. His remark (v. 51) is no ringing confession, but merely a plea for fairness. He appears in the narrative more to demonstrate the Pharisees' intransigence than to mark a stage in his own spiritual development. When their opinions are gently questioned even by one of their own, they are quick to brand the questioner, half in mockery, as a Galilean (v. 52). The intent is not to probe seriously Nicodemus' family background but to rebuke his apparent sympathies with Jesus the Galilean. The Pharisees' parting shot is a corollary of verses 41–42: If the only prophet expected is the Messiah descended from David and born in Bethlehem, then there are no authentic Galilean prophets. Only those ignorant of the Scriptures will follow a Galilean.

Nicodemus disappears as abruptly as he appeared, and the stage is now set for Jesus to confront the Pharisees **again** (8:12), this time not through emissaries but directly. Yet his pronouncement **I am the light of the world** . . . , the sequel to 7:37–38, is not for them exclusively but for **whoever follows me**. It is universal in scope and probably, like 7:37–38, future in its orientation. The desire of Jesus' brothers that he "let the whole world know" about himself (7:4) is coming to realization but with the outcome Jesus foresaw, that the world "hates me, because I keep telling it that its ways are bad" (7:7). Only when the Spirit comes will the outcome be different.

The world's representatives immediately challenge Jesus' authority. The ensuing debate is a virtual re-enactment of 5:30–38. Jesus' claim to be **the light of the world** is invalid because he is testifying on his own behalf (8:13). The Pharisees have in mind the principle of the oral law that witnesses were not to be believed when testifying on their own behalf (the Mishnah, *Ketuboth* 2.9). Jesus had acknowledged this very principle in 5:31, but here he takes exception to it (v. 14). What is different is not the conclusion toward which he is moving but the logic by which he will reach it. His testimony on his own behalf is valid, he says, **because I know where I came from and where I am going**. The reason the Pharisees question his authority is that they do not know these things (v. 14b).

It is not clear how such knowledge validates Jesus' testimony until, in subsequent verses, Jesus makes the same point again in different words: **where I came from** and **where I am going**, it appears, is an indirect way of referring to the Father. Jesus' testimony is valid because he knows the Father. The Father, in fact, is speaking in and through the testimony of

Jesus. Verses 14, 16, and 18 are three progressively clearer ways of saying that there are actually two witnesses, Jesus and the Father, speaking through Jesus' lips. That is why his testimony is self-authenticating. The reader understands this because the same point emerged from the earlier discourse in 5:30–47, but here the Pharisees are baffled by it. A major difference is that the earlier discourse began with a systematic presentation of the relation between the Father and the Son (cf. 5:19–29), whereas here the Pharisees seem to be hearing of the Father for the first time. Not once has Jesus referred to God as his Father throughout this discourse, using instead circumlocutions such as "the one who sent me," or **where I came from**, or **where I am going**. Now he unveils this mysterous Source and Goal as his Father, and the Pharisees do not understand. Even later, in 8:27, it has still not dawned on them that "the one who sent me" means the Father.

Why this apparent regression in terminology? Had the Pharisees forgotten that the very reason Jesus was a wanted man was that he had said "that God was his own Father and in this way had made himself equal with God" (5:18)? It is not likely. The intent of the narrative is rather to dramatize the Pharisees' ignorance of what it *means* for God to be Jesus' Father, that is, their ignorance of all that Jesus taught in 5:19–47. That earlier discourse, though clear and decisive to the readers of the Gospel, was lost on its immediate hearers. A monologue from beginning to end, it is intended by the narrator more for Jesus' followers and would-be followers than for the Jewish authorities. The Temple discourse, on the other hand, is punctuated by sharp exchanges between Jesus and his opponents. Because it aims at actual communication within the actual literary setting, the breakdowns in communication, when they occur, are painfully evident—as, for example, in the Pharisees' question, **Where is your father?** (v. 19).

The Pharisees are not here questioning the legitimacy of Jesus' birth, as some commentators have suggested, but responding to his mention of the scriptural principle that two witnesses are necessary to validate a statement in court (v. 17; cf. Deut. 19:15). There *are* two witnesses, Jesus says: He himself is one, and his Father is the other (vv. 16, 18). **Where is your father?** is the Pharisees' challenge to Jesus to bring on this second witness. They have not yet grasped the point that the second witness speaks not as an identifiable external entity but only through Jesus himself (cf. 5:31–40). To hear Jesus is to hear the second witness as well. To know him is to know his Father. But Jesus' grim verdict in the present case is that **you know neither me nor my Father** (v. 19). The summary statement that "Jesus said all this as he taught in the Temple" (8:20) corrésponds in form to the ending of the synagogue discourse two chapters earlier ("Jesus said this as he taught in the synagogue in Capernaum," 6:59) and so gives the impression that the Temple discourse is now concluded. In fact, the discourse continues to the end of the chapter. What is concluded is merely one stage of the debate between Jesus and the Pharisees, in the Court of Women on the eighth day of the festival. The allusion in verse 20 to the offering boxes (and thus, implicitly, to the Court of the Women) suggests that the festival is now over, yet Jesus does not leave the Temple until verse 59. At some point in the collection of this material, verse 20 may have served to terminate the Temple discourse, but the small word **again** (v. 21; cf. v. 12) allows the Gospel writer to append further discussions probably remembered in connection with the same visit of Jesus to Jerusalem. The seams that are now and then visible in the fabric of the narrative only highlight the Gospel writer's intention to weave a single continous account of Jesus' Temple ministry from 7:14 to 8:59.

The festival ends with Jesus still at large. The Pharisees are no more able to arrest him than the guards they sent out earlier, for still **his hour had not come** (v. 20).

Additional Notes

7:37 / **On the last and most important day of the festival**: The last day of the festival proper was the seventh day, but the eighth day was a distinct celebration in its own right, a time to rejoice and sing the Hallel (i.e., Psalms 113–118). The special festival of the eighth day is discussed at length in the fifth-century midrash, *Pesikta de-Rab Kahana* 28 (ed. W. G. Braude and I. J. Kapstein [Philadelphia: Jewish Publication Society, 1975], pp. 424–44). In the Mishnah (*Sukkah* 4.8) the eighth day is called "the last Festival-day of the Feast," while Josephus (*Antiquities* 3.245) clearly refers to the Festival of Shelters as an eight-day festival. These considerations suggest that v. 37 indeed refers to the eighth day, which, if not most important to everyone, was at any rate a day set apart from all other days for special observance.

7:38 / **As the scripture says**: The passage of scripture being cited remains unidentified. On the assumption that Jesus himself is the source of the water, two of the commonest suggestions have been Ps. 78:16 ("He caused a stream to come out of the rock and made water flow like a river"—referring to the incident described in Exod. 17:1–17) and Zech. 14:8 ("When that day comes [i.e., the day of the Lord], fresh water will flow from Jerusalem, half of it to the Dead Sea and the other half to the Mediterranean"; cf. also Ezek. 47:1–12, and the NT use of this theme in Rev. 22:1–2). A metaphorical identification of Jesus either with the life-giving rock in the Sinai desert (cf. 1 Cor. 10:4) or with the city of Jerusalem itself and its Temple, must be presupposed.

On the assumption that the believer is the source of the water, suggestions include Prov. 18:4; Isa. 58:11; and especially (in the Apocrypha) Sir. 24:28–31: "Now I, like a rivulet from her [wisdom's] stream, channeling the waters into a garden, said to myself, 'I will water my plants, my flower bed I will drench'; and suddenly this rivulet of mine became a river, then this stream of mine, a sea. Thus do I send my teachings forth shining like the dawn, to become known afar off. Thus do I pour out instruction like prophecy" (NAB).

None of these texts comes close to providing a source for any kind of exact quotation. It is likely that the passage Jesus (or the Gospel writer) had in mind contained the striking phrase, **from the heart** (Gr.: *ek tēs koilias autou;* lit. "out of his stomach," or "from within him"), and there is no biblical passage that combines this phrase with the imagery of streams of water. Justin Martyr in the second century (*Dialogue with Trypho* 135.3) identified Christians as "the true Israelite race" because they were "quarried from the heart" [Gr.: *ek tēs koilias*] of Christ like rock from the heart of the earth (cf. also *Dialogue* 114.4). It may be that both he and John were aware of already existing applications to Christ of such texts as Zech. 14:8, Ezek. 47:1–12, and Ps. 78:16, and that John is quoting just such a Christian midrash, or paraphrase, as his **scripture.**

7:40–41 / The Prophet . . . the Messiah: cf. 1:20–21. The real dispute is not between those who say Jesus is the Prophet foretold in Deut. 18:15–18 and those who say he is the Messiah descended from David but between both groups and those who protest that **the Messiah will not come from Galilee.**

7:50 / One of the Pharisees there was Nicodemus. Nicodemus is introduced more abruptly into the conversation than this translation suggests (lit.: "Nicodemus said to them—he who came to him earlier, being one of them—"Does our Law . . .?"

7:52 / No prophet: Every tribe in Israel had had its prophets (cf. Babylonian Talmud, *Sukkah* 27b), and it was not strictly true that no prophets had come from Galilee (Jonah, e.g., came from Gath-hepher in Galilee, 2 Kings 14:25). Because of this, the reading of the GNB margin (**the Prophet**, based on one very early papyrus manuscript, P[66]) is an attractive one, for it would create a parallel with v. 41: **The Prophet**, since he is in fact the Messiah, will not come from Galilee but from Bethlehem in Judea. But there is no evidence that in Jewish expectation there was such a complete merging of the Mosaic Prophet with the Davidic messianic king. More likely, the Pharisees are saying that a prophet is not arising out of Galilee *now*, i.e., this Galilean called Jesus is no true prophet.

8:1–11 / This section (designated as 7:53–8:11 in standard editions of the Greek text and in most English versions) is not found in the earliest manuscripts, and therefore cannot be regarded as an original part of John's Gospel. Most of the later manuscripts that do contain the passage place it here, but some place it in Luke's Gospel (after 21:38), and some at the end of John's Gospel; one manuscript places it after John 7:36, and in one ancient translation it is found after John 7:44. Though it is undoubtedly a true incident in Jesus' life, the story of the adulteress does not belong in the New Testament and specifically does not belong here, where its presence divides one day's action into two and interrupts the narrator's development of 7:37–8:20. Its more appropriate historical setting is that described in Luke 21:37–38, in which Jesus, during the last week of his ministry, spent his nights on the Mount of Olives and his days teaching in the Temple (cf. vv. 1–2), answering questions from the Pharisees and chief priests about the Law.

This helps explain why some late manuscripts insert the passage after Luke 21:38 but not why so many more place it here. Two factors seem to have been at work in this: (*a*) The story illustrates with respect to one woman Jesus' statement to the Pharisees in 8:15: **You make judgments in a purely human way; I pass judgment on no one** (cf. v. 11). (*b*) At the same time it illumines the Johannine theme that judgment nevertheless emerges from Jesus' ministry. By refusing to condemn the adulteress, he condemns the religious establishment before which she stands accused. This implicit theme of judgment on Jerusalem and the Temple may be what impelled later copyists to place the story within the Temple discourse at the Festival of Shelters. Even the detail that it was **the older ones** [or "the elders"] **first** who were put to shame recalls the ancient example of judgment on Jerusalem's first Temple in Ezek. 9:6 (where the "leaders" who are judged first are literally the "elders" of Israel).

8:17 / **Your Law**: It is sometimes urged that Jesus is represented as speaking here as if he himself were not a Jew (cf. the same phrase in 10:34 and the phrase "their Law" in 15:25). This is said to reflect the Gentile, even anti-Jewish, perspective of the author of this Gospel.

Two other factors, however, more plausibly explain Jesus' language in these places. (*a*) The pronouns strengthen his argument by making it *ad hominem*. Jesus' opponents are refuted by the very scripture that they themselves acknowledge and proclaim to be true; the fact that Jesus also acknowledges it is assumed but is not crucial to the argument. (*b*) Jesus may be speaking in the style of OT prophets who at times, in the name of God, stood over against Israel and pronounced judgment on Israel's institutions (e.g., Isa. 1:13: "*your* offerings . . . *your* New Moon festivals, *your* Sabbaths . . . *your* religious gatherings").

8:20 / **In the room where the offering boxes were placed**: lit., "in the treasury." The reference is not to the actual chambers used to store the Temple treasure but probably to the place of access to these chambers, i.e., the Court of the Women (so called to distinguish it from the holy precincts where sacrifices were offered and women were not permitted). Because the Court of the Women was where the candle-lighting ceremony of the eighth day took place (cf. the Mishnah, *Sukkah* 5.2), it is the natural setting for the accompanying discourse.

The fact that it is called the treasury rather than the Court of the Women may simply echo other narratives in which "the treasury" is the scene of Jesus' Temple ministry (e.g., Mark 12:41–44 and Luke 21:1–4, where contributions to the treasury actually figure in the story).

22

Jesus and the Unbelievers

Again Jesus said to them, "I will go away; you will look for me, but you will die in your sins. You cannot go where I am going." ²²So the Jewish authorities said, "He says that we cannot go where he is going. Does this mean that he will kill himself?" ²³Jesus answered, "You belong to this world here below, but I come from above. You are from this world, but I am not from this world. ²⁴That is why I told you that you will die in your sins. And you will die in your sins if you do not believe that 'I Am Who I Am'." ²⁵"Who are you?" they asked him.

Jesus answered, "What I have told you from the very beginning.ˢ ²⁶I have much to say about you, much to condemn you for. The one who sent me, however, is truthful, and I tell the world only what I have heard from him." ²⁷They did not understand that Jesus was talking to them about the Father. ²⁸So he said to them, "When you lift up the Son of Man, you will know that 'I Am Who I Am'; then you will know that I do nothing on my own authority, but I say only what the Father has instructed me to say. ²⁹And he who sent me is with me; he has not left me alone, because I always do what pleases him."

s. What I have told you from the very beginning; or Why should I speak to you at all?

Verses 21–29 serve to document Jesus' indictment of the Pharisees in verse 19, "You know neither me nor my Father." The Father is Jesus' past, and his future. Jesus has come from God and is going to God again, but his hearers understand neither of these things. The earlier bewilderment about where Jesus is going (cf. 7:32–36) is echoed here as well (vv. 21–22), but with the somber added note that **you will die in your sins** (v. 21). His words should be taken not as an absolute pronouncement of doom but as a warning. The Jewish authorities (like everyone else) will die in their sins *if* they **do not believe that "I Am Who I Am"** (v. 24). The reverse side of this warning is the promise of life in verse 51: Whoever obeys my teaching will never die. Even in the nearer context, Jesus can speak more positively: **When you lift up the Son of Man, you will know that "I Am Who I Am"** (v. 28).

Which is it then? Will they die in their sins, or will they come to believe in Jesus and know who he is? The dialogue presupposes the same gulf between the world below and the world above that governed the conversation with Nicodemus in chapter 3. The Jewish authorities **belong to this world** (v. 23) and cannot begin to understand Jesus without a new birth from above. When he says he is going away where they cannot follow, they can only think he is planning suicide (v. 22)! Yet just as a similar misunderstanding had earlier pointed to the profound truth of a mission to the Gentiles (7:35), so here the mention of suicide points forward to Jesus' voluntary death on a cross to take away sin. Not until they **lift up the Son of Man** on that cross will they know who Jesus is and realize that he has spoken the very words of God (v. 28). The reference to a future moment of understanding only serves to accent their present ignorance. **Who are you**? they ask Jesus (v. 25), and are told that **from the very beginning** of his ministry he has been making himself known, if only they would listen (v. 25). There is much he could say now in condemnation, but Jesus refuses to be drawn into bitter argument (v. 26). His intention is rather to deliver the message the Father has given him (vv. 26, 28b).

Insofar as this revelation is a self-revelation, it centers on the strange phrase, **I Am Who I Am** (vv. 24, 28). Literally, the phrase in Greek (*egō eimi*) is "I Am" with no predicate (cf. v. 58). Is a predicate to be supplied from the context—for example, in verse 24, "I am from above," or in verse 28, "I am the Son of Man"? Or does the point of the self-disclosure lie precisely in the *absence* of a predicate, as suggested by the translation **I Am Who I Am**? The latter is more likely. Jesus' identity is not linked to a particular predicate but emerges from all his words and actions up to this point in the Gospel. What the hearers must accept, and what the "lifting up" on the cross will verify, is that he is in fact who he claims (explicitly and implicitly) to be.

Additional Notes

8:25 / **What I have told you from the very beginning**: The Greek is obscure (lit., "the beginning, what I speak to you"). It has been translated "Primarily just what I tell you" and even (as a question) "Why do I speak to you at all?" One ancient papyrus has a longer reading: "I told you in the beginning what I speak to you now," and although this reading is probably not original, it may represent an early paraphrase that captured the intended meaning (the GNB rendering suggests this, as does the NIV: "Just what I have been claiming all along").

8:28 / **When you lift up the Son of Man**: For "lifting up" as an allusion to crucifixion, cf. 3:14. The apparent implication that the Jewish authorities themselves crucified Jesus is surprising in light of 18:31 (which seems to focus on crucifixion as a *Roman* method of execution) but the present passage anticipates, instead, 19:16: "Then Pilate handed Jesus over to them [the Jewish priests] to be crucified." The assumption is that *in some sense* the Jewish authorities (though not the Jewish people) did crucify Jesus.

You will know . . . then you will know: Alongside the striking claim that the Jewish leaders themselves would crucify the Son of Man is an equally surprising note of hope. As a result of Jesus' death, they will come to realize who he is and on whose authority he speaks. The emphasis, however, is not on the faith or repentance of these religious leaders in particular but simply on the fact that Jesus and his claims will be vindicated before the whole world by what happens after he is "lifted up" (i.e., by his subsequent resurrection).

Though this vindication is future, the verse as a whole (together with v. 29) intends primarily to affirm something about the present: Jesus is who he is *now*; he does nothing on his own, but speaks *now* what the Father has instructed him; God is with him, and he lives to please God now and always.

8:29 / **He has not left me alone, because I always do what pleases him**. The argument of the previous section that in the words of Jesus both the Father and the Son speak is here presupposed and continued (cf. v. 16). The reason Jesus is not alone is that he does what pleases the Father (cf. 4:34; 5:30; 6:38). The same terminology is used of Christian believers in 1 John 3:22.

23

Jesus and Those Who "Believed"

JOHN 8:30–59

Many who heard Jesus say these things believed in him. [31]So Jesus said to those who believed in him, "If you obey my teaching, you are really my disciples; [32]you will know the truth, and the truth will set you free."

[33]"We are the descendants of Abraham," they answered, "and we have never been anybody's slaves. What do you mean, then, by saying, 'You will be free'?"

[34]Jesus said to them, "I am telling you the truth: everyone who sins is a slave of sin. [35]A slave does not belong to a family permanently, but a son belongs there forever. [36]If the Son sets you free, then you will be really free. [37]I know you are Abraham's descendants. Yet you are trying to kill me, because you will not accept my teaching. [38]I talk about what my Father has shown me, but you do what your father has told you."

[39]They answered him, "Our father is Abraham."

"If you really were Abraham's children," Jesus replied, "you would do[t] the same things that he did. [40]All I have ever done is to tell you the truth I heard from God, yet you are trying to kill me. Abraham did nothing like this! [41]You are doing what your father did."

"God himself is the only Father we have," they answered, "and we are his true sons."

[42]Jesus said to them, "If God really were your Father, you would love me, because I came from God and now I am here. I did not come on my own authority, but he sent me. [43]Why do you not understand what I say? It is because you cannot bear to listen to my message. [44]You are the children of your father, the Devil, and you want to follow your father's desires. From the very beginning he was a murderer and has never been on the side of truth, because there is no truth in him. When he tells a lie, he is only doing what is natural to him, because he is a liar and the father of all lies. [45]But I tell the truth, and that is why you do not believe me. [46]Which one of you can prove that I am guilty of sin? If I tell the truth, then why do you not believe me? [47]He who comes from God listens to God's words. You, however, are not from God, and that is why you will not listen."

[48]They asked Jesus, "Were we not right in saying that you are a Samaritan and have a demon in you?"

[49]"I have no demon," Jesus answered. "I honor my Father, but you dishonor me. [50]I am not seeking honor for myself. But there is one who is seeking it and who judges in my favor. [51]I am telling you the truth: whoever obeys my teaching will never die."

⁵²They said to him, "Now we know for sure that you have a demon! Abraham died, and the prophets died, yet you say that whoever obeys your teaching will never die. ⁵³Our father Abraham died; you do not claim to be greater than Abraham, do you? And the prophets also died. Who do you think you are?"

⁵⁴Jesus answered, "If I were to honor myself, that honor would be worth nothing. The one who honors me is my Father—the very one you say is your God. ⁵⁵You have never known him, but I know him. If I were to say that I do not know him, I would be a liar like you. But I do know. him, and I obey his word. ⁵⁶Your father Abraham rejoiced that he was to see the time of my coming; he saw it and was glad."

⁵⁷They said to him, "You are not even fifty years old—and you have seen Abraham?"ᵘ

⁵⁸"I am telling you the truth," Jesus replied. "Before Abraham was born, 'I Am'."

⁵⁹Then they picked up stones to throw at him, but Jesus hid himself and left the Temple.

t. If you really were . . . you would do: *some manuscripts have* If you . . . do. u. you have seen Abraham?; *some manuscripts have* has Abraham seen you?

T he reaction of many of the Jewish authorities with whom Jesus has been speaking is to believe in him (v. 30), and the remainder of the discourse is focused on this group of "believers." The prediction that they will realize later who Jesus is (v. 28) appears to be coming true even *before* they lift him up on the cross. It sounds, and it is, too good to be true. Their faith is not genuine (cf. 2:23–25). Jesus has directed their attention toward the future, but they will have none of it. The present is good enough for these "believers," and they are satisfied with their present relationship to God.

To become real disciples, they need time. Only by continued obedience to Jesus' message can they **know the truth** and know what it is to be free (vv. 31–32). The mention of freedom offends them with its implication that they are not already free. As Abraham's descendants, they are proud of having **never been anybody's slaves** (v. 33). Jesus explains that he is using slavery as a metaphor for sin and death (vv. 34–36). Descendants of Abraham or not, they are subject to death like everyone else and, in that sense, slaves (cf. Heb. 2:14–15). Jesus' promise to set them free is a promise of life, an alternative to the grim prospect of dying in their sins (cf. vv. 21, 24). Verse 51 will make the promise explicit without the use of metaphor: **I am telling you the truth: whoever obeys my teaching will never die.**

Two themes—the interplay of life and death, and the significance of being descended from Abraham—are the issues that will drive Jesus and the Jewish "believers" further and further apart and trigger the confrontation with which the Temple discourse comes to an end (v. 59). The descent of these "believers" from Abraham is not in question (v. 37), but their conduct belies their heritage. Physically they are Abraham's descendants, Jesus admits, but neither ethically nor spiritually are they Abraham's children.

Once again Jesus charges that his hearers are trying to kill him (vv. 37, 40), this time in a context in which his identity is known (contrast 7:19). If their behavior means anything, Abraham is not their father; if he were, they **would do the same things that he did** (v. 39). Their deeds give evidence of a very different parentage (v. 41). Jesus links the theme of life and death with that of truth and lies, and both of these with the ancient conflict between God and the Devil (vv. 42–47). God is the giver of life, who through Jesus makes his truth known in the world. The Devil is the source of death, a murderer **from the very beginning** and the **father of all lies**. The references are to the snake's denial of God's truth in the Garden of Eden (Gen. 3:4) and to Cain's murder of Abel, his brother (Gen. 4:8; cf. 1 John 3:12). Death and falsehood go together as surely as life and truth do. When Jesus charges that **you are trying to kill me**, he has in mind simply his hearers' refusal to accept his teaching, **the truth I heard from God** (vv. 37, 40). He equates this **lie** with attempted murder because lies and murder come from the same source and because the one leads inevitably to the other (v. 44). His words are vindicated at the end of the chapter when the "believers" are said to have **picked up stones to throw at him** (v. 59). Though murder was not their intention at the start, Jesus' words uncover the real import of their actions and attitudes. Their inability to hear God's words from the lips of Jesus proves that they belong not to God but to the Devil and are acting out the Devil's intentions (v. 47).

The angry "believers" now grope for the ugliest names they can think of to call Jesus: He is a Samaritan (cf. 4:9) and demon possessed (cf. 7:20). These are not measured charges made to stand up in court, but momentary expressions of rage. Jesus leaves his defense, and the passing of judgment on his adversaries, in the hands of his Father (vv. 49–50) and returns to his initial promise of eternal life to those who obey his teaching (v. 51; cf. vv. 31–32). It is like reopening an old wound. Once more Jesus' claim is rejected by means of an appeal to Abraham (v. 52; cf. v. 33). For Jesus to pretend to give life so that **whoever obeys your teaching will never die** is to put himself ahead of even Abraham and the prophets (vv. 52–53). Life and death are here conceived in purely physical terms, as if Jesus is promising exemption from physical death.

Without pausing to correct the misunderstanding, Jesus addresses the question **Who do you think you are**? (v. 53). His answer in verses 54 and 55 counters the appeal to Abraham with an appeal to God Himself, the supreme Life-giver and Judge of all. But he adds, **Your father Abraham rejoiced that he was to see the time of my coming** [*lit.*, "see my day"]; **he saw it and was glad** (v. 56). Just as there is a specific allusion in 1:51 to Jacob's Bethel experience (Gen. 28:12), it is natural to look for something specific here as well. The apparent reference is to the promise Abraham received that from his offspring blessing would come to the whole world (Gen. 12:1–3). The promise is assumed to be fulfilled in Jesus (cf. Gal. 3:16), but the beginning of its realization is the birth of Isaac and his deliverance from premature death (Gen. 18, 22). It is probably in connection with one or both of these events that Abraham is understood to have seen Jesus' day. The narrator may even have in mind the specific moment when "Abraham looked around and saw a ram caught in a bush by its horns" and knew that his son was spared (Gen. 22:13); this incident was regarded by some early Christian interpreters as pointing to the death of Jesus the Lamb of God (e.g., by Melito of Sardis, in his *Eclogues*; see R. M. Grant, *Second Century Christianity* [London: S. P. C. K., 1957], p. 72).

In an apparently deliberate misunderstanding, the hostile "believers" respond as if Jesus had said that he had seen Abraham, instead of that Abraham had seen his day (v. 57). Their effort to make his claim sound absurd succeeds only in displaying their own willful ignorance. But Jesus' reply is serious, and decisive: **I am telling you the truth . . . Before Abraham was born, "I Am"** (v. 58). With these words, Jesus goes beyond all his previous claims. He *has* seen Abraham; he was alive in Abraham's time, and long before. It is as if the earlier instances of the "I Am" formula (i.e., 4:26; 6:20; 8:24, 28) have been waiting for this one for their deepest meaning. In contrast to them all, there is no content that can be supplied either from the nearer or more remote context: for example, that he is the Messiah, or the Son of Man, or the One from above, or everything that he has claimed to be. He simply *is*. **I Am** in this case is *God's* formula of self-disclosure, just as it is in the Hebrew scriptures (Heb.: *ani hu*, lit., "I he," but normally translated into Greek as *egō eimi*, or "I am"). The formula is clustered especially in Isaiah 40–55, where God uses it to proclaim his uniqueness as Israel's covenant Lord, faithful to his promises and strong to deliver and restore his people (e.g., Isa. 41:4; 43:10–13, 25; 45:18–19; 48:12; 52:6; cf. Deut. 32:39). Its use implies a radical and unqualified monotheism: "Besides me there is no other god; there never was and never will be" (Isa. 43:10b); "there is no other god"

(Isa. 45:18); "no other god is real" (Deut. 32:39). For anyone else to use this formula in the same way was blasphemy (Isa. 47:8; Zeph. 2:15). Here for the first time, the implications of Jesus' use of this formula came through to his hearers; in reaction **they picked up stones to throw at him** (v. 59). There is no doubt that they understood Jesus to be speaking with the voice of God, as if he himself were "the God of Abraham, Isaac, and Jacob" (cf. Exod. 3:6).

The use of the "I Am" form in relation to Abraham recalls Jesus' dispute with the Sadducees in the synoptic Gospels, where he defended the belief in a future resurrection (Mark 12:18–27 and parallels). Jesus' argument on that occasion was that God had said to Moses, "I am the God of Abraham, the God of Isaac, and the God of Jacob," and that God was "the God of the living, not of the dead" (Mark 12:27 and Matt. 22:33; Luke 20:38 explains, "for to him all are alive"). Here in John's Gospel it is Jesus himself who both makes the "I Am" statement and claims to be the giver of life (v. 51). It is not to be assumed that the statement, **Abraham died** (vv. 52–53) necessarily represents the viewpoint of the narrator or Jesus, at least not if it implies death's usual finality. Jesus' opponents, wrong about everything else, are wrong about this as well. He who existed before Abraham and promises eternal life to believers is the source of life and hope even for Abraham himself, and for the prophets. The God of Abraham, and of Isaac and Jacob, is Jesus; he is the only giver of life, and Lord of the resurrection (cf. 5:21, 25, 28). Only Jesus can promise his followers, "I will raise them to life at the last day" (6:39–40; 6:44, 54), and in this passage even Abraham and the prophets are numbered among his followers. The Temple discourse, like the synagogue discourse of chapter 6, ends on the note that God's life is available to human beings only through trust in Jesus and obedience to his teaching.

The self-disclosure is now complete. As for the immediate hearers, their response is marked by neither trust nor obedience. The "believers" of verses 30–31 are unmasked as unbelievers, once and for all. To them, Jesus' claim of identity with the God of Abraham is blasphemy. Their attempted stoning of Jesus is a natural and inevitable reaction, ironically fulfilling what Jesus said was their intent all along. They had tried to kill him (cf. 7:19; 8:37, 40), first by rejecting his message, but now literally. Their attempt on his life fails, just as earlier attempts to arrest him had failed (cf. 7:30, 44). The manner of his escape is not told; mysteriously he **hid himself and left the Temple** (v. 59b). He had come out of hiding to make himself known at the Temple during the Festival of Shelters, and now he goes back in hiding again.

Additional Notes

8:31 / **Those who believed in him**: lit., "the Jews who believed him." The grammatical construction is different from v. 30 (i.e., "believe" followed by a dative, rather than by a preposition designating Jesus as the object of their faith). But in context the two constructions are (as the GNB suggests) equivalents. In this Gospel, to believe *in* Jesus is to believe what he says, and believing his message means believing *in* him as God's messenger. There is no way v. 31 can be made to refer to a less adequate kind of faith than v. 30. In neither verse is it possible to tell from the language that the faith in view is not genuine, even though subsequent events demonstrate that in fact it is not (cf. 2:23–25).

8:31–32 / **If you obey my teaching, you are really my disciples; you will know the truth, and the truth will set you free**. Cf. Jesus' words in his farewell discourse to those who *were* genuinely his disciples: "My Father's glory is shown by your bearing much fruit; and in this way you become my disciples" (15:8); "I no longer speak of you as slaves, for a slave does not know what his master is about. Instead, I call you friends, since I have made known to you all that I heard from my Father" (15:15, NAB). Note that in the latter passage freedom, in contrast to slavery, is defined by knowledge of the truth that Jesus brings, just as it is here.

8:33 / **We have never been anybody's slaves**. The proud spirit of Jewish independence that brought about the Jewish revolt in A.D. 70 can be heard in this pronouncement. The irony sensed by the narrator and his readers is that Israel had lost her independence to Rome almost a century before this statement was made and still had not regained it when the Gospel was written. Though not exactly in slavery, Israel was by no means free of foreign domination.

8:34 / **A slave of sin**: The words **of sin** are missing in a few ancient manuscripts and versions. It is not hard to see why some ancient scribes omitted these words. The emphasis of the verse is on the metaphor of slavery as such, not on that to which one is enslaved. But the stronger manuscript evidence favors the longer reading. The slavery here is to sin, just as it is in Paul's letters (e.g., Rom. 6:16, 20). Sin functions as a middle term between the metaphor (slavery) and the reality (death). Jesus' next pronouncement, "A slave does not belong to a family permanently" (v. 35a), carries forward the metaphor in that it realistically describes a typical household in Jesus' time, yet it also provides a theological interpretation: "slavery" here means death. The Son (i.e., Jesus), on the contrary, has eternal life (v. 35b) and gives that life to those who are dying. In that sense he sets people free (v. 36).

8:38 / **My Father . . . your father**: There are no possessive pronouns in the Greek. An explicit contrast between Jesus' Father (God) and his opponents' father (the Devil) is not introduced until v. 41. It is therefore likely that God is the only Father being referred to in this verse: "I am telling you what I have seen in the Father's presence. Therefore do what you have heard from the Father" (NIV margin).

This translation is supported by the word *oun* ("therefore") in the Greek text. It assumes that the last verb **do** (Gr.: *poieite*) should be taken as an imperative rather than an indicative. Jesus is making one last appeal to his opponents to accept his words as words from God the Father, and put them into practice. But his opponents' answer (v. 39) demonstrates that their Abrahamic descent is more important to them than Jesus' appeal on his Father's behalf.

8:39 / **If you really were . . . you would do**: Some ancient manuscripts continue the note of appeal by making the second verb in this sentence an imperative: **If you are Abraham's children, do** (GNB margin). But the beginning of the following verse in Greek ("*But now* you are trying to kill me") makes it clear that the conditional sentence in v. 39 is contrary to fact: If the opponents were true children of Abraham, they would do what Abraham did, but in fact they are not. Grammatically, the first verb is present tense where an imperfect might have been expected. The effect of this is to heighten the supposition of reality, an effect that the GNB translators have achieved with their rendering, **If you really were . . .**

The same things that he did: lit., "the works of Abraham" (cf. James 2:21–23). In James the reference is to Abraham's willingness to offer up his son Isaac as a sacrifice (Gen. 22:1–14), but here Jesus apparently has in mind Abraham's warm welcome of God's messengers (Gen. 18:1–8). It is to this that he contrasts the hostile behavior of Abraham's self-proclaimed "children" (v. 40).

8:44 / **The children of your father, the Devil**: lit., "you are of the father, the Devil," or even "you are of the father of the Devil" (!). The end of the verse (**he is a liar and the father of all lies**) could also conceivably be read as a reference to the Devil's father (i.e., "even his father is a liar"). Such possibilities may have provided a basis for later Gnostic speculation about the Devil's origins, but in the absence of any such speculations elsewhere in John's Gospel or Epistles, it is virtually certain that the meaning implied by the GNB translation is correct. The first clause of the verse might be paraphrased, "You are 'of the Father,' all right, but your 'Father' is the Devil!" The last clause is lit., "he is a liar, and the father of it" (i.e., of the first lie, "you will not die,"in Gen. 3:4, and therefore all subsequent lies).

8:52 / **Abraham died, and the prophets died**. The statement superficially recalls Jesus' own words in 6:49 ("Your ancestors . . . died," cf. 6:58), but its function in the narrative is different. In chap. 6, Jesus' implication was that God had judged the generation that long ago died in the desert (cf. 1 Cor. 10:5), while those who ate the Bread of life Jesus now offered would live forever. Those who died, he told his opponents, were "your ancestors." Here, however, Jesus' point is that his opponents are *not* Abraham's true descendants (cf. v. 39), nor are they children of the prophets. The pronouncement that Abraham and the prophets are dead is *their* pronouncement, not that of Jesus or of the narrator. The righteous have seen Jesus' day—and they will live! (cf. v. 56, Mark 12:27; note also that Abraham is assumed to be alive in God's presence in Luke 16:22–31).

For an example of Judaism's struggle with the notion that even such a great man as Abraham finally had to face physical death, see *The Testament of Abraham*, trans. M. E. Stone (Missoula, Mont.: Society of Biblical Literature, 1972).

8:56 / **Your father Abraham**: Contrast v. 39, where Jesus denies that Abraham is their father. Here in *ad hominem* fashion, he mockingly throws their own claim in their face (cf. v. 54; "my Father—the very one you say is your God").

See the time of my coming: Ancient Jewish literature testifies to the belief that God revealed "the end of the times" to Abraham (4 Ezra 3:14; cf. also the late rabbinic commentary Genesis Rabbah 44, 22 [*Midrash Rabbah* I (London: Soncino Press, 1961), p. 376] on Gen. 15:18). The reference here, however, is probably not to Abraham's vision in Gen. 15 but to the promise of a son and to the birth and deliverance of the promised offspring.

8:57 / **Not even fifty years old**: It is precarious to argue from this round number, as some have done, that Jesus was approaching fifty years of age (e.g., Irenaeus, *Against Heresies* 1.22.6) or that he looked almost that old (according to Luke 3:23 he was "about thirty years old" when he began his ministry). Compared to the many centuries since Abraham, even an overly generous fifty-year span sounded like only a moment and served well to make the point.

24

The Man Born Blind

JOHN 9:1–12

As Jesus was walking along, he saw a man who had been born blind. ²His disciples asked him, "Teacher, whose sin caused him to be born blind? Was it his own or his parents' sin?"

³Jesus answered, "His blindness has nothing to do with his sins or his parents' sins. He is blind so that God's power might be seen at work in him. ⁴As long as it is day, we must do the work of him who sent me; night is coming when no one can work. ⁵While I am in the world, I am the light for the world."

⁶After he said this, Jesus spat on the ground and made some mud with the spittle; he rubbed the mud on the man's eyes ⁷and told him. "Go and wash your face in the Pool of Siloam." (This name means "Sent.") So the man went, washed his face, and came back seeing.

⁸His neighbors, then, and the people who had seen him begging before this, asked, "Isn't this the man who used to sit and beg?"

⁹Some said, "He is the one," but others said, "No he isn't; he just looks like him."

So the man himself said, "I am the man."

¹⁰"How is it that you can now see?" they asked him.

¹¹He answered, "The man called Jesus made some mud, rubbed it on my eyes, and told me to go to Siloam and wash my face. So I went, and as soon as I washed, I could see."

¹²"Where is he?" they asked.

"I don't know," he answered.

The Temple discourse is over, but Jesus' ministry in Jerusalem continues with no discernible break in the narrative. Having escaped death by stoning, Jesus "left the Temple" (8:59) and, while **walking along** (apparently just outside the sacred precincts), noticed **a man who had been born blind** (v. 1). Despite the smooth transition, it is clear that a new chapter, indeed a new division in the structure of the Gospel, is under way. Jesus' disciples, out of the picture since the end of chapter 6, are with him again (v. 2), and once more Jesus will assume the role of miracle-worker. The healing of the man born blind gives rise to a series of investigations by the religious authorities (vv. 13–34) and finally to the blind man's confession of faith (vv. 35–41) and a new discourse in which Jesus confronts the authorities for the last time with the word of God (chap. 10).

A question from the disciples begins the sequence. The feature of the blind man's predicament that attracted their attention was the fact that he had been blind *from birth*. This fact may have been generally known, or it may have been obvious to onlookers from the man's appearance. In any case, it was this aspect of the man's situation that was thought to require an explanation. Assuming that congenital blindness was a punishment of some kind, was it punishment for the man's own sins or for the sins of his parents? (v. 2). The traditional Jewish notion, "Surely I have been a sinner from birth, sinful from the time my mother conceived me" (Ps. 51:7, NIV) surfaces here in the disciples' initial question and again in the Pharisees' verdict on the man at the end of their series of interrogations (v. 34). Even though Jesus rejects the alternatives posed by the question and shifts the focus from the *cause* (i.e., origin) of the man's affliction to its *purpose* (v. 3), the fact that the man was not only blind but **born blind** remains a highlight of the narrative. This is what sets the story apart from all the synoptic accounts of the giving of sight to the blind (Mark 8:22–26; 10:46–52 and parallels; Matt. 9:27–31). If a man is blind from birth, then the restoring of his sight is nothing less than a new birth. The incident becomes a case study in the experience of which Jesus had told Nicodemus: "No one can see the Kingdom of God unless he is born again." "No one can enter the Kingdom of God unless he is born of water and the Spirit" (3:3, 5).

The blindness of this man, Jesus says, is not the result of someone's sin but the occasion for God's work in his life to be displayed. Like the person mentioned in 3:21 who "comes to the light," the man born blind will demonstrate in his experience that he is God's child. In coming (literally) from darkness to light, he is born again. His story is the case history of a Christian convert. At the beginning he is a beggar and an outcast in the old community of Judaism, and at the end he is a worshiper of Jesus (v. 38). Issues raised theologically in chapter 3 but not resolved with reference to Nicodemus are acted out in the story of the blind man. Though divine election (which shaped the thought of 3:18–21) is not made explicit in the account of the blind man's healing and conversion, it comes to the fore in the theological reflections of chapter 10: The man born blind is one of Jesus' "sheep" because he hears the Shepherd's voice and follows him out of the old community into the new. His response proves that God is *already* at work in his life (cf. 3:21).

This working of God first becomes visible in the work of Jesus. Before he acts, Jesus speaks of the urgency that impels him (vv. 4–5). Earlier he had described this urgency "to obey the will of the one who sent me and to finish the work he gave me to do" as the food that sustained his life (4:34). Here the imagery is that of night and day. Jesus compares his ministry to light in a dark world (cf. 1:9; 3:19; 8:12), a light that like the hours of daylight has its limits and must in time give way to darkness again. Like a laborer determined to finish his job before nightfall, Jesus summons his disciples to join him in taking full advantage of the remaining daylight hours (cf. 11:9–10). It should be remembered that the references to day and night constitute a brief parable about the ministry of Jesus. They do not look beyond it. Elsewhere the Gospel writer can look back on Jesus' ministry with the comment that still "the light shines in the darkness, and the darkness has never put it out" (1:5). From his viewpoint, the time since Jesus' departure from the world is a time for doing "greater things" than he did (14:12), not a time of darkness in which "no one can work." The focus in chapter 9 is on Jesus' impending Passion. The point of verses 4–5 is not that the work of God stops when Jesus' life on earth ends but that Jesus has a certain task assigned to him and a limited time in which to complete it. What he is about to do, therefore, is done under a divine necessity. By including the disciples in that necessity (**we must do the work**, v. 4), Jesus is not so much asking their help with this particular miracle as inviting them to confront with him the approaching reality of the cross. It is an extension of an earlier summons to share in his work (cf. 4:34–38), and it is a summons he will issue several times again before his Passion (cf. 11:7, 15; 12:26; 14:31).

The miracle itself is told simply and briefly (vv. 6–7), setting the pattern for two even briefer repetitions of it by the blind man after his cure (vv. 11, 15). The account recalls the twin stories in Mark's Gospel of the healing of a deaf-mute (Mark 7:31–37) and of a blind man at Bethsaida in Galilee (Mark 8:22–26). In these stories, Jesus does not hesitate to use whatever secondary means are available to bring about healing. In one case he puts two fingers in a man's ears, then spits on his fingers and touches the man's tongue (Mark 7:33); he spits in another man's eyes, puts his hands on him, and afterward touches his eyes again (Mark 8:22, 25). Here he spits on the ground to make a ball of mud that he smears on the man's eyes; then he sends him to the Pool of Siloam to wash the mud away. Such procedures were not uncommon among ancient healers, for saliva (especially when one had been fasting) was believed to have healing properties. Precisely the healing of one's eyes with saliva on the Sabbath was forbidden in the Talmud by some rabbis (*Shabbath* 108a), though the problem over the Sabbath in this case (cf. vv. 14, 16) seems to have arisen because Jesus kneaded the mud into a ball in performing the miracle (the Mishnah, *Shabbath* 7.2, lists "kneading" among thirty-nine activities prohibited on the Sabbath; cf. 24.3).

The narrator's symbolic interpretation of Siloam as **Sent** (v. 7) opens the possibility that the whole procedure described in verses 6–7, vivid and factual though it is, serves a symbolic purpose in the narrative. Irenaeus, writing near the end of the second century, proposed that the "work of God" displayed in these actions of Jesus was nothing less than "the fashioning of man" in the beginning, by which "the Lord took clay from the earth and formed man": what the Word "had omitted to form in the womb"—that is, the man's eyes—he "supplied in public, that the works of God might be manifested in him." Irenaeus uses this to show that the redeemer and Father of Christians is also the world's creator. The washing in Siloam is the "laver of regeneration," the new birth represented by Christian baptism (*Against Heresies* 5.15.2–3; ANF 1.543).

Without insisting on such a direct relationship to Genesis 2:7, one can appreciate this interpretation because of its strong emphasis on new creation or new birth in the story of the blind man. The note that the water by which the man receives his sight is **Sent** (as Jesus is "sent" from God) suggests that the water represents the Holy Spirit. The man born blind is now reborn "of water and the Spirit" (cf. 3:5). The rest of the chapter unfolds all the experiences of a Jewish convert to Christianity: He is born again and baptized; he is questioned by the religious authorities (vv. 13–34); he is finally expelled from the synagogue (v. 34); he confesses his faith in Jesus and worships him as Lord (v. 38).

These things are not, of course, told in the *order* in which they would happen to Christian converts. A person would be expected to confess Jesus as Messiah or Lord *before* receiving baptism, and the interrogations and eventual expulsion from the synagogue would come later. The order of the narrative is determined by the fact that it recounts an actual historical incident. It is not an imaginary story or an allegory. The narrator uses a real incident from the lifetime of Jesus to portray or symbolize several aspects of the experience of Christians from the time of Jesus' resurrection to his own day. The sequence of events is historical, but the point that emerges is theological. It is that God's true children will find their way from the old community to the new even though the transition may not be an easy one.

The transition begins in verses 8–12. The protracted investigation by the Pharisees in verses 13–34 is preceded by a glimpse of his neighbors and those who had seen him earlier as a beggar. After arguing among themselves about the man's identity (vv. 8–9), they confront him directly (vv. 10–12). Was he the same person as the blind beggar they had known before, or wasn't he? Their disagreement recalls certain disputes or "schisms" in the crowd elsewhere in this Gospel over the claims and identity of Jesus himself (e.g., 7:12, 40–43; cf. 9:16; 10:19–21). The man's response (v. 9) is also strangely reminiscent of Jesus. **I am the man**, he says, using the same formula of self-identification that Jesus had used (Gr.: *egō eimi*; lit., "I am"; cf. 6:20; 8:24, 28, 59). These similarities suggest that even though Jesus himself has disappeared from the scene, it is Jesus' power and Jesus' identity that are at stake in the evaluation of this man's experience. In a sense he is Jesus' surrogate in the narrative of verses 8–34 even though he is not yet Jesus' follower. He testifies to what Jesus has done for him (v. 11), and he will doggedly "stick to his story" through a whole series of interrogations. Ironically, he does not know Jesus' whereabouts (v. 12) and (we learn later) fails to recognize him when he sees him.

Additional Notes

9:2 / Was it his own or his parents' sin? Behind the disciples' question is not only the biblical notion that children are sometimes held accountable for the sins of their parents (e.g., Exod. 20:5; discussed and countered in Ezek. 18), but the view proposed by certain rabbis that a child in the womb was already involved in sin (see, e.g., Genesis Rabbah 63, 6[Midrash Rabbah II (London: Soncino Press, 1961), pp. 559–560] based on Gen. 25:22 and Ps. 58:4). It is unlikely that Hellenistic ideas about the pre-existence of the soul contributed to the raising of this question. There is little evidence that such ideas were widely held in Judaism (cf., perhaps, Wisd. 8:20) or that they were used to explain physical misfortune.

9:4 / We . . . him who sent me: There was a tendency in ancient manuscripts to remove the seemingly inappropriate discrepancy between the plural and singular: i.e., either "I must do the work of him who sent me," or "we must do the work of him who sent us." The more difficult reading found in the text is probably correct; the second variant (in which both pronouns are plural) is also difficult, but its wording "him who sent us" is so uncharacteristic of the style of John's Gospel as to make it suspect. "He who sent me" is a fixed Johannine expression, equivalent to "the Father." Its very fixity is what seems to have created the discrepancy between singular and plural in a sentence in which Jesus draws his disciples into the urgency of his own calling.

The plural **we** has the additional effect of giving Jesus' statement a secondary application beyond what he (or probably even the Gospel writer) intended. Christians sometimes apply the text to their own mission in the world between the resurrection of Jesus and his future returning, or Parousia. The **night . . . when no one can work** is then understood as the time after his Parousia, when the mission is complete (cf., e.g., the hymn, "Work, for the Night Is Coming"). But **day** and **night** are not used in that way either in John's Gospel or elsewhere in the NT (to the contrary, cf., e.g., Rom. 13:12; 1 Thess. 5:1-11; 2 Pet. 1:19).

9:5 / **I am the light for the world**. Cf. 8:12. In Matt. 5:14, Jesus uses "light of the world" to describe his disciples. But here, despite the "we" of the preceding verse, the focus is on Jesus in his uniqueness. The light is in the world as long as he continues at work, and the darkness is the hour of his Passion.

9:7 / **(This name means "Sent")**. The etymology of **Siloam** as **Sent** is not artificially created for the sake of the author's symbolism. The water in the pool was, after all, lit. **sent**, or conducted, from the Gihon Spring by way of Hezekiah's tunnel (cf. 2 Kings 20:20; 2 Chron. 32:30; the story is told also by the Siloam Inscription, discovered in the tunnel in 1880 and pictured in R. M. Mackowski, *Jerusalem City of Jesus* [Grand Rapids: Eerdmans, 1980], p. 74). It is uncertain whether or not **sent** (Heb. *shalach*) is the actual derivation of the name **Siloam**. But in any event it is likely that the etymology was already attached to the name when the Gospel was written. The narrator probably took advantage of an existing etymology in order to make a symbolic connection between this pool and the Spirit sent from God (cf. 7:39, in connection with the fact that the water used at the Festival of Shelters was, according to the Mishnah [*Sukkah* 4.9], drawn from this very pool).

25

The Investigation

JOHN 9:13–34

Then they took to the Pharisees the man who had been blind. [14]The day that Jesus made the mud and cured him of his blindness was a Sabbath. [15]The Pharisees, then, asked the man again how he had received his sight. He told them, "He put some mud on my eyes; I washed my face, and now I can see."

[16]Some of the Pharisees said, "The man who did this cannot be from God, for he does not obey the Sabbath law."

Others, however, said, "How could a man who is a sinner perform such miracles as these?" And there was a division among them.

[17]So the Pharisees asked the man once more, "You say he cured you of your blindness—well, what do you say about him?"

"He is a prophet," the man answered.

[18]The Jewish authorities, however, were not willing to believe that he had been blind and could now see, until they called his parents [19]and asked them, "Is this your son? You say that he was born blind; how is it, then, that he can now see?"

[20]His parents answered, "We know that he is our son, and we know that he was born blind. [21]But we do not know how it is that he is now able to see, nor do we know who cured him of his blindness. Ask him; he is old enough, and he can answer for himself!" [22]His parents said this because they were afraid of the Jewish authorities, who had already agreed that anyone who said he believed that Jesus was the Messiah would be expelled from the synagogue. [23]That is why his parents said, "He is old enough; ask him!"

[24]A second time they called back the man who had been born blind, and said to him, "Promise before God that you will tell the truth! We know that this man who cured you is a sinner."

[25]"I do not know if he is a sinner or not," the man replied. "One thing I do know: I was blind, and now I see."

[26]"What did he do to you?" they asked. "How did he cure you of your blindness?"

[27]"I have already told you," he answered, "and you would not listen. Why do you want to hear it again? Maybe you, too, would like to be his disciples?"

[28]They insulted him and said, "You are that fellow's disciple; but we are Moses' disciples. [29]We know that God spoke to Moses; as for that fellow, however, we do not even know where he comes from!"

[30]The man answered, "What a strange thing that is! You do not know where he comes from, but he cured me of my blindness! [31]We know that God does not listen to sinners; he does listen to people who respect him and do what he wants them to do. [32]Since the beginning of the world nobody has ever heard of anyone giving sight to a blind person. [33]Unless this man came from God, he would not be able to do a thing."

---

³⁴They answered, "You were born and brought up in sin—and you are trying to teach us?" And they expelled him from the synagogue.

When their informal interview with the man who had been blind proved inconclusive, his neighbors brought him to the Pharisees (v. 13). The narrator takes the opportunity to add the significant footnote that the miracle happened on a Sabbath. In connection with this, he refers again to the actual procedure Jesus had used (v. 14), for it was this procedure, not the healing itself, that violated the Sabbath law (i.e., the Mishnah, *Shabbath* 7.2). Just as in the case of the Bethzatha healing in chapter 5, the conflict centers on the twin issues of Sabbath breaking and the identity of Jesus (cf. 5:16–18). How is Jesus' unlawful behavior to be reconciled with the notion that he is **from God**? The denial of Jesus' divine origin (v. 16) comes abruptly in the narrative, for Jesus has made no explicit claims for himself in this chapter. The reaction of the Pharisees seems to presuppose to a certain extent the debates of chapters 7 and 8. The Pharisees themselves were divided over Jesus (v. 16), much like the festival crowd in 7:40–43, though the dominant group among them is clearly the group that says he is not from God. Their investigation proceeds in three stages: After their initial interview with the man born blind (vv. 13–17), the Pharisees summoned his parents (vv. 18–23), and when that exchange yielded no answers, they called the man in again for a second round of questioning (vv. 24–34).

As for the man himself, the more he is asked to repeat his story the more his understanding of Jesus grows. To the bystanders he speaks in noncommittal fashion of a **man called Jesus** (v. 11); under formal interrogation he first concludes that Jesus is **a prophet** (v. 17; cf. 4:19); finally, after harsh cross-examination, he throws back at the Pharisees the very phrase with which the controversy began: Jesus is **from God** (v. 33; cf. v. 16). It is this affirmation that gets him expelled from the synagogue (v. 34).

The purpose of questioning the man's parents (vv. 18–23) was to shake, if possible, the testimony implicit in the fact that this man, who now obviously could see, was indeed the Jerusalem beggar known to have been born blind. The identity of this one in whom God's power could be seen at work becomes a clue to the identity of Jesus. The parents were quick to verify the facts of the case (v. 20) but unwilling to venture an explanation. They knew that the question of **how** (vv. 19, 21) was really a question of **who** (v. 21), and they would not discuss Christology. The narrator's explanation (vv. 22–23) suggests that the parents knew (or at least suspected) more than they were telling. The real reason for their silence was not ignorance but fear. The Jewish authorities **had already agreed that anyone who said he believed that Jesus was the Messiah would be expelled from the synagogue** (v. 22). If, as the narrator implies, the parents acted as they did because of this decree, they must have known that their son's healing was the work of Jesus and had a bearing on the issue of his messiahship. Their claim not to know who cured their son (v. 21) was therefore untrue.

To make sense of the parents' action and the accompanying comment, the decree mentioned in verse 22 must be understood against the background of earlier events recorded in this Gospel. Jesus had been wanted by the authorities ever since chapter 5. A crowd in Galilee had proclaimed him "the Prophet who was to come," and had tried to "seize him in order to make him king by force" (6:14–15). At the Festival of Shelters, amid popular speculation over whether he was the Messiah, the guards had tried unsuccessfully to arrest him (7:25–36, 40–52). He was suspected of "misleading the people" (7:13); those who believed in him were called a crowd that "does not know the Law of Moses, so they are under God's curse" (7:49). It comes as no surprise, therefore, when we learn that the authorities tried to rid the synagogue of anyone who claimed to follow Jesus as the Messiah. Their fear of messianic movements is summed up two chapters later at a meeting of the ruling Council: "Look at all the miracles this man [i.e., Jesus, cf. 7:31] is performing! If we let him go on in this way, everyone will believe in him, and the Roman authorities will take action and destroy our Temple and our nation!" (11:48). To confess Jesus as Messiah was politically dangerous; the religious authorities wanted to isolate those who made such a confession so as to avoid giving the Romans the impression that the synagogue was in any way a base for revolutionary activities.

The silence of the man's parents leads to a final confrontation between him and the Pharisees (vv. 24–34). As the exchange goes on, he becomes surer and surer of his ground. First he simply repeats the refrain that **I was blind, and now I see** without making a judgment on the Pharisees' assertion that Jesus is a sinner (v. 25). But he balks at giving the details again: **I have already told you. . . . Why do you want to hear it again? Maybe you, too, would like to be his disciples?** (v. 27). Cursing his sarcasm, the Pharisees bring out what is for the Gospel writer the real issue: They are disciples of Moses, while the man born blind is Jesus' disciple (v. 28). From the writer's perspective, even this is a misunderstanding, for Jesus had said, "If you had really believed Moses, you would have believed me, because he wrote about me" (5:46). Yet the very misunderstanding serves to highlight the situation existing in the writer's own day: There *are* two communities, the disciples of Moses and the disciples of Jesus, each claiming to speak for God. "Judaism" and "Christianity" are becoming distinct, and rival, entities, as the church begins to define itself over against the synagogue.

The Pharisees' words were almost prophetic: The former blind man was in fact transferring his allegiance from one community to the other. But in the same breath, they laid a trap for themselves by admitting that, as far as Jesus was concerned, **we do not even know where he comes from** (v. 29). It was their emphatic way of denying that Jesus was from God (cf. v. 16), but to the man born blind (and to the narrator) it only betrayed their ignorance (cf. 8:14). His last words to them begin on the same note of sarcasm he had used a moment before (v. 30; cf. v. 27) but quickly take a serious turn (vv. 31–33) as he begins to pour out his true convictions. The Pharisees were right: He *is* Jesus' disciple. He is *not* neutral about whether Jesus is a sinner (contrast v. 25). Jesus cannot be a sinner, he concludes, for **God does not listen to sinners** but to those **who respect him and do what he wants them to do** (v. 31). The former blind man attributes his healing to God, with Jesus in the role of intercessor asking God to act. Yet at the same time he can say without hesitation that *Jesus* cured his blindness (vv. 30, 32). His view of miracles coincides perfectly with that of the Gospel writer, and of Jesus as portrayed in this Gospel (cf. 11:41–42). Jesus' works are the works of God (cf. v. 4; 4:34). One cannot assign some miracles to the Father and others to the Son; all that happens redemptively is the work of the Father through the Son (cf. 5:17–29) and can be viewed legitimately from either perspective.

Although the man born blind is spokesman for the absent Jesus throughout this debate and for a theology that bears the implicit endorsement of the narrator, he is nevertheless an individual in his own right. His story is told realistically and with humor. Unlike the sick man of chapter 5, he has personality, a ready wit, and strong convictions. Unlike Nicodemus, he leaves no doubt about what he thinks of Jesus. He is surely one of the most memorable characters in all of the Gospels. His quick, ironic answers (vv. 27, 30), as well as his serious testimony on Jesus' behalf (vv. 31–33), irritated his questioners and pierced their pretensions. In response (ignoring his cure), they simply reverted to the popular notion expressed by Jesus' disciples at the outset of the narrative, that is, that his physical handicap from birth meant that he had been born in sin (v. 34; cf.

v. 2). With this, judging that he had in effect hailed Jesus as the Messiah, **they expelled him from the synagogue** (v. 34; cf. v. 22).

The story of the man born blind is thus framed by references to his sinful birth (vv. 2, 34). The story's intent is neither to affirm nor deny that he was born in sin but to depict his healing as a transformation so total as to constitute a veritable rebirth. Here at last is Nicodemus' opposite number, a Christian convert about whose experience there can be no doubt. If the dialogue with Nicodemus made clear the *impossibility* of entering the Kingdom of God without rebirth, the story of the blind man dramatizes the possibility, indeed the *inevitability*, of entering the Kingdom when a person is truly "born of water and the Spirit" (3:5).

Additional Notes

9:22 / **Expelled from the synagogue**: This expression (Gr.: *aposynagōgos*) occurs in 16:2 with reference to the experience of Christians after Jesus' resurrection and in 12:42 (as here) with reference to a possibility existing already during Jesus' earthly ministry. Many commentators believe that the term is an anachronism in John's Gospel. It is said to reflect a policy instituted about A.D. 90 of excluding Jewish Christians from the synagogues by requiring, as part of the synagogue prayer known as the Eighteen Benedictions (or *Shemoneh Esreh*), a malediction or curse upon the *minim* and *nozrim* (i.e., probably the "heretics" and the "Nazarenes," or Christians; the point was that Jewish Christians could not curse themselves and therefore would have to leave). But expulsion, whether potential or actual, is so integrally a part of the story of the man born blind (cf. v. 34) that perhaps another explanation should be sought. If the controlling word is seen to be **Messiah** (with the political associations that this title had in Jesus' time), then such an agreement as is mentioned in this verse makes good sense in its literary context, and (though it cannot be verified) may reflect the actual situation near the end of Jesus' ministry.

9:24 / **Promise before God that you will tell the truth**: lit., "give glory to God." The expression is used as an idiom to reinforce truthfulness (as, e.g., in Josh. 7:19; cf. GNB with NIV).

9:27 / **And you would not listen**: One ancient papyrus and some ancient versions omit the negative, so as to read, "I told you . . . and you heard." This reading prepares logically for what follows (**Why do you want to hear it again?**), but the reading in the GNB has better manuscript support and echoes Jesus' own words in similar situations in this Gospel (cf. 8:43, 47).

Maybe you, too: The **too** is interesting because it could be taken as a tacit admission by the former blind man that he himself has become Jesus' disciple, something he had not yet acknowledged in so many words.

9:28 / **That fellow's disciple**: The term **that fellow** (Gr.: *ekeinos* here and *houtos* in v. 29), especially in contrast to Moses, carries a derogatory tone, making of Jesus an anonymous figure with no credentials to validate his message.

9:29 / **We do not even know where he comes from**. It may be that the narrator is conscious of the formal contradiction between this statement and 7:27: "But when the Messiah comes, no one will know where he is from. And we all know where this man comes from." The irony of the contrast (if it is deliberate) is that the Pharisees are here unwittingly bearing witness to Jesus' messiahship, the very belief they are committed to stamping out.

Their intended meaning is not, of course, that they are actually ignorant of where Jesus comes from (contrast 6:42; 7:41, 52) but that they do not recognize his credentials.

9:31 / **We know**: This phrase on the lips of the former blind man echoes (and mocks) the Pharisees' use of the same phrase in v. 29. In both cases the appeal is to something commonly acknowledged to be true, yet the purpose of the appeal is to refute an opponent in partisan debate.

9:34 / **You were born and brought up in sin**: lit., "Your whole person was born in sins." The word "whole" (Gr.: *holos*) is used in contrast to the single deficiency of blindness. The Pharisees are saying that there is more wrong with the man from his birth than just blindness (it is, after all, his tongue that is giving them grief). His blindness at birth is a symptom of a far more sweeping moral predicament. The positive side of this view for the Gospel writer is that the restoration of sight can then serve efficiently to represent the spiritual rebirth of a whole person.

There is no real basis in the Greek for a reference here to the man's upbringing (**born and brought up in sin**). The use of the plural, "sins," in the Greek suggests that the Pharisees are thinking not of sin as an abstraction but of specific acts of sin, whether of the child in the womb or of his parents (cf. v. 2).

Trying to teach us: The word **teach** is used here with an authoritarian connotation, like the word "lecture" in some contexts today (cf. 1 Tim. 2:11, where wives are warned against lecturing or bossing their husbands, not against a ministry of teaching; cf. also Matt. 23:8 and perhaps James 3:1).

Expelled him from the synagogue: lit., "threw him out." The context makes it clear that formal exclusion is what is meant (cf. v. 22), not just physical ejection from the place where the interrogation was going on.

26

Spiritual Blindness

When Jesus heard what had happened, he found the man and asked him, "Do you believe in the Son of Man?"

[36]The man answered, "Tell me who he is, sir, so that I can believe in him!"

[37]Jesus said to him, "You have already seen him, and he is the one who is talking with you now."

[38]"I believe, Lord!" the man said, and knelt down before Jesus.

[39]Jesus said, "I came to this world to judge, so that the blind should see and those who see should become blind."

[40]Some Pharisees who were there with him heard him say this and asked him, "Surely you don't mean that we are blind, too?"

[41]Jesus answered, "If you were blind, then you would not be guilty; but since you claim that you can see, this means that you are still guilty."

To complete the story, it remained only for the former blind man to meet Jesus in person. Like a shepherd looking for his lost sheep, Jesus took the initiative in this reunion. He **found** the man after his expulsion from the synagogue (v. 35), just as he had earlier found the sick man in the Temple after the healing at Bethzatha (cf. 5:14). He merely warned the sick man he had healed against further sin, but here he makes a serious attempt to elicit faith: **Do you believe in the Son of Man?** This is the only place in the entire New Testament where **Son of Man** is used as a confessional or creedal term. The reader anticipates instead "Son of God" or "the Messiah" (cf. 1:34; 11:27; 20:31). **Son of Man** was Jesus' own self-designation, but there is little evidence in the Gospels that he expected others to use it or that his contemporaries knew what it meant. It seems originally not to have been a title at all, but to rest on the Aramaic expressions *bar nash* (indefinite, "a son of man" or "a man") or *bar nasha* (definite, "the son of man" or "that man"), used virtually as pronouns (e.g., "someone" or "a certain one").

The present narrative makes perfect sense in light of this background. Jesus asks, "Do you believe in that man [i.e., the man who restored your sight]?" The reply is, "Tell me who he is, sir, so that I can believe in him!" (v. 36). As far as we know, the man born blind had never laid eyes on Jesus. Though he had come back from the pool of Siloam able to see (v. 7), there is no indication that Jesus was waiting for him on his return. When questioned by his neighbors, he had said that he did not know where Jesus was (v. 12). His request in verse 36 (**Tell me who he is, sir, so that I can believe in him**) is therefore a natural one. He has no way of knowing that he is speaking to the very person who gave him back his sight. As soon as Jesus identifies himself (v. 37), the former blind man believes (just as he said he would in v. 36) and falls at Jesus' feet in worship (v. 38).

Such a reconstruction logically explains the incident as it might actually have happened. The only difficulty with it is that in the text as it stands **the Son of Man** looks very much like a title, not merely a pronoun-like expression for an unnamed individual. The question, "Who is this Son of Man?" is asked one more time in this Gospel, by a crowd at the Passover Festival, after Jesus has said that "the Son of Man must be lifted up" (12:34). There the narrator's assumption is that "Son of Man" is Jesus' term for the Messiah (specifically for himself as the suffering Messiah), and that people are trying to square this with their own notion of a Messiah who "will live forever." If the present passage is understood in a similar way, then Jesus is asking the man born blind if he believes in the Messiah. If, as seems likely from the preceding narrative, he has decided that "the man called Jesus" (v. 11) is the Messiah, his request is to know who this Jesus is and, if possible, to meet him. Jesus' self-disclosure in verse 37 then triggers his expression of faith and his act of worship. Aside from the Gospel writer's reinterpretation of **Son of Man** as an explicitly messianic term, the meaning of the conversation in the text of John's Gospel closely parallels the meaning it had in its original setting and probably in the earliest recounting of the incident. The fact that the former blind man's confession of faith comes only *after* his expulsion from the synagogue is strong evidence that the narrator's concern here is historical, not just theological or illustrative. Though the man born blind is presented as a typical convert from Judaism to Christianity, he is also a real person with a real history. The case study is an actual case, not a made-up one, and clearly not a parable or allegory.

The case study ends with the confession of faith at verse 38. From what has happened, Jesus makes a generalization about his mission to the world. He has come for judgment, he says, **so that the blind should see and those who see should become blind** (v. 39). Blindness here becomes a metaphor. The theme of reversal expressed in this metaphor recalls certain sayings of Jesus in the synoptic Gospels: for example, "People who are well do not need a doctor, but only those who are sick. I have not come to call respectable people, but outcasts" (Mark 2:17); or

"But the others . . . hear all things by means of parables, so that 'They may look and look, yet not see; they may listen and listen, yet not understand' " (Mark 4:11–12). Jesus is speaking to no one in particular at this point; his words are recorded for the instruction of the reader. But because "the shoe fits," some of the Pharisees (who up to now have given no evidence of their presence) interject a question: **Surely you don't mean that we are blind, too?** (v. 40).

The question affords Jesus the opportunity to contrast two groups: those like the man born blind who show by their acceptance of Jesus' message that they are his "sheep," and those like the Pharisees who demonstrate by their unbelief that they do not belong to him. This contrast will be the theme of the following chapter. In immediate reply to the Pharisees' question, Jesus reveals that he has been speaking metaphorically and proceeds to apply the metaphor by introducing the notion of sin or guilt (v. 41). Blindness is an appropriate metaphor for sin, even as the ability to see clearly is one for righteousness (cf., e.g., 11:9–10; 12:35–36; 1 John 2:9–11). But the reversal used with the metaphor (v. 39) is present in its application as well: The blind are *not* guilty; the guilty ones are those who claim to see. The blind man was cured; the Pharisees, by their stubborn refusal to accept the reality of the power of God, only proved themselves blind. Their blindness was deeper because it was willful. In their case (*not* the blind man's) the question, Who sinned? (cf. v. 2) was a question that made sense. Their blindness was their sin, not the universal sin of the human condition, but the sin that disclosed itself only with the coming of Jesus into the world (v. 39) and consisted of rejecting his message. Later, in his farewell discourse, Jesus would state this principle clearly: "They would not have been guilty of sin if I had not come and spoken to them; as it is they no longer have any excuse for their sin. . . . They would not have been guilty of sin if I had not done among them the things that no one else ever did" (15:22, 24; cf. 9:32: "Nobody has ever heard of anyone giving sight to a person born blind").

With the words **you are still guilty** (v. 41), Jesus exercises the divine authority he will eventually confer on his disciples, to "retain" (20:23, RSV) the sin of the Pharisees. The verdict passed in the synoptic Gospels that they are "blind guides" (Matt. 23:16, 17, 19) or "blind leaders of the blind" (Matt. 15:14) is solemnly reinforced. Some of the blind they presume to lead enter the Kingdom of God, but they themselves remain in darkness.

Additional Notes

9:36, 38 / **Sir . . . Lord**: The same word in Greek (*kyrie*) is translated **sir** in v. 36 and **Lord** in v. 38. The word is capable of either meaning, depending on the context. **Sir** is appropriate in v. 36 because the former blind man, still ignorant of Jesus' identity, addresses him as a stranger. By v. 38, Jesus has made himself known, and in an expression of faith and worship, **Lord** is the proper translation.

9:37 / **You have already seen him, and he is the one who is talking with you now**. Cf. Jesus' self-disclosure to the Samaritan woman in 4:26 ("I am he, I who am talking with you"). The absence of the "I Am" formula here, where it might have been expected, can perhaps be explained by the preceding words, **You have already seen him**, which put the whole pronouncement into a third-person setting. These words are probably chosen to underscore the fact that the man has now seen Jesus for the first time.

9:39 / **I came to this world to judge**. These words seem to contradict 12:47b ("I came not to judge the world, but to save it"), but cf. 12:48: Jesus' words are the touchstone by which judgment is to be carried out (cf. also 3:17 with 3:18–21).

27

Jesus the Good Shepherd

JOHN 10:1–21

Jesus said, "I am telling you the truth: the man who does not enter the sheep pen by the gate, but climbs in some other way, is a thief and a robber. [2]The man who goes in through the gate is the shepherd of the sheep. [3]The gatekeeper opens the gate for him; the sheep hear his voice as he calls his own sheep by name, and he leads them out. [4]When he has brought them out, he goes ahead of them, and the sheep follow him, because they know his voice. [5]They will not follow someone else; instead, they will run away from such a person, because they do not know his voice."

[6]Jesus told them this parable, but they did not understand what he meant.

[7]So Jesus said again, "I am telling you the truth: I am the gate for the sheep. [8]All others who came before me are thieves and robbers, but the sheep did not listen to them. [9]I am the gate. Whoever comes in by me will be saved; he will come in and go out and find pasture. [10]The thief comes only in order to steal, kill, and destroy. I have come in order that you might have life—life in all its fullness.

[11]"I am the good shepherd, who is willing to die for the sheep. [12]When the hired man, who is not a shepherd and does not own the sheep, sees a wolf coming, he leaves the sheep and runs away; so the wolf snatches the sheep and scatters them. [13]The hired man runs away because he is only a hired man and does not care about the sheep. [14-15]I am the good shepherd. As the Father knows me and I know the Father, in the same way I know my sheep and they know me. And I am willing to die for them. [16]There are other sheep which belong to me that are not in this sheep pen. I must bring them, too; they will listen to my voice, and they will become[v] one flock with one shepherd.

[17]"The Father loves me because I am willing to give up my life, in order that I may receive it back again. [18]No one takes my life away from me. I give it up of my own free will. I have the right to give it up, and I have the right to take it back. This is what my Father has commanded me to do."

[19]Again there was a division among the people because of these words. [20]Many of them were saying, "He has a demon! He is crazy! Why do you listen to him?"

[21]But others were saying, "A man with a demon could not talk like this! How could a demon give sight to blind people?"

v. they will become; *some manuscripts have* there will be.

The brief exchange between Jesus and the Pharisees in 9:39–41 is only the beginning of a discourse extending (with one interruption) through most of chapter 10. The pattern found in chapters 5 and 6, a miracle followed by a discourse interpreting it, is maintained here as well. What chapter 10 inteprets, however, is not the healing of the blind man as such but the events that followed the healing, that is, the former blind man's expulsion from the synagogue and his confession of faith in Jesus. Two contrasts dominate the chapter: the contrast between the Pharisees and Jesus as shepherds of the people and the contrast between the Pharisees and the former blind man as recipients of Jesus' message.

Jesus' address to the Pharisees has two parts (vv. 1–6 and 7–18), each introduced by the characteristic formula **I am telling you the truth** (vv. 1, 7; cf. 1:51). The first is called a **parable** (v. 6); the second makes use of the parable's imagery in two different ways to present yet again the claims of Jesus (vv. 7–10, 11–18). The so-called parable is not what is sometimes designated by that term (i.e., an imaginative story expanding on a metaphor, often with a surprise ending); instead, it is simply a generalized description of a scene from a familiar world in first-century Palestine, that of shepherds and sheep herding. Like many parables in the synoptic Gospels, it could be called a parable of normalcy, a parable that describes what normally takes place in certain everyday situations. Fasting, for example, is normal when someone dies, but not at a wedding celebration (Mark 2:18–20). Doctors are normally for sick people, not those who are well (Mark 2:17). New wine belongs in new bottles (Mark 2:22). Closer to the imagery of the present passage, if a sheep falls into a pit even on the Sabbath, its owner will pull it out (Matt. 12:11). If a shepherd loses track of even one out of a hundred sheep, he will leave the rest to fend for themselves and go out looking for it (Luke 15:4). If not everyday actions, these are at least normal responses to life's emergencies.

The parable of verses 1–5 is of the same type. If we see a man climbing over the wall of a sheep pen to get at the sheep, instead of through the gate, it is probably fair to conclude that he is not the shepherd or owner of the sheep (v. 1). The real shepherd enters by the normal way; the gatekeeper (probably an associate or subordinate shepherd) recognizes him, and even the sheep know the sound of his voice. He in turn calls his sheep by name, and because they know his voice he has no trouble driving them out and leading them to pasture (vv. 2–4). This is all normal procedure, but if a stranger tried to lead them out in similar fashion, they would run away from him, frightened at the unfamiliar voice (v. 5).

The point of this brief glimpse of rural Palestinian life is not at once clear. For the moment, the reader can sympathize with the Pharisees (cf. 9:40–41) who heard Jesus tell the story but **did not understand what he meant** (v. 6). There is definitely a contrast between pseudoshepherds and the real shepherd of the flock (v. 1). The contrast is an ancient one in Judaism, as ancient as Ezekiel 34, with its denunciation of Israel's false leaders (34:1–10) and its proclamation by God Himself that he will assume the role of Shepherd over his people (34:11–31). In Jesus' parable, three things distinguish the true shepherd from the false: He enters by the gate, the gatekeeper lets him in, and the sheep recognize his voice. That the most important of these features is the third is shown by its reiteration in verses 3, 4, and 5. The true shepherd, in contrast to **a thief and a robber** (v. 1), is the one whose voice the sheep recognize and to whom they listen. Applying this understanding to the preceding narrative of the man born blind, we might conclude that Jesus is vindicated as the true shepherd by the fact that the **sheep** (i.e., the formerly blind man) listened to (and followed) him and not the Pharisees.

This conclusion would have merit *if* the question being answered by the parable were Who is the true shepherd? (the answer being, the one who is accepted by the sheep). But the validity of Jesus' mission in John's Gospel does not depend on his being accepted by anyone. He is assumed to be both Messiah and true shepherd of Israel regardless of how people respond to him. If this is so, the question to which the parable is primarily addressed is not Who is the true shepherd? (the answer being obvious— Jesus) but Who are the sheep? (the answer being, those who hear and obey the true shepherd's voice). Not shepherds but sheep are being tested in this chapter. Not Jesus but his hearers are on trial. The man born blind proved himself one of God's flock by trusting in Jesus. How will it turn out for the Pharisees who listen to this parable? Jesus has already pronounced them guilty (9:41), and the subsequent discussion will only reinforce that verdict. It remains for Jesus to apply the language of the parable to the ongoing confrontation between himself and the religious authorities of Judaism. The result is not one unified interpretation of the parable but a number of particular echoes and extensions of its imagery.

This section of the discourse is introduced by the formula **I am telling you the truth** (v. 7) and terminated by a **division** (Gr.: *schisma*) over what Jesus has said (vv. 19–21). It has two subsections, each introduced and punctuated by **I am** pronouncements. The first of these (vv. 7–10) contains the pronouncement **I am the gate for the sheep** (v. 7) and again, **I am the gate** (v. 9). The second (vv. 11–18) has the pronouncement **I am the good shepherd** twice (vv. 11 and 14).

The first subsection immediately answers a question not likely to be asked. A reader might respond to the parable of verses 1–6 by asking about the shepherd or the sheep, but probably not about the identification of the gatekeeper (v. 3), much less the gate! And yet Jesus begins his expansion on the parable, not where one might expect, with "I am the shepherd," but where no one expects, with **I am the gate for the sheep** (lit., "I am the gate of the sheep").

It is true that the gate was mentioned with a certain emphasis near the beginning of the parable. An entrance to the sheepfold "through the gate" (v. 1) is a legitimate entrance. The **gate** might therefore be understood as representing legitimation for those who undertake to be "shepherds" (or leaders) among the people of God. Jesus' pronouncement would then have to be understood as "I am the gate *to* the sheep" (i.e., those who seek access to God's people as their leaders must possess an authority derived from Jesus). Interpreted in this way, the pronouncement has possible relevance to the Christian church at the time the Gospel was written, but it is difficult to know how the Pharisees who heard Jesus would have understood it. Moreover, the most natural interpretation of **the gate for the sheep** is, as that translation suggests, the gate used *by* the sheep to go in and out, not the gate of access *to* the sheep. This is supported by verse 9: **I am the gate. Whoever comes in by me will be saved; he will come in and go out and find pasture**. The metaphor of the gate presents Jesus as the way to salvation (cf. 14:6), not as the validator of ministries. He has come in order that those who believe **might have life—life in all its fullness** (v. 10).

The **gate** metaphor as used in verses 7–10 is only loosely related to the gate mentioned in the parable proper. Before he is the **gate**, Jesus is one who **comes** (vv. 8, 10). This verb—which is no part of the **gate** metaphor—takes priority over the metaphor so as to limit and control it. It is as the Coming One—specifically as the Messiah—that Jesus designates himself **the gate for the sheep**. He is the way to salvation not passively (as **gate** by itself might suggest) but actively, as one who comes to save. It is as the Coming One also that he contrasts himself with **others who came before me** whom he describes as **thieves and robbers** (v. 8), again picking up a phrase from the parable (v. 1). The purpose of the contrast is to make clear that Jesus is the *only* way to salvation. Later he will tell his disciples, "no one goes to the Father except by me" (14:6). In a very different context in the Synoptics, he is represented as urging: "Go in through the narrow gate, because the gate to hell is wide and the road that leads to it is easy, and there are many who travel it. But the gate of life is narrow and the way that leads to it is hard, and there are few people who find it" (Matt. 7:13–14; cf. Luke 13:24). To say that **all . . . who came before me are thieves and robbers** (v. 8) is simply a different way of saying that all other gates are false and all other ways deceptive. Some have found here an allusion to false messianic pretenders (of which there were a number in Jesus' time), but the reference is probably not that specific.

The repetition of the "I am" statement provides a framework within which two distinct points are made. The first statement (v. 7) is followed by the contrast between Jesus and all contrary teachers and teachings (vv. 8, 10a). The second (v. 9a) is followed by an appropriate description of a gate's function: It provides sheep a way into the fold for safety and a way out for freedom and pasture (v. 9b). This is Jesus' function as well: He provides his followers with protection from harm and with abundant life (vv. 9b–10). The contrast with thieves is here repeated, for they do exactly the opposite. They **steal, kill, and destroy** (v. 10a).

A similar pattern exists in verses 11–18. The first instance of **I am the good shepherd** (v. 11) is followed by a contrast with the shepherd who is not so **good** (i.e., the **hired man**, vv. 12–13). The second (v. 14a) is followed by a description of how a good shepherd functions, explicitly referring to the actual redemptive work of Jesus (vv. 14b–18). The unmistakable thrust of the passage is that Jesus is a shepherd **willing to die** for his sheep. This assertion is made right at the outset as the very definition of **good** (v. 11) and again in the middle as part of a revelation or prophecy of the saving work that Jesus is about to accomplish (v. 15). The last two verses in their entirety are then devoted to examining the assertion more closely and reflecting on it theologically (vv. 17–18).

This subsection contains a number of features not found in the introductory parable at all. The **hired man** of verses 11–13 is not to be equated with the **thieves and robbers** mentioned in the parable (v. 1) and in the **gate** polemic of verse 8. Their role is taken over instead by the wolf (v. 12) who **snatches the sheep and scatters them**. The hired man is introduced solely for the sake of the contrast with the good shepherd. The difference between them is that a good shepherd will risk his life to protect the sheep, while a hireling will not. They are not his property and livelihood, after all (v. 12), and their fate does not matter to him in the same way it does to the shepherd. The hired man does not symbolically represent a particular group in Israel (e.g., the Pharisees), nor is the description of him intended as an indictment of Israel's leaders. He is in the discourse only to highlight the fact that, by contrast, a good shepherd is **willing to die** to rescue his sheep from predators. These predators–the **thieves and robbers** and the marauding wolf–are the real enemies of the flock and of the shepherd. Who do they represent? To Jesus, all the forces of evil that he came to overthrow: the demons, or unclean spirits, he drove out of those who were possessed; the "strong man" whom he claimed in one of his parables to have bound and whose captives he claimed to have set free (Mark 3:27); the religious authorities who charged that he himself was in league with Satan (Mark 3:22), and who finally engineered his arrest and execution. To the narrator, the enemies of the sheep represent those same religious authorities, who were already trying to kill Jesus (cf. 5:18; 8:40) and were expelling his followers from the synagogues (9:22, 34); the same group will later condemn him to death and afterward kill, as well as expel from the synagogue, his disciples—all in the name of piety (16:2–3)! The wolf, as well as the thieves and robbers, represents in this Gospel the encroachments of the evil "world," in all its alienation from God, against the followers of Jesus (cf. 15:18–25). It is from the "world" that the sheep need to be protected (cf. 16:33; 17:11, 14–16), and Jesus the shepherd will risk his life, even give his life, to protect and save them.

The notion of the shepherd endangering his life for the sake of the sheep turns almost imperceptibly from a metaphor to a reality as the discourse unfolds. The picture in verse 11 is of a shepherd who is **willing to die** in defense of his sheep by fighting off the attacking wolf. Verses 11–13 are an extended metaphor, in fact a self-contained parable matching the parable in verses 1–5. At the very least they provide a double character sketch (i.e., of the shepherd and of the hired man), but more than that, they tell a real story about a wolf attacking a flock of sheep, with the hired man running away to save his own life. The key to the interpretation of the parable is given first: **I am the good shepherd** (v. 11a). Then the story is told, as a parable should be, entirely in the third person: "The good shepherd lays down his life for the sheep . . . " (v. 11b, NIV; the GNB obscures this shift to the third person).

The parable continues through verse 13, but verses 14–16 are different. The repetition of **I am the good shepherd** necessarily brings Jesus back to the use of the first person, but this time he continues that usage: **As the Father knows me and I know the Father** . . . **I know my sheep and they know me.** . . . **I am willing to die for them** . . . **other sheep which belong to me.** . . . **I must bring them, too**. This is no longer a parable, but a self-revelation of the Son. Though it uses metaphors, it is not itself metaphorical; it is intended, rather, as a literal description of reality. It has nothing to do with shepherds and sheep and everything to do with Jesus, and with his disciples, his Father, and his redemptive death. When Jesus speaks of the mutual knowledge between himself and the Father, and between himself and the disciples (v. 14), his words recall his self-revelation in Matthew 11:27: "No one knows the Son except the Father, and no one knows the Father except the Son and those to whom the Son chooses to reveal him." When he claims to be **willing to die** for his sheep (v. 15), it is clear that he is no longer speaking of fighting physically against wolves, but of dying on the cross to redeem those who believe in him. And when he promises to bring the **other sheep which belong to me that are not in this sheep pen** (v. 16), he is anticipating the church's mission to the Gentiles after his death and resurrection (cf. the narrator's explicit reference to this mission in 11:52). Verses 14–16 thus comprise an unmistakable, though partial, summary of Jesus' mission from its beginning (**As the Father knows me and I know the Father**) to its full realization in history (**one flock with one shepherd**, cf. 11:52; 17:20–23). This summary comes, not from Jesus' disciples in the form of a creed, but from his own lips as revelation.

Yet there is a certain illogic in all this. How can Jesus die, and still be able to gather his sheep into **one flock**? A crucial link in the chain of redemptive events is missing. Jesus must be raised from the dead. The main point of the passage is that Jesus' death results in the unity of the flock, but the unspoken assumption is that unity is possible because of his resurrection. Instead of death followed by resurrection, the pattern is death followed by the gathering of a community, with resurrection as the indispensable link between the two. The same pattern is found in Mark 14:27–28, where Jesus tells his disciples, "The scripture says, 'God will kill the shepherd and the sheep will all be scattered.' But after I am raised to life, I will go to Galilee ahead of you." Here the resurrection is mentioned only in a subordinate clause, and in John 11:52 it is not mentioned at all ("Jesus was going to die for the Jewish people, and . . . to bring together into one body all the scattered people of God").

In the present passage the resurrection becomes explicit in verses 17–18. Jesus explains that he will lay down his life "only to take it up again" (v. 17, NIV). Unlike the stricken shepherd of Zechariah 13:7 (the Scripture he cited in Mark 14:27), Jesus here presents himself as one who dies willingly and at his own initiative: **No one takes my life away from me. I give it up of my own free will. I have the right to give it up, and I have the right to take it back** (v. 18). His own life, like all life (cf. 5:21, 26), is at his disposal. If "the Son gives life to those he wants to" (5:21), it is no surprise that he takes back his own life from the grip of death. And yet the Son is not autonomous (cf. 5:19, 30). Whether in dying, rising from the dead, or gathering a new community, Jesus acts always at his Father's command (v. 18b; cf. 14:31). He has a **right** to do only what the

Father wants done. But both the command and the authority are grounded in the Father's life for the Son (cf. 3:35; 5:20), and love is the Father's response to Jesus' faithful completion of the good shepherd's task (v. 17a).

The brief discourse ends in a **division** (Gr.: *schisma*; cf. 7:43; 9:16) among Jesus' hearers (vv. 19–21). It is significant that what divides them is not only the implicit claim he has just made of a unique relationship to God but also the stubborn fact that he has given sight to the blind (v. 21). The issue raised by the blind man himself in the preceding chapter is still very much alive (9:32–33). Both the words and the works of Jesus continue to challenge his audience and force them toward decision.

Additional Notes

10:3 / **His own sheep**: Some have argued from this phrase that sheep belonging to several shepherds or owners are grouped in one sheepfold. But the phrase "the shepherd of the sheep" in v. 2 suggests, rather, that all the sheep belong to the one shepherd.

The words **his own** (which occur also in the Greek of v. 4) are therefore somewhat redundant, and it is possible that they have been chosen with the application to Jesus already in view. Jesus' disciples are **his own** in a very special and intimate sense (cf. 13:1; and contrast 1:11, where "his own people did not receive him." In the latter part of John's Gospel, Jesus' "own" come to be identified instead with the group mentioned in 1:12 who "believed in him" and received "the right to become God's children").

10:4 / **Has brought them out**: lit., "has driven out all his own." This verse specifies just how the shepherd "leads them out" (v. 3): He enters the sheepfold and literally pushes or drives them through the gate; then when they are out, he goes on in front of them to guide them to pasture. The Greek word for **brought** (*ekballein*) is the same word used for expulsion from the synagogue in 9:34–35, but the parallel is probably coincidental. There is no particular intent here to contrast the "pastoral care" of Jesus with the harsh discipline of the Pharisees.

10:7 / **I am the gate for the sheep**. One ancient papyrus and certain ancient versions read "the shepherd of the sheep." This reading seems to have resulted from scribes being misled by the contrast with "thieves and robbers" into assuming that the shepherd must be in view here. But **gate** is correct.

10:8 / **Before me**: These words are not meant as part of the gate metaphor (i.e., before, or in front of, the gate, seeking entrance; cf., e.g., James 5:9). They are meant temporally: Those who up to now have offered ways of salvation are thieves and robbers.

10:9 / **Come in and go out**: The emphasis here is on the freedom of the sheep to come and go as their needs dictate. The shepherd provides them with both protection and pasture. It is not a question of entering and leaving the realm of salvation.

10:10 / **That you might have life—life in all its fullness**: The GNB correctly indicates that the last phrase is rhetorical. There are not two stages of Christian experience: life, and full or abundant life. The only spiritual **life** this Gospel knows is **life in all its fullness**. It is the "eternal life" that Jesus gives, the only genuine life there is. The close connection between life and freedom recalls 8:32–36.

10:11 / **Is willing to die**: lit., "lays down his life [or soul]." The meaning is that a good shepherd will risk his life (we might say he "puts his life on the line") for his sheep.

The same idiom in v. 15 ("willing to die"), v. 17 ("willing to give up my life"), and v. 18 ("give it up") refers to actual death (the death of Jesus on the cross), not the mere danger of death.

10:16 / **Other sheep**: J. A. T. Robinson (*Twelve New Testament Studies* [Naperville, Ill.: Allenson, 1962], p. 121) has argued that the **other sheep** are Greek-speaking Jews dispersed throughout the world, but the emphasis in John's Gospel on Jesus' mission to the whole world and not just the Jews (e.g., 1:10; 4:42; 12:32) strongly favors their identification as Gentiles (cf. 7:35).

10:17 / **In order that I may receive it back again**: The translation is somewhat misleading. Jesus does not give up his life in order to receive it back but in order to save his sheep. The clause expresses not purpose but result: He gives up his life in death—only to get it back in resurrection (cf. NIV).

For an example of a very early Gnostic reading of this passage, cf. *Gospel of Philip* 9: "Not only when he appeared did he lay down the soul when he wished, but from the day the world came into being he laid down the soul. At the time when he wished, then he came first to take it, since it had been left as a pledge. It was under the robbers and had been taken captive. But he saved it." (*The Gospel of Philip*, trans. R. McL. Wilson, [London: A. R. Mowbray, 1962] pp. 29, 71). Side by side with the literal interpretation stands a speculation about the imprisonment of souls in corrupt bodies until Christ comes to retrieve them (a confusion of the redeemer with the redeemed). The mention of "robbers" echoes John 10:1, 18.

10:19 / **Among the people**: lit., "among the Jews." In all likelihood the same audience is in view here as in 9:40–41 and 10:6, i.e., the Pharisees or the Jewish religious leaders, not **the people** as a whole. Even among the Pharisees there were those who respected Jesus' power to heal (v. 21; cf. 9:16b).

28

Jesus Is Rejected

JOHN 10:22–39

It was winter, and the Festival of the Dedication of the Temple was being celebrated in Jerusalem. ²³Jesus was walking in Solomon's Porch in the Temple, ²⁴when the people gathered around him and asked, "How long are you going to keep us in suspense? Tell us the plain truth: are you the Messiah?"

²⁵Jesus answered, "I have already told you, but you would not believe me. The deeds I do by my Father's authority speak on my behalf; ²⁶but you will not believe, for you are not my sheep. ²⁷My sheep listen to my voice; I know them, and they follow me. ²⁸I give them eternal life, and they shall never die. No one can snatch them away from me. ²⁹What my Father has given me is greater^w than everything, and no one can snatch them away from the Father's care. ³⁰The Father and I are one."

³¹Then the people again picked up stones to throw at him. ³²Jesus said to them, "I have done many good deeds in your presence which the Father gave me to do; for which one of these do you want to stone me?"

³³They answered, "We do not want to stone you because of any good deeds, but because of your blasphemy! You are only a man, but you are trying to make yourself God!"

³⁴Jesus answered, "It is written in your own Law that God said, 'You are gods.' ³⁵We know that what the scripture says is true forever; and God called those people gods, the people to whom his message was given. ³⁶As for me, the Father chose me and sent me into the world. How, then, can you say that I blaspheme because I said that I am the Son of God? ³⁷Do not believe me, then, if I am not doing the things my Father wants me to do. ³⁸But if I do them, even though you do not believe me, you should at least believe my deeds, in order that you may know once and for all that the Father is in me and that I am in the Father."

³⁹Once more they tried to seize Jesus, but he slipped out of their hands.

w. What my Father has given me is greater; *some manuscripts have* My Father, who gave them to me, is greater.

The notation of time and place in verses 22–23 is intended to set the stage for a new encounter between Jesus and the Jerusalem authorities, not to locate the events of 9:1–10:19. The time frame of Jesus' ministry, especially in Jerusalem, is provided by the Jewish religious festivals. The last of these to be mentioned was the autumn Festival of Shelters (7:2), the setting of chapters 7–8. Now it is winter and time for the Festival of Dedication (known today as Hanukkah); the events of 9:1–10:19 are assumed to have taken place in late autumn, between the two festivals.

The Festival of Dedication celebrated Jewish independence, the recapture and reconsecration of the Temple in 165 B.C. under Judas Maccabaeus after its desecration by the Greeks under the Seleucid king Antiochus Epiphanes (see 1 Macc. 4:36–61; 2 Macc. 10:1–18). It was a time for such words as "we are the descendants of Abraham . . . and we have never been anyone's slaves" (8:33) to come alive in the heart of every Jew. Like the other festivals, it was also a time of messianic expectation. Though the Romans respected the Temple precincts and allowed the Jews freedom of worship, this festival was a reminder that the political independence gained under the Maccabees was no longer a reality. For all but the most militant activists the only hope of regaining that independence was the appearing of the Messiah. The question asked in verse 24, however (**are you the Messiah**), represents not a genuine popular longing for the deliverer, but rather the efforts of the authorities to trap Jesus into embracing the messianic role. To say "I am the Messiah" in just those words would be to welcome any and all attempts to make him king (6:15) and so to place himself in jeopardy from the Romans.

The scene is reminiscent of Jesus' interrogation in the other Gospels at his trial. "Are you the Messiah, the son of the blessed God?" (Mark 14:61; cf. Matt. 26:63; Luke 22:67a). Here, as in Matthew and Luke (though not Mark), Jesus' reply is ambiguous: **I have already told you, but you would not believe me** (v. 25; cf. Luke 22:67b–68, "If I tell you, you will not believe me; and if I ask you a question, you will not answer"). The ambiguity lies in the fact that in this Gospel Jesus has *not* already told them (or anyone in a Jewish context) in so many words that he is the Messiah (though he has in a Samaritan setting, cf.4:26). What he means is that he has told them by his *deeds* (v. 25), in particular the healing of the sick man at Bethzatha and the man born blind (cf. v. 21). Such miracles done on the Father's authority testify that Jesus is both Messiah and Son of God (cf. 5:36; 20:31). They do this by virtue of the appended discourses in which Jesus expounds their meaning. Those who reject the unified witness of Jesus' deeds and words prove by their rejection that they are not Jesus' **sheep** (i.e., that they do not belong to him and are not subject to his care). It is another way of saying they are "not from God" (cf. 8:47).

With the words, **for you are not my sheep** (v. 26), Jesus returns to the imagery of verses 1–18. What follows in verses 27–30, however, is best understood not as parable but as a self-revelation of the Son using the metaphor of shepherd and sheep, very much in the style of verses 14–16. The self-identification, "I am the good shepherd," is here implied rather than expressed, but Jesus' activity as shepherd and Son is unfolded similarly in the two sections.

I. Verses 14–16	II. Verses 27–30
a As the Father knows me and I know the Father, in the same way I know my sheep and they know me.	**a My sheep listen to my voice; I know them, and they follow me.**
b And I am willing to die for them.	**b I give them eternal life, and they shall never die.**
c There are other sheep which belong to me that are not in this sheep pen. I must bring them, too; they will listen to my voice, and they will become one flock with one shepherd.	**c No one can snatch them away from me. What my Father has given me is greater than everything, and no one can snatch them away from the Father's care. The Father and I are one.**

Formally, the two sections have in common the revelatory "I"-style in which the speaker is the Shepherd/Son. As to content, they have three features in common: (*a*) the mutual knowledge of sheep and shepherd (based in section I on the mutual knowledge of Father and Son), (*b*) the shepherd's gift of life to his sheep (based in section I specifically on his death), and (*c*) the shepherd's ministry to his sheep (in section I a mission to "other sheep" and the achievement of unity; in section II the security and protection of the flock). Section II is a simplified version of section I, focusing on the safety of the sheep from harm or destruction (cf. vv. 9–12) and using this to illustrate the work carried out in common by the Father and the Son. In chapter 5 the principle that "my Father is always working, and I too must work" (5:17) was illustrated in terms of the giving of life (5:21, 26) and the exercise of judgment (5:22, 27). Here the same principle finds expression in that which is the corollary of the giving of life, that is, the provision of security for those in danger. The commonality of work forms the basis of a syllogism:

If:

no one can snatch them away from me
and
no one can snatch them away from my Father's hand (vv. 28–29)

Then:

The Father and I are one (v. 30)

Jesus and the Father are **one** because they do the same work and stand in the same relation to the sheep. This is not the same as saying merely that Jesus imitates or obeys the Father. Their oneness is not an ethical oneness, or unity of will. They actually do the *same* work, that is, the Father accomplishes his work in the world uniquely through Jesus his Son. Jesus' statement is no less provocative to his audience than was 5:17 (which made the same assertion) or 8:58 ("Before Abraham was born, 'I Am' "). In 5:18, the authorities became "all the more determined to kill him"; in 8:59 "they picked up stones to throw at him"; and here they **again picked up stones to throw at him** (v. 31; the narrator's use of **again** has the precedent of 8:59 clearly in view).

Once more Jesus appeals in his own defense to his **deeds** or works, this time as the **good** works of a **good** shepherd (v. 32; cf. vv. 11, 14). They are **good** because they give life and protection to those in need. They model the kindness of God himself, the Shepherd of his people, for they are, Jesus reiterates, deeds **which the Father gave me to do**. His ironic question, **For which one of these** [good deeds] **do you want to stone me?** (v. 32) presupposes the logic of his defense of his healings in the other Gospels: "Therefore, it is lawful to do good on the Sabbath" (Matt. 12:12, NIV; cf. Mark 3:4). Here in John the issue has already shifted from that of the Sabbath to Jesus' claims of sonship (cf. 5:16–18; 9:16). To the Jewish authorities, the issue is blasphemy: **You are only a man, but you are trying to make yourself God!** (v. 33; cf. 5:18). Their apparent reference is to the claim that **the Father and I are one** (v. 30).

Jesus' reply is surprising, not because he appeals to Scripture, but because of the way he does so: **It is written in your own Law that God said, "You are Gods"** (v. 34). The quotation is from Psalm 82:6: " 'You are gods,' I said; 'all of you are sons of the Most High.' " But Jesus does not quote what precedes ("How ignorant you are! How stupid! You are completely corrupt, and justice has disappeared from the world," 82:5) or what follows ("But you will die like men, your life will end like that of any prince," 82:7). When he says **your own Law**, Jesus does not mean that the Scripture belongs to his opponents and not himself, but rather that an appeal to Scripture (unlike the mysterious appeals he has been making to the authority of his Father) is an appeal in which he and his opponents stand on common ground. The principle that **what the scripture says is true forever** (v. 35), is something on which Jesus and the Jewish authorities are in agreement (cf. Matt. 5:18). To that extent he is serious in his use of the psalm. But what makes his argument seem strange is the fact that those who are called **gods** are by no means being commended. It is true that Jesus' argument is from the lesser to the greater: If those who were merely the recipients of God's message could be called **gods**, why is it blasphemy for Jesus, uniquely chosen by the Father and sent into the world, to call himself at least **Son of God?** Yet Jesus' intent is not to weaken the claim he has made in verse 30 or in any way to lessen the offense taken at his words by the religious authorities. His point is not that he is **Son of God** but not **God**, or that he is **God** in a sense comparable to the way that title was used in Psalm 82:6. His point is rather *that titles as such are irrelevant* in his revelation of himself to the world. Right from the start of the discussion, the Jewish authorities have been trying to talk with Jesus about titles (vv. 23–24, 33), while Jesus responds by referring instead to his works, the **deeds I do by my Father's authority** (v. 25; cf. vv. 25–30, 32, 37–38). Only in verses 34–36 does he address the question of titles, and he does so only to make the point that titles mean nothing. The works of God are all that matter. Jesus could easily have said, "I am God" or "I am God's Son" or "I am the Messiah," but it would not have had to mean any more than God meant when he spoke of "gods" in Psalm 82. The purpose of the quotation is not to claim for Jesus a fixed title but to reduce the whole matter of titles to an absurdity.

In verses 37–38, Jesus resumes, and brings to completion, his own agenda for the discourse: **Do not believe me, then, if I am not doing the things my Father wants me to do. But if I do them, even though you do not believe me, you should at least believe my deeds, in order that you may know once and for all that the Father is in me and that I am in the Father**. The effect of these words is to reiterate the claim of verse 30 that **the Father and I are one**. The point of issue for Jesus is not the title **Messiah** (v. 24), or **Son of God** (v. 36), or even **God** (v. 33), but the relationship between himself and **the Father**, a relationship displayed in such miracles as the healing of the blind man. More even than mutual knowledge (cf. v. 14), this relationship is one of mutual indwelling: The Father is **in** Jesus, and Jesus is **in** the Father. The hearers are not part of this relationship, nor are they invited to be, but Jesus wants them to **know once and for all** that the relationship exists (v. 38). The immediate hearers cannot accept such a claim: **Once more they tried to seize Jesus, but he slipped out of their hands** (v. 39; cf. 7:30, 44; 8:59). The readers of the Gospel can accept it, but at this point in the narrative they are not yet fully prepared to understand it. Mutual indwelling will become a major theme in Jesus' farewell discourses, and only then will the further secret be revealed that Jesus' disciples are **in** him and he **in** them in a way comparable to the relationship that exists between the Father and Jesus (cf., e.g., 14:20; 15:4; 17:21).

Additional Notes

10:22 / **Solomon's Porch**: The porches of the Temple were covered colonnades surrounding the Temple area on all four sides, and facing in toward the sanctuary. The colonnade on the east was called **Solomon's** because it rested on pre-Herodian masonry believed to go back to Solomon himself (Josephus, *Jewish War* 5.184–85; *Antiquities* 15.398–400; 20.221). Such porches were a common feature of Greek buildings and were widely used as places for teaching. From the Greek word for "porch" (*stoa*), the philosophical school of the Stoics took its name. **Solomon's Porch** was a place where the earliest Christians assembled and proclaimed their message (Acts 3:11; 5:12) and an appropriate place as well for Jesus to have engaged in teaching and debate. The author of the Gospel preserves precise historical information at this point.

10:24 / **Keep us in suspense**: lit., "lift up our soul." The idiom is used in the LXX (Pss. 24[25]:1; 85[86]:4: "To you, O Lord, I have lifted up my soul") to refer to a prayer of anticipation. Here the idiom is somewhat different. The element of anticipation is still present, but the anticipation is not a good thing; it connotes uncertainty and is a state that needs to be corrected (for an example illustrating the transition from the LXX to John's Gospel, cf. Josephus, *Antiquities* 3.48). The image is of lifting up, or holding, someone else's breath (i.e., keeping someone in suspense). Walter Bauer's *Greek-English Lexicon of the New Testament* (2d ed., rev. W. F. Arndt, F. W. Gingrich, and F. W. Danker [Chicago: University of Chicago Press, 1979], p. 24) can cite only one instance of this use of the expression—and that from the twelfth century A.D.—yet it is clearly the meaning required by the context (hence the GNB rendering).

10:26 / **You are not my sheep**: lit., "you are not of my sheep" (i.e., you do not belong to my flock).

10:29 / **What my Father has given me is greater than everything**. The neuter singular (**what**) regards Jesus' disciples collectively, as a single, united community (cf. "One flock," v. 16; see also the note on 6:39). The reading followed by GNB is a more difficult one than the variant found in many ancient manuscripts (i.e., "My Father, who gave them to me, is greater") and, for that very reason, more likely to be correct. That the Father is **greater than everything** is obvious to any reader, but in what sense is what the Father has given to Jesus (i.e., the new community of believers) **greater** than anything else? The placing of **my Father** first in the Greek sentence suggests that the greatness of the gift derives from the greatness of the giver and from its preciousness in the giver's sight (cf.

175

the value Jesus places on his disciples, the Father's gift to him, in 17:6–26; also the value of the one lost sheep to the shepherd, the one lost coin to the housewife, and the lost son to his father in Luke 15:4–32).

10:35 / **The people to whom his message was given**: Some of the rabbis applied Ps. 82:6 to the Israelites who witnessed the revelation at Sinai (e.g., the Babylonian Talmud, *Abodah Zarah* 5a). If this is what is in mind in the present context, Jesus' argument is reminiscent of 5:37–38 in that his hearers are being contrasted with those who heard God's message at Sinai. There is no revelation possible for those who reject Jesus, the one whom the Father chose and sent into the world (v. 36; cf. 5:38).

10:36 / **Chose**: lit., "consecrated" or "dedicated" (cf. 17:17, "Dedicate them [the disciples] to yourself"; 17:19, "I dedicate myself to you, in order that they too, may be truly dedicated to you"). The word means to set apart as holy (i.e., for a particular divine purpose). Jesus is set apart for mission to the world, and his consecration (even to death) provides the basis for the consecration, and mission, of his disciples.

10:38 / **Believe my deeds**: The statement involves a paradox. To believe Jesus' deeds, in this Gospel, *is* to believe him, which is the same as believing *in* him. Jesus is not presenting a genuine alternative, but simply indicating another avenue toward belief in him, i.e., by way of his deeds rather than his words. In the last analysis, Jesus' deeds, his words, and he himself are interchangeable as far as faith is concerned. His words and his deeds are simply the means of his self-revelation.

29

From Bethany to Bethany

JOHN 10:40–11:16

Jesus then went back again across the Jordan River to the place where John had been baptizing, and he stayed there. [41]Many people came to him. "John performed no miracles," they said, "but everything he said about this man was true." [42]And many people there believed in him.

[1]A man named Lazarus, who lived in Bethany, became sick. Bethany was the town where Mary and her sister Martha lived. ([2]This Mary was the one who poured the perfume on the Lord's feet and wiped them with her hair; it was her brother Lazarus who was sick.) [3]The sisters sent Jesus a message: "Lord, your dear friend is sick."

[4]When Jesus heard it, he said, "The final result of this sickness will not be the death of Lazarus; this has happened in order to bring glory to God, and it will be the means by which the Son of God will receive glory."

[5]Jesus loved Martha and her sister and Lazarus. [6]Yet when he received the news that Lazarus was sick, he stayed where he was for two more days. [7]Then he said to the disciples, "Let us go back to Judea."

[8]"Teacher," the disciples answered, "just a short time ago the people there wanted to stone you; and are you planning to go back?"

[9]Jesus said, "A day has twelve hours, doesn't it? So whoever walks in broad daylight does not stumble, for he sees the light of this world. [10]But if he walks during the night he stumbles, because he has no light." [11]Jesus said this and then added, "Our friend Lazarus has fallen asleep, but I will go and wake him up."

[12]The disciples answered, "If he is asleep, Lord, he will get well."

[13]Jesus meant that Lazarus had died, but they thought he meant natural sleep. [14]So Jesus told them plainly, "Lazarus is dead, [15]but for your sake I am glad that I was not with him, so that you will believe. Let us go to him."

[16]Thomas (called the Twin) said to his fellow disciples, "Let us all go along with the Teacher, so that we may die with him!"

Jesus' mysterious escape (v. 39) ends the confrontation at Solomon's Porch in the Temple at the Festival of the Dedication (cf. v. 22), just as his earlier escape had ended the confrontation in the Temple at the Festival of Shelters (cf. 8:59). This time he leaves Jerusalem itself, the scene of his activities since 7:14, and returns to Bethany on the other side of the Jordan, where he has spent time with John the Baptist and begun to gather a group of disciples (vv. 40–42; cf. 1:19–51; 3:26).

The earlier narrative implied that Jesus had a place to stay in Bethany (1:38–39), and it was there perhaps that he **stayed** again (v. 40).

The reflection on John the Baptist and his testimony on Jesus' behalf (v. 41) recalls 1:29–34, but the accompanying reminder that **John performed no miracles** drives home the point that John's witness was merely preliminary to the crucial testimony of Jesus' deeds (cf. 10:25–38). The argument of 10:25–42 is comparable to that of 5:30–47 except that the earlier passage began with the witness of John the Baptist (5:33–36) and then moved on to the more decisive witness of Jesus' own words and deeds, whereas the later passage begins with Jesus' deeds and then reflects on John's testimony in postscript.

In this sense, verses 40–42 are a postscript to verses 22–39, but their principal function is to introduce chapter 11. The length of Jesus' stay east of the Jordan is not told, but here, as elsewhere, time spent outside Jerusalem serves as an interlude or period of respite prior to Jesus' major confrontations with the religious authorities in the city. This is the case both with brief transitions like the present one (cf. 2:12; 11:54) and with the entire section comprising Jesus' itinerary from Judea through Samaria to Galilee (3:22–4:54). It is also the case with 7:1, a parallel of particular interest because of similarities (and contrasts) between the ensuing dialogue in 7:2–10 and that of 11:1–16. In each case, the question is whether or not Jesus will return to Judea, where the authorities are seeking his life:

Chapter 7	Chapter 11
Jesus traveled in Galilee (7:1).	**Jesus remained beyond the Jordan** (10:40–42).
His brothers . . . urged him to go to Judea (7:3).	**His disciples** . . . (11:7–8) **urged him *not* to go** (11:8).
Jesus waited, because his time had not yet come (7:6–9).	**Jesus waited for two days** (11:6).
Then he went (7:10). *The result*: Jesus does not die (7:30; 8:20; 59).	**Then he went** (11:9–11, 15). *The result*: **Jesus will die** (i.e., "receive glory," 11:4; cf. 11:16).

What emerges from the comparison is that the visit to Judea and Jerusalem in chapter 7 was not to be the final one, whereas the visit in chapter 11 was. At least it was to be the beginning of Jesus' "final assault" on Jerusalem and the unbelieving world. The assault takes place in two stages: the journey in chapter 11 from Bethany east of the Jordan to Bethany near Jerusalem, and the journey in chapter 12 from Ephraim near the desert (another place of respite, 11:54) to Bethany near Jerusalem a second time (12:1–11) and from there to Jerusalem itself. From 12:12 to the end of chapter 20, Jesus never leaves Jerusalem again, and all that happens there centers on his Passion.

A certain continuity between 10:40–42 and 11:1–16 is presupposed by the wording of 11:6, **he stayed where he was**. The place is of interest to the narrator, not because of the coincidence of its name with the other Bethany (which he never bothers to point out!), but because **there** (Gr.: *ekei*) many people believed in Jesus (10:42). When the question arises of returning to Judea, the disciples point out to Jesus that just recently the Judeans "tried to stone you [cf. 10:31], and yet you are going back there [Gr.: *ekei*]?" (11:8, NIV). It is a question of whether Jesus will leave a place where he is welcomed and accepted for one that has responded to all his appeals with ever-mounting antagonism. There is every reason to believe that the faith of the people east of the Jordan was genuine. The comment that **John performed no miracles** (10:41) would have been pointless unless they were aware of miracles performed by Jesus. Though their faith is a response (long delayed) to the testimony of John the Baptist, it is based not on that testimony alone but on the deeds of Jesus that subsequently verified it (cf. 10:38). In their minds they could have told John the Baptist what the Samaritan villagers told the Samaritan woman (4:42): "We believe now, not because of what you said, but because we ourselves have heard him, and we know that he really is the Savior of the world."

What was it that brought Jesus from this place of acceptance and recognition back to a place of hostility and possible death? Not a carefully planned missionary venture, and not a conscious decision to reveal himself one more time in Jerusalem. What brought him back was a response of love to a dear friend's need (11:3). The narrator pauses to introduce Lazarus (vv. 1–2), and the story begins. Lazarus is identified in relation to Bethany, and Bethany is identified in relation to the two sisters, Mary and Martha, and the story of Jesus' anointing by Mary (cf. 12:3–8). But in referring to this incident, the narrator is not so much getting ahead of his story as linking it up with something already familiar to his readers, a story from the last week of Jesus' ministry that (in one form or another) they had heard ever since they first heard the Gospel (cf. Mark 14:3–9, esp. v. 9). Did they remember the woman who anointed Jesus' feet (or, in some versions, his head)? The friend who was sick was her brother! The identification gives the reader of John's Gospel a point of reference for what follows. Unlike the sick man at Bethzatha, this sick man has a name and an identity. The reader cares from the start what happens to him (one cares deeply about the man born blind as well, but that is because one gets to know him so well as his story unfolds).

On hearing the news of Lazarus' illness, Jesus looks beyond the immediate situation to its **final result**. The end of the matter will not be death, but **glory to God**, and to **the Son of God** (v. 4). The first of Jesus' miracles (2:11) was said to reveal the glory of Jesus (i.e., to make him known to his disciples, cf. 1:14, 31), and now, just before the last of the miracles of his public ministry, **glory** is made explicit once more. The disciples' reaction to Jesus' pronouncement is not recorded. It is not even clear that he is speaking to them. His words are reassuring, yet with a note of mystery about them. Is he promising another miracle, or merely stating in general terms that God will make everything turn out for the best? If he is promising a miracle, the impression given is of a healing like the other healings that he has performed (e.g., 4:46–54; 5:1–9). There is no hint of resurrection, because the apparent meaning of verse 4 is that Lazarus will not die of his illness. Verse 12 makes it clear, in any case, that the disciples are thinking of a natural recovery, not a miraculous healing: Sleep will do Lazarus good, and he will get better. To them the message from Martha and Mary is an annoyance and a threat, summoning Jesus back to a place of danger (v. 8).

The disciples have misunderstood Jesus on two counts. First, they have assumed that Lazarus will not die. Jesus uncovers this assumption by his use of the common sleep metaphor for death (v. 11) but then corrects it by the plain statement, **Lazarus is dead** (v. 14). If Lazarus is dead, the only way the promise of verse 4 can come true is by a miracle of resurrection.

The second (and more serious) misunderstanding is closely related to the first. After his many discourses, the disciples have still not grasped his claims of sovereignty over life and death (e.g., 5:19–29; 6:35–40, 53–58; 8:31–36, 51, 58; 10:14–18, 27–30). They do not understand that the **glory** of which Jesus speaks not only does not exclude death (i.e., the death of Lazarus) but is possible *only* through death—first the death of Lazarus, and then the death of Jesus himself! The **glory of God** is the victory over death won in the case of Lazarus, a victory declared later when Jesus says to Martha, "Didn't I tell you that you would see God's glory if you believed?" (11:40). But beyond the raising of Lazarus, the glory of God is displayed in the "glorification" of God's Son (v. 4b), an expression used in this Gospel for Jesus' death on the cross (cf. 12:23; 13:31–32; 17:1). Jesus is glorified in his death because in this voluntary act of self-giving (cf. 10:18) he completes the work the Father sent him to do and receives the Father's approval.

The possibility of their teacher's death is also very much on the minds of Jesus' disciples, but as a danger to be avoided (v. 8) or an occasion for despair (v. 16), not as a moment of glory. Jesus speaks to their concern about the danger of returning to Judea with a kind of riddle (vv. 9–10), contrasting the safety of the daylight hours with the perils of traveling at night. The riddle is an elaborate way of saying what has been said several times before, that Jesus' hour (i.e., the hour of his death) has not yet come (cf. 2:4; 7:30; 8:20; cf. 7:6, 39) and that until it comes he is perfectly safe. Yet the solemn manner in which Jesus makes this point suggests to the reader that the **twelve hours** of daylight are running out and the time of darkness is near (cf. 9:4–5). When that hour is announced, therefore (12:23, 27, 35; 13:1), the announcement comes as no surprise, but as something signaled well in advance.

The disciples are reading none of the signals. The breakdown in communication between them and Jesus is almost comic. His profound remark in verse 4 draws a blank, as does the significant riddle of verses 9–10. His metaphorical statement that **Lazarus has fallen asleep, but I will go and wake him up** (v. 11; cf. Mark 5:39) is taken literally and misunderstood. Only Jesus' twice-repeated invitation to accompany him back to Judea and their sick friend (vv. 7, 15) gets through to them. The first time they hesitate because of the danger of arrest and stoning (v. 8); the second time Thomas urges them to ignore the danger and face death with their Teacher bravely (v. 16). With its strong emphasis on the prospect of death and its highlighting of the exhortation **Let us go** (vv. 7, 15, 16), the scene is curiously reminiscent of Jesus' summons to his sleeping disciples at Gethsemane (Mark 14:42/Matt. 26:46). Like that scene, it is a summons to the Passion, a challenge to stand with Jesus in his impending hour of crisis and death (this will be even more evident in 14:31).

The implication of verse 16 is that the disciples, in spite of their obtuseness, are able (with Thomas' help) to overcome the false prudence of verse 8 and to respond with courage and good will to the challenge that Jesus puts before them. He neither commends nor rebukes them for their zeal. Thomas' proposal that they follow Jesus even to death expresses an actual Johannine ideal of faithful discipleship (12:26; cf. 6:52–58), yet it has about it something of the rashness of Peter's claim after the last supper that "I am ready to die for you!" (13:37). If Jesus had asked Thomas as he asked Peter, "Are you really ready to die for me?" (13:38), the answer would have had to be no. Thomas and the others were not ready, then or later, yet their aspiration was an authentic one. They were beginning to move, and in the right direction.

A question that remains is why Jesus waited two days (v. 6) before calling his disciples back to Judea. The delay becomes an issue when he arrives and is greeted with the same sorrowful, almost accusing, words from Martha and from Mary: "If you had been here, Lord, my brother would not have died!" (vv. 21, 32; cf. v. 37). Jesus knew (supernaturally) when Lazarus died (v. 14), and his own attitude about the delay is quite different. He tells his disciples, **For your sake I am glad I was not with him, so that you will believe** (v. 15). The blunt question arises, did Jesus wait deliberately until Lazarus was dead so that he might have opportunity to perform a greater miracle? It is not likely. A better solution is that Jesus was no more willing to have his hand forced by Martha and Mary and Lazarus, all of whom he dearly loved (vv. 3, 5), than by his own mother (2:4) or his brothers (7:6–10). The account preserves the authentic memory that Jesus often responded to the initiatives of those in need (cf., e.g., 4:46–54; Mark 1:40–45; 7:24–30) but does so with a characteristically Johannine insistence that *even when this was the case* he still maintained his independence from all human pressures and his accountability to the Father alone. He responds to every cry for help, but in his own time and on his own terms. Neither enemies nor friends set his agenda or control his actions. Though not autonomous, he is "sovereign" in the sense that no one but the Father tells him what to do (cf. 4:34; 10:18). His two-day wait exemplifies that peculiar sovereignty under the Father's direction that distinguishes Jesus' life (especially in this Gospel) from all others.

Additional Notes

10:41–42 / **Came to him . . . believed in him**: For the combination of "coming to" Jesus and "believing," cf. 3:18–21; 6:35; 7:37–38.

11:3 / **Your dear friend**: lit., "one whom you love" (cf. v. 5, where a different word for love is used, but with the same meaning). Besides these two sisters and one brother, the only other person singled out *individually* as an object of Jesus' love is the so-called beloved disciple mentioned in the latter half of this Gospel and identified as the Gospel's author (13:23–25; 21:20–24). Some have speculated that the beloved disciple is indeed Lazarus (who, having been raised from the dead, might naturally be rumored not to die, 21:23), but such a view fails to explain why he would be named in chapters 11–12 and anonymous from there on. Lazarus, Martha, and Mary are never called disciples of Jesus (probably because they do not travel with him), yet it appears that anything said to, or about, the disciples could be said of them as well. They are Jesus' "friends" (vv. 3, 5, 11; cf. 15:13–15); Martha's confession of faith in Jesus (v. 27) corresponds word for word to the confession this Gospel was written to reinforce (cf. 20:31). Unlike the beloved disciple they are not authority figures or quasi-official witnesses to the Gospel tradition; they are instead "ordinary believers," participants in the story with whom the readers of the Gospel (i.e., the Christian community at large) can identify (cf. the royal official in 4:43–54).

11:4 / **To bring glory to God**: see note on 11:40.

The Son of God will receive glory: lit., "be glorified." Jesus in his glorification can be designated **Son of God** (as here), "Son of Man" (12:23; 13:31), "your Son" (17:1), "Jesus" (7:39; 12:16), or with a first person pronoun (17:5). This verse is one of the few instances in which the full confessional term **the Son of God** occurs on the lips of Jesus himself (never in the synoptic Gospels, and in John's Gospel only here and in 3:18; 5:25; and 10:36; Jesus avoids it even in eliciting a confession of faith from the man born blind in 9:35). The term is implicit, however, in Jesus' characteristic language about "the Father" and "the Son" (e.g., 5:19–23), and Jesus' use of it in 10:36 is intended to summarize all his claims for himself both in word and deed (cf. 19:7). The title may have been chosen in the present context for the sake of the parallelism of "glory of God" (v. 4a [lit.]) and **Son of God** (v. 4b); in the rhetoric of Jesus, cf. "Spirit of God" and "Kingdom of God" (instead of Matthew's characteristic "kingdom of heaven") in Matt. 12:28, NIV.

11:6 / **Yet**: The GNB's use of this word is based on the assumption that v. 5 is inserted to explain that Jesus' delay did not indicate a lack of love for his friends: *Even though* he loved them, nevertheless he delayed. But since the Greek particle *oun* means "therefore" or "so" rather than "yet" or "nevertheless," the purpose of v. 5 is probably to explain why Jesus went at all (despite the danger) rather than why he delayed.

11:6 / **Two more days**: There is no symbolic significance in the two days. Lazarus' resurrection is not on the "third day" (to correspond with the resurrection of Jesus) but after four (vv. 17, 39). Nor is a connection plausible between these two days and the length of Jesus' journey to Galilee (2:1) or of his stay at Sychar in Samaria (4:40, 43). The point of the delay is simply to set the stage for Jesus' disclosure that Lazarus is dead (vv. 11–15) and for the ensuing narrative.

11:8 / **The people there**: lit., "the Judeans" or "the Jews." In this instance the reference is geographical because of the accompanying mention of "Judea" (v. 7), yet the specific group in mind is clearly the Jewish religious establishment in Jerusalem (cf. 10:31).

11:12 / **He will get well**: lit., "he will be saved." This is a rare instance of a secular use of the Greek verb *sōzein* ("save") for natural healing or recuperation.

11:16 / **Thomas (called the Twin)**: In Greek, *Didymos* was a proper name with the etymological meaning of "twin." The Hebrew word *te'ōm* (Aramaic: *te'ōmâ*) meant "twin," but was not (as far as we know) a surname. It may, however, have been a nickname. There was a *Greek* name **Thomas** and sometimes in the Hellenistic period a Jewish man who was known to be a twin, or descended from a twin, may have taken (or been given) **Thomas** as his Greek name. If so, in this instance **Thomas** was the disciple's Greek name, while "Didymos," **the Twin**, was an additional Greek name given as a reminder of the Semitic origin and meaning of his name. In later tradition, Thomas was identified with Jude or Judah, the brother of Jesus (cf. Mark 6:3) and regarded as the twin of Jesus himself! (e.g., *Acts of Thomas* 11; also 31; cf. *Gospel of Thomas* 1).

11:16 / **So that we may die with him!**: The GNB translation correctly understands Thomas to refer to dying with Jesus (cf. v. 8). Because of the preceding statement that "Lazarus is dead," (lit., "died," v. 14), it is grammatically possible to understand him to mean dying with Lazarus, but the cause and circumstances of death would be so different from those in the case of Lazarus that such a meaning is highly unlikely.

30

The Raising of Lazarus

When Jesus arrived, he found that Lazarus had been buried four days before. [18]Bethany was less than two miles from Jerusalem, [19]and many Judeans had come to see Martha and Mary to comfort them about their brother's death.

[20]When Martha heard that Jesus was coming, she went out to meet him, but Mary stayed in the house. [21]Martha said to Jesus, "If you had been here, my brother would not have died! [22]But I know that even now God will give you whatever you ask him for."

[23]"Your brother will rise to life," Jesus told her.

[24]"I know," she replied, "that he will rise to life on the last day."

[25]Jesus said to her, "I am the resurrection and the life. Whoever believes in me will live, even though he dies; [26]and whoever lives and believes in me will never die. Do you believe this?"

[27]"Yes Lord!" she answered. "I do believe that you are the Messiah, the Son of God, who was to come into the world."

[28]After Martha said this, she went back and called her sister Mary privately. "The Teacher is here," she told her, "and is asking for you."

[29]When Mary heard this, she got up and hurried out to meet him. ([30]Jesus had not yet arrived in the village, but was still in the place where Martha had met him.) [31]The people who were in the house with Mary comforting her followed her when they saw her get up and hurry out. They thought that she was going to the grave to weep there.

[32]Mary arrived where Jesus was, and as soon as she saw him, she fell at his feet. "Lord," she said, "if you had been here, my brother would not have died!"

[33]Jesus saw her weeping, and he saw how the people with her were weeping also; his heart was touched, and he was deeply moved. [34]"Where have you buried him?" he asked them.

"Come and see, Lord," they answered.

[35]Jesus wept. [36]"See how much he loved him!" the people said.

[37]But some of them said, "He gave sight to the blind man, didn't he? Could he not have kept Lazarus from dying?"

[38]Deeply moved once more, Jesus went to the tomb, which was a cave with a stone placed at the entrance. [39]"Take the stone away!" Jesus ordered.

Martha, the dead man's sister, answered, "There will be a bad smell, Lord. He has been buried four days!"

[40]Jesus said to her, "Didn't I tell you that you would see God's glory if you believed?" [41]They took the stone away. Jesus looked up and said, "I thank you, Father, that you listen to me. [42]I know that you always listen to me, but I say this for the sake of the people here, so that they will believe that you sent me."

[43]After he had said this, he called out in a loud voice, "Lazarus, come out!" [44]He came out, his his hands and feet wrapped in grave cloths, and with a cloth around his face. "Untie him," Jesus told them, "and let him go."

After a brief introduction setting the stage for the action (vv. 17–19), the drama of the raising of Lazarus unfolds in three scenes: one between Jesus and Martha providing a theological interpretation for the whole (vv. 20–27), one in which Jesus reacts to the sorrow of Mary and some Jews who came to mourn with her (vv. 28–37), and one at the tomb recounting the actual procedure by which Jesus raised Lazarus to life (vv. 38–44).

It is not certain how long the journey took from Bethany to Bethany. The purpose of the statement that Lazarus **had been buried four days before** (v. 17) is not to construct a chronology or to help fix the location of the puzzling Bethany east of the Jordan (cf. 1:28). If Lazarus died at about the time Jesus received word of his illness (v. 4), the journey (after a two-day wait) would have taken at least two days. If he died (as is more likely) at about the time Jesus said he had "fallen asleep" (v. 11), it would have taken longer. The purpose of mentioning the four days is to provide a backdrop for Martha's comment in verse 39, and thus for Jesus' dramatic encounter with the grim reality of death in verses 40–44.

The narrator is more interested in Bethany's location in relation to *Jerusalem* (v. 18) than in relation to the other Bethany to the east. Part of the reason may be that he knows this distance and does not know the other, but more significantly, he wants to explain the presence there of some Jews from Jerusalem (v. 19) who will play a small yet crucial role in the story (cf. vv. 31, 33, 36–37, 45–46). The fact that their presence in Bethany needs to be explained (most of the townspeople of Bethany, after all, were Jews!) suggests that here, as frequently in this Gospel, religious authorities of some kind are meant. Because Bethany was as close to Jerusalem as it was, people from Jerusalem had come to join in the mourning, and among these were many of the religious leaders.

Jesus' arrival in Bethany is described like the visit of a conquering king, or in the way the early Christians later expected him to come gloriously to earth a second time in his Parousia (e.g., 1 Thess. 4:15–17; 1 Cor. 15:23; 51–57; like the returning Lord of Paul's expectation, Jesus is coming to Bethany to raise the dead). It is a kind of triumphal entry told in advance, more private than public, in a small village instead of a great city. It is not so much an anticipation of the public entry into Jerusalem (12:12–19) as the beginning of the chain of events leading up to it. To Martha, Jesus was the Coming One (v. 27; cf. 6:14), and when she **heard that Jesus was coming** to her village and her own house she **went out to meet him** (v. 20), like a delegation sent to welcome and escort a victorious emperor into a city (cf. the language used of Jesus' welcome into Jerusalem in 12:13, 18).

Martha's greeting to Jesus (v. 21) recalls his delay in responding to her message. But despite its tone, the intent is not to accuse; even if Jesus had come at once, Lazarus would still be two days dead. Martha's purpose (and Mary's in v. 32) is rather to affirm her confidence in Jesus' power to heal the sick. Even in the present tragic circumstances she does not exclude the possibility of a miracle, though she has no inkling what form it might take (v. 22; for a similar note of anticipation, cf. the remarks of Jesus' mother in 2:5). What *is* clear to her is that Jesus' power is the power of God; if he works a miracle, he must do so not on his own authority but on that of the Father (cf. 5:17, 19). Every miracle of Jesus finally comes down to a miracle of answered prayer (cf. 6:11; 9:31), whether the prayer is expressed verbally or not. In the case of Lazarus, the prayer is explicit. Jesus will ask that Lazarus be made alive, and God will grant it (cf. vv. 41–44).

When Jesus assures Martha that **your brother will rise to life** (v. 23), he is in one breath expressing the common hope he shares with the Pharisees (e.g., Acts 23:6–8; 24:15; cf. John 5:28–29) and announcing what he will do that very day. Martha comprehends the former but not the latter. That her brother **will rise to life on the last day** (v. 24) is something on which she and Jesus can agree. It is a genuine consolation, but it is not something she needed Jesus to tell her, and it does not cut the sorrow of the moment. Instead of addressing the death of Lazarus directly, Jesus speaks to the larger issue of the Jewish resurrection hope (vv. 25–26). Though he says nothing he has not said before in this Gospel (cf. 5:21, 24–26; 6:39–40, 44, 54; 8:51, 58), Jesus quickly does two things that address Martha's immediate concern: He puts himself, and faith in him, squarely at the center of the resurrection hope, and he transforms that hope from a future, somewhat theoretical, expectation into a present experience of the very life of God.

The form of Jesus' reply (vv. 25–26) resembles that of several other of his "I am" pronouncements, in which the "I am" with its predicate is followed by an invitation or promise, introduced by a conditional clause or a participle (cf. 6:35; 8:12; 10:9). In this instance there are two predicates (**I am the resurrection and the life**, v. 25a) and two invitation/promises (**whoever believes in me will live, even though he dies**, v. 25b; **whoever lives and believes in me will never die**, v. 26a). The first of these **whoever** clauses (participles in Greek) explains "I am the resurrection";

the second explains "I am the life." The meaning can be set forth as follows:

a. I am the resurrection—that is, whoever believes in me will live, even though he or she dies.

b. I am the life—that is, whoever lives and believes in me will never die.

The relation of the two parts is best understood when (*b*) is viewed as following logically from (*a*). If it is true that whoever believes in Jesus and dies (e.g., Lazarus) will live again, then it follows that no living believer will ever die—ultimately. The life they have been given is eternal life (cf. 3:16; 10:28). They may die physically, but death's dominion is only temporary. Jesus will "raise them to life on the last day" (6:39–40).

The distinctly Christian note here is that *Jesus* will raise them. He, in his own person, is the resurrection and therefore the life. Life is a relationship to him. As long as Jesus is present, life is present, not simply the life breathed into humanity at the creation (cf. 1:4), but resurrection life, the new life that belongs to "the last day" and will never end.

Martha's response to the pronouncement is entirely appropriate in centering on the person of Jesus (v. 27). This is true despite his lack of interest in titles (cf. 10:34–38) and despite the fact that he neither rebukes nor endorses her confession (he is similarly reserved about the confessions of Nathanael in 1:49, Peter in 6:69, and Thomas in 20:28). Martha acknowledges Jesus as **the Messiah, the Son of God** in the context of his claim to be the giver of life; her explicit **Yes, Lord** to his question, **Do you believe this?** makes this clear. The narrator's endorsement of her confession is seen in his use of the same two titles in stating the purpose for which the Gospel was written (20:31a). He wants his readers to join Martha in her testimony to Jesus, with the explicit intent "that through your faith in him you may have life" (20:31b). Though titles are not an end in themselves, they make sense when they display (as they do in Martha's case) a recognition of Jesus' works and of his power and willingness to give life.

Thus Martha, the practical-minded but troubled hostess of Luke's Gospel (cf. Luke 10:38–42), becomes in the Gospel of John both a woman of words and a woman of faith. Mary's role, surprisingly, is but a faint echo of Martha's (vv. 28–32). She had remained at home, in mourning, and came out to meet Jesus only when Martha came back to summon her (v. 28). Her first words on seeing Jesus duplicate exactly the words of Martha (v. 32; cf. v. 21), but without the added note of hopefulness (cf. v. 22). The narrator seems to know the same traditions about Mary and Martha that are known to Luke, for he portrays Mary always at Jesus' feet (v. 32; cf. 12:3; Luke 10:39). But in the present account at least, hers is a secondary role. She is in the story mainly to weep, and this function she shares with the Jewish leaders who had come from Jerusalem (v. 31; cf. v. 19). The sight of her and these other Jews weeping aroused the emotions of Jesus—sorrow (v. 35), agitation and (surprisingly) anger (vv. 33, 38). He was not angry at Mary and her fellow mourners for losing control (loud weeping was normal and expected in such situations), nor for their lack of faith in what he would do (for they had no way of knowing what that would be). Rather, he was angry at death, the Enemy who holds all human beings captive to uncleanness and shame (cf. Heb. 2:14-15). Death is not here personalized as the Devil, yet the implicit conflict at the tomb of Lazarus is the same conflict with darkness and the "ruler of this world" that emerges in connection with Jesus' own impending death (cf. 12:31; 13:2; 14:30). His anger recalls the anger he sometimes displays in the synoptic Gospels when he faces uncleanness (Mark 1:40-45) or drives out demons (Mark 9:19).

As Jesus proceeds to the tomb, his tears bring a mixed reaction from the Jewish leaders who had come to mourn with the two sisters. His strong emotion gives undeniable evidence of his love for Lazarus, yet there are those who question his power, or his willingness, or both, to have prevented his friend's death (vv. 36-37). The momentary disagreement is a harbinger of a more serious division to come (cf. vv. 45-46).

The miracle itself is told briefly (vv. 38-44). No interpretive discourse follows because Martha has already been given the interpretation (vv. 25-26). Martha, accordingly, is the only witness singled out at the scene of the miracle itself. It is her remark that calls the reader's attention to the stench and foulness of death (v. 39), and it is to her that Jesus renews his promise of **God's glory** (v. 40; cf. v. 4). The promise is immediately fulfilled. When the stone blocking the entrance to the tomb is taken away (in spite of Martha's warning), Jesus looks up to God in prayer. His prayer takes the form of a thanksgiving rather than a petition (cf. 6:11); his relationship to the Father is so close and intimate (cf. 10:38) that he knows his petitions are already answered and that Lazarus will come to life (vv. 41-42). He prays aloud, not because it is necessary, but so that the onlookers will know that he is not acting autonomously. He calls Lazarus by name, with an authority given him from the Father (cf. 5:21, 25-26). As soon as Jesus speaks, Lazarus hobbles from the tomb, **his hands and feet wrapped in grave cloths, and with a cloth around his face** (v. 44). The almost ludicrous sight stands in sharp contrast to the description of the tomb of Jesus on the morning of his resurrection (cf. 20:5–7). The narrator knows (and emphasizes) the difference between the resurrection of Jesus and the resuscitation of Lazarus. Lazarus was raised from death only to die again. After the miracle, he would resume the same kind of life he had known before. Jesus, on the other hand would be raised into a new existence in the presence of the Father and into a new relationship with his disciples. Never again would death touch him. Yet despite the contrast, the narrator uses the resuscitation of Lazarus as a "sign" (cf. 12:18, RSV) of the resurrection to new life, whether of Jesus or of those who belong to him.

In itself, the raising of Lazarus is not qualitatively different from Jesus' other miracles of healing. A resuscitation is a kind of "super-healing," and the two instances in the synoptic Gospels in which Jesus raised the dead (i.e., Mark 5:35–43; Luke 7:11–17) are not singled out from his other healings for special attention. Is is only *as a sign* that the raising of Lazarus stands supreme among Jesus' miracles. But because John's Gospel is interested in Jesus' miracles precisely as signs of his **glory** (i.e., as expressions of his relationship to the Father), this miracle serves the narrator as the fitting conclusion and capstone to the series of signs that comprise Jesus' public ministry.

Additional Notes

11:17 / **Buried four days before**: Many commentators refer to a Jewish belief that for three days after death "the soul hovers over the body, intending to re-enter it, but as soon as it sees its appearance change, it departs" (Midrash *Leviticus Rabbah* 18,1 [Midrash Rabbah IV (London: Soncino Press, 1961), p. 226]). Such a belief is not widely attested, but it was true that in the oral law, if a body was to be identified, it had to be identified within three days after death (on the theory that beyond that interval the physical changes produced by decay would be too extensive to permit certainty; the Mishnah, *Yebamoth* 16.3). It is doubtful that such discussions shed light on the present passage. If the intent was to underscore the fact that Lazarus was truly dead, the detail seems both unnecessary (he was, after all, buried!) and confusing (was Jesus *not* really dead because he was raised within three days?). Rather, the intent is simply to prepare the reader for Jesus' confrontation with death as decay and uncleanness in v. 39.

11:18 / **Less than two miles**: lit., "about fifteen stadia." See note on 6:19.

11:19 / **Judeans**: This is not a helpful translation, because it makes the preceding note of Bethany's distance from Jerusalem unnecessary. Anyone who lived in Bethany would be a "Judean" and in all probability a "Jew," but these **Judeans** (or "Jews") are mentioned because they are from Jerusalem.

11:27 / **Who was to come into the world**: Though technically correct (because from Martha's standpoint **the Son of God** has now come), the translation is open to the misunderstanding that he **was to come** but did not. The intent of the construction (a present participle in Greek) is not to fix the time of the Messiah's coming (as between present and future) but to define his character as a Coming One (i.e., one who invades this world and transforms it). A better translation might be the "Messiah, the Son of God who comes into the world."

11:28 / **Privately**: The need for privacy is shown by vv. 19 and 31. Because Martha wants Mary to have a moment alone with Jesus, she does not want the whole group of mourners present. But the privacy she seeks turns out to be impossible (v. 31).

The Teacher is here. Martha's confessional language (v. 27) does not carry over into the words spoken to her sister. Between the two of them, Jesus is simply **the Teacher**, for they are his disciples. **Teacher**, like "Lord" (the term they use consistently in addressing Jesus) connotes both allegiance and respect (cf. 13:13).

Is asking for you; lit., "calls you." Jesus' words requesting that Mary be summoned are not recorded. It is possible that Martha regards vv. 25–26 as Jesus' "call," whether to herself, or Mary, or any believer. The same verb is used of the calling of Lazarus from the grave (12:17) and of the shepherd calling his sheep by name (10:3); the corresponding noun is used of the "voice" by which the Son of God calls the dead to life (5:25, 28; cf. 11:43). It is more likely, however, that Jesus' request to see Mary had simply been omitted in vv. 20–27 in order to focus attention on Martha's own encounter with Jesus and her momentous confession.

11:33 / **His heart was touched, and he was deeply moved**: lit., "he became angry in his spirit, and shook himself." The note of anger is suppressed in GNB, as in virtually all English translations, both here and in v. 38 (lit., "being angry once more within himself"), but the Greek verbs used unmistakably denote anger and agitation. Whether the agitation (or "shaking") is physical as well as emotional is difficult to say; the active voice ("he shook himself") suggests that it is. The anger seems to be on the inside, while the shaking or trembling is the outward expression of it. The first question an interpreter or translator should ask is not Why would Jesus shake with anger? but What do the words actually mean?

11:35 / **Jesus wept**. The word for **wept** here is different from the word used for the weeping of Mary and the Jewish leaders. The latter (vv. 31, 33) means "wail" (like the customary wailing at a funeral of the time), whereas the word used of Jesus means simply "to shed tears." That Jesus' emotions were deep and genuine, however, is shown by vv. 33 and 38.

11:37 / **He gave sight to the blind man, didn't he?** Cf. 10:21. In itself, the remark could be used to cast doubt on the reality of the healing of the blind man (i.e., the fact that he did not prevent Lazarus from dying makes it doubtful that he healed the blind man at all). But following as it does on v. 36, its intent is rather to call into question the genuineness of Jesus' love (i.e., the healing of the blind man proves he had the power to prevent his friend's death; what must have been lacking was the willingness to do so).

11:40 / **Didn't I tell you that you would see God's glory if you believed?** To what previous statement is Jesus referring? He had promised Martha that her brother would be raised to life (v. 23); he had also spoken to her about "believing" (vv. 25–26), and she had indeed "believed" (v. 27). But there had been no explicit promise of **God's glory**. He had mentioned the glory of God in v. 4, but not to Martha.

An intriguing possibility is that v. 4 was not intended as a word spoken to the disciples who were with Jesus east of the Jordan, but actually as a response sent back to the sisters in answer to their message about Lazarus' illness (v. 3). If so, v. 40 may refer specifically to v. 4. Though v. 4 is not explicitly said to be a message sent from a distance, neither is it said to be spoken to the disciples, and the disciples give no evidence of having heard it (contrast v. 7, where Jesus explicitly addresses "the disciples"). In any event, vv. 4 and 40 are closely linked by the notion that the glory of God was displayed in the raising of Lazarus from the dead (cf. also the continuing vision promised to Jesus' disciples according to 1:51).

11:44 / **Untie him . . . and let him go**. All three resuscitations in the Gospels end with a similarly warm human interest touch in which Jesus meets an additional, comparatively minor, need (cf. Mark 5:43; Luke 7:15). It is possible also that the release of Lazarus from the bands of cloth that bound him is intended to suggest the biblical imagery of "loosing" for victory over death and the powers of evil (e.g., Matt. 16:19; Luke 13:16; Acts 2:24; cf. John 8:32–36).

31

The Verdict against Jesus

JOHN 11:45–54

Many of the people who had come to visit Mary saw what Jesus did, and they believed in him. [46]But some of them returned to the Pharisees and told them what Jesus had done. [47]So the Pharisees and the chief priests met with the Council and said, "What shall we do? Look at all the miracles this man is performing! [48]If we let him go on in this way, everyone will believe in him, and the Roman authorities will take action and destroy our Temple and our nation!"

[49]One of them, named Caiaphas, who was High Priest that year, said "What fools you are! [50]Don't you realize that it is better for you to have one man die for the people, instead of having the whole nation destroyed?" [51]Actually, he did not say this of his own accord; rather, as he was High Priest that year, he was prophesying that Jesus was going to die for the Jewish people, [52]and not only for them, but also to bring together into one body all the scattered people of God.

[53]From that day on the Jewish authorities made plans to kill Jesus. [54]So Jesus did not travel openly in Judea, but left and went to a place near the desert, to a town named Ephraim, where he stayed with the disciples.

T he public ministry of Jesus, which began with the cleansing of the Temple (2:13–22), exhibits throughout features that in the Synoptics had been associated with Passion week in Jerusalem: first, his practice of teaching in the Temple (e.g., 7:14–8:59; 10:22–39; cf. Luke 21:37–38), and second, the theme implicit in that teaching that both he and his audience are involved in a trial, calling their respective witnesses and seeking vindication (e.g., 5:30–47; 8:12–20).

Compared to the synoptic records of Jesus' trial before the Jewish ruling Council, or Sanhedrin, (cf. Mark 14:53–65; 15:1; Matt. 26:57–68; 27:1–2; Luke 22:66–71), this is a long trial indeed. If there is anything corresponding to his momentous self-disclosure before the High Priest (Mark 14:62; Matthew 26:64; cf. Luke 22:69), it is the exchange in Solomon's Porch in the Temple in 10:22–39. Even here, Jesus points back to claims made earlier, whether in word or deed (10:25). The synoptic trial of Jesus is frequently divided into the "Jewish trial" and the "Roman trial," and it is the Jewish trial that in John's Gospel is replaced by the public ministry. Only the Roman trial, the hearing before Pilate, is left for the Passion narrative (18:33–38; cf. Mark 15:2–4; Matthew 27:11–14; Luke 23:1–5). But in order to be concluded, a trial must reach a verdict. Verses 47–53 record the "verdict" of the Sanhedrin against Jesus, not a formal or official verdict, but simply the final determination that he must die.

The verdict comes as a direct result of the raising of Lazarus. The Jews who had been mourning at the house of Martha and Mary are split into two groups over the miracle. **Many** believed in Jesus but **some** went and told the Pharisees what he had done (v. 45; though the word "division" or "schism" is not used, the situation recalls the "divisions" mentioned in 7:43; 9:16; and 10:19–21; cf. also the dispute described in vv. 36–37, within this very company of mourners). It was the report of the unbelieving faction to the Pharisees that precipitated the gathering of the Sanhedrin. The Pharisees and chief priests were alarmed, not simply by the raising of Lazarus, but by **all the miracles this man is performing** (v. 47). They feared a mass movement based on faith in Jesus, and consequent reprisals by the Roman government (v. 48; that revolutionary ideas were abroad is shown by the attempt in Galilee to make Jesus a king by force, 6:15).

The proposal of Caiaphas the High Priest (vv. 49–50) is not quite so obvious as it might first appear. His intent is not merely to do away with Jesus before he brings down on Israel the wrath of Rome, but to maneuver Rome itself into doing away with him. Better for Rome to destroy one man than the whole nation. In this sense, according to Caiaphas, Jesus must **die for the people** (v. 50).

The narrator seizes on the phrase **die for the people** and gives it a quite different interpretation in verses 51–52. He gives himself the liberty to do this on the grounds that Caiaphas (as High Priest) must have been a prophet as well; consequently his words are from God and have a deeper meaning than appears on the surface. Jesus will **die for the Jewish people** (as the good shepherd, "willing to die for the sheep" v. 51; 10:11, 15). As shepherd, too, he will **bring together into one . . . all the scattered people of God** (v. 52; cf. 10:16). Jesus' death is redemptive; by it the Jewish people have an opportunity to be spared—spared not merely from political destruction, as Caiaphas hoped, but spared from death itself (cf. v. 26). More than that, Jesus' death is unifying; by it all who believe, of every race, will not only receive eternal life, but will (with the Jews) be gathered into a single community, safe from all external dangers (10:16, 28–29; cf. 17:11, 20–23). This is the vision of Jesus in John's Gospel, a vision the Gospel writer has taken up and—through the eyes of

Caiaphas—made his own. The writer's assumption is that Caiaphas' words far transcended his personal knowledge and intent. Like Balaam (cf. Num. 24) he spoke more wisely than he knew, and his evil designs were turned to a divine purpose.

Verses 51–52 interrupt the record of the Council. On the advice of Caiaphas, the religious authorities made their decision **to kill Jesus** (v. 53). In a practical sense, the outcome was nothing new. The authorities had been "determined to kill him" ever since the first confrontation over the Sabbath law (5:18), and from that time on Jesus had been a wanted man. Again and again the terminology used is that they were "trying to kill" him (7:1, 19, 25; 8:37, 40), a phrase more suggestive of mob violence than of formal judicial proceedings. He had called them murderers, and children of the first murderer, the Devil (8:44); the Sanhedrin "verdict" simply made final a murderous intent that had been present all along.

For one last time the familiar pattern of flight from danger to a place of relative seclusion repeats itself. This time the retreat is **a town named Ephraim** near the desert (v. 54), a place, in all likelihood, where Jesus had stayed before (like the Bethany east of the Jordan) and where he knew he could find refuge.

Additional Notes

11:47 / **The Council**: lit., "the Sanhedrin," the highest ruling body among the Jews in Judea. The Sanhedrin was composed of the chief priests, the elders or lay nobility of the people, and the scholars or scribes (including Pharisees) and was presided over by the ruling High Priest. This body had the final authority in both the religious and secular affairs of the Jews as long as its decisions did not encroach on the authority of the Roman procurator. It is debated whether at this time the Sanhedrin had the authority to carry out the death penalty (the stoning of Stephen in Acts 7 suggests that it did, but John 18:31 is customarily cited as evidence that it did not; but see the discussion of 18:31).

What shall we do? The expression (a present indicative rather than a deliberative subjunctive) could also be translated, "What are we doing?" (with the implied answer "Nothing" or "The wrong thing"). But the GNB rendering agrees with the context and is probably correct.

11:48 / **Everyone will believe in him**. Cf. the use of similarly sweeping language in 1:7; 3:26; 12:32, and esp. 12:19. The "universalism" is not merely a groundless fear on the part of the priests and Pharisees (cf. 12:11) but belongs to the Gospel writer's perspective. Yet such language is not intended literally. For the Gospel writer, it simply points in a general way to the accomplishment of God's will in the mission of Jesus and of his followers.

Our Temple: lit., "our place." The term could refer either to the holy place (i.e., the **Temple**, as in GNB), or to the holy city of Jerusalem. It is likely, on the basis of contemporary usage, that the **Temple** is meant; e.g., Acts 6:13-14; 7:7, and esp. John 4:20, where the Greek text reads "in Jerusalem is the place where one must worship" (in the latter instance, ironically, the GNB has incorrectly understood the "place" as the city: "Jerusalem is the place where we should worship God").

11:49 / **That year** (cf. v. 51; 18:13): There is no implication that the High Priest served only one year. Such an implication would be mistaken. In theory, the High Priest served for life (cf. Num. 35:25), and in practice he served either for life or until the Romans deposed him. Caiaphas served no less than eighteen years (cf. Josephus, *Antiquities* 18.35, 95). The phrase **that year** is probably used rhetorically, in the sense of "that fateful year of our Lord's Passion"; cf. "that day" (v. 53), and "that time" (lit., "that hour," 19:27), both in relation to Jesus' Passion.

11:51 / **Prophesying**: The narrator seems to assume that Jewish High Priests had the gift of prophecy. Josephus attributes prophecy to John Hyrcanus who was High Priest from about 135 to 104 B.C., but with some indication that this was, if not unique, at least not the general rule (*Wars* 1.68-69; *Antiquities* 13.299-300). An earlier High Priest, Jaddus, had received a revelation in connection with the visit to Jerusalem of Alexander the Great, and Alexander himself had received a corresponding relevation (*Antiquities* 11.327, 333-334). But the narrator is not so much concerned with generalizing about the prophetic powers of High Priests as simply interpreting one specific utterance as a prophecy. The fact that Caiaphas was High Priest made it slightly more appropriate for the narrator to do so, and he seized the opportunity.

11:52 / **One body**: The word **body** is not in the Greek text, and it somewhat confuses the picture by introducing the Pauline body metaphor (as, e.g., in 1 Cor. 12:12-27). The narrator probably has in mind simply the concept of oneness; if a metaphor is involved at all, it is the metaphor of "one flock," as in 10:16.

Scattered people of God: lit., "scattered children of God." The "children of God" is here a designation for those who had been chosen for salvation (contrast 1:12, where the term denotes what people become as a result of believing in Jesus); "children of God" is thus equivalent to "sheep" (specifically the "other sheep . . . not in this sheep pen," in 10:16. A more remote metaphor that may have contributed to the choice of language here is that of the church as broken bread "scattered on the mountains" that was "gathered together and made one" (*Didache* 9.4; cf. John 6:12-13).

11:54 / **Did not travel openly in Judea**: The situation corresponds closely to that described in 7:1, except that in that instance Jesus stayed in Galilee.

A town named Ephraim: The exact location of this place is unknown. Eusebius in the fourth century located it about twenty miles north of Jerusalem and five miles east of Bethel (*Onomasticon* 28.4; 90.19). The sixth-century Madeba map also places "Ephron or Ephraea: the Lord was there" northeast near Rimmon, in the hill country adjoining the Jordan valley. If these traditions are correct, "Aenon, not far from Salim" (3:23) would be some distance to the north, and it is possible (though it cannot be proven) that Ephraim is where Jesus' disciples carried on a baptizing ministry (3:22). Modern identifications of the site have centered either on the Arab village of et-Taiybe (once called "Afra"), or the valley of Ain Samniya slightly to the northeast.

With the disciples: It is uncertain whether the **disciples** with whom Jesus stayed were the same group of disciples that traveled with him to Bethany (cf. 11:16), or a community of disciples who lived in Ephraim, or both. Probably Thomas and his companions joined Jesus in his retreat, but if Ephraim was familiar territory, there may have been a group of disciples there who provided them lodging. (cf. 3:22, 26; 4:1).

32

The Last Passover

JOHN 11:55–12:11

The time for the Passover Festival was near, and many people went up from the country to Jerusalem to perform the ritual of purification before the festival. [56]They were looking for Jesus, and as they gathered in the Temple, they asked one another, "What do you think? Surely he will not come to the festival, will he?" [57]The chief priests and the Pharisees had given orders that if anyone knew where Jesus was, he must report it, so that they could arrest him.

Six days before the Passover, Jesus went to Bethany, the home of Lazarus, the man he had raised from death. [2]They prepared a dinner for him there, which Martha helped serve; Lazarus was one of those who were sitting at the table with Jesus. [3]Then Mary took a whole pint of a very expensive perfume made of pure nard, poured it on Jesus' feet, and wiped them with her hair. The sweet smell of the perfume filled the whole house. [4]One of Jesus' disciples, Judas Iscariot—the one who was going to betray him—said, [5]"Why wasn't this perfume sold for three hundred silver coins and the money given to the poor?" [6]He said this, not because he cared about the poor, but because he was a thief. He carried the money bag and would help himself from it.

[7]But Jesus said, "Leave her alone! Let her keep what she has for the day of my burial. [8]You will always have poor people with you, but you will not always have me."

[9]A large number of people heard that Jesus was in Bethany, so they went there, not only because of Jesus but also to see Lazarus, whom Jesus had raised from death. [10]So the chief priests made plans to kill Lazarus too, [11]because on his acccount many Jews were rejecting them and believing in Jesus.

For the third time in John's Gospel, the Passover is near (v. 55; cf. 2:13; 6:4), and for the second and last time (cf. 2:13), Jesus travels to Jerusalem to keep the festival. The early visit to Jerusalem involving the cleansing of the Temple (2:13–22) had given the impression that Jesus' Passion was about to begin, but it did not. Now the Passion *is* soon to begin, and the narrator creates an atmosphere of expectancy for his story. He does not immediately state that "Jesus went to Jerusalem" (2:13), but says that **many people** (v. 55) did so, and that when they arrived, they looked for Jesus, asking **What do you think? Surely he will not come to the festival, will he?** (v. 56). Jesus first returns to Bethany (12:1), and then triumphantly enters Jerusalem (12:12–19). The suspense builds as the Passover draws ever closer: **near** (11:55), **six days before** (12:1), "the next day" (i.e., five days before, 12:12), "the day before" (13:1). Jesus' "assault" on the city, leading to his arrest, death, and resurrection, develops step by step.

Who were the **many** who **went up from the country** so as to be in Jerusalem early for the festival and perform the necessary rites of self-purification? Were they Jews from all over Israel, or a more specific group? The fact that the word **country** in verse 55 is the same word translated "place" in verse 54 suggests that they may have come from the same region where Jesus was staying. That they were **looking for Jesus** and speculating as to whether he would come to the festival (v. 50) is natural if they were acquainted with him and knew his previous whereabouts. It is not likely that his name was such a household word that people from all over Israel would be asking this question.

At any rate, the worshipers described in verses 55–56 (unlike the "Jewish authorities" in 7:11, a similar passage in some ways) are not hostile to Jesus, but neutral (more like the "crowd" in 7:12). If they knew where Jesus had previously been staying, they did not tell the authorities. The identification and continuity of the crowds of people mentioned throughout chapter 12 is a difficult matter, and it is natural to ask whether the **large number of people** in 12:9 who came to Bethany to see Jesus and Lazarus can be identified with the group looking for Jesus according to 11:55–56. The crowd in 12:9 was clearly in violation of the command given by the **chief priests and the Pharisees** (11:57) that **if anyone knew where Jesus was, he must report it**. They learned that he was in Bethany and did not report it, but instead went there themselves to see him. It is perhaps no accident that the command of the priests and Pharisees is first mentioned in connection with the group **from the country** that was looking for Jesus in the Temple (vv. 55–57). Though his transitions are not always smooth or clear, the narrator has left open the possibility (though no more than that) that there was one particular crowd of worshipers (from Ephraim) that looked for Jesus at Jerusalem before the festival (vv. 55–56), found him at Bethany (12:9), and finally bore witness to his miracle of raising Lazarus from the dead (12:17). To some extent, the continuity can be tested as we go along, but there is no way to prove (or disprove) the notion that the crowd came first from Ephraim.

Embedded between the search for Jesus and the finding of him is the story of his anointing at Bethany by Mary (12:1–8). The narrator has already alluded to this incident in introducing Lazarus (11:2), but now recounts it in full and in its proper sequence. It is recognizably the same

199

anointing as the one said to have taken place in Bethany at the home of a leper named Simon, according to Mark 14:3–9 and Matthew 26:6–13. The differences in John's Gospel are that Simon is not named, and that the dinner (in Jesus' honor) is given probably in celebration of the raising of Lazarus from the dead. If the host is anonymous (v. 2), no one else is. All the familiar faces from chapter 11 are present: Martha, helping to serve (cf. Luke 10:40); Lazarus, reclining at table (v. 2); and Mary, at Jesus' feet as always (v. 3; cf. Luke 10:39; John 11:32). The only new figure is Judas Iscariot (vv. 4–6) who has been mentioned (6:71) but who has had no role in the narrative to this point.

The story is best understood as a foreshadowing of Jesus' last meal with his disciples (13:1–30) and the accompanying farewell discourses (esp. 13:36–14:31). It is frequently observed by commentators that the telling of the story has been influenced at certain points by the memory of a somewhat similar incident in Galilee found only in Luke (7:36–50): for example, Jesus' feet are anointed, rather than his head (contrast Mark 14:3), and Mary impulsively wiped his feet with her hair (for both of these details, cf. Luke 7:38). In Luke an unknown woman used her hair to wipe her *tears* from Jesus' feet and only afterward anointed them with perfume; in John, Mary pours perfume on his feet only to wipe it off immediately! (v. 3). It is argued that such details are at home in the Lukan story of an impulsive forgiven prostitute but illogical in John's account of the devotion of Jesus' close and dear friend, and therefore that the two situations have merged to some degree in the telling. This may be true, but it should not be forgotten that the washing—and drying—of feet is an act of decisive significance elsewhere in John's Gospel itself (i.e., 13:1–17). Before coming to the astonishing reversal of a teacher washing the feet of his disciples (13:8), the narrator describes the more normal or natural situation of a disciple anointing the feet of her teacher. What was odd was not the act of anointing as such, but the costly perfume that Mary used, and the quantity of it.

Mary is first of all simply a model of servanthood; this role she has in common with Martha (v. 2), but it is Mary's servanthood that is accented here. She is commended for the reckless extravagance of her devotion—and in this respect she does resemble the woman in Luke 7:36–50. Such a large amount of perfume (v. 3) filled the whole house with a sweet smell. Yet none of this is regarded in the Gospel as an end in itself. It is simply the measure of her love for Jesus, and of her commitment to serve him. The main similarity between the present passage and Jesus' farewell discourse is that in each a symbolic action representing servanthood (cf.

13:1–17) occasions the disclosure that Jesus must go away (vv. 7–8; cf. 13:33; 13:36–14:31). The parallel is strengthened by the presence of Judas in both situations (vv. 4–6; cf. 13:2, 11, 21–30). Here Judas is given the lines that in the other Gospels are assigned generally to "some of the people there" (Mark 14:4) or to "the disciples" (Matthew 26:8), protesting the wastefulness of Mary's action (v. 5). Though not missing the opportunity to comment on Judas' character and his impending betrayal of Jesus (vv. 4, 6; cf. 6:71), the narrator uses his complaint as the setting for Jesus' revelation: What Mary has done (whether she realizes it or not) is, in effect, to embalm his body ahead of time in preparation for burial (v. 7).

The implication is that soon he will be gone (v. 8; cf. 13:33). If the Sanhedrin verdict made his death historically certain, the anointing by Mary dramatizes its certainty to those closest to him. The prospect of Jesus' absence in his concluding words, **you will not always have me** (v. 8), remains, for the moment, untempered by any hint of reunion with him or promise of his renewed presence. Only later does he extend a word of hope to servants like Mary, whose love for him is stronger than death: "Whoever serves me must follow me; and where I am, my servant also will be. My Father will honor the one who serves me" (v. 26, NIV; cf. 14:3; 17:24). The same issue of Jesus' absence and how it is to be overcome dominates more than half of his farewell discourse, but for the time being it is left unresolved.

The celebration was interrupted by the arrival at Bethany of the crowd of worshipers from Jerusalem (v. 9). Picking up the thread of the Sanhedrin's decree in 11:47–53, the narrator adds the postscript that Lazarus, too, was wanted by the authorities. He was the living proof of the miracle; because he was alive **many Jews** had come to believe in Jesus (v. 11; cf. 11:45). The decision to kill Jesus therefore had to include plans to kill Lazarus as well (v. 10). The irony that it was not enough to "let one man die for the people" (11:50), but that there had to be two, was lost on Caiaphas and the chief priests! The narrator adds the postscript about Lazarus at this point because of his earlier statement that the visiting crowd came to see Lazarus as well as Jesus (v. 9). In not going directly to the chief priests, the crowd was defying the Sanhedrin and protecting two fugitives rather than one.

Additional Notes

11:55 / **To perform the ritual of purification**: It was necessary for those celebrating the Passover to be ritually pure (cf. Num. 9:6–12; 2 Chron. 30:17–18), and it is likely that rites of purification were assumed to be necessary for Jews living among or near Gentiles.

11:56 / **Surely he will not come?** The form of the question in Greek indicates that a negative answer is expected, but the GNB somewhat overtranslates. The fact that they were looking for Jesus at all suggests a real possibility that he would be there. A more subtle rendering would be: "What do you think? Will he come to the festival?"

12:2 / **They prepared a dinner**: **They** is impersonal, and has no antecedent. The meaning is "a dinner was prepared."

12:3 / **A whole pint**: lit., "a pound" (Gr., *litra*, the Roman pound of twelve ounces). This was obviously an enormous amount, enough to have lasted for many years; cf. the extravagant amount of spices later used to embalm the body of Jesus (19:39).

A very expensive perfume made of pure nard: The verbal agreement with Mark 14:3—extending to the common use of some very rare words—is striking and suggests that the two accounts are not only based on the same incident but on the same narration of that incident. *Nard*, or spikenard, was a plant, native to India, the oil of which was used as an ointment or perfume. The word translated **pure** (lit., "faithful" or "trustworthy"; hence "genuine" or "unadulterated") is used in this way only here and in Mark 14:3. It may have been the trade name under which the product was marketed.

Filled the whole house: There is a tradition of interpreting this phrase symbolically to mean something equivalent to Mark 14:9: The news of Mary's good deed filled the whole world just as the sweet smell of the perfume filled the house (the late Midrash on Ecclesiastes 7:1 [Soncino ed., *Midrash Rabbah VIII* (London: Soncino Press, 1961), p. 166] said, "[The scent of] good oil is diffused from the bedchamber to the dining-hall while a good name is diffused from one end of the world to the other"). It is more likely that the phrase, like the mention of "pure nard" and other such details, simply reflects the vivid recollection of someone actually present at the scene.

12:5 / **Three hundred silver coins**: The coin in question was specifically the Roman *denarius*. A *denarius* was a laborer's wage for one day (cf. Matt. 20:2), so three hundred of them would indeed have kept a poor family alive for quite some time.

12:6 / **He was a thief. He carried the money bag and would help himself**. That Judas was the treasurer among Jesus' disciples is noted also in 13:29, but his thievery is mentioned only here. Judas is always seen as the betrayer in John's Gospel, but without direct indication that his betrayal was for money. The present passage affords a useful glimpse in retrospect of Judas' character (for a perspective on thieves, cf. 10:1, 10). The narrator introduces the information at this point in order to make it clear that the immediate issue is not right or wrong attitudes toward the poor (an issue that the story in itself might easily have raised), but the presence or absence of Jesus (see note on 12:8).

12:7 / **Let her keep what she has for the day of my burial**: lit., "Let her alone, that she may keep it for the day of my burial." The GNB translation is misleading if it implies that Mary had not poured out all the perfume. The references to "a whole pint" (v. 3), its precise cost (v. 5), and the smell of it filling the whole house (v. 4), all suggest that she had used it all. Therefore the purpose clause in Jesus' statement must be a purpose realized in the present, not the future: "Let her keep it [as she has done] for the day of my burial." It was, of course, too late for Judas to prevent Mary from doing what she did, but Jesus' point is that neither Judas nor anyone else should rebuke her for it. Mark's Gospel brings out the meaning more clearly and in more detail ("Leave her alone! Why are you bothering her? She has done a fine and beautiful thing for me . . . She did what she could; she poured perfume on my body to prepare it ahead of time for burial," 14:6, 8; cf. Matt 26:10, 12). It is possible that the terse, almost enigmatic saying in John actually represents the earliest form of the saying, while Mark and Matthew have preserved a slightly later (and correct) clarification of it.

12:8 / **You will always have poor people with you**. Mark 14:7 has the same statement, but with the additional words "and any time you want to, you can help them." Far from encouraging a casual or neglectful attitude toward the poor, Jesus (in Mark) is urging attention to their needs (cf. Deut. 15:11). Matthew 26:11 lacks the additional words, perhaps because he has already emphasized so strongly in 25:31–46 the point that, during the period of Jesus' absence, good works done for those in need are done for Jesus himself. John lacks them, however, simply because the question of the poor is not the question he is addressing at the moment. He dismisses it as a smoke screen raised by the thief, Judas. Though his suggestion that Judas did not care about the poor (v. 6) has implied in passing that Christians *should* care, John's emphasis falls not on the first part of the pronouncement, **You will always have poor people with you**, but on what it leads up to: **you will not always have me**. He is concerned with the single question of the impending separation of Jesus from his disciples.

12:10 / **So the chief priests made plans to kill Lazarus too**. Even though the verb for **made plans** is a simple past tense, not a pluperfect, it appears that the narrator is providing further information about the Council that met in 11:47–53, not describing a new decision occasioned by the crowd's present visit to Bethany. (The word **so** in the GNB translation seems to imply the latter.) If the authorities knew of the visit to Bethany, it is hard to see why they would not simply have arrested Jesus (and Lazarus) at Bethany instead of passing more decrees. A better translation might be: "The chief priests had decided [or, "made plans"] to kill Lazarus as well." If the reference is back to 11:47–53, then the "many Jews" who were "believing in Jesus" (v. 11) are those referred to in 11:45, not the group now visiting Jesus in Bethany.

33

The Triumphant Entry into Jerusalem

JOHN 12:12–19

The next day the large crowd that had come to the Passover Festival heard that Jesus was coming to Jerusalem. [13]So they took branches of palm trees and went out to meet him, shouting, "Praise God! God bless him who comes in the name of the Lord! God bless the King of Israel!"

[14]Jesus found a donkey and rode on it, just as the scripture says,

[15]"Do not be afraid, city of Zion!
Here comes your king,
    riding on a young donkey."

[16]His disciples did not understand this at the time; but when Jesus had been raised to glory, they remembered that the scripture said this about him and that they had done this for him.

[17]The people who had been with Jesus when he called Lazarus out of the grave and raised him from death had reported what had happened. [18]That was why the crowd met him—because they heard that he had performed this miracle. [19]The Pharisees then said to one another, "You see, we are not succeeding at all! Look, the whole world is following him!"

T he next day the scene changes. The narrator picks up the story from the point of view of the growing Passover crowds in Jerusalem. The crowd received news that Jesus was on his way into the city (v. 12). How this news reached them the text does not say—until later (vv. 17–18). Not even the reader has been told in so many words that Jerusalem was Jesus' destination—though an attentive reader would have guessed. Before analyzing the reasons for the crowd's action or attempting to link the scene with the preceding one, the narrator simply describes, as briefly as possible, what the crowd did and what Jesus did. As they came out to meet him with palm branches, shouting praises to God and blessings on their coming King, Jesus **found a donkey and rode on it** (vv. 13–14a). That is all there is to the account of Jesus' entry into Jerusalem. The rest (vv. 14b–19) is commentary.

The comments of the narrator are in three parts: a Scripture citation (vv. 14b–16), an added note distinguishing two crowds and explaining which was which (vv. 17–18), and a significant last reflection on the whole scene by the Pharisees, functioning like a chorus in a Greek drama (v. 19). The Scripture citation is a very free quote of Zechariah 9:9, much freer than Matthew 21:5. (Matthew is the only other Gospel to include this quotation in its account of the entry.) The interest is in the correspondence between certain words in the quotation and certain words in the accompanying narrative (including the crowd's exclamation in v. 13). On the one hand, the passage in Zechariah **said this about him**, and on the other, the crowd **had done this for him** (v. 16). The correspondence centers on two words: *comes* (i.e., **him who comes**, v. 13; **here comes**, v. 15; cf. also **Jesus was coming to Jerusalem**, v. 12) and *king* (i.e., **King of Israel**, v. 13; **your king**, v. 15). A subsidiary correspondence exists between **rode** (lit., "sat") in verse 14 and **riding** (lit., "seated") in verse 15, also between **donkey** in verse 14 and **young donkey** in verse 15. The correspondences point to the theme of Jesus the coming King seated on a donkey as on a throne. Jesus' kingship has been mentioned only twice before in this Gospel, once in a more or less positive way (1:49), and once negatively (6:15). But in the Passion narrative it will become the dominant category in which Jesus and his claims are presented—for the last time—to the world (cf. 18:33–38; 19:12–16, 19–22). The accent on kingship in the story of Jesus' entry into Jerusalem suggests that in a very real sense (just as the Passover notice in 11:55 intimated) the Passion narrative is already under way.

The appropriateness of the Zechariah quotation, and therefore of kingship as the proper category for understanding Jesus, was only apparent to his disciples, the narrator adds, **when Jesus had been raised to glory** (v. 16). **Raised to glory** (lit., "glorified") is an expression embracing in itself both Jesus' death and his resurrection. His glorification is complete only when he has been raised from the dead (and the Spirit is ready to come, 7:39), yet it begins as soon as he first looks death in the eye (12:23; cf. 11:4). Verse 16 is an acknowledgment that the interpretation of the triumphal entry represented by the Scripture quotation is postresurrection (like the interpretation of the Temple cleansing given in 2:17, 22), yet the future impinges on the present. The "glorification" is about to begin (v. 23); the paradoxical nature of Jesus' kingship is about to be revealed (vv. 24–33).

Left unanswered in verse 12 was the question of what precipitated the joyous welcome in the first place. How did the great Passover crowd learn **that Jesus was coming to Jerusalem**? Verses 17–18 were appended to the narrative to answer that question, but in so doing they raise questions of their own. First, they complicate the picture of the triumphal entry with their distinction between those **who had been with Jesus** and those who met him with palm branches. Second, because of an uncertainty in the text, they leave in doubt the identity of the first of these groups. If the crowd that **had been with Jesus** was (as GNB indicates) with him **when** (Gr.: *hote*) he raised Lazarus from the grave, it must have been the crowd that came to comfort Martha and Mary (11:19, 31, 33), many of whom afterward believed in Jesus (11:45). But according to some ancient manuscripts, "the crowd that had been with Jesus" reported to the crowd assembled in Jerusalem for Passover "that" (Gr.: *hoti*) Jesus had raised up Lazarus. In this case it is more plausible to identify the former crowd as the crowd that had gone to Bethany to see Jesus and Lazarus (v. 9) and then, presumably, returned to Jerusalem again. Although the manuscript support is not as strong for this reading as for the other, it provides continuity between the triumphal entry and what precedes it. If the crowd mentioned in verse 9 is not the same crowd that brings back its testimony in verse 17, it is hard to see why it is in the text at all. On the other hand, the group of Jewish leaders who consoled Mary in chapter 11 have already served a definite function in the unfolding story (11:45–46), and their testimony has already had its effect (v. 11). The additional factor that brought about the triumphal entry seems to have been the verification provided by the crowd visiting Bethany in verse 9. Because of the strange placement of verses 17–18 (almost as if they were an afterthought), and especially because of the textual uncertainty, this "explanatory" footnote makes the account of the entry more confusing than it would otherwise be. The one thing it brings out clearly, however, is that Jesus' royal welcome into the city (and therefore all that happened afterward) was directly traceable to the raising of Lazarus from the grave. Jesus' promise is being fulfilled: The illness of Lazarus has become "the means by which the Son of God will receive glory" (11:4).

The last wry comment belongs to the Pharisees (v. 19). To them it must have seemed that Caiaphas' dire prediction was coming true. Everyone was acting as if they believed in Jesus (cf. 11:48); the whole world was following in his train. The narrator senses the irony of their remark and uses it to full advantage. Jesus himself had once asked, "Does a person gain anything if he wins the whole world but loses his life?" (Mark 8:36). Now he stood, with the world at his feet, about to lose his own life—"so that the world may live" (cf. 6:51). The paradox has now been introduced, but its many dimensions remain to be explored.

Additional Notes

12:13 / **Praise God!**: lit., "Hosanna," an Aramaic expression meaning "Save now!" used either literally as a petition for deliverance or as a technical term ascribing praise to God. The Hebrew form of the expression is used as a petition in Ps. 118:25 (the apparent source of the crowd's acclamation), but the New Testament writers seem to have in mind a shout of praise. Both here and in Mark 11:9–10/Matthew 21:9, the Greek text leaves the Aramaic untranslated (cf. also *Didache* 10.6: "Hosanna to the God of David"). Luke, instead of leaving the phrase untranslated or translating it literally, brings out his interpretation of it by the use of the paraphrase: "the large crowd of his disciples began to thank God and praise him in loud voices for all the great things that they had seen: 'God bless the king who comes in the name of the Lord!' " (19:37–38; for a more literal rendering of "hosanna," cf. Rev. 7:10, NIV: "Salvation belongs to our God"). A modern example of how prayer can become an ascription of praise is "God save the queen!"

God bless him who comes in the name of the Lord. This part of the crowd's acclamation is a quote from Ps. 118:26, one of the so-called Hallel Psalms (115–118) used in the liturgy of Passover. It is not, however, cited as Scripture (the operative Scripture citation is, rather, Zech. 9:9 in v. 15) but is simply a spontaneous cry, based in part on the liturgy and echoing terminology for Jesus used elsewhere in this Gospel (for **him who comes**, cf. 1:15, 27; 3:31; 6:14; 11:27; for the **King of Israel** in the next line, cf. 1:49).

12:15 / **Do not be afraid, city of Zion**: lit., "daughter of Zion," in the OT, a synonym for Zion itself, the city of Jerusalem. Zech. 9:9 is different ("Rejoice greatly, daughter of Zion," RSV), but cf. Zeph. 3:16: "Do not fear, O Zion" (RSV; Zion here is synonymous with "daughter of Zion" in 3:14). The tone of assurance suggested either by **Do not be afraid** or "Rejoice greatly" is based on elements in the text not explicitly cited in John, though perhaps implied: "He comes triumphant and victorious, but humble . . . " (Zech. 9:9).

12:16 / **His disciples did not understand**: There is no blame placed on the disciples for their failure to understand. The accent is not on their lack of understanding now, but on their clear understanding later (cf. 2:22; 20:8–9). The comment helps set the stage for redefining Jesus' kingship as death and resurrection.

34

Jesus Speaks of His Death

JOHN 12:20–36

Some Greeks were among those who had gone to Jerusalem to worship during the festival. [21]They went to Philip (he was from Bethsaida in Galilee) and said, "Sir, we want to see Jesus." [22]Philip went and told Andrew, and the two of them went and told Jesus. [23]Jesus answered them, "The hour has now come for the Son of Man to receive great glory. [24]I am telling you the truth: a grain of wheat remains no more than a single grain unless it is dropped into the ground and dies. If it does die, then it produces many grains. [25]Whoever loves his own life will lose it; whoever hates his own life in this world will keep it for life eternal. [26]Whoever wants to serve me must follow me, so that my servant will be with me where I am. And my Father will honor anyone who serves me.

[27]"Now my heart is troubled—and what shall I say? Shall I say, 'Father, do not let this hour come upon me'? But that is why I came–so that I might go through this hour of suffering. [28]Father, bring glory to your name!"

Then a voice spoke from heaven, "I have brought glory to it, and I will do so again."

[29]The crowd standing there heard the voice, and some of them said it was thunder, while others said, "An angel spoke to him!" [30]But Jesus said to them, "It was not for my sake that this voice spoke, but for yours. [31]Now is the time for this world to be judged; now the ruler of this world will be overthrown. [32]When I am lifted up from the earth, I will draw everyone to me." ([33]In saying this he indicated the kind of death he was going to suffer.) [34]The crowd answered, "Our Law tells us that the Messiah will live forever. How, then, can you say that the Son of Man must be lifted up? Who is this Son of Man?"

[35]Jesus answered, "The light will be among you a little longer. Continue on your way while you have the light, so that the darkness will not come upon you; for the one who walks in the dark does not know where he is going. [36]Believe in the light, then, while you have it, so that you will be the people of the light."

After Jesus said this, he went off and hid himself from them.

The principle that the "whole world is following" Jesus (v. 19) finds immediate illustration in **some Greeks** who were among the worshipers at the festival (v. 20). Their request to see Jesus was directed at Philip (cf. 1:43–44), ceremoniously passed along by him to Andrew, and by the two of them to Jesus (vv. 21–22). These two disciples have been seen together twice before: first as Jesus' agents in initially gathering a group of followers (1:35–45), and later as the two whose faith

Jesus tested before the feeding of the five thousand (6:5–9). Again they are a team, this time in presenting to their Teacher the longings of the Gentile world and receiving from him the revelation, indirect though it may be, of how the Gentile world soon will **see** him.

In asking to **see** Jesus, the Greeks were merely requesting an interview, but Jesus has in mind a redemptive and universal vision (cf. 6:40: "For what my Father wants is that all who see the Son and believe in him should have eternal life"). He therefore does not answer their question directly; the reader never learns whether or not the interview was granted. Instead, Jesus announces that his **hour has now come** (contrast 2:4), the hour **for the Son of Man to receive great glory** (v. 23). Only when he is "glorified" in death and resurrection will the Greeks (and all other Gentiles) be able to **see** him redemptively.

That the momentous **hour** was indeed the hour of death was implied in two earlier uses of the term in this Gospel. Twice Jesus had escaped death "because his hour had not yet come" (7:30; 8:20). Now he speaks again of death, this time in the language of parable (v. 24). The parable, like several of Jesus' parables of the Kingdom of God in the Synoptics, is a parable of a growing seed (cf., e.g., Mark 4:1–9, 26–29, 30–32; Matt. 13:24–30. But Jesus, instead of being the sower who plants the seed (as, e.g., in Matt 13:37), is in this instance himself the **grain of wheat**. It is he who must die, and by his death produce **many grains**. His death will make possible a rich harvest, in that it will bring salvation to the Gentiles.

The sequel to verse 24 is verse 32. When verses 24 and 32 are placed side by side, they look like two stanzas of a single pronouncement:

a. I solemnly assure you, unless the grain of wheat falls to the earth and dies, it remains just a grain of wheat. But if it dies, it produces much fruit (v. 24, NAB).
b. And I—once I am lifted up from the earth—will draw all men to myself (v. 32, NAB).

The symmetry between *a*. and *b*. centers on the contrast between the phrases "to the earth" in the first, and "from the earth" in the second. The contrast stands out against the formal similarity of the two stanzas. Both are built around conditional clauses. The first begins with a negative "if" (i.e., "unless") clause reminiscent of others in this Gospel (e.g., 3:3, 5; 6:53) and concludes with a positive "if" clause ("but if it dies, it produces much fruit"). The positive conditional form ("once [i.e., "if"] I am lifted up") carries over into the second stanza, which completes the thought of the first and at the same time interprets it. The "grain of wheat" is now, by the emphatic "I," specifically identified as Jesus, while the reference to producing "many grains," or "much fruit," is defined as drawing everyone to himself. Jesus, the "grain of wheat," falls "to the earth" in death, and is "lifted up from the earth" in resurrection, like a plant in its full growth. It appears that Jesus has applied a parable of growth, similar to those found in the synoptic Gospels, to his own Passion and resurrection.

What Jesus and the earliest forms of the tradition have done, however, is not necessarily identical to what the Gospel writer has done. In the Gospel as it stands, verses 24 and 32 are not joined together, and verse 32 is interpreted as referring not to Jesus' resurrection but to his death on the cross (v. 33; cf. 3:14). The Gospel writer is not so much interested in a sequence (i.e., first Jesus died; then he rose), as in focusing significantly on the death of Jesus, and on that alone. He sees Jesus' death, to be sure, from the perspective of the resurrection, but he is not concerned with the resurrection itself as a distinct event. Because he knows and believes that Jesus was raised from the dead, he is able to interpret Jesus' death on the cross as a victory, a "glorification." He superimposes the contours of the resurrection, and its significance, on the crucifixion. Seen in this way, a dark tragedy becomes a glorious victory. The gruesome "lifting up" of Jesus on a cross becomes his exaltation to a place of honor in God's presence (cf. Acts 2:33; 5:31) and his vindication before the whole world. By it he will grant eternal life to "everyone who believes" (3:15) and **will draw everyone** to himself (v. 32).

To the Gospel writer, verses 24 and 32 are two different images for the same reality, the death of Jesus, and both make the point that latent *in the death itself* is the power and reality of the resurrection. The paradox inherent both in nature and in grace is that life comes only through death (cf. 1 Cor. 15:36). This paradox is brought to bear, not only on Jesus' experience, but on that of his disciples (v. 25). Just as in Mark's Gospel the first prediction of the Passion was immediately followed by teaching on discipleship (Mark 8:31–38), so here the announcement of Jesus' **hour** becomes the basis for a decisive call to self-denial and servanthood (vv. 25–26). Even death cannot separate Jesus from his disciples if, like Mary (cf. vv. 3–8), they **serve** him (v. 26). Serving Jesus in the new situation to come, however, will be defined not merely by Mary's example, but by Jesus' own (cf. 13:1–17). To serve him is to **follow** or imitate him (v. 26), that is, to be the same kind of servant that he was (cf. 13:13–16). Jesus later puts this teaching in the context of being hated and persecuted by the world (15:18–21). He never tells his disciples to hate the world in return, but he does tell them to hate their **own life in this world** and so gain **life eternal** (v. 25). What is required of a disciple in the face of the Teacher's death is to give up the vested interest he or she has in the world and follow Jesus in the way of servanthood. When that requirement is met, Jesus says, **my servant will be with me where I am** (v. 26a). He does not specify where that will be; all that his disciples need to know for the moment is that they will be with him, and that his love is stronger than death. Later he will make it clear that they will join him in the Father's presence (14:1–3) and there see in its fullness the glory he received from the Father (17:24). For now he offers only the general assurance that **my Father will honor anyone who serves me** (v. 26b). These verses afford a glimpse of issues that will be addressed in greater detail in the farewell discourses.

Having spoken to his disciples (vv. 22–26), Jesus will now turn his attention to the Father (vv. 27–28), and finally to the crowd (presumably the "large crowd" of vv. 12 and 18) standing around him (vv. 29–36). John's Gospel has no record of Jesus' prayer at Gethsemane (by the time Jesus is in the garden, the issue is already settled, 18:11). The closest equivalent to the synoptic Gethsemane is his prayer out of a troubled heart (v. 27) concerning the **hour** that is upon him. Momentarily undecided as to what his prayer should be, Jesus first asks that the hour of suffering might not come, but immediately withdraws that request in favor of another: **Father, bring glory to your name** (vv. 27–28a; cf. Mark 14:36: "Father . . . All things are possible for you. Take this cup of suffering away from me. Yet not what I want, but what you want"). What changes his petition is the acknowledgment that **that is why I came—so that I might go through this hour of suffering** (v. 27). Just as in Mark, the decisive factor is his commitment "to obey the will of the one who sent me and to finish the work he gave me to do" (4:34). Jesus has "come down from heaven to do not my own will but the will of him who sent me"; (6:38). The prayer he must choose, therefore, is "your will be done," or (its equivalent) **Father, bring glory to your name!** (v. 28a).

A reader familiar with the Lord's Prayer could almost imagine that Jesus was starting to recite it, in a form close to that of Luke ("Father, hallowed be your name," Luke 11:2). If that was the case, he never finished, for a voice from heaven answered immediately: **I have brought glory to it, and I will do so again** (v. 28b). The two "glorifications" are surprising, but emerge as distinct from one another in two subsequent passages as well (13:31–32; 17:4–5). God brings glory to his name, first, through the obedience of his Son (signaled by the obedient prayer just uttered) and, second, by reuniting the Son to himself through death and resurrection (cf. esp. 17:5). None of this made sense to the onlookers. What impressed them was the power and majesty of the voice (v. 29), not what the voice was saying. And yet, like Jesus' dramatic prayer at the raising of Lazarus (11:41–42), the voice was for their sake and not his (v. 30). Like that prayer, it was a bridge between Jesus and heaven, an unusually concrete example of "heaven open and God's angels going up and coming down on the Son of Man" (1:51) and a reminder that Jesus was acting not on his own, but always and only on the Father's initiative.

As he turns his attention to the crowd, Jesus announces to them the coming of the hour, just as he had earlier announced it to the disciples (cf. v. 23). Because the hour is now seen in relation to the world rather than to Jesus personally, the emphasis is on judgment instead of glory (v. 31; cf. 3:19; 5:22, 27). Although John's Gospel records none of the incidents found in the other Gospels in which Jesus cured those who were demon possessed, it is striking that the judgment of the world is described here as one great exorcism: **Now the ruler of this world will be overthrown** (lit., "thrown out," the term commonly used for the exorcism of demons, e.g., in Mark 1:39; Matt. 10:8; 12:28). The interest of this Gospel is not in a plurality of demonic forces but solely in the Devil, Jesus' one great Adversary and the evil **ruler of this world** (cf. 14:30; 16:11). The passage is reminiscent of Jesus' parable in the three other Gospels about his conflict with "Satan" or "Beelzebul, the chief [i.e., ruler] of the demons": "No one can break into a strong man's house and take away his belongings unless he first ties up the strong man; then he can plunder his house" (Mark 3:27/Matt. 12:29; cf. Luke 11:21–22). The imagery in John is different—Satan is driven out rather than bound—but the reality is much the same. Jesus defeats **the ruler of this world** and sets his captives free. **When I am lifted up from the earth,** he says, **I will draw everyone to me** (v. 32).

When the "lifting up" is understood as Jesus' resurrection (i.e., when v. 32 is paired with v. 24), the drawing of everyone to himself could be understood as the raising of the dead at the last day through the power of the Risen One (cf. 5:25–29; 6:39–40, 44, 54). But when the "lifting up" is understood primarily with reference to the crucifixion (as v. 33 demands), the drawing of everyone is more naturally seen as mission, the transformation of a single grain into **many grains** (v. 24) or the gathering of scattered sheep into "one flock" (10:16; cf. 11:52). In John's Gospel it is by the *cross*—followed and completed by resurrection, to be sure, but essentially by the cross—that mission becomes reality (cf. 10:15–16; 11:51–52; 12:23–25). The cross is like a magnet to which **everyone** (Jew and Greek alike) is drawn. Whether it is Jesus (v. 32) or the Father (cf. 6:44) who draws people, it is to the cross, and the crucified one, that they come. To be drawn to the cross is to be drawn into the pattern of discipleship represented in verses 24–26—or in 6:53–58, under the metaphor of eating Jesus' flesh and drinking his blood.

The crowd seemed to hear nothing of what was involved in Jesus' promise to draw everyone to himself. Only the "lifting up" caught their attention. But when they heard "lifting up," did they think of exaltation, or crucifixion? The meaning of verse 34 hinges on the answer. If they understood the "lifting up" as exaltation (cf. Acts 2:33; 5:31), then they are saying: The Law tells us that the Messiah is to be the Exalted One who endures forever and rules over Israel, but you say it is this mysterious "Son of Man" (i.e., their problem is with the term **Son of Man**). But if they understand the "lifting up" as crucifixion, they are saying: The Law tells us that the Messiah will endure forever, but you say the "Son of Man" (by which we assume you mean the Messiah) will die by crucifixion (i.e., their problem is with the notion of a dying Messiah).

The second alternative is the more likely. The crowd's terminology echoes more closely Jesus' words in 3:14 ("the Son of Man must be lifted up") than his words in the present context (neither the title **Son of Man** nor the verb **must** are found in v. 32). The analogy of "the bronze snake on a pole in the desert" made it clear that 3:14 referred to the crucifixion, and the crowd's use of the language of that verse (especially right after the parenthetical comment of v. 33) demonstrates that this is their understanding here as well. How they came to this conclusion on the basis of what Jesus actually said in verse 32 is more difficult to determine. They did not, after all, have the benefit of the narrator's comment in verse 33! But in any case, the exchange in verse 34 serves to remind the readers of the Gospel that Jesus' Jewish contemporaries had as much difficulty with the idea of a crucified Messiah as did the Jews with whom they themselves came in contact.

Jesus' last words to the crowd continue to emphasize his impending death. He uses the familiar imagery of light and darkness in much the same way as in 9:4–5 and 11:9–10; that is, the light is the time during which Jesus is on earth, and the darkness is the period after his departure. But the two previous passages used this imagery to accent Jesus' own urgency about his mission, whereas the present passage uses it to underscore the urgency for his hearers to believe in him before it is too late. The light is more than simply the time when Jesus is present; the light is Jesus himself, the one in whom they must believe.

The outcome of this last appeal—and of all the appeals that preceded it—is sketched in verses 37–50. The crowd of bystanders to whom he speaks is seen by the narrator as representative of all who heard Jesus' message in his earthly ministry as well as all who have heard it since that time. The metaphor of the light and darkness is flexible, not fixed, in its application. The darkness did not fall once and forever when Jesus went away. The light is still shining (cf. v. 46; 1:5; 8:12), and the words of verses 35–36 are as appropriate in the narrator's world (and ours) as in the historical setting of Jesus' last Passover. When Jesus **went off and hid himself** from the crowd (v. 36b), a particular sequence in his self-revelation came to an end (cf. 8:59), but the story goes on. The rest of the story will be seen largely through the eyes of his disciples, who will continue to hold before the world the urgent appeal of verses 35–36.

Additional Notes

12:20 / **Greeks**: The term refers to Gentiles by birth, not to Greek-speaking Jews (cf. 7:35). Those in view here may have been actual converts to Judaism, or simply Gentiles who respected and worshiped the God of the Jews (like the Ethiopian eunuch in Acts 8:27, or Cornelius in Acts 10:2). In any case, they were among the crowds worshiping at the Jewish Passover.

12:23 / **Answered them**: that is, Philip and Andrew, not the Greeks. Vv. 23–26 are directed to the disciples, not outsiders, and deal with issues related to discipleship.

12:24 / **And dies**: The use of the verb **dies** to describe the germination of a seed is not intrinsic to the metaphor. The choice of this word is perhaps occasioned by the image of falling to the ground (probably not **into the ground**, as GNB has it, which suggests burial); the word **dies**, with its intimation of human death, anticipates v. 25.

12:33 / **Indicated**: lit., "signified" or "gave a sign." The verb is related to the characteristic noun for "sign" or "miracle" in this Gospel. To the Gospel writer, the "lifting up" of Jesus on the cross is a sign of his victory over death. In referring to this event verbally, Jesus himself was revealing the sign in advance (cf. 18:32, as well as the verbal sign to Peter, regarding Peter's death, in 21:19).

12:34 / **Our Law tells us that the Messiah will live forever**: lit., "remain forever." The reference is to the Scriptures generally, not to a legal code or to the Pentateuch in particular (cf. perhaps Ps. 110:4 or Isa. 9:6–7). The belief that the

Messiah would remain forever was not confined to those who conceived of him as a supernatural or transcendant figure. The crowd may have had in mind passages in which God promised that the messianic line of descendants of King David would never fail (e.g., 2 Sam. 7:13; Ps. 132:10–12; and esp. Ps. 89:36, which is closest of all to the present passage in actual terminology). That Jesus too will "remain forever" despite being lifted up in death is seen in this Gospel in a parabolic context in 8:35.

12:35 / **Continue on your way**: lit., "walk." This verb stands parallel to "believe" or "continue to believe" (present tense) in verse 36, both verbs being qualified by the clause **while you have the light**. This "continuing" or "walking" is not a neutral stance toward Jesus, but a life lived in faith (cf. 8:12). The use of the present tense does not here imply that the crowd already believed. Jesus' point is simply that for the time being they **have the light** (v. 35) because he is present among them, and he wants this to continue even when he has (physically) gone away.

35

Unbelief or Belief?

Even though he had performed all these miracles in their presence, they did not believe in him, ³⁸so that what the prophet Isaiah had said might come true:

"Lord, who believed the
message we told?
To whom did the Lord
reveal his power?"

³⁹And so they were not able to believe, because Isaiah also said,

⁴⁰"God has blinded their eyes
and closed their minds,
so that their eyes would
not see,
and their minds would not
understand,
and they would not turn to me,
says God
for me to heal them."

⁴¹Isaiah said this because he saw Jesus' glory and spoke about him. ⁴²Even then, many Jewish authorities believed in Jesus; but because of the Pharisees they did not talk about it openly, so as not to be expelled from the synagogue. ⁴³They loved the approval of men rather than the approval of God.

⁴⁴Jesus said in a loud voice, "Whoever believes in me believes not only in me but also in him who sent me. ⁴⁵Whoever sees me sees also him who sent me. ⁴⁶I have come into the world as light, so that everyone who believes in me should not remain in the darkness. ⁴⁷If anyone hears my message and does not obey it, I will not judge him. I came, not to judge the world, but to save it. ⁴⁸Whoever rejects me and does not accept my message has one who will judge him. The words I have spoken will be his judge on the last day! ⁴⁹This is true, because I have not spoken on my own authority, but the Father who sent me has commanded me what I must say and speak. ⁵⁰And I know that his command brings eternal life. What I say, then, is what the Father has told me to say."

Jesus' last plea to the crowd was "believe in the light" (v. 36), and the first note struck in the narrator's concluding summary (v. 37) is that **they did not believe in him.** Jesus' public ministry is summarized as a series of **miracles** (lit., "signs") intended to nourish faith, but the result instead was unbelief. The very purpose of John's Gospel, as stated in 20:30–31, was to reverse that result, but in order to do so realistically the strength and stubbornness of unbelief had to be presented in the most graphic of terms. The summary in verse 37 is reminiscent of Moses' speech to Israel in Deuteronomy 29:2–4: "You saw for yourselves what the Lord did to the king of Egypt. . . . You saw the terrible plagues, the miracles, and the great wonders that the Lord performed. But to this very day he has not let you understand what you have experienced." Yet this is *not* the passage to which the narrator appeals. Probably because he wants something even stronger and more poignant, he draws instead on the experience of the prophet Isaiah (vv. 38–41). First he finds in the words of Isaiah 53:1 an equivalent to the idea that people **did not believe** in Jesus: **Lord, who believed the message we told?** (with the implicit answer, "No one"). That the early Christians appealed to this verse in their frustration over Israel's unwillingness to acknowledge Jesus as the Messiah is shown by Paul's use of it in Romans 10:16. Here the Gospel writer finds the same rejection and frustration already in the experience of Jesus (cf. 15:18–21).

The second stage of his argument is that the people did not believe because **they were not able** to do so (v. 39). In support of this stark judgment, he appeals to Isaiah 6:10 (v. 40). Jesus himself is represented in the synoptic Gospels as quoting this verse from Isaiah in connection with his practice of teaching in parables (Mark 4:12; Matt. 13:13–15; Luke 8:10). There are two differences in the narrator's use of it in John's Gospel: It refers to the whole of Jesus' ministry, not just to his teaching in parables, and it attributes to God explicitly (not just implicitly) the blinding of the people's eyes and the closing of their minds. The accent on negative election (i.e., on God's withholding of the truth from some to prevent them from coming to faith) is, if anything, stronger here than in the other Gospels. In the immediate context, the reference to spiritual blindness follows naturally after the appeal to walk in the light in verses 35–36. In the larger context, the Isaiah quotation recalls Jesus' pronouncement of judgment on the Pharisees in 9:39–41. His very coming into the world has the purpose of blinding as well as giving sight, and his verdict against the Pharisees coincides perfectly with the narrator's verdict in the present passage against all who rejected Jesus' message. But never in this Gospel does the notion of God's choice or nonchoice of individuals for eternal life foreclose an appeal to their free will. Election, especially negative election, is always introduced *after the fact*, as an explanation of why someone did or did not believe. It is never a judgment, or an impossibility, declared in advance.

The legitimacy of appealing to Isaiah is established not simply on the basis that Isaiah was writing Scripture or that analogies existed between Isaiah's experience and that of Jesus but on the basis that Isaiah was referring directly to Jesus himself (v. 41). This is done by linking Isaiah 6:10 to its context, Isaiah's vision in the Temple: "I saw the Lord. He was sitting on his throne, high and exalted, and his robe [LXX: "his glory"] filled the whole Temple. Around him flaming creatures were standing. . . . They were calling out to each other: 'Holy, holy, holy! The Lord Almighty is holy! His glory fills the whole world' " (Isa. 6:1–3). The narrator boldly identifies "the Lord" in Isaiah's vision with Jesus, and "his glory" with the glory of Jesus. Like Abraham, who rejoiced to see the time of Jesus' coming (8:56), Isaiah is depicted here as a Christian disciple long before the Christ, glimpsing the glory that would some day be revealed in Jesus' ministry and death (cf. 1:14; 2:11; 11:40; 12:23).

It is surprising that the narrator builds his connection between Isaiah's testimony and Jesus on the second of his citations rather than the first. The first citation (Isa. 53:1) comes within the memorable fourth Servant Song of Isaiah, which begins (according to the LXX): "Behold, my servant will have understanding, and he will be lifted up and glorified exceedingly (Isa. 52:13; GNB is different). John's Gospel has been using the same two verbs, "lifted up" (v. 32; cf. 3:14; 8:28) and "glorified" (vv. 16, 23; cf. 11:4) in reference to Jesus and his approaching death; it is likely that his choice of these words presupposes (as do many other NT passages) the identification of Jesus with the suffering servant whose career is prophetically sketched in Isaiah 52:13–53:12. Perhaps the narrator simply assumes his readers' familiarity with this connection and calls their attention instead to a less obvious point of reference. The comment in verse 41 takes for granted, in any case, a rather subtle acquaintance with the circumstances of Isaiah's call. It is not impossible that the argument as a whole is built on an already well developed system of Christian interpretation of the Jewish Scriptures, a system worked out after Jesus had been "raised to glory" (v. 16) or "raised from death" (2:22).

The alternative to unbelief is belief, and the writer seems ready to present that alternative in verse 42. What he presents, however, turns out to be no alternative at all. The statement that **many of the Jewish authorities believed in Jesus** is at once canceled by the fact that **they did not talk about it openly** for fear of expulsion from the synagogue. What group is in view? Apparently a group characterized by the same pseudo-faith mentioned in 2:23–25 and 8:30–31. Like the "believers" of 2:23–25 who, it turned out, loved "the darkness rather than the light" (3:18), these people **loved the approval of men rather than the approval of God** (v. 43; cf. also 5:41, 44). The only feature possibly distinguishing this group from the others is that they are **authorities** (lit., "leaders") among the people. But "those who believed in him" in 8:31 are literally "the Jews," a term often denoting Jewish authorities, whereas the one named example of the "many" who believed according to 2:23 was "a Jewish leader named Nicodemus" (3:1; cf. 3:10).

The somber reference to these secret (and therefore false) believers in such a strategic place, right at the end of his summary of Jesus' public ministry, suggests that the narrator assigns to them special importance. Unlike the man born blind, they did not make a public confession of their faith. They did not want to risk expulsion from the synagogue (cf. 9:22, 34), so they kept quiet about their faith in Jesus as the Messiah and continued to function in positions of leadership in the Jewish community. The verdict of John's Gospel is that such a position is an untenable one. Not to decide is to decide. Such people have, by their silence, chosen human approval over the approval of God (v. 43). The narrator writes of them with a sense of tragedy, as if aware that there were people like that in the synagogue of his own city (in Asia Minor or wherever it might have been). Jews who publicly identified themselves as Christians could under some circumstances face expulsion from the synagogue or even death (cf. 16:2). Not all were willing to pay the price or to follow the way of discipleship marked out for them in verses 24–26 (cf. 6:53–58). Those who were willing were those who "came to the light" (cf. 3:21) by openly declaring their faith and receiving Christian baptism (cf. 3:1–21).

No evidence suggests that the indictment in verses 42–43 was aimed at the Jews who believed in Jesus according to 11:45 and 12:11, or the crowd that testified to his miraculous power according to 12:17. The Gospel has offered many instances of genuine faith in Jesus (cf. 2:11; 4:41–42, 53; 6:69; 7:31; 9:38; 10:42), but the summary in verses 37–43 focuses entirely on unbelief. The narrator leaves it for Jesus himself to speak of true faith (vv. 44–46), and then not in relation to a specific group who **believed** (as in v. 42) but as part of a reflection on the purpose and the consequences of his mission to the world (vv. 44–50). Because Jesus has gone into hiding (v. 36), this tiny discourse has no audience and no historical context, only a literary context. Poised between Jesus' speeches to the crowds and his words of farewell to his disciples, it summarizes the alternatives left by the former, while at the same time helping to introduce the latter.

Much of the content of the section echoes things said earlier. It appears that the Gospel writer has gathered sayings of Jesus that were either handed down without reference to a particular time and place, or else originally preserved in connection with one or more of the major discourses of this Gospel—for example, Jesus' first Passover (3:11–36 or 5:19–47) or the Temple discourse (7:14–8:59). If the Gospel writer was selective in assembling the material for these discourses (as he surely was in narrating Jesus' deeds: 20:30 and 21:25), there would have been a stock of sayings known to him but not included in the great discourses. Though the writer's style testifies that he is not afraid of being redundant, the similarity of these sayings to material already included would probably have produced more redundancy than he wanted. It is likely that verses 44–50 are drawn from such a stock of "leftover" sayings, already formulated in the characteristically "Johannine" way as a result of having been repeated, taught, and reflected upon in Christian communities known to the author.

Jesus' brief message begins and ends with what he has been saying all along: that he is the Father's representative because the Father has sent him (vv. 44–45, 49–50); to believe in him is to believe in the Father (v. 44; cf. 14:1); to see him is to see the Father (v. 45; cf. 14:9). God is the one with whom believers and unbelievers alike have to do. How a person responds to Jesus has eternal consequences. Jesus' mission is redemptive: He has **come into the world as light. . . . not to judge the world, but to save it** (cf. 1:5, 9; 8:12). Yet the *results* are not inevitably so (witness vv. 37–43). Those who reject Jesus, the man and the prophet, must face God, the Judge of all (v. 48a). The words spoken by Jesus will condemn such a person at the last day, not because they are Jesus' words, but because they are words from God (vv. 48b, 49).

With respect to all this, the small discourse looks back at the message Jesus has already proclaimed and the mixed response to it. Where verses 37–43 saw only the negative response, verses 44–50 see the alternatives of faith and unbelief together and examine (however briefly) the implications of both. At the very end, there is a turning toward the future and an anticipation of a renewed appeal (v. 50). The principle operative in both past and future is that **the Father who sent me has commanded me what I must say and speak** (v. 49). This command means **eternal life** and not death (v. 50; cf. 6:63, 68).

Jesus' final reference to **what I say** . . . (v. 50) should be understood as what he now intends to say. The structure of this pronouncement resembles that of 14:31, which is also pointed toward the future:

12:50 (lit.): So the things which I speak, just as the Father told me, *thus I speak*.

14:31 (lit.): And just as the Father commanded me, *thus I do*.

In the same way that 14:31 looks forward to what Jesus will *do* in the Passion, so verse 50 looks forward to what he will *say* in a new set of discourses oriented toward the Passion. Both are grounded in the Father's

command (cf. 10:18) and in Jesus' identity both as Son and Prophet, who the Lord had said would "tell the people everything I command" (Deut. 18:18).

Additional Notes

12:43 / Approval: Gr.: *doxa*, the same word translated "glory" in v. 41 and in most of its other NT occurrences (though cf. the rendering "praise" in 5:41, 44). The use of this word permits a play on words between the uses of "glory" and "glorify" earlier in the chapter and the verdict expressed here. In choosing to seek human praise or "glory," these people were actually rejecting "the glory of God" revealed in Jesus.

12:44 / Said in a loud voice: lit., "cried out." The fact that this expression occurs twice in the Temple discourse (7:28, 37), marking off three of its major divisions, could suggest that that discourse was the original setting of 12:44–50. Yet the same term is used in 1:15 to introduce a saying of John the Baptist that (like vv. 44–50) is without any real context. No firm conclusions about the origin of these verses can be based, therefore, on this expression.

12:47 / I will not judge him. Cf. 3:17, 18; 8:15, but contrast 5:22, 27, 30. See note on 5:22.

36

Jesus Washes
His Disciples' Feet

JOHN 13:1–20

It was now the day before the Passover Festival. Jesus knew that the hour had come for him to leave this world and go to the Father. He had always loved those in the world who were his own, and he loved them to the very end.

²Jesus and his disciples were at supper. The Devil had already put the thought of betraying Jesus into the heart of Judas, the son of Simon Iscariot.ʸ ³Jesus knew that the Father had given him complete power; he knew that he had come from God and was going to God. ⁴So he rose from the table, took off his outer garment, and tied a towel around his waist. ⁵Then he poured some water into a washbasin and began to wash the disciples' feet and dry them with the towel around his waist. ⁶He came to Simon Peter, who said to him, "Are you going to wash my feet, Lord?"

⁷Jesus answered him, "You do not understand now what I am doing, but you will understand later."

⁸Peter declared, "Never at any time will you wash my feet!"

"If I do not wash your feet," Jesus answered, "you will no longer be my disciple."

⁹Simon Peter answered, "Lord, do not wash only my feet, then! Wash my hands and head, too!"

¹⁰Jesus said, "Anyone who has taken a bath is completely clean and does not have to wash himself, except for his feet.ᶻ All of you are clean—all except one." (¹¹Jesus already knew who was going to betray him; that is why he said, "All of you, except one, are clean.")

¹²After Jesus had washed their feet, he put his outer garment back on and returned to his place at the table. "Do you understand what I have just done to you?" he asked. ¹³"You call me Teacher and Lord, and it is right that you do so, because that is what I am. ¹⁴I, your Lord and Teacher, have just washed your feet. You, then, should wash one another's feet. ¹⁵I have set an example for you, so that you will do just what I have done for you. ¹⁶I am telling you the truth: no slave is greater than his master, and no messenger is greater than the one who sent him. ¹⁷Now that you know this truth, how happy you will be if you put it into practice!

¹⁸"I am not talking about all of you; I know those I have chosen. But the scripture must come true that says, 'The man who shared my food turned against me.' ¹⁹I tell you this now before it happens, so that when it does happen, you will believe that 'I Am Who I Am.' ²⁰I am telling you the truth: whoever receives anyone I send receives me also; and whoever receives me receives him who sent me."

y. The Devil . . . Simon Iscariot: *or* The Devil had already decided that Judas, the son of Simon Iscariot, would betray Jesus. *ᶻSome manuscripts do not have* except for his feet.

The new division in John's Gospel is marked by a long, loosely connected, almost breathless comment by the narrator (vv. 1–3) in which he tries to gather up the themes of chapters 1–12 and 13–17 alike and use them as his stage setting. The first element in this setting has to do with time and circumstances: The notice that **it was now the day before the Passover Festival** (v. 1a) brings the temporal notices of 11:55 ("the time . . . near"), 12:1 ("six days before"), and 12:12 ("the next day") up to date; the further indication that **Jesus and his disciples were at supper** (v. 2a) is a necessary minimum for making sense of verses 4–5. On the basis of the synoptic Gospels, the **supper** is commonly assumed to be Jesus' last meal with his disciples, a Passover meal at which he instituted the Lord's Supper (Mark 14:12–26/Matt. 26:17–30/Luke 22:7–23; cf. vv. 21–30). But if this is the case, the author of John's Gospel has ignored the institution of the Eucharist altogether (even though 6:52–58 suggests that he probably knew of it) and has focused instead on a different "sign" or symbolic act of Jesus. And instead of identifying the meal as a Passover, he has consciously placed it just **before the Passover Festival** (v. 1). It is unlikely, therefore, that the narrator attaches any particular significance to the supper itself (any more than to the "dinner" at Bethany [same word in Greek] mentioned in 12:2). It is simply the occasion for Jesus to "say . . . what the Father has told me to say" (12:50) both by sign and by word.

More important to the narrator than the external circumstances are the theological factors that go into his brief setting in verses 1–3, that is, what **Jesus knew** (vv. 1b, 3) and what **the Devil** had done (v. 2b). The things Jesus knew (that **the hour had come for him to leave this world and go to the Father**, that **the Father had given him complete power**, and that **he had come from God and was going to God**) will provide several of the major themes of Jesus' farewell discourse (13:31–17:26). A postscript appended to the first of these (**He had always loved those in the world who were his own, and he loved them to the very end**) centers attention on what is immediately to follow, the washing of the disciples' feet (vv. 4–20), while the accompanying remark about the Devil's power over Judas (v. 2b) sets the stage for the subsequent designation of Judas as the betrayer and his exit into the night (vv. 21–30).

The procedure by which Jesus washed the feet of each of his disciples is described in very few words (vv. 4–5). Attention centers less on the act itself than on Jesus' explanation of what it means. The interpretation is given in two parts: first, a somewhat confusing exchange with a somewhat confused Simon Peter (vv. 6–11), and second, a clearer and more complete explanation in a brief monologue addressed to the disciples as a group (vv. 12–20). Each part ends mysteriously with a reference to Jesus' betrayal by Judas (vv. 11, 18–20), anticipating verses 21–30.

Simon Peter's initial question (v. 6) highlights the fact that Jesus, by girding himself with a towel and washing the disciples' feet, has reversed the customary practice. In the world of Jesus' day, servants might wash the feet of their master on his return from a journey, a wife might wash her husband's feet, or students the feet of their teacher. But not the other way around. Peter's address to Jesus as **Lord** (v. 6), while customary among individual disciples in this Gospel (cf., e.g., 6:68; 11:21, 27, 32, 39; 13:36, 37; 14:5, 8, 22), has a special aptness here in accenting the incongruity of the situation. Why a **Lord** or master should act out the servant's role toward those who are actually his servants is indeed hard to fathom, and for the moment Jesus provides no explanation. Though Peter and the other disciples **do not understand now** what his strange behavior means, they **will understand later** (v. 7). The expression **later** (Gr.: *meta tauta*; lit., "after these things"), when not used simply as part of a narrative (as in 5:1; 6:1, 7:1), can refer either to the future in a general sense or to future events mentioned in prophecies about the last days (e.g., Rev. 1:19). The promise of specific knowledge or belief or remembrance at some future time (usually after the resurrection) is a fairly common one in John's Gospel (cf. 2:22; 12:16; 13:19, 29; 16:4, 25), and the immediate impression left by verse 7 is that the disciples will understand what the footwashing means *after* Jesus has been crucified and raised from the dead.

Peter, less than satisfied, still presses his question, this time in the form of a protest. For a teacher to wash his disciples' feet is inappropriate, and Peter will not participate (v. 8). Jesus' response is just as direct. If Peter does *not* let Jesus wash his feet, he is no disciple. Without explaining precisely what it means, Jesus here states unmistakably that footwashing (i.e., having one's feet washed by Jesus) is not optional but a necessity for anyone desiring to follow him. To be a disciple, one must be **clean**. Peter grasps the point at last, and begs to be clean all over (v. 9), but Jesus makes a distinction based on the metaphor of someone returning home from the public baths (v. 10). Such a person is clean, except for the feet, which have picked up the dust of the road. What is needed is not a second bath, but only the routine washing of feet. Applying the metaphor to the disciples, Jesus tells them that, having bathed, they too are **clean**. They do not need a second bath (as Peter's request implies), but only the washing of their feet.

Jesus' metaphorical reply to Peter leaves behind more questions than it answers. In what sense are the disciples **clean**? What is their first bath that makes a second unnecessary? And there is still the question: What does the footwashing itself represent? Many commentators find here a reference to the once-and-for-all spiritual cleansing involved in Christian baptism, and it is easy to see how the first readers of the Gospel might have made this application. But though the Gospel offers glimpses of the disciples' baptizing activity in the days of John the Baptist (3:22; 4:1-2), it shows no particular interest in their own baptism (presumably at the hands of John). More to the point is Jesus' subsequent remark to them that "you have been made clean already by the teaching I have given you" (15:3). In the course of Jesus' public ministry they were separated from the world and united to Jesus by their acceptance of his message. The unbelieving among them were in turn separated from their number, so that finally they were established as a community of faithful disciples (cf. esp. 6:60-71). In this sense they are now **clean**, and Jesus is almost ready to address them as the faithful community that will continue his work in the world. The key to their identity and their mission in the world is somehow represented in the symbolic act of footwashing, but Jesus defers his explanation of how that is so until verses 12-20. For the moment, one obstacle remains. It is not *quite* true that **all of you are clean** (v. 10). Jesus had spoken earlier of "the ones that would not believe" and also of one who "would betray him" (6:64). The former had been unmasked and had gone away (6:66), but the latter was still present (6:70-71). Before presenting Jesus' interpretation of the footwashing, the narrator pauses momentarily to mention the betrayer and to underscore Jesus' awareness of his presence (v. 11; cf. 6:64, 71). The brief aside anticipates a somewhat longer reflection on the betrayal theme in verses 18-20.

The entire conversation between Jesus and Peter takes place in the course of carrying out the procedure described in verses 4-5, and verse 12 takes up where verse 5 left off. But when Jesus asks the disciples **Do you understand what I have just done to you?** (v. 12b), it comes as a surprise because he has already stated that they will only understand **later** (v. 7). More surprising still is the comment in verse 17 that concludes his explanation: *Now that you know this truth,* **how happy you will be if you put it into practice**. The assumption is that the **later** time mentioned in verse 7 has arrived! *Now* they understand what Jesus is doing (cf. 15:15). Though verse 7 in its context seemed to point beyond the resurrection, it turns out to have its fulfillment just a few moments later, around the same table and in the same chapter. In John's Gospel, "post-resurrection truths" (i.e., things that become true when Jesus is raised from the dead to rejoin the Father) have a way of making their appearance already within Jesus' ministry, especially as the Passion draws near. The future is superimposed on the present.

But what is it here that differentiates nonunderstanding in verse 7 from understanding in verse 17? Only Jesus' few simple words of explanation, built on an argument from the greater to the lesser. If Jesus, whom they rightly address as Teacher (cf. 1:38; 11:28)) and Lord (cf. vv. 6, 9; 6:68; 11:21, 27, 32, 39) has humbled himself as a servant to wash their feet, how much more should they be willing to wash one another's feet? Jesus' act of menial service is meant as an **example** to be followed (vv. 13–15). The principle that **no slave is greater than his master, and no messenger is greater than the one who sent him** (v. 16), which refers elsewhere (15:20; cf. Matt. 10:24) to the inevitability of persecution, is used here to reinforce the logic of verses 13–15. If **no slave is greater than his master**, then they should not be too proud to do what Jesus has done; if **no messenger is greater than the one who sent him,** then the servant role that belongs to Jesus' mission cannot be considered foreign to their own.

The heart of Jesus' pronouncement is verse 14, which can be laid out in the form of a triangle, with the statement **I, your Lord and Teacher, have just washed your feet** represented by a vertical line pointed downward (indicating something bestowed from above, or from someone greater), and the statement **you, then, should wash one another's feet** represented by a horizontal line pointed either way (indicating mutuality between or among human beings). This yields the following diagram:

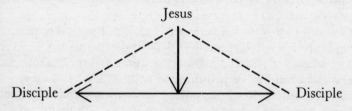

The point of such a "triangular" sentence is that God's actions of grace toward humanity, through Jesus, find their completion and full realization in things that the recipients of this grace do for one another. This will be seen in other triangular statements in Jesus' farewell discourses, centering on divine love: for example, 13:34b, "As I have loved you, so you must love one another," and 15:12, "My commandment is this: love one another, just as I love you" (cf. also 1 John 4:11, "Dear friends, if this is how God loved us, then we should love one another," and Eph. 4:32, "Instead . . . forgive one another, as God has forgiven you"). For the author of John's Gospel, footwashing is both a symbol and a concrete expression of self-giving love. To **wash one another's feet** (v. 14) is to "love one another," and because the imagery is that of cleansing, it is likely that the mutual forgiveness of sins is implied as well.

The initiative in love, in forgiveness, and specifically in the washing of the disciples' feet, rests with Jesus. It is the initiative of the cross. The tone for the narrative (as well as for the discourse to follow) has been set in the first three verses of the chapter: He who **loved . . . his own** was about to **leave this world and go to the Father**, for he **had come from God and was going to God**. The self-giving expressed in the washing of feet foreshadows the self-giving involved in Jesus' death on the cross. The Teacher who washes the feet of his disciples corresponds to the Good Shepherd who lays down his life for his sheep (cf. 10:11, 15, 17; cf. 15:13). The extension of the latter principle can be seen in the triangular statement found in 1 John 3:16–18: "This is how we know what love is: Christ gave his life for us. We too, then, ought to give our lives for our brothers! If a rich person sees his brother in need, yet closes his heart against his brother, how can he claim that he loves God? My children, our love should not be just words and talk; it must be true love, which shows itself in action." Just as there is no one way in which disciples "give their lives" for each other, so there is no one way in which they **wash one another's feet**: Mutual love is the key, but this love may express itself in material help, deeds of kindness, forgiveness of wrongs committed, protection from persecution, even death in another's place—all the things that God himself provides for his children. This is what Jesus means by describing the footwashing as an **example** (v. 15). Not only is it absolutely essential to be "washed" in this sense by Jesus (v. 8); it is also necessary to "wash the feet" of others (cf. Matt. 10:8: "You have received without paying, so give without being paid"). The **should** of verse 14 is a genuine obligation, not merely good advice. It is something that Jesus' followers "owe" (Gr.: *opheilete*) to one another (cf. 1 John 4:11) and consequently, to everyone (Rom. 13:8; cf. 1 John 2:6, where the obligation is to "live just as Jesus Christ did"). Jesus allots one of this Gospel's two beatitudes (i.e., expressions with the Greek word *makarios*, "blessed" or "happy," akin to Matt.

5:3–12 and Luke 6:20–23) to those who faithfully pay their debt of love (v. 17, **how happy you will be**; cf. the beatitude in Luke 11:28).

The strong emphasis on "doing" or "putting into practice" the teaching of Jesus (vv. 15, 17) complements and balances the fourth Gospel's characteristic accent on "believing" in him as the way to eternal life (contrast, e.g., the other Johannine beatitude, 20:29: "How happy are those who believe without seeing me!"). Jesus' teaching in connection with the footwashing in John's Gospel is thus surprisingly close to the teaching with which he concludes the Sermon on the Mount in the synoptic Gospels (Matt. 7:16–27/Luke 6:43–49): for example, "You will know them by what they do" (lit., "their fruits," Matt. 7:16a; cf. 7:20); "Not everyone who calls me 'Lord, Lord' will enter the kingdom of heaven, but only those who do what my Father in heaven wants them to do" (7:21); "So then, anyone who hears these words of mine and obeys [lit., "does"] them is like a wise man who built his house on rock" (7:24; cf. 7:26).

The scope of the disciples' responsibility is not specified. Clearly, they have an obligation to **one another** (v. 14), but the reference in verse 16 to being **sent** hints at a wider mission as well. Strictly speaking, verse 16a (**no slave is greater than his master**) is sufficient to make the point that they must follow their master's example in the way they treat each other. Verse 16b (**no messenger is greater than the one who sent him**) appears at first to have been retained by the author simply because the two sayings were remembered and handed down in the church as a pair (like the pair found in Matt. 10:24). But on closer examination, verse 16b proves to have a function of its own. The word **messenger** (Gr.: *apostolos*) is literally "apostle" (the only occurrence of this word in John's Gospel), and it may be that verse 16b serves as a subtle reminder that the group addressed so decisively in verses 12–17 was in fact "the Apostles" (elsewhere in this Gospel referred to as "the Twelve" (6:67, 70; 20:24). In any case, the emphasis on sending in verse 16b is not accidental, for it is reinforced in verse 20, a pronouncement with close parallels of its own in the synoptic Gospels (e.g., Matt. 10:40/Luke 10:16; Matt. 18:5). All of this suggests that, in washing the disciples' feet, Jesus is preparing them for a mission to the world. Their servanthood to one another (v. 14) is not an end in itself but a means toward the greater end of continuing and extending Jesus' own mission. Far from being merely parenthetical, verses 16 and 20 are crucial to the understanding of verses 1–20 as a whole. This will become clear as Jesus explains more fully in his farewell discourses the significance of what he has done and will do (cf., e.g., 15:16; 17:17–19).

The common theme of sending supports the view that verses 18–20, despite their apparent reference to the traitor Judas, belong with verses 1–17, not 21–30. In a sense, they serve the same function in relation to verses 12–17 that verse 11 serves in relation to verses 6–10. But it should be noted that the reference to Judas in verses 18–20 is not explicit (in v. 11 it became explicit only as a comment of the narrator). Jesus mentions Judas neither by name nor by such an expression as "he who betrays me" (cf. v. 11). His words do not even have to be understood as referring to one betrayer in particular. Verse 20 suggests that their most immediate application is to the mission of the disciples after Jesus has sent them forth. The three verses are a kind of prophetic oracle, warning of the danger of betrayal among those supposedly committed to Jesus and his mission. There are several New Testament examples of such oracles:

Men will hand over their own brothers to be put to death, and fathers will do the same to their children; children will turn against their parents and have them put to death (Matt. 10:21; cf. Mark 13:12).

I came to set sons against their fathers, daughters against their mothers, daughters-in-law against their mothers-in-law; a man's worst enemies will be the members of his own family (Matt. 10:35–36; cf. Luke 12:52–53).

Many will give us their faith at that time; they will betray one another and hate one another (Matt. 24:10).

The behavior described in such pronouncements stands in total contrast to the behavior demonstrated in the footwashing.

Jesus ties his oracle to a biblical text, Psalm 41:10, which he says **must come true** in his experience and in that of the disciples (v. 18; an allusion to Mic. 7:6 in Matt. 10:35–36 accomplishes the same purpose, but without the fulfillment formula). The text deals with betrayal within a family or close-knit community (i.e., among those who eat at the same table). Though the narrator surely thinks of Judas as the prime historical example of such betrayal (vv. 21–30), there is no reason to assume that he (or Jesus) has Judas *exclusively* in mind. The pain of discord and treachery is to be just as real an experience within the Christian community as the pain of persecution, and Jesus wants his disciples to be prepared. When professed believers "betray one another and hate one another" (Matt. 24:10), Jesus wants it known that he has warned of these very things in advance (cf. 16:4a, where he makes the same point about persecution). Those who remember his warnings (cf. Mark 13:23/Matt. 24:25) will maintain, in the face of every disappointment, their faith in Jesus as all that he claimed to be (i.e., that **"I Am Who I Am,"** v. 19), and in so doing find their faith vindicated. They are the ones who prove themselves truly "apostles" or "sent ones," and to them the promise of verse 20 is given. The brief mission oracle ends appropriately with a prophetic guarantee of the authority of the messengers (cf. the placement of Matt. 10:40–42 and Luke 10:16 at the end of substantially longer missionary discourses).

Jesus is thus vindicated as God, the **I Am** and the giver of life (cf. 8:58), in the mission of his disciples, with its setbacks as well as its triumphs, not (despite 18:5–8) in his personal betrayal by Judas. But now, having spoken generally of betrayal in the context of his disciples' impending mission, Jesus is ready to address the specific betrayal (and betrayer) immediately at hand.

Additional Notes

13:1 / **The day before**: lit., "before." The translators have supplied the information that it was just one day before the Passover Festival on the basis of the chronology of John's passion narrative. The time is said to be "night" in v. 30, and there is no indication of a new day until 18:28 ("early in the morning"). But the GNB becomes confusing with its translation **the day before the Passover** (lit., "the preparation of the Passover") in 19:14. What is meant there is the day of the killing of the Passover lamb, obviously part of the Passover Festival but the day before the actual eating of the Passover meal. The confusion might have been avoided by a vaguer translation (e.g., "just before the Passover Festival") in 13:1. Such a rendering would keep alive the impression left by 11:55 and 12:1, 12 that the festival was drawing nearer and nearer, yet without prematurely raising questions of chronology.

Those in the world who were his own: There are echoes here of the prologue: "The Word was in the world . . . yet the world did not recognize him. He came to his own country, but his own people did not receive him. Some, however, did receive him" (1:10–12). In the present passage, the "some" who received him are identified as **his own**, for now they have displaced "his own people" who rejected him. Still Jews, they belong to the new Israel that Jesus began almost immediately to gather around himself (cf. 1:31, 47–51; 2:11). The statement that they are **in the world** is not as redundant as it may sound to the casual reader, but hints at the fact that they will have a mission in the world after Jesus' departure (cf. 17:11).

He loved them to the very end. Some translations tend to connect this statement with the footwashing in particular (e.g., NIV: "he showed them the full extent of his love"; *BDF* par. 207[3]: "he gave them the perfect love-token"), but it is more likely that the phrase, **to the very end** (Gr.: *eis telos*) has a temporal as well as a qualitative sense, and that the statement points beyond the footwashing to what the footwashing itself represents, Jesus' death on the cross.

13:2 / At supper: lit., "while supper was going on." Some ancient manuscripts read "when supper was finished." This reading, while quite well attested, probably rests on a copyist's error (perhaps an error of hearing), for the supper was by no means finished (cf. vv. 21–30).

The Devil had already put the thought of betraying Jesus into the heart of Judas: lit., "the Devil having already put it into the heart that Judas . . . should betray him." The GNB margin reads **the Devil had already decided that Judas . . . would betray Jesus**. The question is whether the Devil puts the thought into *Judas'* heart to betray Jesus (text) or whether the Devil puts it into *his own* heart (a Semitic idiom meaning "to decide") that the betrayal should take place (margin). The meaning represented by the text is more plausible, for it is unlikely that the narrator would reflect on the thought processes of the Devil. Some ancient manuscripts tried to make this meaning more obvious by actually putting **Judas** in the genitive case (**the heart of Judas**, just as GNB has it). But the best manuscripts have **Judas** as nominative. The text as it stands is difficult; the reference is simply to **the heart**, but since the narrator's purpose is to make a comment about *Judas'* motivation (cf. v. 27; 6:71), **the heart** is implicitly the heart of Judas.

13:6 / Are you going to wash my feet, Lord? No readable English can convey the emphasis of the Greek (lit. "Lord, you? of me? wash the feet?"). The placement of **Lord** and the two pronouns together at the beginning of the sentence strongly accents the incongruity of the situation as Peter saw it.

13:8 / You will no longer be my disciple: lit., "you do not have a part with me." A "part" (Gr.: *meros*) with Jesus refers to a place in the community of believers and a share in the unique destiny they enjoy of being with Jesus forever (cf. 14:3). Other NT uses of *meros* refer to an eternal destiny, whether of punishment or blessing (Matt. 24:51/Luke 12:45; Rev. 20:6; 21:8).

13:10 / Except for his feet: These words are omitted in one ancient Greek manuscript, but the vast majority of manuscripts, including the most ancient, preserve the longer reading. If the shorter variant is adopted (as many commentators suggest), either: *(a)* the **bath** referred to is not the footwashing, in which case the point of the pronouncement is that no footwashing is necessary; or *(b)* the **bath** referred to *is* the footwashing, in which case Jesus is saying that the disciples are **completely clean** by virtue of the footwashing itself. But *a* contradicts the whole thrust of the passage (v. 8 in particular), while *b* is rendered (at least) difficult by the assertion in 15:3 that the disciples are clean by virtue of Jesus' *teaching*. It is better to follow the lead of the best manuscripts (as GNB has done) and adopt the longer reading, with its implication that the footwashing represents not the initial **bath** but a second cleansing (i.e., the practice of love and forgiveness by the community of faith.) It is possible, though by no means certain, that the narrator has in mind baptism as the accompaniment to receiving Jesus' teaching in the church of his own day and is making the point that baptism is not to be repeated. The emphasis of the passage as a whole, however, is not on the once-and-for-all character of baptism but on the absolute necessity of footwashing, however the latter is understood.

All of you are clean—all except one: lit., "And you are clean—but not all." The difference is subtle, but it is worth noting that the words actually attributed to Jesus, both here and in v. 11, do not refer explicitly to **one** person. It is the narrator (in v. 11a) who makes the connection with Judas explicit. Although Jesus' literal words allow an application to Judas, they also allow (if **you** is understood as looking beyond the Twelve to the entire Christian community) a wider application as well. The phrase "but not all" anticipates v. 18 ("I am not talking about all of you") and the warning given there that betrayal—and betrayers—will be a continual thorn in the side of those chosen by Jesus and sent into the world.

13:15 / **An example** . . . **so that you will do**: The context shows that Jesus has in mind primarily a moral example. But a liturgical example (i.e., that the disciples in their worship should literally act out the symbolism of the footwashing) is by no means excluded. This is especially true in light of the fact that, in this Gospel, the symbolic act of footwashing replaces the symbolic act of the institution of the Lord's Supper. Possibly John either knows of, or is advocating, the practice of footwashing in the Christian communities with which he is familiar. Such a practice would be a way for the Christian community to dramatize the responsibility of its members to be servants to one another and so bring to full realization in the world the forgiveness and love of Jesus. It is not likely, however, that John intends an "ordinance" or "sacrament" of footwashing to displace the Lord's Supper at the center of Christian worship. His omission of the Lord's Supper is probably to be explained by the earlier inclusion of the synagogue discourse on the bread of life (esp. 6:52–58), which made an account of the institution superfluous. If John envisioned footwashing as a liturgical practice, he probably viewed it as part of what happened around the Lord's table, perhaps as a preparation for the Eucharist proper.

13:17 / **Now that you know**: lit., "if you know." The translation is justified because the first class conditional clause in Greek assumes reality, i.e., that in fact they do know the truth Jesus speaks. The conditional clause in the same verse, **if you put it into practice**, is a different grammatical construction referring to something that may or may not take place in the future rather than to something already true in the present.

13:18 / **I know those I have chosen.** These words must be understood as qualifying 6:70. Jesus chose the Twelve as a group, but Judas will shortly be seen *not* to have been truly chosen as an individual.

The man who shared my food turned against me. Some commentators have noticed that **shared my food** (lit., "ate my bread") uses the same unusual Greek word for "eat" found in 6:54, 56–58 and have proposed that John has chosen this word (instead of the commoner word found in the LXX of Ps. 41:10) for the sake of supposed eucharistic implications. More likely it is either a word he was in the habit of using purely as a matter of style, or else the LXX manuscripts with which he was familiar had it in their texts of Ps. 41:10. It is true, however, that what was violated, both by Judas and by subsequent betrayers in the ancient church, was (at least at one level) the fellowship of the Lord's table (cf. Mark 14:18, "one of you will betray me—one who is eating with me").

The phrase **turned against me** (lit., "raised his heel against me") rests on an ancient gesture of contempt probably carrying the connotation of trampling someone underfoot, or perhaps shaking the dust of his city from one's feet. Such a gesture is to this day regarded by Arabs as an insult (cf. E. F. F. Bishop, *Expository Times* 70 [1958–59], pp. 331–32).

37

Jesus Predicts His Betrayal

JOHN 13:21–30

After Jesus had said this, he was deeply troubled and declared openly, "I am telling you the truth: one of you is going to betray me." [22]The disciples looked at one another, completely puzzled about whom he meant. [23]One of the disciples, the one whom Jesus loved, was sitting next to Jesus. [24]Simon Peter motioned to him and said, "Ask him whom he is talking about."

[25]So that disciple moved closer to Jesus' side and asked, "Who is it, Lord?"

[26]Jesus answered, "I will dip some bread in the sauce and give it to him; he is the man." So he took a piece of bread, dipped it, and gave it to Judas, the son of Simon Iscariot. [27]As soon as Judas took the bread, Satan entered into him. Jesus said to him, "Hurry and do what you must!" [28]None of the others at the table understood why Jesus said this to him. [29]Since Judas was in charge of the money bag, some of the disciples thought that Jesus had told him to go and buy what they needed for the festival, or to give something to the poor.

[30]Judas accepted the bread and went out at once. It was night.

Verse 21 marks a solemn and troubling moment for both Jesus and the disciples. The words **after Jesus had said this** (Gr.: *tauta eipōn*) terminate the minidiscourse comprising verses 12–20 and introduce a new sequence of events (cf. 18:1, where the same expression terminates the farewell discourses as a whole). The reference to Jesus being **deeply troubled** (lit., "he was troubled in the spirit") recalls his anguish at the tomb of Lazarus (11:33) and again at the prospect of the "hour" of his death (12:27). The betrayal of which he is about to speak is a betrayal to death, and (as before) it is the nearness of death and of the Devil that agitates his spirit. He makes his declaration both **openly** and solemnly, as one bringing a formal testimony: **I am telling you the truth: one of you is going to betray me.** The narrator has kept this betrayal ever before the eyes of his readers (cf. 6:64, 71; 12:4, 6; 13:11), but to the disciples it comes as a shock: Who can the traitor be? (v. 22).

At this tense moment a new character comes into the story, a disciple never identified by name, but only as **the one whom Jesus loved** (v. 23; cf. 19:26–27; 20:2–8; 21:7, 20–24). Just as the identity of all the disciples rests on the fact that Jesus "loved them to the very end" (v. 1), so this disciple's identity as an individual rests on Jesus' love for him. His position at the table, next to Jesus, was regarded by the disciples as a place of special honor (cf. Mark 10:35–40). Not even Simon Peter sat as close to Jesus as he (v. 24). Though the identification of this disciple with John, the son of Zebedee, is more plausible than any other that has been proposed (see Introduction) the fact remains that, as the Gospel's author (21:24), he has chosen to remain anonymous, and the commentator has no choice but to respect his anonymity.

As soon as he has been introduced, the disciple whom Jesus loved becomes the recipient of a revelation (vv. 24–30). Simon Peter asks him to find out from Jesus the traitor's identity, and Jesus arranges a private signal for him by which to recognize who it is: **I will dip some bread in the sauce and give it to him; he is the man** (v. 26). When the bread is dipped and given to Judas, the beloved disciple (but apparently no one else) knows that Judas is the betrayer. The narrator remarks that **as soon as Judas took the bread, Satan entered into him**, almost as if he remembers actually seeing it happen. If the signal was indeed for him, his fascination with Judas as an instrument of Satan through much of his Gospel (cf. 6:70–71; 13:2; 17:12) is understandable.

Whether the narrator is himself the beloved disciple or whether he is drawing on eyewitness material that comes from this person, he seems to assume the beloved disciple's place at the table and to write from his standpoint. The ignorance of the rest of the disciples is illustrated by their misunderstanding of Jesus' last words to Judas, **Hurry and do what you must!** (v. 27). The statement that **None of the others** [lit., "none of those"] **at the table understood why Jesus said this to him** (v. 28) gives evidence of being written from the beloved disciple's point of view. The narrator seems, by making him the observer, to exclude the beloved disciple from the generalization that no one at the table knew what was going on. The narrator sees the action through the beloved disciple's eyes. Though this does not prove the two are the same person, nothing in the narrative is inconsistent with that supposition. The beloved disciple is the one person seated at the table other than Jesus and Judas himself who understands the significance of Judas' departure. Whether he even shared his insight with Peter, whose request first drew him into the situation, the reader is not told. As the one disciple with insight into what had just transpired, he is also the appropriate one to preserve and put in perspective Jesus' last revelations and instructions.

Verse 30 picks up the flow of external dramatic action from verse 26, after the significant interpretive aside represented by verses 27–29. Judas, as soon as he received the piece of bread, made his exit **at once,** in apparent obedience to Jesus' command, **Hurry and do what you must!** in verse 27. The narrator adds that **it was night,** probably as a dramatic comment on Judas' fate. In his last pronouncement to the religious authorities, Jesus had said, "The light will be among you a little longer. Continue on your way while you have the light, so that the darkness will not come upon you; for the one who walks in the dark does not know where he is going" (12:35). For Judas, the curtain of night had now fallen; having left the circle of the disciples to do his evil work, he was walking in darkness.

Additional Notes

13:23 / **Sitting next to Jesus**: lit., "reclining at Jesus' side." The reclining posture was characteristic of formal meals in the Greek world, and among Jews was optional (except at Passover when it was obligatory; the Jewish *Passover Haggadah* says, "on all other nights we eat and drink either sitting or reclining, but on this night we all recline"). John's choice of words here suggests to some commentators that he is describing a Passover meal (other details, such as the dipping of bread in v. 26 and the mention in v. 31 that the meal took place at night also support such a theory). If it is a Passover meal, however, it is obviously a private one celebrated at least one day in advance (cf. v. 1). The author clearly does not regard it as the Passover in a literal, chronological sense. Possibly it is a solemn meal held in lieu of the Passover one precisely because "Jesus knew that the hour had come for him to leave this world" (v. 1); by the time the official meal was to be eaten, he would be gone. Yet the disciples, at any rate, were still expecting to celebrate the official Passover with him (v. 29).

The word for Jesus' "side" (Gr.: *kolpos*) is the same word used in the statement in the prologue that Jesus was "at the Father's side" (1:18), and may have been chosen here to accent the intimacy that existed between Jesus and the disciple whom he loved. The word translated "side" in v. 25, however, is a different word (Gr.: *stēthos*, "chest" or "breast").

13:25 / **Moved closer**: The Greek text (at least several of the most important ancient manuscripts) has here the adverb *houtōs* ("thus" or "like this," left untranslated in GNB), which captures something of the storyteller's excitement about his narrative, and perhaps also the graphic recollection of an eyewitness (i.e., the beloved disciple himself?). See note on 4:6.

13:26 / **Dip some bread in the sauce**: lit., "dip the morsel." A morsel for dipping in broth or sauce was normally a piece of bread, but according to the *Passover Haggadah*, a small wad of bitter herbs was used for dipping in a sauce at the Passover meal. The question whether the morsel here is bread or bitter herbs is therefore tied in with the question of whether Jesus regarded this as a Passover

236

meal (note, however, that GNB supplies the word **bread** even in Mark 14:20 and its parallels). Some have argued from v. 18 (lit., "he who ate my bread") that bread is meant here, but the connection is precarious. **Bread** is probably meant, but in any case the narrator's emphasis is on the ritual act of dipping and giving, not on the menu; **sauce,** for example, is not mentioned in the text at all, but is supplied by the translators ("broth" would have been just as plausible).

13:27 / **As soon as Judas took the bread**: lit., "after the morsel." Though Judas' acceptance of the morsel is implied here, it is not explicit until v. 30.

Jesus said to him: The untranslated Greek particle *oun* allows the possibility that Jesus said this as he offered the morsel of bread to Judas (v. 26). The intervening statement that "after the morsel, Satan entered him" despite being woven skillfully into the narrative as if seen by an eyewitness, is essentially a theological judgment, whether made on the spot by the beloved disciple or in retrospect as the story was told and written down.

13:29 / **To go and buy what they needed for the festival, or to give something to the poor**: The first of these suppositions reinforces the impression given by v. 1 that the Passover Festival had not yet begun, that the meal described in this chapter was not a Passover in any sense, and that the disciples still expected that they would all celebrate the Passover together (see note on 13:23). The reference to the poor recalls 12:5–6 and, in light of that exchange, strikes a note of irony: The disciples who thought Judas was collecting for the poor could hardly have been more mistaken.

13:30 / **Judas accepted**: The Greek particle *oun* is again left untranslated in GNB (cf. note on v. 27); like the *oun* of v. 27, it is probably meant to resume the thought of v. 26. V. 30 would follow smoothly after v. 26 with nothing in between. This resumptive *oun* could be appropriately translated "so."

38

Three Decisive Pronouncements

JOHN 13:31–35

After Judas had left, Jesus said, "Now the Son of Man's glory is revealed; now God's glory is revealed through him. [32]And if God's glory is revealed through him, then God will reveal the glory of the Son of Man in himself, and he will do so at once. [33]My children, I shall not be with you very much longer. You will look for me; but I tell you now what I told the Jewish authorities, 'You cannot go where I am going.' [34]And now I give you a new commandment: love one another. As I have loved you, so you must love one another. [35]If you have love for one another, then everyone will know that you are my disciples."

The transition from narrative to discourse is accomplished by the repetition in verse 31 of the verb **left** (lit., "went out"; Gr.: *ex-ēlthen*) from verse 30. As soon as Judas was gone, Jesus began to speak again. The material from verse 31 to the end of chapter 17 comprises the farewell discourses and the so-called high priestly prayer of the Johannine Jesus. The major themes of the discourses and the prayer are set forth programmatically in three distinct pronouncements in verses 31–35. The three pronouncements consist of verses 31–32, verse 33, and verses 34–35 respectively. The first deals with glorification, the second with Jesus' departure from the world, and the third with love.

The discourse material that follows the pronouncements can be divided into two parts. The first, 13:36–14:31, consists of a series of questions and answers built around the second of the three pronouncements (i.e., the prediction of Jesus' departure in v. 33); no particular attention is given to the first or last of the three. The second great block of discourse (and prayer) material, 15:1–17:26, develops all three of the themes presented in verses 31–35, in reverse order. Thus, the theme of love (with its corollary of hatred and persecution) comes to fuller expression in 15:1–16:4a; the theme of departure is expounded for a second time in 16:4b–33; and the theme of Jesus' glorification is picked up and made the basis of

Jesus' last prayer in 17:1–26. The proposed outline can be set forth concisely as follows:

Glorification (13:31–32)	Love (15:1–16:4a)
Departure (13:33)	Departure (16:4b–33)
Love (13:34–35)	Glorification (17:1–26)

The pronouncement on glorification (vv. 31–32) reiterates and draws together earlier sayings of Jesus about his own glorification (11:4; 12:23) and the glory of God (11:4, 40; 12:28). The two belong inseparably together. God is glorified in the doing of his will, and his will for the Son of Man leads to "glorification" on the cross. Verse 32 is intended to explain verse 31, by stating in a different way (in GNB with an "if" clause, though see note) how the glory of God and the glory of the Son of Man are interrelated. God will glorify the Son of Man **in** [or in relation to] **himself,** that is, not with a display of outward splendor, but simply by reuniting Jesus to himself in the cross and resurrection.

There is a sense of imminency in all this. The glorification of the Son of Man in death will take place **at once** (cf. "**Hurry and do what you must!**" v. 27; "Judas . . . went out at once," v. 30). Jesus adds **My children, I shall not be with you very much longer** (lit., "only a little while [Gr.: *eti mikron*] am I with you"), and speaks bluntly to his disciples of what his glorification will mean for them. For them it is not a source of joy or consolation; Jesus' glorification means only his departure and the pain of his absence. The disciples will be no better off than the religious authorities whom Jesus twice rebuffed with the harsh words, **You cannot go where I am going** (cf. 7:34; 8:21). What sort of **glory** was this? For a moment, the question remains unresolved.

Verses 34–35 provide the interpretive key to the footwashing account in verses 1–20 and will in turn be interpreted by Jesus' teaching on love and mission in 15:1–16:4a. The recurrence in verse 34 of the triangular pattern of verse 14 (**As I have loved you, so you must love one another**) suggests that love (with its corollary, the pain of betrayal) was the theme of Jesus' words and actions from the start. The washing of feet, for Jesus, epitomized love in action. This love command was **new,** not intrinsically, for even the Jewish sectarians of Qumran were told to "love all the children of light," (1QS iii.13) but in its basis in the self-giving love of Jesus on the cross ("As I have loved you . . . " cf. v. 1). The **new commandment** is John's equivalent of the "new covenant" mentioned by Luke and Paul (Luke 22:20; 1 Cor. 11:25; cf. Mark 14:24; Matt. 26:28). All our literary witnesses agree that something decisive happened at Jesus' last meal with his disciples, but Paul and the synoptic writers connect that something with the liturgy of the Lord's Supper; for John it has to do with everyday life and the disciples' practical demonstration of love for each other. To be sure, John's Gospel allows a liturgical dimension as well (see note on 13:14), whereas Luke makes room in the immediate context for practical teaching on servanthood (Luke 22:24–27). Yet the prevailing emphases are different.

The last of the three pronouncements concludes by hinting again at the theme of mission: The **new commandment** of mutual love is not an end in itself but a means to the end that **everyone will know that you are my disciples** (cf. 17:21, 23; 15:16; for a different perspective on the same theme, cf. 13:18–20; 15:18–16:4a). All the themes of the farewell discourses, in fact, are present in verses 31–35, simply awaiting fuller development. If the **new commandment** is regarded as the resolution of the problem posed in verse 33 by the absence of Jesus (in the sense that the disciples find Jesus again in loving one another), then verses 31–35 become almost a tiny farewell discourse complete in itself, comparable to the short discourse in verses 12–20. One might imagine, in fact, a very early stage of the Gospel tradition in which verses 12–20 and 31–35 were the only "farewell discourse" there was. This is especially plausible if, as is often assumed, the Passion narrative took shape first and Jesus' last discourses were then fitted to it so as to provide a theological interpretation of the Passion from Jesus' own lips. Such a theory is speculative, and yet the transition from 13:1–35 to 18:1 is a smooth one. The words "after Jesus had said this" (Gr.: *tauta eipōn*; see note on 18:1), correspond exactly to the words at the beginning of 13:21 following the brief speech of verses 12–20. The notice that Jesus "left" (Gr.: *exēlthen*) with the disciples across the Kidron brook (18:1) forms a sequence with the terse statement that Judas "went out" (Gr.: *exēlthen*) after receiving the morsel that Jesus offered him (13:30).

If such an early stage of the tradition could be isolated with certainty, it would reveal a form of John's Gospel much closer to the Synoptics than the present one in the ratio of narrative to discourse in the context of Jesus' Passion. But if this "primitive" Gospel of John once existed, it exists no more. Verses 31–35 were *not* allowed to stand without further development and explanation, and it is the two resulting collections of last words from Jesus to his disciples (13:36–14:31; 15:1–17:26) that largely make John's Gospel what it is.

Additional Notes

13:32 / **If God's glory is revealed through him**: These words are omitted in a number of significant ancient manuscripts. Though the omission might easily have happened by accident, because of the duplication of the clause **God's glory is revealed through him**, the external evidence favors the shorter reading. If this reading is adopted, v. 32 is not a reiteration of v. 31 as a whole, but only of the clause "now the Son of Man's glory is revealed," i.e., **God will reveal the glory of the Son of Man in himself, and he will do so at once** (the words **at once** help explain the dramatic "now" with which the pronouncement begins). This reading is probably to be preferred.

In himself: lit., "in him" (Gr.: *en autōi*). The sense requires that the Greek be read with a rough breathing (or *h* sound) at the beginning: *en hautōi* (**in himself**). The Father glorifies the Son **in himself** (i.e., in, or in relation to, the Father); to say that he glorifies the Son in the Son would make no sense.

39

The Impending Departure I

"Where are you going, Lord?" Simon Peter asked him.

"You cannot follow me now where I am going," answered Jesus; "but later you will follow me."

[37]"Lord, why can't I follow you now?" asked Peter. "I am ready to die for you!"

[38]Jesus answered, "Are you really ready to die for me? I am telling you the truth: before the rooster crows you will say three times that you do not know me.

[1]"Do not be worried and upset," Jesus told them. "Believe[a] in God and believe also in me. [2]There are many rooms in my Father's house, and I am going to prepare a place for you. I would not tell you this if it were not so.[b] [3]And after I go and prepare a place for you, I will come back and take you to myself, so that you will be where I am. [4]You know the way that leads to the place where I am going."

[5]Thomas said to him, "Lord, we do not know where you are going; so how can we know the way to get there?"

[6]Jesus answered him, "I am the way, the truth, and the life; no one goes to the Father except by me. [7]Now that you have known me," he said to them, "you will know[c] my Father also, and from now on you do know him and you have seen him."

[8]Philip said to him, "Lord, show us the Father; that is all we need."

[9]Jesus answered, "For a long time I have been with you all; yet you do not know me, Philip? Whoever has seen me has seen the Father. Why, then, do you say, 'Show us the Father'? [10]Do you not believe, Philip, that I am in the Father and the Father is in me? The words that I have spoken to you," Jesus said to his disciples, "do not come from me. The Father, who remains in me, does his own work. [11]Believe me when I say that I am in the Father and the Father is in me. If not, believe because of the things I do. [12]I am telling you the truth: whoever believes in me will do what I do—yes, he will do even greater things, because I am going to the Father. [13]And I will do whatever you ask for in my name, so that the Father's glory will be shown through the Son. [14]If you ask me[d] for anything in my name, I will do it.

[15]"If you love me, you will obey my commandments. [16]I will ask the Father, and he will give you another Helper, who will stay with you forever. [17]He is the Spirit, who reveals the truth about God. The world cannot receive him, because it cannot see him or know him. But you know him, because he remains with you and is[e] in you.

[18]"When I go, you will not be left all alone; I will come back to you. [19]In a little while the world will see me no more, but you will see me; and because I live, you also will live. [20]When that day comes, you will know that I am in my Father and that you are in me, just as I am in you. [21]"Whoever accepts my commandments and obeys them is the

one who loves me. My Father will love whoever loves me; I too will love him and reveal myself to him."

²²Judas (not Judas Iscariot) said, "Lord, how can it be that you will reveal yourself to us and not to the world?"

²³Jesus answered him, "Whoever loves me will obey my teaching. My Father will love him, and my Father and I will come to him and live with him. ²⁴Whoever does not love me does not obey my teaching. And the teaching you have heard is not mine, but comes from the Father, who sent me.

²⁵"I have told you this while I am still with you. ²⁶The Helper, the Holy Spirit, whom the Father will send in my name, will teach you everything and make you remember all that I have told you.

²⁷"Peace is what I leave with you; it is my own peace that I give you. I do not give it as the world does. Do not be worried and upset; do not be afraid. ²⁸You heard me say to you, 'I am leaving, but I will come back to you.' If you loved me, you would be glad that I am going to the Father, for he is greater than I. ²⁹I have told you this now before it all happens, so that when it does happen, you will believe. ³⁰I cannot talk with you much longer, because the ruler of this world is coming. He has no power over me, ³¹but the world must know that I love the Father; that is why I do everything as he commands me.

"Come, let us go from this place.

a. Believe: or You believe. b. There are . . . were not so; or There are many rooms in my Father's house; if it were not so, would I tell you that I am going to prepare a place for you? c. Now that you have known me . . . you will know; some manuscripts have If you had known me . . . you would know. d. Some manuscripts do not have me. e. is; some manuscripts have will be.

The single theme of the first block of teaching material is developed in dialogue form, with a series of questions and answers (13:36–14:24) ending with a postscript in the form of a monologue (14:25–31). Each question is occasioned by a previous statement of Jesus, so that each interchange has three parts: Jesus' initial statement, the question that it occasions, and Jesus' answer to the question. In all, four disciples take their turn as inquirers: Peter, Thomas, Philip, and Judas (not "the son of Simon Iscariot," but another disciple named Judas).

The Question of Peter (13:36–14:4)

Peter's question, **Where are you going, Lord?** builds on Jesus' statement in verse 33, "You cannot go where I am going." It is a natural question, because Jesus' destination has not yet been established, but it is not a mere request for information. Behind it is the plaintive cry, Why are you going? or Why must you go? The discourse that follows (13:36–14:31) is Jesus' response to that cry as well as his formal answer to the question explicitly asked.

Jesus' initial assertion that he was going away had pointed back explicitly to similar statements made earlier to the Jewish authorities (7:33–36; 8:21). It is the common NT scandal of the cross (cf. 1 Cor. 1:23), but it is seen here as an offense even to Christian believers. For them it is the scandal of an absent Lord.

Instead of answering Peter's question directly by saying that he is going to the Father, Jesus begins by qualifying his initial statement, "You cannot go where I am going." In verse 36b he says, **You cannot follow me now where I am going . . . but later you will follow me.** The experience of the disciples is not entirely parallel to that of Jewish authorities, for the disciples' separation from Jesus will be only temporary. Jesus' response is directed first to Peter personally; he will follow later, presumably in the experience of martyrdom (cf. 21:18–19). Embedded within this part of Jesus' response to the scandal of his departure is a reference to Peter's own personal "scandal" (using the word in a somewhat different sense). Peter professes his willingness to follow Jesus even to death (and he will), but in the more immediate future he will deny his Lord three times (vv. 37–38). This prediction, though a fixed part of the tradition (cf. Mark 14:27–31 and parallels) is not elaborated. The thread of it is picked up in 18:15–18, 25–27, and probably 21:15–17, but it plays no real part in the argument here.

In 14:1 Jesus widens the application of his words to all the disciples as the pronouns change from singular to plural. The recurrence of the words **where I am** (14:3) and **where I am going** (14:4), however, indicate that the statement in 13:33, which occasioned the whole series of questions, is still in mind. The scandal of Jesus' absence is here alleviated by an emphasis on hope. Jesus' assurance to the disciples is that their separation from him will be only for a limited time. The purpose of his departure is to make room for them all in the **Father's house**. He will return for them, and they will join him there forever (vv. 2–3; cf. 12:26). The reference is to Jesus' future coming (cf. 1 John 2:28) and to the resurrection of those who believe in Jesus (cf. 6:39–40, 44, 54). In principle both Peter's question and his plaintive cry, both the "where" and the "why," have now been answered. Yet the dialogue goes on.

The Question of Thomas (14:5–7)

The statement prompting Thomas' question is part of the answer to Peter: **You know the way that leads to the place where I am going** (v. 4). The words **where I am going** still echo 13:33 and 36. Jesus' answer to Thomas' question, **How can we know the way to get there?** (v. 5), introduces the new thought that Jesus himself is the way (v. 6). Jesus' answer centers on himself; it is neither necessary to know *where* he is going, in the sense of Jewish apocalyptic speculations about the structure of the heavens, nor the *way*, in the sense of a formula for escaping this world and attaining salvation (as in Gnosticism and the Hellenistic mystery religions). What is necessary is simply to know Jesus in personal faith and to trust him as the only one who can lead the searching disciple to the Father. Thomas' question changes the focus of discussion from the destination to the way to reach it, while at the same time underscoring the fact that Jesus has not yet answered *Peter's* question in so many words (**Lord, we do not know where you are going**, v. 5). Even though it is occasioned by Jesus' mention of the way, it is still basically a rephrasing of Peter's **Where are you going?** in 13:36 (now with particular reference to the implied corollary, "Where are *we* going when we follow you later?"). Jesus has implied that he is going to the Father's house (v. 2), but he has not said what this really means. He speaks more explicitly in v. 6: **No one goes to *the Father* except by me**. The simultaneous stress is on Jesus as the Way and on the Father as the Destination. The center of interest is no longer *time* (**later you will follow**) but *persons* (Jesus and the Father).

The Question of Philip (14:8–21)

The Father now becomes the subject of the third interchange. The terms **where I am going** and **the way** have now been replaced by "the Father" and "the Son" respectively. Thus Jesus' introductory statement, **Now that you have known *me* . . . you will know *my Father* also** (v. 7), echoes Thomas' complaint, **Lord, we don't know *where you are going*; so how can we know *the way?*** (v. 5). So when Philip asks Jesus to reveal the Father (v. 8), he is actually raising for a third time the question **Where are you going?** The problem is still what it was back in 13:33: If Jesus is going away, the disciple is no better off than the Jewish authorities who rejected Jesus.

The parallels between this exchange and Jesus' debate with "the Jews" in 8:12–20 are especially instructive. There, in the context of a debate over the credibility of Jesus' testimony to himself, the expression "where I came from and where I am going" (8:14) was used as an indirect way of referring to the Father. Jesus' real indictment of his hearers was that they did not know his Father (8:19), but to say that they did not know the Father was the same as saying they did not know where Jesus came from or where he was going. This passage sheds light on chapter 14 both in its similarities and its differences. Its major theme is the validation of legal testimony by two witnesses, Jesus and the Father (8:17–18), with Jesus' departure from the world as a subsidiary minor note (though it comes to the fore in 8:21). In chapter 14, the departure is the major theme, with the question of the validity of Jesus' testimony as a side issue (**Believe in God and believe also in me**, v. 1; cf. vv. 10–11). Thomas' acknowledgment that **we do not know where you are going** (v. 5) corresponds to Jesus' claim in 8:14 that his questioners "do not know where I come from or where I am going." Philip's request in verse 8 to **show us the Father** is formally similar to the question "Where is your Father?" in 8:19a, but in substance there is a world of difference. Where they in their sarcasm were challenging Jesus to produce his second witness, Philip is restating in personal terms the question of Peter and Thomas, **Where are you going?** The immediately preceding comment to Philip and the others, **Now that you have known me . . . you will know my Father also** (v. 7a) corresponds closely to what he said to the Jewish authorities in 8:19b ("If you knew me, you would know my Father also") but with a crucial difference in the tenses (the contrary-to-fact condition has become a condition assuming reality, like "now that you know the truth" in 13:17), and an added assurance that **from now on you do know him and you have seen him** (v. 7b).

With these words, the thrust of the argument shifts once and for all from the future to the present. To Jesus' disciples, the fact that he will be with them only a little while longer (13:33) makes it imperative to realize what his presence on earth has already meant (**for a long time I have been with you all**, v. 9), and to respond in faith to his revelation in words and works (vv. 9–11). The way to the Father is more than the resurrection at the last day (cf. vv. 2–3). It is a way accessible right now to any disciple who hears Jesus' words in faith as the Father's words and sees his works as the works of the Father. This is what the eleven disciples at the table had not yet done (v. 9), and what the readers of the Gospel were expected to do.

Though the emphasis here is on the Son's historical revelation on earth, there is no sharp distinction between this period and the impending time of Jesus' absence. The shift from the one to the other in verse 12 is easy and natural, in contrast to Jesus' earlier warning about the night "when no one can work" (9:4; cf. 11:9–10). The public ministry as a whole drew its urgency from the warning with which it concluded: "The light will be among you [only] a little longer. Continue on your way while you have the light, so that the darkness will not come upon you. . . . Believe in the light, then, while you have it, so that you will be the people of the light" (12:35–36). But in chapter 14, Jesus' departure to the Father means, not an end to the works of God, but **greater things** (v. 12) accomplished by the disciples, with the assurance that Jesus, now with the Father, will answer their prayers (vv. 13–14). The situation of the public ministry has been transcended; what is true for the disciples is not at all the same as what is true for the world. Despite their failure thus far to understand or believe that Jesus is in the Father and the Father in Jesus (v. 10), the opportunity exists **from now on** to recognize exactly that (vv. 7b, 11).

After each of the four questions that punctuate this first farewell discourse, Jesus, in addressing the disciples, shifts at some point from singular to plural (cf. vv. 1–3, 7, 11–21, 24b). These plurals suggest that generalized discourse material has been worked into the question-and-answer framework. The longest block of pure discourse consists of verses 11–21, where the content almost (but not quite) submerges the question-and-answer form. This content consists of a series of promises held out to those who "see" (vv. 7, 9) and **believe** (v. 11) Jesus and his revelation. Jesus promises them the power to do **greater things** than even he has done (v. 12) and, closely associated with this, the privilege of having their prayers answered (vv. 13–14). But the most important promise is the one on which the first two depend: Jesus' own continuing presence with them (vv. 15–21).

The brief monologue introducing the last disciple's question (v. 22) is constructed according to a simple pattern repeated in verses 15–20 and verse 21. In answer to the last question, Jesus does not carry the thought further, but simply repeats the pattern for a third time, only now with a negative corollary (vv. 23–24). The section as a whole yields the following picture:

Verses 15–20	Verse 21	Verses 23–24
If you love me, you will obey my commandments (v. 15).	**Whoever accepts my commandments and obeys them is the one who loves me. My father will love whoever loves me; I too will love him and reveal myself to him** (v. 21).	**Whoever loves me will obey my teaching. My father will love him, and my Father and I will come to him and live with him** (v. 23)
I will ask the Father, and he will give you another Helper.... When I go, you will not be left all alone; I will come back to you.... When that day		

comes, you will
know that I am in
my Father and that
you are in me, just
as I am in you (vv.
16–20).

> Whoever does not
> love me does not
> obey my teaching.
> And the teaching
> you have heard is
> not mine but comes
> from the Father who
> sent me (v. 24).

The framework for the love command is somewhat different here from the triangular framework of chapter 13: Love moves first of all in an upward direction; the disciples are to love Jesus, and in turn they will receive the divine love. The sequence is as follows:

a. The disciple is to love Jesus and keep his commandments.
b. Consequently the Father (and Jesus) will love the disciple and grant him a revelation.

The only reference in this first discourse to the love between the Father and the Son has the love moving in the same upward direction: Jesus loves the Father and does what the Father commands him (v. 31; contrast 15:9–10). This simple pattern is best described as "covenantal." In Judaism, the core of God's demand was summed up in the daily prayer known as the Shema, taken from Deuteronomy 6:5–6: "Love the Lord your God with all your heart, with all your soul, and with all your strength. Never forget these commands which I am giving you today." Loving God and keeping his commandments became a common way of describing the duty of Israel (e.g., Exod. 20:6; Deut. 5:10; 7:9; 11:1). The emphasis was on love as a demand and, consequently, more on people's love for God than on God's love for them. Jesus' language at this point recalls his answer in the synoptic Gospels to the scribe who asked, "Which commandment is the most important of all?" (Mark 12:28–34/Matt. 22:34–40/Luke 10:25–28), except that in John it is love for *Jesus* rather than love for God that stands at the center (cf. 21:15–17). In a manner typical of this Gospel, Jesus identifies himself so closely with the Father that as far as the *disciple* is concerned, the two are virtually equivalent (cf. 10:30; vv. 9, 23).

The Question of Judah (14:22–24)

The name Judah can be used to distinguish this disciple (cf. Luke 6:16; Acts 1:13) both from Judas the traitor and from Jude the brother of Jesus (cf. Mark 6:3/Matt. 13:55; Jude 1). Judah's question, which at first glance seems overshadowed by the preceding discourse material, is actually a key to understanding the whole, for it picks up details from Jesus' promises in verses 16–20 that might otherwise have passed unnoticed. Judah asks, **Lord, how can it be that you will reveal yourself to us and not to the world?** (v. 22). Jesus had spoken in verses 16–17 of **another Helper** (Gr.: *paraklētos*) whom he called **the Spirit, who reveals the truth about God** (lit., "the Spirit of truth"). Of this **Helper**, Jesus said, **The world cannot receive him, because it cannot see him or know him. But you know him, because he remains with you and is in you** (v. 17). Again in verse 19 he had picked up the language of his opening pronouncement in 13:33, but now with a crucial qualification: **In a little while** [Gr.: *eti mikron*; cf. 13:33] **the world will see me no more, but you will see me; and because I live, you also will live**. This is what calls forth Judah's question. The world will not see Jesus after he departs. As far as the world is concerned, he is absent; a real (and permanent) separation has taken place. But for the believer, *the separation is not real*. Even though Jesus goes away in the sense of departing from human view, the disciple continues to **see** him (v. 19; cf. vv. 7b, 9) by sharing his life and by knowing the other **Helper**, the Spirit of truth who takes his place. Jesus departs from the world only to be closer to his disciples than ever before. Because he goes to the Father, he says, his disciples will one day know **that I am in my Father and that you are in me, just as I am in you** (v. 20; cf. 10:38). Paradoxically, it is in departing that he returns, for in his reunion with the Father he unites himself (and his Father) with the disciples as well (cf. 20:19–23).

Here most decisively the scandal of Jesus' absence is overcome. At the beginning (13:33) the disciples seemed to have no advantage over the world, for they could not follow where Jesus went. In answer to Peter's question, this was qualified: They would follow, but only later, when Jesus had prepared a place for them (13:36; 14:3). Now the full truth comes out: For those who have faith there is no real separation from Jesus. His departure means that he and the Father will be together again and that in the Spirit both will be present, and accessible, to the believing disciple. Judah's question is a natural one, for Jesus' words seem to resist the claims of sense experience. What the eyes see—Jesus' departure from the world by death—is an illusion. What is real—the presence of the Spirit, and Jesus' union with the Father and with his disciples—cannot be seen in the usual (i.e., the world's) sense of the term. Judah is simply asking why the disciples and the world see things so differently. Jesus' answer (vv. 23–24) sounds at first as if he has not heard the question, but the negative corollary that he adds in verse 24 speaks to the issue that Judah raises by defining (in a way characteristic of John's Gospel) the difference between the church and the world: **Whoever does not love me does not obey my teaching**. The "world" consists of those who do not love Jesus, while the "church" (a term never used in this Gospel) consists of those who love and obey him (vv. 15, 21). The Spirit will come only to those who know the Spirit (v. 17; cf. 1 Cor. 2:11–14); Jesus and the Father are present only to those who have the eyes to see them (v. 19). Judah's question is based on the common early Christian expectation that Jesus will return to earth with a "dazzling presence" (2 Thess. 2:8) so that "everyone will see him" (Rev. 1:7). This outlook responds to Jesus' absence by affirming his visible presence—but in the future. John's Gospel responds instead by affirming his *in*visible presence here and now, with those who love him. Even when the coming is future, as in verse 3, it is a coming specifically to the believer, to **take you to myself**, not a public epiphany of the Son of God upon the earth. For John, that epiphany has already taken place in the ministry of Jesus. The world has made its decision and shown itself to be blind. John therefore feels no necessity to submit his assertions of Jesus' coming to the tests of ordinary sense experience. Outward appearances to the contrary, Jesus and the Father will come to make their home with the disciples (v. 23), in and through the **Helper** (v. 16) who will be with them forever. Thus, the heart of chapter 14 is the reinterpretation of the *eti mikron* ("not . . . very much longer") of 13:33 with a corresponding *eti mikron* (**in a little while**) in 14:19. The former has to do only with sense experience; the latter introduces what is for John the core of Christian existence—new life in the Father and the Son.

Conclusion (14:25–31)

Only in the last few verses of the chapter does the question-and-answer framework give way to monologue. The concluding summary, marked off by the formula **I have told you this** . . . (v. 25; cf. 15:11; 16:1, 4, 25, 33; 17:1) continues to speak of the **Helper** (v. 26) and of Jesus' departure and return (v. 28), with some indications that the disciples' anxiety about their impending separation from Jesus has not been entirely relieved. Jesus describes more concretely than before the "helping" ministry of **the Helper, the Holy Spirit, whom the Father will send in my name**—he will **teach you everything and make you remember all that I have told you** (v. 26)—with the particular purpose of calming their fears (cf. 16:4b; also Mark 13:11; Matt. 10:19–20; Luke 12:11–12). It is not surprising that at this point Jesus repeats his earlier reassurance, **Do not be worried and upset** (v. 27; cf. v. 1). More surprising is his use of a contrary-to-fact condition, **If you loved me you would be glad that I am going to the Father** (v. 28), especially in view of the fact that he has just defined *the world* as those who do not love Jesus (v. 24). Until the disciples have overcome their grief and fear, they cannot be said to love Jesus perfectly (cf. 1 John 4:18), and to that degree they are still on the same footing as the world.

Here for the first time in the discourse is the implicit recognition of a crisis to come that will test the faith and love of the disciples. It is a crisis of separation, and even though Jesus has gone to great lengths to show that the separation is not ultimately real, he tacitly admits that it will be real to them, at least for a time. It is a temptation, a cause for anxiety, and though it has already been overcome in the words of Jesus, it must still be overcome in the disciples' experience. To this end Jesus leaves with them his wish of peace, given **not as the world does** (v. 27). It is not a peace to be measured by outward circumstances but a peace within the disciples themselves, not the kind that depends on freedom from conflict, but the kind that remains constant when trouble comes.

There is thus a certain tension between the four questions and answers that comprise most of the farewell discourse and the summary with which it concludes. If 13:36–14:31 is viewed as a farewell discourse complete in itself, verses 25–31 can be regarded as John's way of making a transition from the idealism of the discourse to the realism of the Passion narrative. The crisis will come in the person of Satan, **the ruler of the world** (v. 30), and Jesus calls the disciples to join him in confronting this their greatest foe (**Come, let us go from this place**, v. 31). It is significant that a discourse built on the announcement that Jesus was going where the disciples could not follow should end with a summons for them to go out *with Jesus* to meet the adversary. This final call to immediate action (used differently in the synoptic Gospels, Mark 14:42/Matt. 26:46) preserves here the distinctly Johannine emphasis on Jesus' unity with his disciples as he turns his face toward the cross.

Additional Notes

13:37 / **I am ready to die for you**: lit., "I will lay down my life for you." The idiom is the same as that used by Jesus in 10:11, 15, 17.

14:1 / **Do not be worried and upset:** lit., "Don't let your heart be troubled." The same verb was used of Jesus in 11:33; 12:27; and 13:21. Having quieted his own heart in preparation for the Passion, Jesus now begins to prepare his disciples for what lies ahead.

Believe in God and believe also in me. The two verbs can be read either as imperatives (as here) or indicatives (i.e., "You do believe in God, and you believe in me"); or one can be read as indicative and the other as imperative (i.e., "You do believe in God; therefore believe in me"). But consistency favors translating the two verbs in parallel fashion, and the double indicative would be trite and redundant at this point. The GNB rendering is therefore preferable; Jesus is not speaking of belief in God (or himself) in a generalized sense but in relation to a specific hope for the future: "Trust God and trust me; this is what will happen, and there is no cause for fear."

14:2 / **Many rooms in my Father's house**: The "many mansions" of the AV has been changed in most modern versions because of the incongruity of "mansions" within a **house**. **Rooms** is literally "dwelling places" (Gr.: *monai*), the original meaning of "mansion" (from the Latin *manere*, "to dwell"); cf. Jesus' promise in v. 23 that he and the Father will come and "live with" (lit., "make a dwelling [*monē*] with") the person who loves and obeys Jesus.

The phrase **my Father's house** recalls 2:16–17, where similar terminology was used of the Temple in Jerusalem. Here it refers metaphorically to heaven. The metaphor, however, is probably that of an actual house or household (cf. 8:35–36), not the "heavenly temple" of Jewish and Christian apocalyptic literature (as, e.g., in Rev. 4). The emphasis is not on individual "compartments" in heaven but simply on the assurance that there is plenty of room for all who belong to Jesus.

I would not tell you this if it were not so. It is better to follow the GNB margin in taking the sentence as a question: **If it were not so, would I tell you that I am going** [lit., "going away"] **to prepare a place for you?** Grammatically, this translation is preferable because it takes account of the conjunction **that** (Gr.: *hoti*), which otherwise has to be ignored. The difficulty it presents is its implication that Jesus had said *on a previous occasion* that he was going away to prepare a place for his disciples. Nowhere else in the Gospel did he say this in so many words, but he did state clearly that he was going away (e.g., 7:33; 8:21), and it may be that the preparing of a place for believers was regarded as implicit in such passages as 6:39; 10:16; and 12:32.

14:6 / **I am the way, the truth, and the life**. The main thrust of the context is carried by Jesus' claim that he is **the way**; the other two self-designations are corollaries of this (cf. NIV: "I am the way—and the truth and the life"; or NEB: "I am the way; I am the truth and I am life"; but Moffatt's "I am the real and living way" goes too far in this direction).

14:7 / **Now that you have known me . . . you will know**. Some ancient manuscripts make the condition contrary-to-fact (**If you had known me . . . you would know**, GNB margin; cf. 8:19, as well as Jesus' later rebuke to the disciples for their lack of love and joy in v. 28). The stronger manuscript evidence, however, favors the text as given. Both Jesus' immediate positive statement that **from now on you do know him and have seen him** (i.e., the Father, v. 7b) and his surprised question, "Yet you do not know me, Philip?" (v. 9) also support the notion that Jesus is assuming knowledge—not the lack of it—on the part of his disciples.

14:12 / **Greater things**: lit., "greater works." The works the disciples will perform after Jesus' departure are **greater** than Jesus' works not in intrinsic value or glory but in scope: The disciples will do the works of God on a much wider scale as they bring the message of eternal life to the whole world, Gentiles as well as Jews (cf. 10:16; 11:52; 12:32).

14:14 / **If you ask me for anything in my name, I will do it**. A characteristic of this first farewell discourse is its terminology of prayer: Prayer is made not only in Jesus' name, but *to* Jesus (rather than to the Father), and Jesus himself is the one who answers prayer (some early manuscripts omit **me**, perhaps because it seemed awkward with **in my name**, but it is retained in the most important of the ancient textual witnesses). Jesus' assumption here is that because he is "going to the Father" (v. 12b), he shares in the Father's work of answering prayer, and in fact guarantees the answer. The phrase **in my name** means "on my authority"; the prayer is answered when the petitioner and the One being petitioned are united in faith and love, i.e., when the conditions described in verses 15–21 are in effect.

14:16 / **Another Helper**: **Another** implies that Jesus too is a **Helper** (Gr.: *paraklētos*; cf. 1 John 2:1, which speaks of the *risen* Jesus helping believers by serving as their advocate before God). The Spirit is here characterized as continuing to do for believers all that Jesus did for them while he was on earth—especially teaching and encouraging them. The Spirit's function is a revelatory and a pastoral one. He (or she; the term *paraklētos* in any case accents the personality of the Spirit) is a **Helper** in the specific sense of illuminating the revelation from God that Jesus brought and applying it to the ever-changing needs of Jesus' followers.

14:17 / **He remains with you and is in you**. The tenses are present, but Jesus is referring to the future: when the Spirit comes, he will come to stay and will live in the disciples' hearts. Some manuscripts make the second verb a future (GNB margin: **will be in you**) as if Jesus were distinguishing between the Spirit's presence *with* the disciples even then and *in* them after his departure. But such a distinction is foreign to the text; in NT references to union with God, **in** by no means implies greater intimacy than **with** (cf. Phil. 1:23; 1 Thess. 4:17), and here the two are virtually interchangeable.

14:18 / **All alone**: Gr.: *orphanous* (lit., "orphaned" or "abandoned").

14:19 / **Because I live, you also will live**. The words **because I live** refer to Jesus' resurrection; the promise that **you also will live** probably points both to the disciples' hope of future resurrection and to their present possession of spiritual life through the risen Jesus (cf. 6:57).

14:26 / **Make you remember all that I have told you**: Such language was used especially of warnings about trouble and persecution (cf. 13:18; 16:4; and perhaps 14:29), but memory also played an important part in the interpretation of Jesus' deeds (cf. 2:17, 22; 12:16). The writer of this Gospel probably saw himself as one to whom **the Helper, the Holy Spirit**, had given special insight and perspective, after the fact, on the words and deeds of Jesus as he wrote them down.

14:28 / **For he is greater than I**. Even though Jesus and the Father are "one" (10:30), Jesus can still characterize the Father as **greater** because there are certain aspects of their relationship that are not reciprocal or reversible: The Father sent Jesus, Jesus did not send the Father; Jesus goes away to rejoin the Father, the Father does not come to him. Functionally, the Father is **greater**. The disciples should be glad that the human being who eats with them as friend and teacher is not the end in himself, but the Way to God, the Beginning and the End of all things.

14:29 / **Before it all happens, so that** . . . **you will believe**: Before what happens? The only answer possible from the context is Jesus' departure, i.e., all the events associated with his Passion. When did they believe? One possible answer is 20:28–29; another (assuming that the specific belief was that Jesus had gone to the Father) is 20:8, where the beloved disciple "saw and believed" simply on the basis of the empty tomb.

14:30 / **He has no power over me**: lit., "in me he has nothing." It may be that even though the Devil is ultimately in view here, Jesus has in mind first of all the Devil's embodiment in Judas, who because of 13:21–30 now "has nothing" in Jesus. As the farewell discourse draws to a close (v. 31), Judas is indeed "coming" (cf. 18:2–3); he and the Roman soldiers he will bring are the immediate enemy to be faced.

40

Jesus' Love and
the World's Hatred

"I am the real vine, and my Father is the gardener. ²He breaks off every branch in me that does not bear fruit, and he prunes every branch that does bear fruit, so that it will be clean and bear more fruit. ³You have been made clean already, by the teaching I have given you. ⁴Remain united to me, and I will remain united to you. A branch cannot bear fruit by itself; it can do so only if it remains in the vine. In the same way you cannot bear fruit unless you remain in me.

⁵"I am the vine, and you are the branches. Whoever remains in me, and I in him, will bear much fruit: for you can do nothing without me. ⁶Whoever does not remain in me is thrown out like a branch and dries up; such branches are gathered up and thrown into the fire, where they are burned. ⁷If you remain in me and my words remain in you, then you will ask for anything you wish, and you shall have it. ⁸My Father's glory is shown by your bearing much fruit; and in this way you become my disciples. ⁹I love you just as the Father loves me; remain in my love. ¹⁰If you obey my commands, you will remain in my love, just as I have obeyed my Father's commands and remain in his love.

¹¹"I have told you this so that my joy may be in you and that your joy may be complete. ¹²My commandment is this: love one another, just as I love you. ¹³The greatest love a person can have for his friends is to give his life for them. ¹⁴And you are my friends if you do what I command you. ¹⁵I do not call you servants any longer, because a servant does not know what his master is doing. Instead, I call you friends, because I have told you everything I heard from my Father. ¹⁶You did not choose me; I chose you and appointed you to go and bear much fruit, the kind of fruit that endures. And so the Father will give you whatever you ask of him in my name. ¹⁷This, then, is what I command you: love one another.

¹⁸If the world hates you, just remember that it has hated me first. ¹⁹If you belonged to the world, then the world would love you as its own. But I chose you from this world, and you do not belong to it; that is why the world hates you. ²⁰Remember what I told you: 'No slave is greater than his master.' If they persecuted me, they will persecute you too; if they obeyed my teaching, they will obey yours too. ²¹But they will do all this to you because you are mine; for they do not know the one who sent me. ²²They would not have been guilty of sin if I had not come and spoken to them; as it is, they no longer have any excuse for their sin. ²³Whoever hates me hates my Father

also. ²⁴They would not have been guilty of sin if I had not done among them the things that no one else ever did; as it is, they have seen what I did, and they hate both me and my Father. ²⁵This, however, was bound to happen so that what is written in their Law may come true; 'They hated me for no reason at all.'

²⁶"The Helper will come—the Spirit, who reveals the truth about God and who comes from the Father. I will send him to you from the Father, and he will speak about me. ²⁷And you, too, will speak about me, because you have been with me from the very beginning.

¹"I have told you this, so that you will not give up your faith. ²You will be expelled from the synagogues, and the time will come when anyone who kills you will think that by doing this he is serving God. ³People will do these things to you because they have not known either the Father or me. ⁴But I have told you this, so that when the time comes for them to do these things, you will remember what I told you.

Just as it is possible to imagine a stage of the tradition when the only farewell discourse was 13:31–35 (see chapter 30), so it is possible to imagine a stage when the discourse extended to 14:31 but no further. There is a smooth transition from that verse's summons to "go from this place," to the statement in 18:1 that Jesus "left with his disciples and went across the brook called Kidron." At the end of chapter 14, the reader expects the group to leave and the discourse to end. Instead, the discourse continues, as Jesus seems to make a new beginning.

In a manner reminiscent of the public ministry, he combines a particularly vivid and concrete metaphor with an "I am" formula (cf. "I am the bread of life," 6:35, 48; "I am the gate for the sheep," 10:7, 9; "I am the good shepherd," 10:11, 14). As in each previous example, the key pronouncement occurs twice: **I am the real vine** (v. 1) and **I am the vine** (v. 5). But unlike the previous examples, the pronouncements here add a second identification to each of the "I am" formulas (**my Father is the gardener,** v. 1; **you are the branches,** v. 5). The result is not a full-blown parable (both 10:1–5 and 10:12–13 are more like parables in the sense of telling a real story), but something similar to the interpretations attached in the synoptic Gospels to the parables of the sower (Mark 4:13–20 and parallels) and of the weeds in the field (Matt. 13:36–43). Jesus identifies himself in relation to the Father in verses 1–4, and in relation to the disciples in verses 5–8.

The vine or vineyard metaphor is an ancient one for describing the people of Israel under God's care (cf. Ps. 80:14–18; Isa. 5:1–7). Though the identification with Israel remains implicit and undeveloped (cf. 1:43–51), the metaphor calls attention not only to Jesus himself but to the disciples and their relationship to him. Even in verses 1–4, where Jesus defines his identity first in relation to the Father (vv. 1–2), the disciples are quickly brought into the picture (**you**, vv. 3–4), whereas verses 5–8 center almost entirely on them, the **branches**, and how they **bear fruit**. Most of the other "I am" sayings in this Gospel are accompanied by an invitation to "come" to Jesus, or "believe" in him (e.g., 6:35; 8:12; 10:9; 11:25–26; 14:6), but **I am the vine** focuses instead on those who have already come and has as its corollary the command to "remain in" (or "united to") him in whom they have believed. The vine metaphor seems, in fact, to have been introduced at this point in the discourses primarily to dramatize the single imperative of "remaining" (Gr.: *menein*) spiritually united to Jesus in a life-sustaining relationship.

The first "I am" sequence (vv. 1–4) provides a kind of metaphorical history of the disciples' experience. The care of the branches is in the hands of the Father, who **breaks off** (Gr.: *airei*) fruitless branches and **prunes** (Gr.: *kathairei;* NIV: "trims clean") those that are productive (v. 2). This summary of the Father's work serves as an interpretation of chapter 13 as a whole: Judas, the fruitless branch, has been "broken off" (cf. 13:21–30), while the rest of the disciples are **clean** (Gr.: *katharoi*) as a result of Jesus' teaching (v. 3; cf. 13:10) and ready to **bear more fruit** (v. 2).

The end of the first sequence (v. 4) anticipates the second. The key to "bearing fruit" is remaining united to Jesus, the source of all life, yet this "remaining" is not a passive thing. It consists of more than simply allowing Jesus to rule in one's heart by default. It begins to take shape in the second "I am" sequence (vv. 5–8), and it comes to concrete expression in the summons to love and mission that immediately follows (vv. 9–17). After the heading, **I am the vine, and you are the branches** (v. 5a), the second sequence falls into a chiastic (*a b b a*) pattern:

a. **Whoever remains in me, and I in him, will bear much fruit;**
b. **for you can do nothing without me** (v. 5).
b′. **Whoever does not remain in me is thrown out like a branch and dries up; such branches . . . are burned** (v. 6).
a′. **If you remain in me and my words remain in you, then you will ask for anything you wish, and you shall have it. My Father's glory is shown by your bearing much fruit; and in this way you become my disciples** (vv. 7–8).

The point of the sequence as a whole is that when branches remain with the vine they bear fruit, and when they do not they die. Clearly, *a* and *a'* are promises, while *b* and *b'* are warnings or threats. In *b* the negative point is made briefly; in *b'* it is developed at some length. Similarly, in *a*, the positive point is made briefly, and in *a'* more elaborately. A saying about answered prayer has been woven into *a'* as a specific example of fruit-bearing (v. 7; cf. 14:13–14), and at the end Jesus' thought circles back to the **Father's glory** as the ultimate reason for **bearing much fruit** and so becoming disciples (v. 8).

What do these words and images mean concretely in human experience? Christian discipleship, a clear enough notion in itself, seems confusing in the present context because Jesus, instead of assuming that his disciples *are* disciples, speaks of the possibility of them *becoming* disciples (v. 8)! It is helpful to remember a clue dropped much earlier when Jesus was addressing a group of "believers" who turned out not to be believers at all: "If you obey [lit., "If you *remain* in"] my teaching, you are really my disciples" (8:31). The clue was that discipleship involved more than just *believing* (i.e., establishing a relationship to Jesus); it demanded also *remaining* (i.e., maintaining and nurturing that relationship). This had to be done by hearing and obeying Jesus' "teaching" (8:31), which was exactly what the counterfeit "believers" of 8:30–59 refused to do. In the present passage, discipleship is similarly defined in terms of remaining in Jesus, and in verse 7 he significantly adds the condition that **my words remain in you.** It is the "teaching," after all, that has made them clean (v. 3), and one dimension, at least, of remaining in (or united to) Jesus is remembering his teaching and continuing to obey it (cf. the many biblical injunctions to Israel to remember and obey the words of the Lord; e.g., Deut. 6:4–9).

The familiar triangular pattern of chapter 13 is reaffirmed in verses 9–17. Remaining in Jesus and reflecting on his words is first defined more precisely as remaining in his love, a command based on the Father's love for Jesus as well as Jesus' love for the disciples (v. 9). Remaining in Jesus' love is equated with obeying his commands, based on the precedent of Jesus remaining in his Father's love by obeying his Father's commands (v. 10; cf. the references to Jesus' obedience in 10:18; 12:49–50; and 14:31). Such a precedent proves that the obedience of which Jesus speaks is not the obedience of a slave (cf. v. 15), for its motivation is love and its purpose is joy (v. 11). Jesus' commands come to a focus in the one great command to **love one another, just as I love you** (v. 12; cf. v. 17). Here the triangular pattern becomes explicit, and for the moment Jesus and his disciples are back in the world of chapter 13, especially 13:12–17. "Remaining" is at last defined concretely as "doing" something (v. 14; cf. 13:15, 17), specifically, loving one's **friends** (i.e., one's brothers and sisters in the community of disciples) and giving one's life for them (v. 13). This is the example Jesus sets, symbolically in the footwashing and literally in his death on the cross. To remain in him is to follow his example of servant-hood by loving others, even at the cost of one's own life (cf. 1 John 3:16–18). Verses 9–17 simultaneously interpret the vine imagery of verses 1–8 and reinforce the interpretation already given of the footwashing two chapters earlier.

Here, ironically, just at the point in the Gospel where servanthood is given its most profound expression, servanthood is transcended. Jesus has referred to the disciples as his servants (12:26, 13:16) and, despite what he says in verse 15, he will do so again almost immediately (v. 20, citing 13:16 verbatim). Yet the term "servant" (Gr.: *doulos*, sometimes translated "slave" in GNB) has its limitations. "A slave [or servant] does not belong to a family permanently," Jesus had once said, "but a son belongs there forever" (8:35). Though a servant might be loved by his master, Jesus selects another word, **friend** (Gr.: *philos*, vv. 13–15), to call particular attention to his love for the disciples (v. 12) and to keep that love ever before them (cf. 13:1; also 13:23, the disciple "whom Jesus loved"). But the distinction goes deeper. A master's love for his servants does not involve telling them his business (except for what they need to know to do their jobs), but shared knowledge and insight is an important part of true friendship (v. 15).

Friendship is here defined in terms of both *revelation* and *imitation*. Almost at the beginning of his ministry, Jesus had said: "What the Father does, the Son also does. For the Father loves [Gr.: *philei*] the Son and shows him all that he himself is doing" (5:19b–20). Now that Jesus has told his disciples everything he has heard from the Father (v. 15b), they in turn **know** what Jesus is doing (v. 15a), and must **do** what he commands (v. 14). This means doing what Jesus himself has done, for Jesus' commands are based on his example (**love one another, just as I love you**, v. 12; cf. 13:15). At this point, Jesus' words powerfully reinforce what he had said in 13:17: "Now that you know this truth, how happy you will be if you put it into practice." Friendship finds its realization in loving service. Friendship and servanthood are not set against each other as contradicting ideals, for the contrast is used solely to highlight the importance of revelation. The unfulfilled promise of 8:32 is at last coming true—though not for those who first heard it—"you will know the truth, and the truth will set you free."

In chapter 15 as in chapter 13, mutual love among Jesus' disciples does not stay within the community of disciples but inevitably results in mission to the world (cf. 13:18–20). The brief positive glimpse of this mission in 15:16–17 serves as the transition to a longer and largely negative portrayal of its difficulties and dangers in 15:18–16:4a. Verses 16–17 are linked to what follows by the notion that the disciples are chosen for their task (vv. 16, 19; cf. 13:18), but even more closely to what precedes by a last reference to fruit-bearing (v. 16) and a last repetition of the command to **love one another** (v. 17). If remaining in Jesus is defined concretely as loving one another, the consequent bearing of fruit must be defined as reproducing oneself and one's relationship to Jesus spiritually in the lives of others—that is, as what later, and more ecclesiastically minded, Christians have called evangelism (cf. 12:24: a single grain of wheat "dies" in order to produce "many grains," lit., "much fruit"). The evangelization of the world in this Gospel does not arise out of the disciples' conscious love or compassion for the world itself, or the masses of people in it, but out of their "in-house," familial love for each other. "If you have love for one another," Jesus is still saying, "then everyone will know that you are my disciples" (cf. 13:35). The entire section from verses 9 to 17 is best understood not only as an interpretation of the vine metaphor in its immediate context, but as a crucial exposition in retrospect of Jesus' washing of the disciples' feet two chapters earlier.

The prospect that "everyone will know" Jesus' disciples by their love for one another does not mean that everyone will believe. In the first discourse the "world" was defined as those who did not love Jesus (14:22–24). Here the indictment of **the world** is even sharper. If the disciples are known by their love, **the world** is defined by its hatred—for Jesus first and then for those who belong to him. The root of this hatred is alienation. Jesus is "from above" (3:31), and those who "belong to this world here below" cannot begin to understand him (8:23). Because the disciples did not "come down from heaven" as Jesus did (3:13; cf. 6:32–42), it might appear that they, unlike Jesus, in some sense **belong** to the world. But this is not the case; the fact that Jesus chose them to be his messengers alienates them from **the world** just as surely as if they had literally come down from above (v. 19; cf 17:14).

Building on pronouncements similar to two that he had used in connection with the footwashing (i.e., 13:16 and 20), as well as similar sayings found in the synoptic Gospels (e.g., Matt. 10:24–25, 40; Luke 10:16), Jesus predicts that the disciples will face persecution (vv. 18–21).

It is difficult to tell whether Jesus' self-citation in verse 20 stops with **no slave is greater than his master** (and is therefore based entirely on 13:16a) or whether it includes the rest of verse 20 as well. His point is that if he has been hated and persecuted by his contemporaries, his followers should not be surprised that the same fate awaits them. Verse 20 is probably the citation of a saying to that effect not found verbatim in any of our Gospels but represented in variant forms in John 13:16 and in Matthew 10:24–25 (the "if" clauses with which v. 20 concludes find their parallel in Matt. 10:24b). Jesus' point is therefore not the same as in 13:20, or in Matthew 10:40 or Luke 10:16. His mission is seen here as the historical precedent for that of his disciples, not as something identical with it or embodied in it. Though the disciples' mission is seen as a continuation of Jesus' own, Jesus does not blur the distinction between them or superimpose one upon the other. Instead, he focuses the disciples' attention first on his own mission and its consequences (vv. 22–25), and then, more specifically than before, on what lies ahead for them (15:26–16:4b).

The summary of his public ministry (vv. 22–25) recalls Jesus' indictment of the Pharisees in 9:39–41. Directed not against a particular group of questioners but against the world itself, it is the universal indictment of which 9:39–41 was a particular instance. In the entire Gospel, only 1:10–11 and 3:19 are comparable in scope. The solemn verdict is formally repeated in two stanzas of parallel structure:

a. **They would not have been guilty of sin**	a'. **They would not have been guilty of sin**
b. **if I had not** come and spoken to them;	b'. **if I had not** done among them the things that no one else ever did;
c. **as it is,** they no longer have any excuse for their sin.	c'. **as it is,** they have seen what I did, *and they hate both me and my Father* (v. 24).
Whoever hates me hates my Father also (vv. 22–23).	

In each stanza, the world's sin is understood concretely in relation to the coming of Jesus into the world. If Jesus had not come, there would have been no **sin** (cf. 9:41), for sin is defined solely as hatred of Jesus and, consequently, as hatred of the Father who sent him. Drawing once more on the experience of the psalmists of Israel, Jesus adds a supporting

Scripture quotation: "They hated me for no reason at all" (Pss. 35:19; 69:5; cf. *Ps. Sol.* 7.1). If the one great commandment is love, the one great transgression is hatred.

Now that the precedent of hatred has been set, the disciples can be under no illusions about what their own mission entails. Whereas 13:18–20 dealt with the single experience of betrayal by members of one's own community, 15:26–16:4a alludes to a whole range of troubles. Jesus' disciples will be expelled from their synagogues, just as the blind man was (9:34), or even killed by religious zealots intent on murder as a sacred duty (16:2; cf. the example of Saul of Tarsus in Acts 9:1–5). Like Jesus before them, they will be mistreated by people who **have not known either the Father or me** (16:3).

The unspoken assumption of all these prophecies is the departure of Jesus, which will be made explicit in 16:5 (cf. 13:36–14:31). Though Jesus' coming was decisive in bringing to light the world's sin, there is yet another "coming" that affects—even determines—the disciples' situation in the world after he has gone: the coming of the **Helper** (v. 26; cf. 14:16–17, 26). Jesus' absence is clearly indicated by the promise that he will **send** the Spirit to the disciples **from the Father** (v. 26). Even more than in the first discourse, the Spirit's presence with the disciples is promised especially in situations of persecution, when they would feel Jesus' absence most keenly. To this extent the Spirit's function is the same as it is in the synoptic Gospels: to enable the disciples to stand firm under hostile questioning and to testify faithfully about Jesus to their persecutors (vv. 26–27: cf. Mark 13:11; Matt. 10:19; Luke 12:11–12).

Though this is the main import of the promise of the Spirit in its historical and literary context, it is likely that the first readers of the Gospel (like many readers today) regarded it as the conferral of authority in a more general sense on those who had been with Jesus **from the very beginning** (v. 27; cf. 1 John 1:1–3). Those who had witnessed his words and deeds on earth were the ones uniquely qualified to be the vehicles of the Spirit's witness from heaven. But if Jesus, or the Gospel writer, has in mind here a justification of apostolic authority, he keeps it strictly subordinate to the more immediate purpose of encouraging Christians in the face of persecution. His primary concern, he tells the disciples, as well as the primary object of the Spirit's ministry, is **that you will not give up your faith** (v. 1) at the prospect of expulsion from the synagogue or even death (v. 2). The expression "to give up" or "give up one's faith" (lit., "be scandalized") was used earlier when the disciples drew back in horror at the thought of sharing in Jesus' violent death (6:60–61). The possibility of martyrdom continued to be present through much of the Gospel (cf. 12:24–26; 13:36–38), and now Jesus refers explicitly to the danger of being killed for his sake (v. 2)—even as he had bluntly charged his enemies all along with trying to kill him (7:19; 8:37, 40). The thrust of Jesus' prophetic vision is that all the hatred directed against him from the beginning of his ministry, expressing itself in persecution (5:16) with the intent to kill (5:18), will be redirected at his disciples after his departure. His hope is that the disciples will remember his warnings, and be reassured by two things: first, by knowing why the religious authorities are persecuting them (**because they have not known either the Father or me**, v. 3); and second, by knowing that Jesus was not taken by surprise, but saw beforehand what was in store for them as clearly as he saw his own calling and destiny (v. 4a; cf. 13:19; 14:29).

Additional Notes

15:6 / **Thrown out like a branch**: What was stated in v. 2 as a metaphor ("He breaks off every branch in me") appears here in the form of a simile. The description in v. 6b of the gathering and burning of the dried-up branches is not a theological statement but is drawn from observation of everyday life. But does the imagery imply that those who belong to Jesus can lose the salvation they have by virtue of their relationship to him? The answer depends on one's assessment of the spiritual condition of Judas the betrayer. If Judas was at first a true disciple of Jesus, one may conclude that a genuine believer may in fact be **thrown out like a branch**. But if Judas was never truly a child of God, then his case is *not* that of a believer losing his salvation. Such terms as "a devil" (used of Judas as early as 6:70) and "the man who was bound to be lost" (17:12) suggest that the latter alternative is the correct one. Judas was a "fruitless branch" because he had no life-giving connection with Jesus in the first place. His expulsion simply made visible (to the beloved disciple at least) what was already the case in his heart. It is fair to draw the tentative conclusion that the same is true of whatever other "fruitless branches" the Gospel writer may have in mind in his own congregations.

15:16 / **The kind of fruit that endures**: lit., "that your fruit might remain" (Gr.: *menēi*, the word used throughout the chapter for "remaining" in Jesus). The hope expressed is that the disciples' converts will be firmly established in their new faith and will realize among themselves the same mutual love that Jesus desires for the first generation of believers (cf. 17:20).

And so the Father will give you whatever you ask. This expression of Jesus' intent is probably to be taken as synonymous with the immediately preceding intent that the disciples **go and bear much fruit** (cf. vv. 7–8). Prayer is an integral part of the disciples' mission; they will fulfill their mission precisely by asking the Father for a rich "harvest" of new believers (cf. Matt. 9:37–38/Luke 10:2; also perhaps Ps. 2:8). The supreme example of prayer as the key to mission is Jesus' own prayer in 17:9–23.

15:20 / **If they obeyed my teaching**: The context (v. 21 in particular) makes it clear that Jesus is using irony here: **If they obeyed my teaching**—which they did not—**they will obey yours too**. Though some will respond positively to the disciples' mission (cf. 17:20), Jesus is not looking at that possibility here.

15:21 / **Because you are mine**: lit., "for the sake of my name," or simply "for my sake."

15:25 / **Their Law**: The terminology indicates that Jesus' indictment is directed against the same Jewish religious establishment that has been persecuting him and seeking his life. See note on 8:17.

15:26 / **I will send**: In the second discourse (here and in 16:7), Jesus is the one who sends the Spirit from the Father. Contrast the terminology of the first discourse in which the Father himself sends the Spirit, though in response to Jesus' request (14:16, 26).

16:2 / **Expelled from the synagogues**: Cf. 9:22; 12:42, where expulsion from the synagogue was viewed as a possibility even within Jesus' earthly ministry. Here the experience is placed in a prophetic context, pointing to the experience of Christians in the decades after Jesus' resurrection. At least for the last decade of the first century, there is Jewish evidence that such expulsions actually took place. See note on 9:22.

Serving God: lit., "offering worship to God." Even as good works such as prayer, almsgiving, and fasting were regarded by Jews after the destruction of the Temple as equivalent to sacrifice, so would the "good work" of ridding the world of heretics be counted as an act of sacred worship.

16:4 / **When the time comes for them to do these things**: lit., "when their hour comes." This could mean "when the hour comes for these things [i.e., the things of which Jesus had just spoken] to be fulfilled," or "when the persecutor's hour comes" to do what they have to do. The second alternative is the more likely (cf. Luke 22:53b: "But this is your hour to act, when the power of darkness rules").

41

The Impending Departure II

JOHN 16:4b–33

"I did not tell you these things at the beginning, for I was with you. ⁵But now I am going to him who sent me, yet none of you asks me where I am going. ⁶And now that I have told you, your hearts are full of sadness. ⁷But I am telling you the truth: it is better for you that I go away, because if I do not go, the Helper will not come to you. But if I do go away, then I will send him to you. ⁸And when he comes, he will prove to the people of the world that they are wrong about sin and about what is right and about God's judgment. ⁹They are wrong about sin, because they do not believe in me; ¹⁰they are wrong about what is right, because I am going to the Father and you will not see me any more; ¹¹and they are wrong about judgment, because the rule of this world has already been judged.

¹²"I have much more to tell you, but now it would be too much for you to bear. ¹³When, however, the Spirit comes, who reveals the truth about God, he will lead you into all the truth. He will not speak on his own authority, but he will speak of what he hears and will tell you of things to come. ¹⁴He will give me glory, because he will take what I say and tell it to you. ¹⁵All that my Father has is mine; that is why I said that the Spirit will take what I give him and tell it to you.

¹⁶"In a little while you will not see me any more, and then a little while later you will see me."

¹⁷Some of his disciples asked among themselves, "What does this mean? He tells us that in a little while we will not see him, and then a little while later we will see him; and he also says, 'It is because I am going to the Father.' ¹⁸What does this 'a little while' mean? We don't know what he is talking about!"

¹⁹Jesus knew that they wanted to question him, so he said to them, "I said, 'In a little while you will not see me, and then a little while later you will see me.' Is this what you are asking about among yourselves? ²⁰I am telling you the truth: you will cry and weep, but the world will be glad; you will be sad, but your sadness will turn into gladness. ²¹When a woman is about to give birth, she is sad because her hour of suffering has come; but when the baby is born, she forgets her suffering, because she is happy that a baby has been born into the world. ²²That is how it is with you: now you are sad, but I will see you again, and your hearts will be filled with gladness, the kind of gladness that no one can take away from you.

²³"When that day comes, you will not ask me for anything. I am telling you the truth: the Father will give you whatever you ask of him in my name.ᶠ ²⁴Until now you have not asked for anything in my name; ask and you will receive, so that your happiness may be complete.

²⁵"I have used figures of speech to tell you these things. But the time will come when I will not use figures of

speech, but will speak to you plainly about the Father. ²⁶When that day comes, you will ask him in my name; and I do not say that I will ask him on your behalf, ²⁷for the Father himself loves you. He loves you because you love me and have believed that I came from God. ²⁸I did come from the Father, and I came into the world; and now I am leaving the world and going to the Father."

²⁹Then his disciples said to him, "Now you are speaking plainly, without using figures of speech. ³⁰We know now that you know everything; you do not need to have someone ask you questions. This makes us believe that you came from God."

³¹Jesus answered them, "Do you believe now? ³²The time is coming, and is already here, when all of you will be scattered, each one to his own home, and I will be left all alone. But I am not really alone, because the Father is with me. ³³I have told you this so that you will have peace by being united to me. The world will make you suffer. But be brave! I have defeated the world!"

f. the Father will give you whatever you ask of him in my name; *some manuscripts have* if you ask the Father for anything, he will give it to you in my name.

The second farewell discourse runs most closely parallel to the first precisely where it is most properly a "farewell" (i.e., where it addresses directly the question of Jesus' impending departure; cf. 13:33). Here, inevitably, is also where the differences between the two discourses become most noticeable. Whereas the first discourse was largely structured around a series of questions by various disciples, here the question-and-answer method seems to be consciously abandoned. The earlier discourse began with Peter's "Where are you going, Lord?" in 13:36, but here Jesus makes the specific statement that **none of you asks me where I am going** (v. 5b). The reference is not simply to questions but to the *specific* question that touched off the whole discourse comprising 13:36–14:31. It is as if Jesus shows awareness of 13:36 but makes a conscious effort to do things differently. Such a development from "questions" to "no questions" might be appropriate if it made the point that now the questions were answered and no further inquiry was necessary. But the point is not that the disciples have no *need* to ask (because they know) but that they are too overcome with sorrow to put into words the question uppermost in their minds. They are no more knowledgeable here than in chapter 14. If anything, they are more confused and upset. **These things** that cause their grief (v. 4b) are best understood, not as the announcement that Jesus is going away (which he has so far made only in passing in v. 5a), but as the whole discourse up to this point, especially 15:18–16:3. The announcement of Jesus' departure also disturbs them, though primarily in light of what has just preceded it; it means they will have to face the world's hatred alone.

The abandonment of the question-and-answer form in verse 5b has the immediate function of accenting how overcome the disciples are with sorrow. But later, when the same emphasis on "no questions" appears again under somewhat happier circumstances (vv. 23, 30), it suggests that another motivation may also be at work. The change in form serves to make the theological point that the initiative in revelation lies not with the church but with Jesus. The literary technique of using questions to solicit divine revelation was a familiar one in Jewish and Christian apocalyptic literature and in Gnostic writings. John's Gospel itself makes use of questions (or statements) based on misunderstanding as a foil for Jesus' self-disclosure (cf., e.g., 3:4; 4:11, 15, 33; 6:34; 7:35–36; 8:22; 11:12; 13:9). This is to some extent characteristic of the questions in the first farewell discourse, and even in the present situation the disciples are similarly puzzled as they ask each other what Jesus means by **a little while** (vv. 17–18). Here Jesus knows their question before they ask it and takes the initiative in granting them an answer (vv. 20–22). The attitude taken toward questions as an aid to revelation in this chapter is articulated a half century later in the *Shepherd of Hermas*, an edifying Christian narrative of a series of visions originating in the church at Rome. True prophecy (i.e., a "spirit which is given from God") is distinguished from false prophecy by the fact that it is "not asked questions" or consulted like an oracle. A spirit that is consulted speaks on human initiative and is therefore earthly and powerless (Hermas, *Mandates* 11.5–6). It is perhaps for a similar reason that Jesus is depicted throughout this chapter as one who takes the initiative in revelation—not only at the beginning, when the disciples are too troubled to give voice to their anxieties, but at the end (v. 30), when they acknowledge explicitly that Jesus knows everything and has no need to be questioned because he has made all things clear.

These differences between the first discourse and the second should not be exaggerated. Obviously the disciples still have questions (essentially the same questions as before), and Jesus still provides the answers. And even in the first discourse, the initiative lay in a sense with Jesus because each of the four questions was triggered by a previous statement of his. What happens in the second discourse is simply that the monologue form, which in the first farewell discourse became dominant only in the summary (14:25–31), is made the vehicle for the *whole* discourse. And along with the form of 14:25–31, its concern about an impending crisis reappears as well from 15:18 on, and is made ever more explicit.

Jesus' answer to the question of his departure does not differ in its general outline from that found in chapter 14. It includes promises of the **Helper** (vv. 7–15), of renewed fellowship between the disciples and Jesus (vv. 16-22), and of answered prayer (vv. 23-24, 26). The most conspicuous difference is that the Helper's ministry has to do with the world (vv. 8–11) as well as believers (vv. 12–15). In chapter 14 the Helper was to speak only to the disciples, for the world could neither accept nor recognize him (14:17). In 15:26–27, however, the Helper gives testimony about Jesus, and the disciples are regarded not merely as recipients of this testimony but as instruments or co-workers of the Spirit in presenting it. The same is true in 16:8–11; though the Helper will be sent **to you** (the disciples, v. 7) his mission is to **prove to the people of the world that they are wrong about sin and about what is right** [lit., "justice"] **and about God's judgment** (v. 8). This the Spirit will do, not by some inward testimony in the hearts of **the people of the world**, but by the outward testimony of words spoken by Jesus' disciples in the course of their mission (cf. 15:27).

Verses 8–11 summarize the content of this testimony; they are perhaps the nearest thing we have to a distinctly Johannine formulation of the basic Christian message as first proclaimed to unbelievers. The summary is in three parts, each part defining a single key concept: sin, justice, judgment. The definitions are thoroughly characteristic of John's Gospel yet at the same time consistent with the understanding of these same three concepts in the earliest examples of the Christian proclamation in the book of Acts. **Sin** is defined not as breaking a set of laws but as rejecting Jesus (v. 9; cf. Acts 2:23; 3:13–15). "Justice," or **what is right**, is defined not as obeying a set of laws but as divine vindication, the raising of Jesus Christ from the dead (cf. Acts 2:24, 36; 3:15); the Johannine way of putting it is, **I am going to the Father and you will not see me any more** (v. 10). Only **judgment** is understood somewhat differently than in the sermons of Acts (where it is characteristically future, Acts 10:42; 17:31). **Judgment** is identified here, as elsewhere in this Gospel (5:29 being the only exception), with Jesus' victory over Satan, especially in his Passion (12:31; cf. 14:30; in the Synoptics, cf. Mark 3:23–27). Because the Passion is almost upon him, Jesus can claim that the world's evil ruler is **already** judged (v. 11; cf., "now" in 12:31).

What is this **world** that the Helper and the disciples will confront? Is it the world of the Jews, or of the Gentiles? The preceding references to expulsion from synagogues and to violent persecution as a religious duty (v. 2) suggest that a mission to Judaism is primarily in view, and this is supported by the three definitions in verses 8–11. The Jewish antagonists to the church would know about sin, justice, and judgment, but the definitions would be new to them: Sin is rejecting *Jesus*; justice is what God has done for *Jesus*; judgment is what *Jesus* has accomplished already by his death. The message of verses 8–11 amounts to a Christian redefinition of all that was of vital concern to the Jews. Yet the same message will confront the pagan world as well (cf. 18:33–38). Paul's confrontation with the Roman governor Felix aptly illustrates these verses; when Paul spoke to this pagan official and his Jewish wife about "goodness [lit., "justice"], self-control, and the coming Day of Judgment" (Acts 24:25), the governor was afraid and told Paul to leave.

Nowhere is it made plainer than in the present chapter that the Christian message is forever on a collision course with the **world**, whether of Jew or Gentile. The greater the willingness to acknowledge the world's reality and to recognize concretely what it means for Christians to live there, the greater the possibility of a negative or even hostile view of the world. In chapter 14, the disciples and the world moved, for the most part, on tracks that never met, but in chapters 15–17 they do meet and come into conflict, even though Jesus traces only faintly the precise contours of that conflict. **I have much more to tell you**, he says to his disciples, **but now it would be too much for you to bear** (v. 12). He leaves it to the Spirit to spell out more clearly **things to come** (v. 13), that is, the nature of the disciples' mission and of the world's opposition to it, and the final outcome of all their efforts. Jesus takes this opportunity to make the most sweeping statements about the Spirit's ministry to be found anywhere in the discourses. The Spirit of truth will lead the disciples into **all the truth** (v. 13). Such a phrase, taken out of context, could refer to all the philosophical and scientific truth of the universe, but here Jesus focuses specifically on truth that he says is **mine**. Jesus can speak of his truth as **all the truth** because **all that the Father has is mine** (v. 15; cf. 17:10); everything the Spirit reveals comes from the Father and therefore from Jesus. The accent here is not on what human beings can learn anyway by rational inquiry or by the use of their five senses but on the **much more** (v. 12) that Jesus would like to tell the disciples, but cannot, about their life and mission in the world. The teaching ministry of the Spirit builds on and develops the teaching ministry of Jesus himself. By making explicit what in Jesus' historical teaching was only implicit, the Spirit will prepare the disciples to face new enemies and seize new opportunities to extend Jesus' mission in the world. The implication is that the Spirit has done so precisely in this Gospel and in these last discourses.

The long monologue is briefly interrupted by a question (vv. 17–18), not a question directed at Jesus, but one that the disciples **asked among themselves**. The question is triggered by a kind of riddle (v. 16) built around the phrase **a little while** and reminiscent of the departure saying in 13:33 that had triggered the first farewell discourse (cf. 14:19). Here the phrase **a little while** (Gr.: *mikron*) occurs twice, and the disciples are confused. Jesus in his explanation moves from riddle (vv. 16, 19) to parable (vv. 20–21) to plain speech (vv. 22–28).

In resolving the problem raised by Jesus' statement in 13:33, chapter 14 had spoken of a single brief interval. "In a little while" the world would not see Jesus, but the disciples would see him (14:19). In chapter 16 his absence is acknowledged even as far as the disciples are concerned (**in a little while you will not see me any more**, v. 16a; cf. v. 10, **you will not see me any more**). But the absence is only temporary, because after a second brief interval the disciples will see him again (**and then a little while later you will see me**, v. 16b). In the first discourse, faith and unbelief perceived reality differently; here they perceive it in the same way but make different value judgments about what they see. The reality is the departure of Jesus from the world; at this, the disciples **will cry and weep, but the world will be glad** (v. 20). Jesus then introduces a parable about a woman in labor to dramatize the point that the disciples' sadness will later give way to joy (v. 21). The reversal implied by this imagery seems at first to demand that at the moment when the disciples' sadness turns to joy, the world's joy turns bitter. The metaphor of birth pangs (cf. 1 Thess. 5:3), as well as such distinctly eschatological terms as **that day** (vv. 23, 26) and the word used for **suffering** (Gr.: *thlipsis*, v. 21), suggest a revelation that is visible both to the world and the church, and one that puts the world decisively to shame—a kind of culmination of the Spirit's ministry as described in verses 8–11. All of these factors support the notion that the first **little while** of verse 16 refers to Jesus' physical departure from this world in death, and the second, to his visible return to earth at this Second Coming (or Parousia, as many early Christians called it). This can be shown as follows:

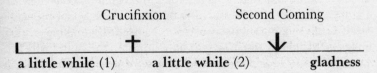

The first **a little while** is the short time that remains before Jesus' death. The second is the whole age of the church and of the church's mission.

This is the period of Jesus' absence, a time of **sadness** and **suffering**. The time of **gladness** is that future time, after Jesus' return, when faith becomes sight. The pattern is clear enough; the designation of the whole age of the church as only a **little while** is perfectly consistent with the early Christian conviction that "the end is near" (1 John 2:18; cf. James 5:8; 1 Pet. 4:7; Rev. 1:1, 3; 22:6, 10).

But there is a difficulty with this pattern. In verses 23–24 Jesus makes specific statements and gives specific instructions about the practice of prayer in **that day** of gladness, after the disciples have seen Jesus again. These statements, especially the invitation, **ask and you will receive, so that your happiness** [or "gladness" as in vv. 20–22] **may be complete** (v. 24b), are appropriate to the time of the church's mission but inappropriate to the time of consummation, after Jesus' Second Coming. They are commands that the author and his readers would naturally understand as directed to them, in their own time and situation (cf. 14:13–14; 15:7, 16). The completion of their gladness or joy corresponds to what Jesus prays for in 17:13. Nor can this gladness be differentiated from that mentioned in verses 20–22. Verses 23–24, and therefore verse 22 as well, belong wholly to what the Gospel writer regards as present experience, not to some transformed future state of bliss. If verses 23–24 are brought to bear on the interpretation of what precedes, a new and more satisfactory paradigm emerges for understanding verses 16–22:

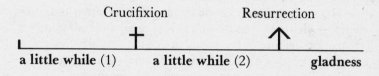

The first **little while** is again the short time remaining before Jesus' death. The second is the two or three days between the crucifixion and Easter morning, when Jesus is in the tomb. The two intervals are about equal in length, and both are literally short. The time of **gladness** is that time of renewed fellowship with Jesus after his resurrection (cf. 20:20, "The disciples were filled with joy at seeing the Lord"), a time signaling for them a continuing relationship with Jesus in the Spirit until their mission in the world is complete (cf. 14:18–20). The time of the disciples' mission is viewed here not as suffering and estrangement from Jesus but as joy and a more intimate union with him than was possible during his lifetime on earth (cf. 14:20). It is the time when Jesus' promise of answered prayer goes into effect because Jesus is with the Father (v. 24,

Until now you have not asked for anything in my name; ask and you will receive; cf. 14:12–14).

Surely this second paradigm is more "Johannine" than the first. Despite all that has been said about betrayal and persecution, the author is conscious of living in an age of joy and not sadness. He writes as one for whom Jesus is present and not absent: "The light shines in the darkness, and the darkness has never put it out" (1:5). Jesus' next-to-last pronouncement in chapter 16 is **The world will make you suffer**, but his very last word is **Be brave! I have defeated the world!** (v. 33). It is likely that both the riddle of verse 16 and the parable of verse 21 were sayings of Jesus remembered by his disciples after his resurrection and subject to either of two interpretations, depending on the circumstances of the interpreters. A suffering or oppressed church might well read it according to the first paradigm; a church rejoicing in worship, with a strong consciousness of the presence of Christ in the Spirit, would be more likely to read it according to the second. John is sensitive to the first, so sensitive in fact as to be ambiguous, but it is the second paradigm that finally represents his own interpretation of Jesus' pronouncements. Though Jesus will one day come again for all the world to see and will raise the dead from their graves (5:28–29; cf. 14:3), this is not the "second coming" that matters most in John's Gospel. The emphasis rather is on Jesus' reunion with his disciples by virtue of his own resurrection from the dead (cf. 20:19–23) and his continuing presence with them in their mission through the ministry of the Helper. Transcending the sadness of persecution and betrayal, Jesus confers a **gladness that no one can take away from you** (v. 22).

A conspicuous feature of this postresurrection period is free and open communication between God and his children. One side of this is, of course, the privilege of asking in Jesus' name, with the promise that all such prayers will be answered (vv 23b–24, 26). But intertwined with the promise of answered prayer is the promise of revelation (v. 23a [see note], 25, 29–30). If the disciples are able to speak freely to God in prayer, God will also be able—and willing—to speak freely to them. Though the Spirit is not mentioned here explicitly, Jesus anticipates that he will speak to his disciples **plainly about the Father** (v. 25) through the Helper, or Spirit of truth (cf. 15:26; 16:7). He anticipates that after his departure—and because of it—the veil will be drawn aside, and things now puzzling to the disciples will be made clear. He has **much more** to say (v. 12), and he will say it all, through the Spirit, in due time.

In verse 25, Jesus makes a distinction between **figures of speech**, the mode of his revelation in the present, and speaking **plainly** when the time for full revelation comes. The **figures of speech** can refer only to the riddle of verse 16, the parable about the woman in labor in verse 21, and perhaps to the metaphor of the vine in 15:1–17. To characterize the whole discourse as **figures of speech** is an exaggeration, to about the same degree as the statement in Mark 4:34 that Jesus would not speak to the people "without using parables." No sooner is the distinction between "figures of speech" and plain speech out of Jesus' mouth than he begins to speak as **plainly** as it is possible for anyone to do! (vv. 27–28; esp. v. 28: **I did come from the Father, and I came into the world; and now I am leaving the world and going to the Father**). The disciples immediately recognize this open revelation for what it is: **Now you are speaking plainly, without using figures of speech. We know now that you know everything; you do not need to have someone ask you questions. This makes us believe that you came from God** (vv. 29–30).

The decisive interjection by the disciples breaks the long monologue; for the first time in the entire second discourse, the disciples speak to Jesus directly. They are no longer *afraid* to ask questions, but now they have no *need* for questions, and they know it, because Jesus is the perfect Revealer. The key to this dramatic exchange is the expression **the time is coming and is already here**, which Jesus had used on two earlier occasions to highlight certain pronouncements (4:23; 5:25), and which he will use almost immediately again (v. 32). In the present instance, Jesus allows the disciples to finish the expression for him: He promises in verse 25 that **the time will come** for speaking plainly, and the disciples respond in verse 29 that the time is **now**. Their observation that Jesus already speaks plainly is quite accurate, and their acknowledgment that he comes from God (v. 30) confirms what he had said they believed in verse 27. The text offers no clue that the conclusion reached here by the disciples is in any way misguided or premature. It is likely that their words, no less than the preceding words of Jesus, serve as a vehicle for the narrator's own perspective on the events he describes. This perspective is that the future Jesus speaks of in verses 22–26 has already broken in upon the present. The future is now; the free and open revelation characteristic of the age of the Spirit is already at work, not in a series of events or experiences subsequent to the Gospel story, but in the text of the Gospel itself: To Jesus, **the time is coming**, but to the narrator and his readers, **it is already here**.

The disciples' confession that Jesus **came from God** (v. 30) is seldom counted among the great confessions of the fourth Gospel (e.g., 1:29, 34, 49; 6:69; 11:27; 20:28), for several reasons: (1) It is attributed to the disciples as a group rather than to one particular disciple (no individual disciples, in fact, are ever named anywhere in this second farewell discourse); (2) it employs no memorable christological title such as "Son of God," "Messiah," or "Lord"; (3) it is anticlimactic after Jesus' statement in verse 27 that the disciples **have believed that I came from God**; and (4) its force seems blunted by Jesus' skeptical-sounding reply (v. 31) and his immediate prediction that the disciples **will be scattered, each one to his own home, and I will be left all alone** (v. 32). But over against all these considerations stands the stubborn fact that the great prayer of chapter 17 is firmly built on this confession (e.g., 17:8: "they know that it is true that I came from you, and they believe that you sent me"). More than anything else, the disciples' explicit acknowledgment in verse 30 that Jesus has come from God is what occasions the long prayer, and specifically the commendation of the disciples in 17:6–8. It provides a positive setting for the prayer in that it signals to Jesus that his work is finished (17:4): The group of followers that his Father has given him is now ready to continue his mission in the world

Negatively, the setting of the prayer is the ominous prediction that the disciples will be **scattered** (v. 32) and will desert Jesus in his time of need (cf. Mark 14:27/Matt. 26:31). Where the first discourse had glanced momentarily at Peter's individual "scandal" of denying his Lord (13:38), the second (as always) deals with the disciples as a group, focusing on the embarrassing truth that all of them fled for their lives at Jesus' arrest (cf. Mark 14:50/Matt. 26:56). If verse 30 is a moment of great insight for the disciples, verse 32 reveals their coming moment of abject failure. The thought of verses 29–33 swings back and forth like a pendulum between positive and negative poles: The disciples believe (vv. 29–30), *but* they will be **scattered** and Jesus will be alone (vv. 31–32); *but* he is not really alone; the Father is with him, and in him they have peace (vv. 32–33); *but* the world will make them suffer (v. 33), *but* Jesus has defeated the world (v. 33). The farewell prayer of chapter 17 rises out of this patchwork. If those for whom Jesus prays are those whom the Father has given him out of the world (17:6, 9), they are also those who are **scattered** in the world (v. 32). The famous prayer for unity (17:11, 21, 23) is first of all a prayer for the dispersed, "to bring together into one . . . all the scattered people of God" (11:52). If the prayer of chapter 17 celebrates the confession of verse 30, it also aims at overcoming the failure and frustration intimated in verse 32. In the immediate sense, the dispersed are the eleven disciples who deserted Jesus on the occasion of his arrest, but in the narrator's larger perspective, they are Jesus' followers even in subsequent generations (cf. 17:20) who find themselves scattered and vulnerable in a hostile world, cut off from each other and seemingly cut off from their Lord. For them, Jesus prays "that they may all be one, Father! May they be in us, just as you are in me and I am in you" (17:21).

Chapter 16 affords yet one more clue about the prayer in chapter 17: It is to be Jesus' *last* prayer for his disciples, not only because he is leaving the world, but because his return to the Father makes possible for the believer a new relationship to God in prayer. To pray to the Father **in Jesus' name** (vv. 23, 24, 26) is to have *direct* access to the Father. Jesus will not be a sort of go-between who takes the disciples' requests and presents them to the Father (v. 26). He does not see his role with the Father as that of a heavenly intercessor. Even though there is NT testimony elsewhere that the risen Jesus "lives forever to plead with God" for believers (Heb. 7:25), Jesus' interest here is not in his own future high priestly role but in assuring his troubled disciples that **the Father himself loves you** (v. 27). Because of what Jesus has done, they will be able to approach God directly in prayer, and their loving Father will hear and answer them. But now, for one last time before he departs, Jesus *will* pray to the Father on their behalf. Christian tradition for the last two centuries has referred to John 17 as Jesus' "high-priestly" prayer. The designation is apt, if it is kept in mind that Jesus is not seen here as the heavenly high priest already at God's right hand interceding for his church, but rather as the Christ of Calvary, poised between earth and heaven. The prayer is part of the once-and-for-all priestly work by which Jesus consecrates himself to death and his redeemed followers to their world mission (cf. 17:17, 19).

Additional Notes

16:4 / **For I was with you**: Jesus' language implies that in a certain sense he is no longer **with** his disciples, for he is already on his way to the Father (cf. v. 5: "But now I am going"). The impression of distance is stronger in chapter 17, where consistently Jesus speaks of the disciples in the past tense (e.g., 17:12, "While I was with them"; cf. 17:11, "And now I am coming to you; I am no longer in the world"). In Luke, it is the *risen* Jesus who speaks this way (Luke 24:44). In John's Gospel, **the beginning** when Jesus was **with** his disciples probably refers to the time of his public ministry, before he began to speak explicitly of his departure or death.

16:8 / **He will prove . . . that they are wrong**: lit., "he will convict." The verb "convict" goes appropriately with **sin** (in Greek as in English) but not so appropriately with "justice" and **judgment**. Jesus is represented here as expanding the familiar expression "to convict of sin" (cf. 8:46) into a three-part pronouncement. GNB has chosen the translation **prove . . . wrong** because it comes close to the meaning of "convict" and yet is appropriate with all three nouns.

16:10 / **You will not see me any more.** Because it is the "people of the world" who are being proved wrong, the reader expects "*they* will not see me" (cf. 14:19!), but **you** is chosen instead in order to anticipate the "you" of v. 16. That v. 10 is still in mind in vv. 16-22 is shown by the disciples' puzzled reference in v. 17 to the clause **because I am going to the Father,** which has occurred only in v. 10.

16:22 / **I will see you again.** The form of the saying in v. 16 leads one to expect "*you* will see *me* again," but Jesus' promise here emphasizes once again his own initiative in self-revelation.

16:23 / **You will not ask me for anything**: lit., "you will not ask me anything." The word for **ask** (Gr.: *erōtesete*) can mean either to ask questions or to make a request. By itself, the statement refers more naturally to the asking of questions: The disciples will not have to ask Jesus any questions because he reveals everything freely (cf. v. 30).

The GNB translation is based rather on the immediate context (v. 23b), which has to do with prayer: The disciples will make their requests (i.e., pray), not to Jesus, but to the Father in Jesus' name, and the Father will grant their requests. The emphatic position of **me** (Gr.: *eme*) before the verb (lit., "me you will not ask anything") seems to support this conclusion, yet the parallel with v. 30 is decisive in favor of **ask** as "ask questions." The twin themes of open revelation and open prayer are introduced in vv. 23a and 23b–24 respectively (separated by the solemn formula **I am telling you the truth**), and then developed more fully in vv. 25-30 (revelation, in vv. 25, 29–30; prayer, in vv. 26–27). The placement of **me** just before the verb **ask** in v. 23a corresponds perfectly to the placement of "you" (Gr. *se*) immediately before the same verb in v. 30.

16:26 / **Ask him on your behalf**: Here, in distinction from verses 23 and 30, the Greek verb *erōtan* means to make request or pray. This is because it is followed by the preposition *peri* ("for" or "concerning"); the same construction is used, e.g., in 17:9: "I pray for them. I do not pray for the world."

16:31 / **Do you believe now?** These words can be taken either as a skeptical question (as here) or as a glad exclamation. Because the context indicates that the disciples' faith is genuine (even though qualified by the prediction of v. 32), a better translation would be "Now you believe!"

16:32 / **I am not really alone.** The prediction that the disciples will leave Jesus all alone at his arrest is immediately corrected in light of the principle laid down in 8:16 and 29 that Jesus is never alone because the Father is always with him.

42

Jesus Prays for His Disciples

JOHN 17:1–26

After Jesus finished saying this, he looked up to heaven and said, "Father, the hour has come. Give glory to your Son, so that the Son may give glory to you. [2]For you gave him authority over all mankind, so that he might give eternal life to all those you gave him. [3]And eternal life means to know you, the only true God, and to know Jesus Christ, whom you sent. [4]I have shown your glory on earth; I have finished the work you gave me to do. [5]Father! Give me glory in your presence now, the same glory I had with you before the world was made.

[6]"I have made you known to those you gave me out of the world. They belonged to you, and you gave them to me. They have obeyed your word, [7]and now they know that everything you gave me comes from you. [8]I gave them the message that you gave me, and they received it; they know that it is true that I came from you, and they believe that you sent me.

[9]"I pray for them. I do not pray for the world but for those you gave me, for they belong to you. [10]All I have is yours, and all you have is mine; and my glory is shown through them. [11]And now I am coming to you; I am no longer in the world, but they are in the world. Holy Father! Keep them safe by the power of your name, the name you gave me,[g] so that they may be one just as you and I are one. [12]While I was with them, I kept them safe by the power of your name, the name you gave me.[h] I protected them, and not one of them was lost, except the man who was bound to be lost— so that the scripture might come true. [13]And now I am coming to you, and I say these things in the world so that they might have my joy in their hearts in all its fullness. [14]I gave them your message, and the world hated them, because they do not belong to the world, just as I do not belong to the world. [15]I do not ask you to take them out of the world, but I do ask you to keep them safe from the Evil One. [16]Just as I do not belong to the world, they do not belong to the world. [17]Dedicate them to yourself by means of the truth; your word is truth. [18]I sent them into the world, just as you sent me into the world. [19]And for their sake I dedicate myself to you, in order that they, too, may be truly dedicated to you.

[20]"I pray not only for them, but also for those who believe in me because of their message. [21]I pray that they may all be one. Father! May they be in us, just as you are in me and I am in you. May they be one, so that the world will believe that you sent me. [22]I gave them the same glory you gave me, so that they may be one, just as you and I are one: [23]I in them and you in me, so that they may be completely one, in order that the world may know that you sent me and that you love them as you love me.

[24]"Father! You have given them to me, and I want them to be with me where I am, so that they may see my glory, the glory you gave me; for you loved me before the world was made.

²⁵Righteous Father! The world does not know you, but I know you, and these know that you sent me. ²⁶I made you known to them, and I will continue to do so, in order that the love you have for me may be in them, and so that I also may be in them."

g. Keep them safe by the power of your name, the name you gave me; *some manuscripts have* By the power of your name keep safe those you have given me. h. I kept them safe by the power of your name, the name you gave me; *some manuscripts have* By the power of your name I kept safe those you have given me.

If chapters 15–17 are viewed as an expansion in reverse order of three pronouncements found in 13:31–35, then chapter 17 is built on Jesus' solemn reference to glorification in 13:31–32. Glorification is at any rate the theme of verses 1–5. In verse 1, Jesus prays, **Father, . . . Give glory to your Son, so that the Son may give glory to you.** In verse 5, he prays again, **Father! Give me glory in your presence now, the same glory I had with you before the world was made.** Superficially, it appears that these two petitions frame the first major division of the prayer. On this assumption, many commentators divide the prayer into four parts: Jesus' petition for his own glorification (vv. 1–5), his petitions for his disciples gathered around him to hear his last words (vv. 6–19), his petitions for later generations of believers (vv. 20–23), and his concluding petitions for a final reunion with his loved ones (vv. 24–26).

There are, however, significant breaks in thought after verses 3 and 8 that call such an outline into question. Between verses 3 and 4, Jesus' solemn references to himself in the third person (**your Son, the Son, Jesus Christ whom you sent**) abruptly give way to a more direct first person: **I have shown your glory on earth; I have finished the work you gave me to do** (v. 4). There is also a temporal shift: Verses 1–3 are oriented toward the future, while verses 4–8 are oriented, for the most part, toward the past. Jesus' opening petition, **Give glory to your son** (v. 1), clearly points to his impending death (cf. 12:23, 27–28; 13:1, 31–32), whereas the next clause **so that the Son may give glory to you** looks still further into the future.

To what is Jesus referring? The explanation is given in verse 2. The purpose clause

so that **the Son may give glory to you** (v. 1b) is made specific by a second purpose clause, structured identically:

so that **he might give eternal life to all those you gave him** (v. 2b)

278

The Son will give glory to the Father *after* his death on the cross, and this glorification is defined as the giving of eternal life. Eternal life, in turn, is defined as the knowledge of God, and the definition is skillfully woven into the petition itself. Eternal life means **to know you, the only true God, and to know Jesus Christ, whom you sent** (v. 3). The Son will give glory to the Father, then, by making him known in the world. He will be able to do this because the Father has given him **authority over all mankind** (v. 2a; cf. Matt. 28:18). Jesus has in view in these opening verses the world mission to be carried out by his disciples after his death. Through their testimony, the Son will give glory to the Father by granting life and knowledge to all who believe (i.e., **to all those you gave him**, v. 2). Verses 1–3 set the tone for the entire prayer, and their scope is universal. They (and not vv. 1–5) mark the prayer's first major division.

Verses 4–8 (with the exception of v. 5) are not petitions at all. They are, instead, a kind of last report to the Father of what Jesus has done on earth in the course of his ministry. On the basis of what he has accomplished, he renews his prayer for glorification (v. 5; cf. v. 1), but the emphasis of the section as a whole is on the resumé that undergirds the petition more than on the petition itself. Verse 5, in fact, is almost parenthetical, coming as it does between two parallel descriptions of Jesus' accomplishments so far:

I have shown your glory on earth; **I have finished the work you gave me to do** (v. 4);

I have made you known **to those you gave me out of the world** (v. 6).

Just as in verses 1–3, the Son's work of "glorifying" the Father is defined as making him known, but in this case the revelation is to the specific group of eleven disciples gathered to hear Jesus' last instructions. The phrase **those you gave me** focuses on this limited group in contrast to **all those you gave him** (out of **all mankind**) in verse 2. Such phrases as **they have obeyed** (v. 6), **now they know** (v. 7), **they received it, they know, they believe** (v. 8) are Jesus' testimony to the Father that the revelation has taken place; his work is indeed finished. He bases his testimony explicitly on the disciples' confession in 16:30, enlarging on his exclamation in 16:31, "Now you believe!" The eleven disciples are the living trophies of his mission on earth. As he reiterates his plea for **glory in your presence** (v. 5), he presents them to the Father with the acknowledgment that they **belonged to you, and you gave them to me**—as tangible evidence that his work is done.

With this, the intercession begins: Jesus prays in verses 9–19 for the Eleven, while in verses 20–23 he turns his attention to **those who believe in me because of their message**. The latter section is short because the petitions of verses 9–19 are assumed to apply also to the larger group. Verses 20–23 simply make the extension explicit and bring to particular focus for the church the themes of unity and mission. The transition from the disciples to the later church is made inevitable by the fact that the prayer stands within a Gospel. Its primary theme must be Jesus and the disciples as they appeared on the stage of history, yet at the same time there must be bridges from this past history to the Gospel writer's own day and his own churches. Usually these bridges are simply taken for granted; the reader is expected to know that Jesus' instructions to his immediate disciples were meant to apply to the contemporary church as well. But occasionally the bridges become visible—for example, in Mark 13:37 ("What I say to you then, I say to all: 'Watch' ") and Luke 12:41 ("Peter said, 'Lord, does this parable apply to us, or do you mean it for everyone?' "). In the present instance, a visible bridge is appropriate because of the universal scope of verses 1–3; with the explicit notice at verse 20, Jesus is returning to horizons already set at the beginning of the chapter. The point of the transition is not to distinguish between the two groups in any sharp way or to assert specific things about one that are not true of the other. On the contrary, the purpose of verses 20–23 is to affirm continuity from one generation of disciples to the next. In general, it makes little difference whether any particular statement appears before or after verse 20.

If there is a development in the petition, it has to do with the relationship of Jesus' disciples to the world. The same ambiguity that characterized chapter 16 is present here as well. The world is the enemy, the source of persecution, yet before the prayer is over, it becomes the object of a loving purpose expressed in mission. As for the disciples, they are seen in verses 9–13 as persecuted and in need of the Father's protection; in verses 14–19 (introduced by the words, **I gave them your message**) they are seen as carrying out a mission, though still persecuted and still in need of the Father's protection; in verses 20–23, **those who believe . . . because of their message** are seen as fulfilling their mission, and persecution is no longer part of the picture. Their unity is seen in verse 11 as a corollary of being kept safe by the power of God, while in verses 21–23 it is the means by which the world will come to believe and know what Jesus wants it to know. The disciples' stance in the world, passive at the beginning of the long petition, becomes more and more active as Jesus moves toward his conclusion. The petition that began with the disclaimer, **I do not pray for the world** (v. 9), ends with the expressed intent that **the world will believe** [or "know"] **that you sent me** (vv. 21, 23).

Jesus' delight in these followers whom God has given him is carried over from verses 4–8. His acknowledgment to the Father that **they belong to you** (v. 9) recalls verse 6, while the claim that **my glory is shown through them** (v. 10) further explains **I have shown your glory on earth** (v. 4)—thereby reinforcing the explanation already provided in verses 4–8. The dividing line, in fact, between report or presentation (vv. 4–8) and petition (vv. 9–23) is not hard and fast. Woven into the petition are further statements looking back at Jesus' ministry: **while I was with them, *I kept them safe.* . . . *I protected them,* and not one of them was lost** [cf. 6:39, 10:28]. . . . *I gave them your message,* **and the world hated them** (vv. 12, 14). At every point, Jesus' past activity undergirds his future-directed request: He kept the disciples safe (v. 12), and now he asks the Father to keep them safe when he is gone (vv. 11, 15); he gave them God's message (v. 14), and now he asks the Father to **dedicate them to yourself by means of the truth; your word** [i.e., "your message"] **is truth** (v. 17). In short, Jesus called them out of the world (cf. 15:19). They no more belong to the world than he himself does (vv. 14, 16), yet he recognizes that they will still be physically present there even when he is not. If they are in the world without belonging to it, they are there as those who have been sent (v. 18). They are there in the same way that Jesus was (cf. 1 John 4:17), sent to their own home as strangers (cf. 1:10–11). They cannot withdraw from the world any more than he did. Jesus did not leave the world until his work was finished, and when he left, his departure was not a withdrawal but a victory. Therefore he does not ask the Father **to take them out of the world, but . . . to keep them safe from the Evil One** (v. 15; cf. v. 11, also the last petition of the Lord's Prayer: "Keep us safe from the Evil One," Matt. 6:13).

To live in the world and carry the Father's message, the disciples must be "dedicated" (Gr.: *hagiazein*, lit., "to make holy," vv. 17, 19) or "consecrated" (v. 19, RSV) to the Father. If they are **sent** as Jesus was sent (v. 18), they are "dedicated" or set apart for their mission just as he was in the beginning (cf. 10:36, where GNB renders *hagiazein* as "chose"). But their sending, and their consecration, has a new basis as well. Jesus does not say to the Father, as 10:36 might lead us to expect, "As you dedicated me (when you sent me into the world), so I dedicate them," but rather, **I**

dedicate myself to you, in order that they, too, may be truly dedicated to you (v. 19). The word **dedicate** takes on here a different meaning than was apparent in verse 17 or in 10:36. How does Jesus dedicate himself? Simply by making a strong commitment in his heart to fulfill his mission? In a sense, yes, but his mission on earth is already complete—except for his redemptive death. Therefore, **I dedicate myself** can only mean consecration *to death*. Jesus dedicates or consecrates himself as a priest would consecrate a sacrifice! He is priest and sacrificial victim at the same time (cf. Heb. 9:12). It is solely on the basis of the one word **dedicate** or "consecrate" in verse 19 that the traditional designation of chapter 17 as Jesus' "high-priestly prayer" is justified. His self-dedication to the Father benefits the disciples. It is **for their sake** (Gr.: *huper autōn*, v. 19) just as the Good Shepherd's death is "for the sheep" in 10:11, 15 or as Caiaphas prophesies Jesus' death "for the Jewish people" in 11:52 or as Jesus speaks of giving his life "for his friends" in 15:13.

But what exactly are the benefits of Jesus' dedication of himself to death? What does his death accomplish for the disciples? The answer is given in a series of four purpose clauses (introduced in Greek by the conjunction *hina*) referring to the disciples (vv. 19, 21a, 22b, 23a); these are interspersed with two more purpose clauses (also with *hina*) referring to the world (vv. 21b, 23b). The four purpose clauses referring to the disciples span the division in the prayer at verse 20 and link Jesus' intent for his immediate disciples with his intent for the subsequent generations:

in order that **they, too, may be truly dedicated to you** (v. 19)

that **they may all be one. . . . May they be in us, just as you are in me and I am in you** (v. 21a)

so that **they may be one, just as you and I are one** (v. 22b)

so that **they may be completely one** (lit., "perfected into one," v. 23a)

It is not sufficient to say merely that the disciples are "saved" or receive "eternal life" through Jesus' death—although that is true. Their salvation is described here in a particular way. They are not only a "saved" but a "saving" community. Jesus' death has implications for them on at least three levels:

First, the intent that the disciples be **truly dedicated** to the Father (v.

19) reinforces Jesus' prayer for their dedication in verse 17, along with the accompanying statement that **I sent them into the world, just as you sent me into the world** (v. 18). This means that Jesus' death is the key to the mission of which he has been speaking since the beginning of verse 14 (with the words, "I gave them your message . . . "). The notion that the death of Jesus is the only thing that makes a world mission possible for his disciples is already familiar to the reader of this Gospel from 10:15–16 ("And I am willing to die for them. There are other sheep. . . . I must bring them, too"), 12:24 ("a grain of wheat remains no more than a single grain unless . . . it dies"), and 12:32 ("When I am lifted up from the earth, I will draw everyone to me").

Second, the description of the disciples as **truly dedicated to you** (v. 19b) also follows closely in the wake of Jesus' pronouncement **I dedicate myself to you** in verse 19a. If Jesus' self-dedication to the Father implies his death, does the dedication of the disciples hold open the possibility of their deaths as well? If "eating the flesh" and "drinking the blood" of Jesus implied following him in the way of discipleship and mission even to death (cf. 6:53–58), and if the principle that a grain of wheat must "die" in order to reproduce itself was applied to the disciples as well as to Jesus (cf. 12:25–26), it appears that here too, martyrdom is within the scope of Jesus' vision. If the world hates the disciples as it hated Jesus (v. 14; cf. 15:18–21; 16:1–4), there is no guarantee that their lives will end differently from his own. The earlier petition that they be **kept safe** (vv. 11, 15) should not be understood as referring to sheer physical survival (despite 18:8–9!) but probably to "remaining" spiritually united to Jesus and one another (cf. 15:1–8) in the completion of their mission on earth, no matter what the cost.

Third, the petitions for oneness (vv. 21a, 22b, 23a; cf. v. 11b) must be understood against this background of mission and discipleship. The spiritual unity of which Jesus speaks is not an abstraction. For his disciples and for all subsequent believers, to be **truly dedicated** to the Father is to become **one**, and to become **one** in the Father and the Son is to be **truly dedicated** to God for the task of bringing Jesus' message to the whole world. Unity and mission are inseparable in this Gospel. Unity is sought not for itself, but for the sake of mission, whereas mission has unity as both its presupposition and its goal.

Earlier, Jesus stated his desire to bring all his sheep into "one flock with one shepherd" (10:16), and in the next chapter the narrator commented that Jesus' death would "bring together into one . . . all the scattered people of God" (11:52). Here, the unity of the disciples serves a still wider purpose, expressed in the two additional purpose clauses referring to the world:

so that the world will believe that you sent me (v. 21b)

in order that the world may know that you sent me and that you love them [i.e., believers in Jesus] as you love me (v. 23b; cf. 13:35, "then everyone will know that you are my disciples")

None of these purposes, either for the disciples or for the world, should be regarded as already realized from the narrator's standpoint. Though the unity of believers with (and in) the Father and the Son is accomplished in principle by Jesus' resurrection from the dead (cf. 14:20), it is not accomplished concretely apart from the completion of the disciples' mission. The unity of Jesus' followers challenges the world to believe and to recognize the love of God displayed in Jesus, but the world's actual response remains undecided. The narrator's verdict on Jesus' earthly ministry is largely negative; only a remnant believed (cf. 1:10–12; 3:19–21; 12:37–43). But one way or another, Jesus will realize his intention: Either the world will believe and know the truth redemptively as the disciples have done already (and in this way cease to be the world), or it will be brought unwillingly to the recognition that it is in the wrong, and that Jesus and his disciples are the true messengers of God (cf. 16:8–11). In the latter case, the world is simply a theater for the vindication of Jesus' followers as those beloved of God. Both possibilities are held open, but the accent throughout the prayer is more on the believers and their vindication than on settling in advance the fate of the world.

This is clearly seen in the prayer's conclusion (vv. 24–26). In verse 24, petition gives way to a straightforward declaration of intent: I want them to be with me where I am (cf. 12:26; 14:3). Jesus desires for his disciples a vision of his own glory, the glory I had with you before the world was made (cf. v. 5). The glory that Jesus and his loved ones share is rooted in the Father's love for Jesus; it antedates the world and it will outlast the world (v. 24). This glory will be seen at Jesus' coming, when he raises his own to new life at the last day (5:25; 6:39–40). Verse 24 and verses 25–26 are set off from each other and from the rest of the prayer by the repetition of the address Father! and Righteous Father! in verses 24 and 25. Verses 25–26 bring the prayer to a close, not with a request, but with a concise summary of the entire prayer in the setting of the farewell discourses.

Despite the larger intent **that the world may know** (v. 23), the present fact is still that the **world does not know** God (v. 25). With the confession of 16:30 still in mind, Jesus points yet again to his disciples who **know that you sent me** (cf. vv. 6–8). And the same balance between past and future that shaped his language at other points in the prayer (e.g., vv. 4–5, **I have shown your glory**, . . . **Give me glory**; vv. 11–12, **Keep them safe**. . . . **I kept them safe**) is functioning here as well: **I made you known to them**. . . . **I will continue to do so** (v. 26). Though the "Helper," or "Spirit who reveals the truth about God," is not mentioned explicitly in Jesus' prayer, it is surely the Spirit whom Jesus has in mind. Jesus will continue to make the Father known in the world through the Spirit and, in turn, through the disciples (cf. 15:26–27).

The last three divisions of the prayer (after vv. 23, 24, and 26) are also linked appropriately by the theme of God's love. The triangular pattern introduced with the sign of the footwashing controls the farewell discourses to the very end:

that you love them as you love me (v. 23)

for you loved me before the world was made (v. 24)

that the love you have for me may be in them, and so that I also may be in them (v. 26)

Jesus' prayer for his disciples (and all subsequent believers) reinforces and displays his love for them (cf. 13:1), now clearly articulated as God's unique love for his Son extended to a whole people, a new community of faith. All that remains is the final outpouring of that love in Jesus' death on the cross.

Additional Notes

17:1 / **Looked up**: lit., "lifted up his eyes." The same Greek expression occurs in 4:35 ("take a good look"), 6:5 ("Jesus looked around"), and 11:41 ("Jesus looked up"). In each instance a crowd is either approaching Jesus or standing nearby. There is no crowd in chapter 17, but the use of this expression at the very beginning of the chapter may suggest the universal scope of Jesus' prayer. The parallel with 11:41–42 is especially striking: "I thank you, Father, that you listen to me. . . . I say this for the sake of the people here, *so that they will believe that you sent me*" (cf. 17:21, 23).

17:10 / **All I have is yours, and all you have is mine**. The clause is parenthetical, making a generalization of the immediately preceding statement that the disciples "belong to you." The second part of the generalization draws on 16:15 ("All that my Father has is mine"). The two halves of the pronouncement complement each other by making the same point in two different ways: The Father has given everything he possesses to his Son, yet in being given it remains forever his own possession (cf. Matt. 11:27/Luke 10:22).

17:11 / **And now I am coming to you; I am no longer in the world**. Jesus speaks here as if his departure has already begun (cf. "while I was with them," v. 12; "and now I am coming to you," v. 13). This perspective is characteristic, not of the prayer alone, but of the preceding farewell discourses as well (see note on 16:4).

17:11, 12 / **The name you gave me**: Some ancient manuscripts read in v. 11, **By the power of your name keep safe those you have given me**, and in v. 12, **By the power of your name I kept safe those you have given me** (GNB margin)— in both cases referring to the disciples, as in v. 6. The better-supported text, however, clearly states that the Father has given to Jesus his own name. The giving of the Father's name to Jesus is perhaps analogous to the giving of his glory (cf. v. 24), and is surely included in the **all** of v. 10. But what specific name is meant? A comparison with Phil. 2:9–11 might suggest that the name "Lord" (Gr.: *kurios*; the Greek equivalent of the Hebrew *Yahweh* or *Jehovah*) is in view, and Thomas' confession in 20:28 could be understood as bearing out this conclusion. A related, and more likely, suggestion is that the name is "I Am" (Gr.: *egō eimi*; Heb.: *ani hu*), the self-designation of God in the OT (especially in Isaiah) that Jesus adopted at several crucial points in this Gospel and made his own (cf. 6:20; 8:24, 28; 13:19; 18:5–6; and above all, 8:58).

17:12 / **So that the scriptures might come true**: The scripture fulfillment is mentioned in order to explain why there was one exception—Judas—to the general principle that **not one of them was lost**. The scripture in mind is probably the one cited in 13:18 (i.e., Ps. 41:10). The single exception proves the rule: Any true community of faith may harbor traitors or apostates, but the presence of such cannot endanger God's elect, who are **kept safe** by the power of his name.

17:18 / **I sent them into the world**. It is difficult to be sure of the time reference of these words. Their similarity to 20:21 ("As the Father sent me, so I send you") suggests to many scholars that they are intended to anticipate the sending described there. Yet their correspondence with other first person verbs in vv. 12 and 14 (**I kept them safe. . . . I protected them. . . . I gave them your message**; cf. **I have made you known**, v. 6; **I gave them the message**, v. 8) makes it more likely that they refer back to a mission that began *within* Jesus' ministry (i.e., **while I was with them**, v. 12). Whether Jesus is represented as sending his disciples early in his ministry, as in 4:38 ("I have sent you to reap"; cf. Matt. 9:37–38/Luke 10:2), or after his resurrection, as in 20:21, it is the same mission. From the standpoint of the prayer in chapter 17 it is already under way, even though Jesus is only now, through his impending death, dedicating the disciples to their task.

17:19 / **Truly dedicated to you**: lit., "dedicated in truth" (**to you** is implied). The word "truth," carried over from v. 17, is more than adverbial, and refers once more to the "word" or "message" from God that Jesus commits in turn to his disciples.

17:21 / **May they be in us**. Some ancient manuscripts read "one in us." The shorter text as it stands is to be preferred, but in the context there is no real difference in meaning, because in any case Jesus has just prayed **that they may all be one** (v. 21a). For believers to be **in** the Father and the Son is to be **one** with God and with each other. For this reason, GNB has correctly (though unnecessarily) supplied the whole phrase, **may they be one**, in the next sentence, just before the expressed intent **that the world will believe** (v. 21b).

17:23 / **Completely one**: lit., "completed [or "perfected"] into one." The adverbial expression is redundant, for how can an entity that is **one** be less than **completely one**? The grammatical construction in Greek is somewhat analogous to that used in 11:52 ("bring together into one"), though with a different verb. Both passages speak of a process that has unity as its goal.

17:24 / **You have given them to me**: lit., "that which you have given to me." For the use of the neuter singular to refer to believers corporately, see notes on 6:39 and 10:29.

43

The Arrest of Jesus

JOHN 18:1–14

After Jesus had said this prayer, he left with his disciples and went across Kidron Brook. There was a garden in that place, and Jesus and his disciples went in. ²Judas, the traitor, knew where it was, because many times Jesus had met there with his disciples. ³So Judas went to the garden, taking with him a group of Roman soldiers, and some temple guards sent by the chief priests and the Pharisees; they were armed and carried lanterns and torches. ⁴Jesus knew everything that was going to happen to him, so he stepped forward and asked them, "Who is it you are looking for?"

⁵"Jesus of Nazareth," they answered.

"I am he," he said.

Judas, the traitor, was standing there with them. ⁶When Jesus said to them, "I am he," they moved back and fell to the ground. ⁷Again Jesus asked them, "Who is it you are looking for?"

"Jesus of Nazareth," they said.

⁸"I have already told you that I am he," Jesus said. "If, then, you are looking for me, let these others go." (⁹He said this so that what he had said might come true: "Father, I have not lost even one of those you gave me.")

¹⁰Simon Peter, who had a sword, drew it and struck the High Priest's slave, cutting off his right ear. The name of the slave was Malchus. ¹¹Jesus said to Peter, "Put your sword back in its place! Do you think that I will not drink the cup of suffering which my Father has given me?"

¹²Then the Roman soldiers with their commanding officer and the Jewish guards arrested Jesus, tied him up, ¹³and took him first to Annas. He was the father-in-law of Caiaphas, who was High Priest that year. ¹⁴It was Caiaphas who had advised the Jewish authorities that it was better that one man should die for all the people.

Jesus' exit with his disciples from the place where they had eaten supper (v. 1) corresponds to the notice in Mark (14:26) that "they sang a hymn and went out" to Gethsemane and the Mount of Olives. Though John's Gospel does not give the name "Gethsemane" to the place where they stopped, and though *only* John's Gospel calls it a **garden** (Gr.: *kēpos*), it is clearly the same place and the same occasion. Perhaps because of the long prayer in chapter 17, there is no prayer in the garden, no exhortation to the disciples to stay awake and pray, and consequently no failure on their part. Attention is centered entirely on Jesus' arrest by the Roman soldiers and the temple guards. The synoptic Gethsemane scene is echoed only in Jesus' rebuke to Peter for trying to defend him with a sword: **Put your sword back in its place! Do you think that I will not drink the cup of suffering which my Father has given me?** (v. 11; cf. Mark 14:36 and parallels).

The **garden** is described as an enclosed area; Jesus and his disciples "went into it," according to verse 1 (NIV), and in verse 4 Jesus "went out" (NIV) to speak with those who had come to arrest him. The explanation that it was a favorite meeting place for Jesus and his disciples (v. 2) hints at an aspect of his Jerusalem ministry that the Gospel nowhere explicitly describes. But if Jesus spent time privately with his disciples outside the city (e.g., 3:22; 10:40–11:16; 11:54), why not also at Jerusalem? Was it to this **garden**, for example, that Nicodemus had come long before with his questions? Evidently Jesus' private instructions and prayers with his disciples were not confined to the one occasion recounted in chapters 13–17 but characterized his ministry all along. Although the Gospel outline divides Jesus' life into a public ministry comprising chapters 2–12 and a private ministry comprising 13–17, it is likely that in reality Jesus' ministry had both a public and a private dimension from beginning to end.

The narrator mentions Jesus' custom of private meetings with the disciples to explain how Judas knew where they might be found. Judas brings to the garden not only **temple guards**, as in the other Gospels, but **Roman soldiers** as well (v. 3), a whole cohort of them (GNB: simply **group**, but in the Greek, *speira*, normally one tenth of a legion, or six hundred men!). John's Gospel will emphasize more than the others the role of Pontius Pilate and the Romans in Jesus' trial and execution, and they are seen here as participants from the outset.

Jesus is in control of the situation at every step. Twice he asks the assembled soldiers and guards who they are looking for; twice they say, **Jesus of Nazareth**; and twice, with the declaration **I am he**, Jesus identified himself (vv. 4–5, 7–8). On the face of it, the simple words **I am he** (lit., "I am"; Gr: *egō eimi*) merely identify him as **Jesus of Nazareth**, the object of the group's search. But they also correspond exactly to the formula by which Jesus revealed himself *as God* according to 8:24 and 28 ("I Am Who I Am"), and especially 8:58 ("I Am"; in each case, Gr.: *egō eimi*). Only by attributing equal significance to the **I am he** of the present passage can the reader explain the reaction of the crowd of soldiers and temple guards: **They moved back and fell to the ground** (v. 6). As he repeats his self-revelation (v. 8), Jesus adds, **If, then, you are looking for me, let these others go**. The **others** are his disciples gathered with him in the garden. Jesus has literally "kept them safe by the power of your name, the name you gave me" (17:12a). The "name" is "I Am," and its power has driven back the tenth part of a Roman legion! Yet Jesus' intention is not to overwhelm his antagonists but to surrender to them—on the condition that his disciples be spared.

At this point, the narrator makes explicit the link between Jesus' action here and his prayer in the preceding chapter. Jesus' unique surrender fulfills what he had said immediately *after* the claim to have kept the disciples safe by the power of the divine name: "Father, I have not lost even one of those you gave me" (v. 9; cf. 17:12b, "I protected them, and not one of them was lost"; cf. also 6:39). The only exception is Judas the traitor, "the man who was bound to be lost" (17:12b), and in the present scene he has already been placed on the other side, with the adversaries, **standing there with them** as they were driven back by Jesus' self-revelation (v. 5). The narrator's comment in verse 9 makes the physical safety of Jesus' disciples an illustration of their spiritual well-being. Jesus himself takes full responsibility for their flight at the time of his arrest and incorporates it into the divine purpose. They are indeed "scattered, each one to his own home" (16:32), yet Jesus' prayer has restored them in principle and made them one. As Good Shepherd, he will not allow the approaching wolves to scatter and devour the sheep who belong to him (cf. 10:12–15). The disciples' moment of disgrace is transformed into Jesus' moment of triumph.

As Good Shepherd, too, Jesus makes sure that "no one takes my life away from me. I give it up of my own free will. I have the right to give it up and I have the right to take it back. This is what my Father has commanded me to do" (10:18). The Father's command is a **cup of suffering which my Father has given me**, and Jesus will not allow Simon Peter to defend him with the sword (v. 11). The arrest proceeds to its inevitable conclusion: The soldiers and temple guards, regaining their composure, take Jesus into custody. He is brought first to Annas, the father-in-law of Caiaphas the High Priest. Though Annas is mentioned in connection with Jesus' passion only in this Gospel, he is not the center of interest. The narrator calls the readers' attention instead to the High Priest himself, with a reminder of his earlier advice to **the Jewish authorities that it was better that one man should die for all the people** (cf. 11:49–52). That Jesus has put his fate in the hands of this man means that the **cup of suffering** is now unavoidable and that the time for it is rapidly drawing near.

Additional Notes

18:1 / **After Jesus had said this prayer**: lit., "After Jesus had said these things" (Gr.: *tauta eipōn*). The word **prayer** is supplied only because the prayer of chapter 17 immediately precedes. But at earlier stages in the compilation of the material, 18:1 may have followed 13:35 or 14:31. The same expression occurs in 13:21, at the end of Jesus' brief discourse on servanthood in 13:12–20.

Across Kidron Brook: **Brook** is literally "winter torrent," i.e., a wadi flowing with water in the rainy season but dry the rest of the year. John is the only Gospel that mentions Jesus' route out of the city in this way. The terminology, which agrees with that of the LXX, accurately describes the Kidron and probably helped to fix what later became the traditional locations of Gethsemane near the foot of the Mount of Olives.

18:3 / **Lanterns and torches**: The detail serves as a reminder that it was still night, as in 13:30. Judas' departure had taken place only a few hours earlier. In Luke, Jesus tells those who have come to arrest him, "This is your hour to act, when the power of darkness rules" (Luke 22:53).

18:4 / **Jesus knew everything that was going to happen**. The statement resembles in form the notices at the beginning of the footwashing narrative: *Jesus knew* that the hour had come for him to leave this world and go to the Father" (13:1); "*Jesus knew* that the Father had given him complete power; he knew that he had come from God and was going to God" (13:3). The same knowledge presupposed in the washing of the disciples' feet and in the farewell discourses continues to govern Jesus' words and actions throughout the Passion narrative (cf. also 19:28). Nothing that happens will take him by surprise.

18:9 / **So that what he had said might come true**: The fulfillment formula used here (Gr.: *hina plerōthē*) corresponds exactly to a formula used elsewhere for citing the fulfillment of OT Scripture (e.g., 13:18; 15:25, and frequently in Matthew's Gospel). Jesus' spoken words are already being accorded an authority comparable to that of "what is written."

18:10 / **Simon Peter** ... **Malchus**. The incident of the cutting off of the High Priest's servant's ear is told in all the Gospels, but only in John are the participants named. Mark 14:47 attributes the act to "one of those standing by." Matt. 26:51 is the same, but with an added warning to the disciples that "all who take the sword will die by the sword" and that what is to happen must happen in order to fulfill Scripture (26:52–54; here v. 11 serves a similar function). In Luke 22:50–51, Jesus says, "Enough of this!" and immediately heals the victim's ear!

The naming of Annas in the immediate context (v. 13) suggests that John's Gospel may be drawing on a source that freely identifies particular individuals. The identification of Simon Peter accomplishes two things: It avoids the implication that *all* of Jesus' disciples were armed (cf. Luke, who in 22:38 limits the number of swords to two), and it anticipates the account of Peter's failure in vv. 15–18, 25–27). The same one who was ready to defend Jesus with a sword was later unwilling even to acknowledge that he was Jesus' disciple.

18:13 / **Annas**: Annas and Caiaphas are mentioned together as "high priests" at the beginning of John the Baptist's ministry in Luke 3:2, and Annas is specifically called "the High Priest" in Acts 4:6, yet John's Gospel clearly identifies Caiaphas as **High Priest that year** both in this verse and in 11:49, 51. Annas is the High Priest's father-in-law (a fact revealed only in this Gospel) and a man of considerable authority but not (at this time) the High Priest.

44

Jesus and the High Priest

JOHN 18:15–27

Simon Peter and another disciple followed Jesus. That other disciple was well known to the High Priest, so he went with Jesus into the courtyard of the High Priest's house, [16]while Peter stayed outside by the gate. Then the other disciple went back out, spoke to the girl at the gate, and brought Peter inside. [17]The girl at the gate said to Peter, "Aren't you also one of the disciples of that man?"

"No, I am not," answered Peter.

[18]It was cold, so the servants and guards had built a charcoal fire and were standing around it, warming themselves. So Peter went over and stood with them, warming himself.

[19]The High Priest questioned Jesus about his disciples and about his teaching. [20]Jesus answered, "I have always spoken publicly to everyone; all my teaching was done in the synagogues and in the Temple, where all the people come together. I have never said anything in secret. [21]Why, then, do you question me? Question the people who heard me. Ask them what I told them—they know what I said."

[22]When Jesus said this, one of the guards there slapped him and said, "How dare you talk like that to the High Priest!"

[23]Jesus answered him, "If I have said anything wrong, tell everyone here what it was. But if I am right in what I have said, why do you hit me?"

[24]Then Annas sent him, still tied up, to Caiaphas the High Priest.

[25]Peter was still standing there keeping himself warm. So the others said to him. "Aren't you also one of the disciples of that man?"

But Peter denied it. "No, I am not," he said.

[26]One of the High Priest's slaves, a relative of the man whose ear Peter had cut off, spoke up. "Didn't I see you with him in the garden?" he asked.

[27]Again Peter said "no"—and at once a rooster crowed.

A relatively brief interrogation of Jesus by the High Priest (vv. 19–24) is framed by a two-part account of Peter's denial (vv. 15–18, 25–27). The division of the denial into two scenes follows a precedent reflected in Mark (14:54, 66–72) and Matthew (26:58, 69–75; Luke on the other hand, puts the material in one continuous narrative, 22:54–62). As in Mark, the vivid picture of Peter warming himself by the enemy's fire is the point at which the narrative breaks off (v. 18) and later resumes. But unlike Mark and Matthew, which use the first scene only to set the stage for the three denials, John's Gospel assigns the first denial to his first scene (vv. 16–18) and the other two to the second (vv. 25–27).

The High Priest's house, and its courtyard, is the setting for all that happens in this section. Annas, mentioned in passing in verse 13, is forgotten until verse 24, where the narrator belatedly supplies the information that Jesus had been sent on, still bound (cf. v. 12), from Annas to **Caiaphas the High Priest,** who must, accordingly, be understood as the interrogator in verses 19–23.

Simon Peter and another, unnamed disciple have followed Jesus on this circuit. There is no specific evidence linking this disciple with "the one whom Jesus loved," mentioned in 13:25, though the identification has been often made. Because the other disciple was **well known to the High Priest** (v. 15), he was admitted to the courtyard of the High Priest's house (though presumably not into the house itself) and secured Peter's admittance as well (v. 16). The question of the girl at the gate (v. 17) seems to reflect the same interest in the identity of Jesus' disciples that the High Priest himself shows in his questioning of Jesus. Inside the house the High Priest was asking Jesus **about his disciples** as well as his teaching (v. 19), while outside the girl was asking Peter, **Aren't you also one of the disciples of that man?** Peter, despite Jesus' successful effort to ensure the disciples' safety (v. 8), and despite the fact that the identity of his fellow disciple was already known (v. 15), did not want to be so identified and stubbornly denied any connection whatever with Jesus (vv. 17, 25, 27). Like Judas (cf. v. 5), he stands with Jesus' enemies, warming himself at their fire in the courtyard (vv. 18, 25). The synoptic Gospels tell the story in such a way as to imply that the account of Peter's denial probably came from Peter himself, but here another disciple is present as a potential witness against Peter, and it is possible that the story is told, at least in part, from his viewpoint. If this disciple, who was **well known to the High Priest,** is the source for the narrative of both the arrest and the interrogation, it is understandable that Malchus, the High priest's slave, would be named (v. 10) and also that Peter's third questioner (v. 26) would be identified as Malchus' relative. The latter identification serves as an ironic link between Peter's misguided zeal in the garden in verse 10 and his abject cowardice in the High Priest's courtyard. But whoever the narrator is at this point, he follows the precedent of the synoptic writers in calling the reader's attention to the crowing of the cock, in exact fulfillment of Jesus' prediction (cf. 13:38).

If Peter feared for his life, it is doubtful that his fear was well grounded. Jesus had already secured the disciples' safety (vv. 8–9), and the apparent fact that Peter's companion was publicly identified as one of them does not seem to have put him in any particular danger. In asking Jesus

about his disciples, the High Priest probably wants their names, but not in order to arrest them. More likely, he wants to question them about Jesus' teaching. The concern **about his disciples and about his teaching** is a single concern. In reply, Jesus indicates that the identification of a fixed group of people as his **disciples** is irrelevant because his **teaching** is in any case a public matter. He has said nothing privately to his disciples that he has not said **publicly to everyone . . . in the synagogues and in the Temple, where all the people come together** (v. 20).

Jesus' concise answer gathers up in itself the discourses of his public ministry in the Temple at Jerusalem (8:20; cf. 10:22–24) and in the synagogue at Capernaum (6:59). Jesus' "trial" here before the High Priest is no trial at all, because Jesus merely refers back to the ongoing trial that was the public ministry and issued finally in the verdict reached by the Sanhedrin in 11:47–53. The answer seems to overlook the more private instructions Jesus had given to his disciples after their meal together in chapters 13–17. Though these teachings were never said to be **in secret,** they were intended for the specific group to whom Jesus referred when he prayed "for those you gave me" out of the world (17:6, 9). But Jesus' answer to the High Priest is based on the assumption that everything he said privately to his own disciples was implicit already in what he said openly to all the people—if only they had listened and understood! (cf. 12:39–40). At times his words to the disciples echoed—with subtle but crucial differences—things he had said to the religious authorities or the crowds in the Temple (as, e.g., 13:33 with 7:34 and 8:21 or 14:7 with 8:19 or 16:27–28 with 8:42). Nothing he said was subversive; there were no secret instructions for a select group engaged in plotting against either Rome or the Jewish priesthood. To learn the substance of his teaching, no list of disciples, no interrogation of them one by one, was necessary. The High Priest could question anyone who had heard Jesus on any number of occasions—his own priestly associates in fact—and draw his own conclusions.

The exchange ends, like the Sanhedrin trial in Mark (14:65) and Matthew (26:67), with Jesus being subjected to physical abuse (v. 22). The reasons, however, are different. There is no "mocking" scene here. Instead, one of the guards, interpreting Jesus' response as a refusal to answer the High Priest's question, and therefore as a sign of contempt, rebuked Jesus and struck him, probably because of Exodus 22:28 ("You must not speak evil of the ruler of your people"). The Apostle Paul is described as showing respect for this principle in Acts 23:2–5. But while Paul apologizes for his behavior by pleading ignorance, Jesus squarely denies the charge of evil speaking: **If I have said anything wrong, tell everyone here what it was. But if I am right in what I have said, why do you hit me?** (v. 23). The incident is probably told for the sake of this final unanswered challenge, which points back not merely to Jesus' statement to the High Priest in verses 20–21 but (like that statement itself) to Jesus' entire public ministry. The reason he cannot be charged with "insult" or "speaking evil" of anyone is that he has always spoken the truth, and the truth is incompatible with evil (cf. 8:46, "Which one of you can prove that I am guilty of sin? If I tell the truth, then why do you not believe me?"). The purpose of Jesus' answer to the guard is simply to reinforce and punctuate his answer to the High Priest.

Additional Notes

8:15 / **Another disciple . . . well known to the High Priest**: Some ancient manuscripts have the definite article—"the other disciple"—furthering the identification of this individual with the beloved disciple of chap. 13 (cf. the terminology of 20:2, 3, 4, 8). But the best manuscripts have it indefinite, as the GNB suggests. It was probably this verse that gave rise to later traditions that John the Gospel writer was himself a priest (Eusebius, *Ecclesiastical History* 2.31.3). The disciple mentioned here was probably not a Galilean, and not necessarily one of the Twelve, but a resident of Jerusalem who had come to believe in Jesus (cf., e.g., 11:45; 12:11). He is the "narrator" at this point to the extent that some of what happens is seen through his eyes and based on his testimony, but there is no compelling reason to identify him as the Gospel's author. Even an author who was himself an eyewitness would, where possible, have based his narrative on the eyewitness testimony of others besides himself (cf. 1:32–34; 19:35).

18:18 / **A charcoal fire**: Only John's Gospel mentions a **charcoal fire** (Gr.; *anthrakia*; Mark and Luke speak more generally of a fire or firelight). The vivid detail anticipates the scene by the lake in 21:9 where a "charcoal fire" also provides the setting for Peter's threefold affirmation and apparent restoration (21:15–17).

18:19 / **About his teaching**: Jesus' real answer to all questions **about his teaching** is found in 7:16–17: "Whoever is willing to do what God wants" will know the one essential thing about Jesus' teaching—that it is not his own, but comes from God. Having already answered the High Priest's question, Jesus does not answer it again but merely directs attention back to his public ministry, especially the self-revelation at the Festival of Shelters in chapters 7–8.

18:20 / **Everyone . . . all the people**: The world translated **everyone** is literally "the world" (Gr.: *kosmos*), and the phrase **all the people** is literally "all the

Jews": "The world" and "the Jews" are implicitly equated because Judaism—its synagogues and especially its Temple in Jerusalem—was the stage on which Jesus' confrontation with the whole world was taking place (cf. 1:10–11, "the world did not recognize him . . . his own people did not receive him"; also 7:3–4, "go to Judea. . . . let the whole world know about you!"; 12:19, "Look, the whole world is following him!").

18:24 / **Then Annas sent him**: The context requires that this statement be understood as a remark of the narrator looking back on something that had happened earlier (i.e., before v. 19). It is best taken parenthetically: e.g., "(Annas, of course, had sent Jesus, still bound, to Caiaphas the High Priest)." Such a conclusion is permitted by Greek particle *oun* (translated **then** in GNB) and by the tense of the verb **sent.** It is demanded by the fact that only Caiaphas is called **High Priest** in John's Gospel, and the High Priest is clearly said to be the questioner in vv. 19–23. One ancient Syriac version has the whole of vv. 13–24 in a different sequence (i.e., vv. 13, 24, 14–15, 19–23, 16–18), and a few later manuscripts have resorted to other rearrangements, even transcribing v. 24 *twice* in two different locations! Such scribal liberties, as well as modern scholarly conjectures to much the same effect, are to be rejected. The simplest solution is that when the narrator reached v. 24, he realized that his earlier remarks about Annas and Caiaphas in vv. 13–14 might have left the reader in doubt as to who the interrogator was. V. 24 was an effort to clarify the matter without rewriting the two earlier verses.

45

Pilate and the Condemnation of Jesus

JOHN 18:28–19:16a

Early in the morning Jesus was taken from Caiaphas' house to the governor's palace. The Jewish authorities did not go inside the palace, for they wanted to keep themselves ritually clean, in order to be able to eat the Passover meal. ²⁹So Pilate went outside to them and asked, "What do you accuse this man of?"

³⁰Their answer was, "We would not have brought him to you if he had not committed a crime."

³¹Pilate said to them, "Then you yourselves take him and try him according to your own law."

They replied, "We are not allowed to put anyone to death." (³²This happened in order to make come true what Jesus had said when he indicated the kind of death he would die.)

³³Pilate went back into the palace and called Jesus. "Are you the king of the Jews?" he asked him.

³⁴Jesus answered, "Does this question come from you or have others told you about me?"

³⁵Pilate replied, "Do you think I am a Jew? It was your own people and the chief priests who handed you over to me. What have you done?"

³⁶Jesus said, "My kingdom does not belong to this world; if my kingdom belonged to this world, my followers would fight to keep me from being handed over to the Jewish authorities. No, my kingdom does not belong here!"

³⁷So Pilate asked him, "Are you a king, then?"

Jesus answered, "You say that I am a king. I was born and came into the world for this one purpose, to speak about the truth. Whoever belongs to the truth listens to me."

³⁸"And what is truth?" Pilate asked.

Then Pilate went back outside to the people and said to them, "I cannot find any reason to condemn him. ³⁹But according to the custom you have, I always set free a prisoner for you during the Passover. Do you want me to set free for you the king of the Jews?"

⁴⁰They answered him with a shout, "No, not him! We want Barabbas!" (Barabbas was a bandit.)

¹Then Pilate took Jesus and had him whipped. ²The soldiers made a crown out of thorny branches and put it on his head; then they put a purple robe on him ³and came to him and said, "Long live the King of the Jews!" And they went up and slapped him.

⁴Pilate went back out once more and said to the crowd, "Look, I will bring him out here to you to let you see that I cannot find any reason to condemn him." ⁵So Jesus came out, wearing the crown of thorns and the

purple robe. Pilate said to them,
"Look! Here is the man!"

⁶When the chief priests and the
temple guards saw him, they shouted,
"Crucify him! Crucify him!"

Pilate said to them, "You take him,
then, and crucify him. I find no
reason to condemn him."

⁷The crowd answered back, "We
have a law that says he ought to die,
because he claimed to be the Son of
God."

⁸When Pilate heard this, he was
even more afraid. ⁹He went back into
the palace and asked Jesus, "Where
do you come from?"

But Jesus did not answer. ¹⁰Pilate
said to him, "You will not speak to
me? Remember, I have the authority
to set you free and also to have you
crucified."

¹¹Jesus answered, "You have
authority over me only because it was
given to you by God. So the man who
handed me over to you is guilty of a

worse sin."

¹²When Pilate heard this, he tried to
find a way to set Jesus free. But the
crowd shouted back, "If you set him
free, that means that you are not the
Emperor's friend! Anyone who claims
to be a king is a rebel against the
Emperor!"

¹³When Pilate heard these words,
he took Jesus outside and sat down on
the judge's seat in the place called
"The Stone Pavement." (In Hebrew
the name is "Gabbatha.") ¹⁴It was then
almost noon of the day before the
Passover. Pilate said to the people,
"Here is your king!"

¹⁵They shouted back, "Kill him!
Kill him! Crucify him!"

Pilate asked them, "Do you want
me to crucify your king?"

The chief priests answered, "The
only king we have is the Emperor!"

¹⁶Then Pilate handed Jesus over to
them to be crucified.

The sentencing of Jesus to death takes place within the framework of a series of exchanges between the Roman governor Pilate and the Jewish religious authorities. The time is from early morning (18:28) to noon (19:14) of the day after Jesus' arrest. The structure of the narrative is determined by the fact that the Jewish authorities, for reasons of ritual purity, would not go inside the palace that served as Pilate's headquarters (v. 28). Contact with the dwelling of a Gentile—even a temporary dwelling, for Pilate's official residence was at Caesarea—would render them ceremonially unfit to eat the Passover meal. Because of this, the action shifts back and forth constantly between the inside and outside of the palace. Pilate himself is always in the center of the action, whether addressing the Jewish authorities outside the palace (18:29–32, 38b–40; 19:4–8, 12–16a) or dealing with Jesus within (18:33–38a; 19:1–3, 9–11). Each of these encounters makes its own contribution to an understanding both of Pilate himself and of the factors that inevitably led even such natural enemies as Pilate and the Jewish authorities to cooperate in Jesus' death. The narrative may conveniently be divided into six scenes:

Pilate and the Jewish authorities (18:29–32). Pilate's question about the charges against Jesus (v. 29) is presumably one to which he already

299

knows the answer. Roman soldiers would hardly have participated in Jesus' arrest (cf. v. 3) without his knowledge and permission. But the question had to be asked as a matter of procedure. The answer of the Jewish authorities (v. 30) probably reflects their impatience at this formality, as if to say, "You know very well what the charges are. Let's get on with it." Pilate's initial cooperation in the arrest probably stemmed from what he saw as an opportunity to bring a potential troublemaker under questioning and learn whether he was dangerous to the political order or not. If the Jewish authorities could be assisted in curbing subversives among their own people, so much the better. Pilate's preference is that now that Jesus is in custody, the Jews themselves should **take him and try him according to your own law** (v. 31).

His assumption is obviously that they have not already done so. Although the synoptic Gospels speak of Jesus being condemned by the assembled priests and elders in the High Priest's house and by the Sanhedrin, there is reason to doubt that he had been *formally* tried and found guilty by the Jews. If he had been found guilty of such a charge as blasphemy or deception of the people, he would have been put to death by stoning like his brother James the Righteous, the leader of the Jerusalem church, in A.D. 62 (Josephus, *Antiquities* 20.200; Eusebius, *Ecclesiastical History* 2.23.4–18) or like Stephen in the book of Acts (7:54–60). The reply of the Jewish authorities to Pilate, **We are not allowed to put anyone to death** (lit., "We are not allowed to kill anyone"; Gr.: *apokteinein*), is most naturally understood as referring to the sixth commandment of the Decalogue ("Do not commit murder"). The issue was not whether the Jews had the right of capital punishment under *Roman* law but rather what *their own* law did not permit them to do. If they executed someone not formally convicted of a crime, they would be guilty of murder according to the Law of Moses. If some of the religious authorities judged that a person deserved to die (cf. 19:7) but were either unable to make their charges stick or unwilling to press their case for fear of a popular uprising (cf. Mark 14:2/Matt. 26:5/Luke 22:2), their only recourse was to manipulate the Romans into carrying out the judgment on their behalf. Jesus had said all along that the Jewish authorities were trying to "kill" him (Gr.: *apokteinein*, 7:20; 8:37, 40); the narrator (5:18; 7:1) and even the crowds in Jerusalem (7:25) had confirmed that this was the case. The result of the only meeting of the Sanhedrin mentioned anywhere in the Gospel was not a formal conviction but simply a plan by the Jewish authorities "to kill Jesus" (11:53). When these same authorities now told Pilate, "We are not allowed to kill anyone," they were condemning their own actions and exposing their own hypocrisy. The narrator's viewpoint is that they would indeed "kill" Jesus as surely as if they were to drive the nails and thrust the spear with their own hands. Yet their hesitancy to act on their own authority without a formal conviction meant that Jesus would die by a Roman rather than a Jewish method of execution. Instead of being crushed by stoning, he would be "lifted up" in gruesome death by crucifixion, and in this prospect the narrator sees the fulfillment of Jesus' own words (cf. 3:14; 8:28; 12:32–33). Nothing that happens will take Jesus by surprise; all the devious plans of the religious authorities and all the vacillations of Pilate stand under a divine necessity: The Son of Man "must" be lifted up in a redemptive, and therefore triumphant, death (cf. 3:14–16).

Pilate and Jesus (18:33–38a). Back inside the palace, Pilate questions Jesus for the first time. The theme of their conversation is kingship, a theme that will dominate the narrative from this point until Pilate places the inscription "Jesus of Nazareth, King of the Jews" on Jesus' cross and insists that it stand as written (19:19–22). The title **king of the Jews** occurs first in Pilate's opening question to Jesus (v. 33). The question **Are you the king of the Jews?** is found in all four Gospels, and in each of the Synoptics Jesus' answer is noncommittal ("So you say," Mark 15:2/Matt. 27:11/Luke 23:3), the equivalent of no answer at all. In this Gospel, however, the question is asked twice (vv. 33, 37a); in each case Jesus' answer builds on the enigmatic "*so you say*," but moves beyond it to deeper issues (vv. 34, 37b):

Does this question come from you [lit., "*Do you say so* on your own"] **or have others told you about me?** (v. 34).

You say **that I am a king. I was born and came into the world for this one purpose, to speak about the truth. Whoever belongs to the truth listens to me.** (v. 37b).

The first reply (v. 34) addresses Pilate at a very personal level, as if to ask him, "Do you really want to know the answer for your own sake, or are you simply carrying out your duty as magistrate?" Pilate deflects the personal thrust by freely admitting that it is not his own question. He is not a Jew and has no interest in Jewish disputes about kingship. He only wants to get at the facts in Jesus' case. As if to elicit from Jesus himself the charges that the Jewish authorities are bringing against him, Pilate asks, **What have you done?** (v. 35), but Jesus will not be drawn into specifics.

Instead, returning to Pilate's first question, he redefines kingship. He has a kingdom but it **does not belong to this world** (lit., "is not from this world," v. 36). Like Jesus himself, it is "from above" (cf. 8:23). To see it or enter it, a person must be "born again" or "born from above" (3:3). Jesus is not speaking of the kingdom's location, but of its *source*—and therefore of its nature. Its source is God, even as Jesus comes from God. As God sends Jesus, so God and God alone brings the kingdom to realization. It is not established by armed violence; Jesus is not the sort of king who needs, or permits, the protection of the sword (cf. vv. 10–11).

Jesus' redefinition has stretched the meaning of kingship almost to the breaking point. Pilate, somewhat confused, can only repeat his initial question: **Are you a king, then?** (v. 37a; cf. v. 33). This time Jesus' reply (v. 37b) builds even more explicitly on the traditional "so you say," and in so doing seems to move beyond the theme of kingship to the more characteristically Johannine theme of revelation. **I was born and came into the world**, he says, **for this one purpose, to speak about the truth**, adding, significantly, for Pilate's benefit, **Whoever belongs to the truth listens to me** (v. 37b; cf. 8:47). Even here, Jesus is not repudiating kingship but continuing the redefinition of it that he began in verse 36. Ultimately he is King, but for the present his role is **to speak about the truth**. He is the Revealer of God (cf. 1:1, 18). His purpose is not to call attention to himself but to the truth that God sent him to make known. Once when his revelation led to the conclusion that he was "the Prophet who was to come into the world," Jesus had fled from the consequent attempt "to make him king by force" (6:14–15). And though his followers acknowledged him on occasion as "King of Israel" (1:49; 12:13), his full revelation as Revealer and King has awaited the "hour" of his death and resurrection (cf. 12:16, 23).

Jesus' second reply to Pilate, even more than the first, confronts the governor personally with the force of his claims. The statement **Whoever belongs to the truth listens to me** implies the question Do *you* belong to the truth, Pilate? Are *you* listening to me? In discourse after discourse, Jesus has confronted the world of Judaism, and now, in one brief but significant exchange, he confronts the whole Gentile world in the person of a single Roman magistrate. Pilate's parting shot, **And what is truth?** (v. 38), leaves the issue unresolved. The intent of Jesus' last prayer "that the world may know that you sent me" (17:23; cf. 17:21) is not yet realized, but in his brief conversation with Pilate, the mission to the Gentiles has begun (cf. Paul's allusion to this scene in 1 Tim. 6:13).

Pilate and the Jewish Authorities (18:38b–40). On the basis of his interview with Jesus, Pilate makes the first of three declarations of Jesus' innocence under Roman law (v. 38b, cf. 19:4, 6; also Luke 23:4, 14, 22). He proposes that Jesus be released, in accordance with a familiar Passover custom, but by repeating the provocative term **king of the Jews** (v. 39), he reminds the Jewish leaders of what, in their eyes, was Jesus' crime and so fuels their wrath once again. The point is probably not that Pilate was being hypocritical, but that he could not resist an opportunity to make fun of the Jews for worrying about such a pitiful **king**. In any event, they rejected his proposal and demanded instead the release of a certain **Barabbas**, identified only in this Gospel as a **bandit** (though cf. Mark 15:7; Luke 23:19). The narrator allows the irony of the rejection of the Son of God in favor of this notorious criminal to speak for itself (for a more explicit reflection on this irony, cf. Acts 3:14).

Pilate, Jesus, and the Jews (19:1–8). The note of ridicule in Pilate's use of the phrase **king of the Jews** in 18:39 comes vividly to the fore in this section. Pilate decides to dramatize to everyone present what a pitiful and harmless figure Jesus is and what a pitiful race of people the Jews are for taking him seriously, whether as a king or as a dangerous pretender and blasphemer. All that happens—presumably inside the palace—in verses 1–3 is preliminary to the presentation of Jesus to the **chief priests and temple guards** outside the palace in verses 4–8, and all of it—the beating and slapping, the thorny crown, the purple robe, and especially the mocking shout **Long live the King of the Jews!**—is the product of Pilate's sick and anti-Semitic sense of humor. He seems obsessed throughout with the grim joke that Jesus is the Jews' king. The words with which he presents Jesus to the assembled Jewish leaders—**Look! Here is the man!** (v. 5)—are intended to arouse not so much pity as a sense of the ridiculous. To the Gospel writer, however, they are profoundly significant as a reminder of who it is who is going to be presented as king (v. 14) and then crucified (v. 18). It was as "Son of Man" that Jesus was to be both "glorified" (12:23; 13:31) and "lifted up" (3:14; 8:28; 12:34), and **man** is the closest a Roman Gentile could be expected to come to the idiomatic Jewish expression "Son of Man." Like the High Priest Caiaphas (11:51–52), Pilate is understood here as speaking more wisely than he knows. His elaborate joke serves the narrator and his readers as nothing less than the last decisive announcement of Jesus' paradoxical "glorification" in the face of death and shame.

Pilate's words, and the sight of Jesus robed in purple and crowned with thorns, agitates the assembled priests and guards all the more as they shout: **Crucify him! Crucify him!** (v. 6a). Up to a point this exchange between Pilate and the religious authorities virtually re-enacts their first encounter in 18:29–32. Pilate's reply, **You take him, then, and crucify him** (v. 6b) reiterates his earlier advice to **take him and try him according to your own law** (18:31). It also makes clear that, as far as Pilate was concerned, they had the power to carry out the death penalty if they so decided. Though they were unwilling or unable to do so, probably out of a lack of broad-based support, they remained firmly convinced that **We have a law that says he ought to die** [i.e., the law of blasphemy, Lev. 24:16] **because he claimed to be the Son of God** (v. 7).

The mention of the title **Son of God** for the first time in the Passion narrative recalls earlier disputes between Jesus and the Jewish authorities (e.g., 5:18; 10:33, 36). It was the understanding that Jesus was claiming to be "God," or "equal with God," that led all along to charges of blasphemy (10:33), attempts to stone him (8:59; 10:31), and the fixed determination that sooner or later he must die (5:18). To Pilate, however, divine sonship was a new factor in the discussion, and it awakened in him a new emotion (as far as the present narrative is concerned)—fear. Unlike the Jews, he heard the title **Son of God** in a polytheistic rather than monotheistic framework, and if he was dealing not with a pitiful and amusing mock **king of the Jews** but with some kind of favored messenger from the gods, the joke was no longer so funny as he had thought!

Pilate and Jesus (19:9–11). Pilate's superstitious fear comes to expression at once with the question, **Where do you come from?** (v. 9). Jesus has already answered the question implicitly. If his kingdom comes not from this world, but from above, so too does he (cf. 3:31; 8:23). He chooses not to make the answer explicit, and in fact gives Pilate no answer at all. Yet when Pilate makes the claim that Jesus' fate is in his hands (v. 10), Jesus responds significantly that not only his origin but his destiny is from above, in the sense that it rests with God and with him alone. Pilate's claim of authority over Jesus, when translated literally, sounds like a feeble echo of Jesus' own claim in 10:18. The similarities can be shown as follows:

10:18	19:10 (lit.)
No one takes my life away from me. I give it up of my own free will. *I have the right* [Gr.: *exousian echō*] to give it up, and *I have the right* [*exousian echō*] to take it back. This is what my Father has commanded me to do.	Do you not know that *I have the right* (Gr.: *exousian echō*] to release you and *I have the right* [*exousian echō*] to crucify you?

When Jesus says in answer to Pilate, **You have authority** [*exousia*] **over me only because it was given to you by God** (lit., "from above," v. 11), he is reasserting his own claim from 10:18. In relation to all human beings and institutions, Jesus' fate is in *his own* hands. But in relation to the Father (10:18b) he has received a command that he must obey. Pilate's authority over him is therefore a derived authority; it is "from above." Pilate is but an unknowing instrument in the hands of God, while Jesus is the Father's loving Son and obedient servant. Jesus is not speaking in abstract or universal terms about a divinely given authority that the state has over matters of justice and human life but of his own mission in particular and of the specific plan by which the Father has chosen to "glorify" his only Son.

It is clear that Jesus does not view Caiaphas (**the man who handed me over to you**) or the Jewish authorities in quite the same way he views Pilate. Jesus does not hesitate to judge both Caiaphas and Pilate guilty of sin (cf. 9:41; 15:22), but he pronounces Caiaphas, and those he represents, **guilty of a worse sin** (v. 11b). The reason is not that they stand outside God's sovereignty but that (as they are seen in this Gospel) they are arrayed on the other side altogether, with their "father, the Devil" (8:44), the "ruler of the world" (12:31; 14:30; 16:11). Like him, and like his child Judas, they have "no power over" Jesus (14:30) and nothing to do with God's redemptive plan. Their actions, no less than Pilate's, help bring that plan to realization, yet their role is somehow different. Pilate "belongs to the earth [Gr.: *gē*; 3:31] and speaks about earthly matters"; like John the Baptist he cannot "have anything unless God gives it to him" (3:27). But Caiaphas and his allies "belong to this world" [Gr.: *kosmos*; 8:23] and to this world's ruler; like him, they are liars and murderers because they have rejected Jesus' teaching and relentlessly sought his life (cf. 8:37–38, 44–45). Pilate is but a pawn, while they are the Enemy. Though they are Jewish, it is not their Jewishness that distinguishes them or makes their sin greater. It is, rather, their consistent identification with the "world" in all its unbelief and darkness and their consequent murderous intent toward Jesus the true light (cf. 1:5–9; 3:19–21).

Pilate, Jesus, and the Jews (19:12–16a). It is difficult to know what Pilate made of Jesus' remarks. The narrator appears to be condensing a longer account so as to bring the story more quickly to its conclusion. The phrase *tried to find a way* in verse 12 (Gr.: *ezētei*, imperfect tense) suggests that Pilate may have made several attempts, not specified in the text, to have Jesus released. Already afraid that Jesus might have power with the gods, Pilate had now been reminded of his own accountability to higher powers (v. 11). But when he tried to use the authority he claimed he had to free Jesus, he found his efforts blocked by the political realities of his own situation. The upshot of all his efforts was that at some point the religious authorities played their trump card: **If you set him free, that means that you are not the Emperor's friend! Anyone who claims to be a king is a rebel against the Emperor!** (v. 12). The bottom line was that if the Emperor were to learn that Pilate was protecting a claimant to kingship, Pilate's status as "friend of Caesar" (a title of privilege bestowed by the Emperor as a reward for faithful service) would be in jeopardy—so would his official position, and perhaps his very life.

The blunt personal threat had an immediate and remarkable effect on Pilate. He brought Jesus outside the palace for one last time, presenting him to the assembled Jewish leaders with the words **Here is your king!** (v. 14). The parallel between this expression and **Here is the man!** in verse 5 could suggest that he is merely resuming the mockery of verses 1–5 and bringing to an end his grotesque mock coronation. But something has changed. There is a seriousness in Pilate's behavior and a bitter solemnity here that was not present before. Realizing that the Jewish authorities have forced him to accede to their demands, Pilate takes his revenge. By sitting in the judge's seat, he gives to the announcement **Here is your king!** a ceremonial and quasi-official character. The ultimate insult he can hurl at the Jews is that this truly *is* their king, the one they deserve and the only one they will ever have. His insult finds its mark, for it draws from them in angry response the ultimate blasphemy of the God of Israel: **The only king we have is the Emperor!** (v. 15). In denying Jesus, they deny in the end their own Jewishness, and in a strange turn of phrase, Pilate is said to have **handed Jesus over to them** [the Jews] **to be crucified**—a *Roman* method of execution!

The narrator is careful to fix precisely the time and the place of all this. It is **the day before Passover**, the so-called day of preparation; the hour is about noon; the place is called **The Stone Pavement**, also designated by the Semitic name **Gabbatha** (vv. 13–14). Why is the incident so momentous as to warrant such fullness of detail? The most plausible answer is that it is Jesus' long-awaited "glorification." If the cross is the ironic moment of Jesus' "lifting up," is not his formal presentation as king outside the governor's palace the ironic moment of his glory? Is it only coincidence that the place of crucifixion and the place of the presentation are each carefully designated with both Greek and Semitic names

(vv. 13, 17)? It appears that the two events are intended to form a pair, with the precise time reference of verse 14 placed between them to do service for both. They are joined not simply for the sake of chronological accuracy but to allow Jesus' kingship and his crucifixion to illumine and interpret each other (**Do you want me to crucify your king?** Pilate asked). Jesus in this Gospel reigns as King—of the Jews and of all people—not from a throne, but from a cross; and his death is not the tragic and shameful defeat it appears to be but the decisive revelation of his kingship, and of the glory of God.

Additional Notes

18:28 / **Jesus was taken. . . . The Jewish authorities did not go inside**: lit., "they took Jesus. . . . and they [emphatic] did not go inside." The first "they" is purposely undefined or impersonal (correctly rendered in GNB by the passive voice). The larger context suggests that Jesus was brought to Pilate by the "Roman soldiers . . . and the Jewish guards" who had arrested him in the first place (v. 12), but the indefinite expression allows the narrator to focus instead on those who had sent the temple guards in the first place, i.e., "the chief priests and the Pharisees" (v. 3). Designated here only by the emphatic pronoun (Gr.: *kai autoi*), and referred to in the ensuing narrative as "the people" (lit., "the Jews," see note on 18:38), they are Pilate's antagonists throughout (cf. the expression "the chief priests and the temple guards" in 19:6).

The governor's palace (Gr.: *to praitōrion*, a transliteration of the Latin *praetorium*): The term referred to any official residence of the Roman military governor in occupied territory. In Palestine, it was natural to seize and make use of Herodian buildings for this purpose (e.g., the "governor's headquarters" in Caesarea in Acts 23:35 is literally "the praetorium of Herod"). In Jerusalem, Pilate's official residence was either in the Antonia, a Hasmonean fortress on a height just north of the Temple area that Herod the Great converted into a palace, or in the more elaborate palace that Herod later built for himself on the western height of the city, near the present Jaffa Gate. The former became the dominant identification in Christian tradition after the Crusades (the Antonia is the starting point of the traditional Via Dolorosa), but the latter is more probable on literary and archaeological grounds. See R. M. Mackowski, *Jerusalem City of Jesus* (Grand Rapids: Eerdmans, 1980), pp. 91–111; also J. Wilkinson, *Jerusalem as Jesus Knew It* (London: Thames & Hudson, 1978), pp. 137–44.

Ritually clean, in order to . . . eat the Passover meal: The statement indicates that the Passover meal has not yet been eaten (cf. 19:14, "the day before the Passover") and that therefore Jesus' last meal with his disciples in chapter 13 is not to be understood, in this Gospel, as the Passover. It also underscores a terrible irony: These men who were so scrupulous about the slightest contact with a

Gentile or the residence of a Gentile nevertheless had no hesitation about maneuvering that Gentile into doing what their own law forbade them to do—killing an innocent man (v. 31)!

18:36 / **My followers**: The word is not "disciples" or "servants" but the same word that in vv. 3, 12, 18, and 22 is translated "guards." The word is chosen on the (contrary-to-fact) assumption that his kingdom belongs "to this world." If it did, his disciples would be "guards" like the guards who arrested him and would meet force with force (as Peter tried to do). But because it is not, he has no "guards." His disciples have an entirely different role, determined by his own single purpose "to speak about the truth" (v. 37).

18:38 / **The people**: lit., "the Jews." The GNB translation—in its effort to *avoid* anti-Semitism!—gives the misleading impression that the Jewish people as a whole demanded Jesus' execution—(see note on 6:41). This is not the case. "The Jews" here refers to the religious authorities, a limited group of leaders among the people acting as self-appointed representatives of the nation.

18:39 / **According to the custom you have**: This policy of amnesty is mentioned also in Mark 15:6 and Matt. 27:15 (by the respective Gospel writers rather than by Pilate), but it is not mentioned outside the New Testament. The reason for the silence of the Jewish sources may be that the custom prevailed for a relatively short period of time—only during Pilate's term of office, perhaps, or (at the most) over those decades in which insurrections were more frequent and there were more political prisoners than before. It was probably not a Jewish custom as such, but a Roman concession to raise public morale.

18:40 / **A bandit**: The term can denote anyone who commits armed robbery, but it was frequently used by Josephus to refer to a particular kind of terrorist who combined plunder with riot and insurrection (cf. Mark 15:7; Luke 23:19).

19:3 / **And came to him and said . . . and they went up and slapped him**: The translation does not do justice to the imperfect tense of all the verbs in this verse: "and they kept coming at him, saying . . . and they slapped him again and again."

19:8 / **Even more afraid**: Pilate's fear has not previously been mentioned. Probably no comparison is intended with a previous state of mind; the comparative is used simply to express the idea that Pilate was very frightened by the phrase "Son of God."

19:11 / **The man who handed me over**: The verb "hand over" (Gr.: *paradidonai*) is the same word translated "betray" when it is used of Judas (cf. 6:64, 71; 12:4; 13:2, 21; 18:2, 5). But Judas did not hand Jesus over *to Pilate*. The reference is rather to the Jewish authorities (cf. 18:30, 35) and probably (because it is singular) specifically to Caiaphas.

19:12 / **When Pilate heard this**: lit., "from this" (i.e., either "from this time on," or "as a result of this"); the connection is not so close or specific as it is in vv. 8 and 13.

The Emperor's friend: The phrase in Latin *amicus Caesaris* ("Caesar's friend") was a technical term for a privileged status awarded by the Emperor. There is evidence that Pilate may have enjoyed this status by virtue of his association with the strongly anti-Semitic Aelius Sejanus (Tacitus wrote in *Annals* 6.8 that "whoever was close to Sejanus had a claim on the friendship of Caesar"). But Sejanus lost his own status in the year 31, and for this reason Pilate may have been especially vulnerable—especially to threats from the Jews.

19:13 / **Sat down on the judge's seat**: It is debated whether the verb is intransitive or transitive, i.e., whether Pilate himself sat down or whether he seated Jesus on the judge's seat (as part of an elaborate mocking ceremony). The latter interpretation is reflected in second-century traditions in which Jesus is mockingly commanded, "Judge us" (Justin Martyr, *First Apology* 35), or, "Judge justly, O king of Israel" (*Gospel of Peter* 7). But the **judge's seat** (Gr.: *bēma*) is not, strictly speaking, a throne, and the verb "to sit" (Gr.: *kathizein*) is normally intransitive when used of someone functioning as a judge. Josephus, in fact, uses this very expression of Pilate himself in *Jewish Wars* 2.172. The seriousness with which Pilate proceeds at this point suggests that he is not now mocking Jesus but pronouncing his own verdict on the Jewish priests and people.

The Stone Pavement (Gr.: *lithostrotos*): This place is frequently identified with an ancient pavement of massive stone slabs (over two thousand square yards) at the site of the Fortress Antonia, under the present-day Sisters of Zion hospice and the Church of the Flagellation, excavated in 1870. Although this is possible, it is likely that any large square in Jerusalem (whether from this period or after its Roman rebuilding in the second century) would have the same general appearance that this site has. The discovery therefore cannot be used with confidence to settle the location of the praetorium (see note on "governor's palace" in 18:28). The *lithostrotos* is mentioned as if it were something more specific than a vast paved square—perhaps a small raised platform (see note on **Gabbatha**) on which the judge's seat was placed. As in the case of Bethzatha, the narrator writes as if the place could still be identified in his time, but (unlike Bethzatha) the **Stone Pavement** cannot be identified with certainty today.

Gabbatha is not the Hebrew translation of **Stone Pavement**. It is in fact an Aramaic word, probably meaning a height or a ridge, but whether it was a natural elevated place or something man-made (e.g., an elevated stone platform) is unclear.

19:14 / **Almost noon**: lit., "about the sixth hour." According to the Jewish reckoning of hours from 6:00 A.M. this would be about noon (see note on 1:39). In the interest of harmonizing with the synoptic Gospels (e.g., Mark 15:25: "It was nine o'clock in the morning when they crucified him"), some have argued that John's Gospel was following the Roman time reckoning from midnight, so that "the sixth hour" was 6:00 A.M. This is possible, though it crowds a great deal of action between "early in the morning" (18:28) and 6:00 A.M. while leaving the three hours between 6:00 and 9:00 A.M. unaccounted for. It also raises the question of why John would fix the time of Jesus' presentation as king so carefully and the time of his crucifixion not at all. Whatever the resolution of the chronologies, a solemn reference to noon in this verse does correspond symbolically to the synoptic notice that "at noon the whole country was covered with darkness" (Mark 15:33 and parallels).

The day before the Passover: lit., "the Preparation of the Passover." The term "preparation" (Gr.: *paraskeuē*) by itself commonly referred to Friday, the day of preparation for the Sabbath (cf. vv. 31, 42), but in conjunction with **Passover** it refers to the day when the Passover lamb was slaughtered and preparations were made for the Passover meal. The chronology presupposed in this Gospel is that in the year Jesus died the Passover was also a Sabbath.

19:16a / **Pilate handed Jesus over to them**. There is a somber mutuality in the execution of Jesus: First the Jewish authorities "handed over" Jesus to Pilate (18:30, 35), and now he **handed Jesus over to them**. For the strange implication that in a sense the Jewish authorities themselves crucified Jesus see note on 8:28.

46

Crucified, Dead, and Buried

So they took charge of Jesus. [17]He went out, carrying his cross, and came to "The Place of the Skull," as it is called. (In Hebrew it is called "Golgotha.") [18]There they crucified him; and they also crucified two other men, one on each side, with Jesus between them. [19]Pilate wrote a notice and had it put on the cross. "Jesus of Nazareth, the King of the Jews," is what he wrote. [20]Many people read it, because the place where Jesus was crucified was not far from the city. The notice was written in Hebrew, Latin, and Greek. [21]The chief priests said to Pilate, "Do not write 'The King of the Jews,' but rather, 'This man said, I am the King of the Jews.'"

[22]Pilate answered, "What I have written stays written."

[23]After the soldiers had crucified Jesus, they took his clothes and divided them into four parts, one part for each soldier. They also took the robe, which was made of one piece of woven cloth without any seams in it. [24]The soldiers said to one another, "Let's not tear it; let's throw dice to see who will get it." This happened in order to make the scripture come true:

"They divided my clothes
        among themselves
    and gambled for my robe."

And this is what the soldiers did.

[25]Standing close to Jesus' cross were his mother, his mother's sister, Mary the wife of Clopas, and Mary Magdalene. [26]Jesus saw his mother and the disciple he loved standing there; so he said to his mother, "He is your son."

[27]Then he said to the disciple, "She is your mother." From that time the disciple took her to live in his home.

[28]Jesus knew that by now everything had been completed; and in order to make the scripture come true, he said, "I am thirsty."

[29]A bowl was there, full of cheap wine; so a sponge was soaked in the wine, put on a stalk of hyssop, and lifted up to his lips. [30]Jesus drank the wine and said, "It is finished!"

Then he bowed his head and died.

[31]Then the Jewish authorities asked Pilate to allow them to break the legs of the men who had been crucified, and to take the bodies down from the crosses. They requested this because it was Friday, and they did not want the bodies to stay on the crosses on the Sabbath, since the coming Sabbath was especially holy. [32]So the soldiers went and broke the legs of the first man and then of the other man who had been crucified with Jesus. [33]But when they came to Jesus, they saw that he was already dead, so they did not break his legs. [34]One of the soldiers, however, plunged his spear into Jesus' side, and at once blood and water poured out. ([35]The one who saw this happen has spoken of it, so that you also may believe.[i] What he said is true, and he knows that he speaks the truth.) [36]This was done to make the scripture come true: "Not one of his bones will be broken." [37]And there is

another scripture that says, "People will look at him whom they pierced."

[38]After this, Joseph, who was from the town of Arimathea, asked Pilate if he could take Jesus' body. (Joseph was a follower of Jesus, but in secret, because he was afraid of the Jewish authorities.) Pilate told him he could have the body, so Joseph went and took it away. [39]Nicodemus, who at first had gone to see Jesus at night, went with Joseph, taking with him about one hundred pounds of spices, a mixture of myrrh and aloes. [40]The two men took Jesus' body and wrapped it in linen cloths with the spices according to the Jewish custom of preparing a body for burial. [41]There was a garden in the place where Jesus had been put to death, and in it there was a new tomb where no one had ever been buried. [42]Since it was the day before the Sabbath and because the tomb was close by, they placed Jesus' body there.

i. believe; *some manuscripts have* continue to believe.

The use of **they** in verse 16b preserves the impression that it was the Jewish authorities who took Jesus out to the place of crucifixion. Though the verb **took charge** is, strictly speaking, used impersonally (i.e., Jesus "was taken into custody"; see the first note on 18:28), its close link with verse 16a suggests the continuing involvement of the chief priests (and the temple guards) in all that happened. Clearly, they are present, as is Pilate himself (vv. 19–22). The presence of Roman soldiers is not indicated until verse 23, where the reader finally learns that it was these soldiers who had actually nailed Jesus to the cross (in v. 18).

Verses 16b–22 are, in an important sense, an extension—the conclusion, in fact—of the running battle of wills between Pilate and the Jewish authorities from 18:28 to 19:16a. Yet one more time, thwarted in every effort to set Jesus free, Pilate makes his grim joke at the Jews' expense—this time in writing. Ceremoniously, in three languages, for all the world to read, he places on the cross where Jesus is crucified the solemn inscription **Jesus of Nazareth, the King of the Jews** (v. 19). He has lost the substantive point at issue, but he has won the war of nerves. When urged to modify the inscription so as to state only that kingship was Jesus' claim, Pilate mocks the Jews' traditional and well-known reverence for the written word with the terse reply: **What I have written stays written** (v. 22). Jesus, "glorified" in the presentation as king at Gabbatha, "The Stone Pavement," has now been "lifted up" as king—and so designated in writing—at **Golgotha, "The Place of the Skull,"** (v. 17). The narrator's careful concern about the time (v. 14) and the exact place (Gr.: *topos*, vv. 13, 17) of these great redemptive events may reflect the beginnings of Christian interest in holy places and in some kind of liturgical calendar.

Some details in vv. 16b–22 do *not* particularly accent themes from the preceding section but (like much of what follows in vv. 23–42) rest simply on the concern of Christian eyewitnesses (i.e., the beloved disciple and the women mentioned in v. 25) to preserve in the church's memory impressions of things they had seen. As Jesus left the vicinity of the palace and the Stone Pavement, he was **carrying his** [own] **cross** (i.e., probably the crossbeam; in all likelihood, Golgotha was a customary place for crucifixions, where large vertical stakes were permanently in place). There is no interest in the Via Dolorosa as such, and therefore none in Simon of Cyrene who, according to the Synoptics, was at some point conscripted to help Jesus carry the cross (Luke 23:26) or to carry it for him (Mark 15:21; Simon and his sons are evidently known to Mark's readers). Instead, the action shifts immediately to the place of execution, where Jesus is crucified with **two other men, one on each side, with Jesus between them** (v. 18). These men are not identified as "bandits" (Mark 15:27) or "criminals" (Luke 23:32), nor is any exchange recorded between them and Jesus. They are introduced solely to set the stage for the contrast between them and Jesus in verses 31–33: Their deaths are hastened by the breaking of their legs, but none of Jesus' bones are broken (v. 36).

Aside from Pilate's inscription naming Jesus **King of the Jews**, the narrator is less interested in the crucifixion procedure itself than in what happened during the time Jesus was on the cross, and even after his death, just before the removal of the victim's bodies (vv. 23–30, 31–37). The story unfolds in a series of distinct scenes or vignettes, centering first on four Roman soldiers (vv. 23–24), then on Jesus and his closest disciples (vv. 25–27), then on Jesus alone in his death (vv. 28–30), and finally on certain unique physical circumstances noted by an eyewitness in connection with his death (vv. 31–37). Three of these scenes (the first, third, and fourth) are explicitly understood by the narrator as fulfillments of Scripture (vv. 24, 28, 36–37).

Many commentators find symbolism in the reference to Jesus' robe **made of one piece of woven cloth without any seams in it** (v. 23). It is thought to represent either the unity of Christian believers (cf. 17:21, 23) or Jesus' unique role as Christian High Priest (cf. Josephus' description of the Jewish High Priest's robe in *Antiquities*, 3.161). But the symbolism is doubtful. The narrator calls attention to the way the robe was woven only to explain why it was impossible to tear it without ruining the cloth. Because of this, the soldiers threw dice for it and so fulfilled Psalm 22:18 down to the smallest detail. The verse is poetry. Its two parts,

"They gamble for my clothes and divide them among themselves" (Ps. 22:18, GNB, based on the Hebrew text) are an example of Hebrew parallelism; they say the same thing twice. But as the verse is quoted here, two distinct things are being said, and a distinct fulfillment is found for each:

They divided my clothes among themselves . . . (fulfilled in v. 23a), **and gambled for my robe** (fulfilled in vv. 23b–24).

Though the narrator understands perfectly well the nature of poetic parallelism, he takes the opportunity (as any rabbinic Jewish interpreter would do) to extract separate meaning from each part if it fits the historical information he is trying to explain. The same interpretive technique is found in Matthew 21:2–7, where Jesus used both a donkey and its colt in the triumphal entry, and in Acts 4:25–27, where David is understood to have spoken both of Israel and the Gentiles.

Beyond the interest in the fulfillment of Scripture, the significance of the first scene is that Jesus is shown having let go of his possessions, specifically his clothing. The second scene shows him letting go of his family, specifically his mother, whereas in the third scene he lets go of life itself. Exaggeration of the symbolic element is as much a danger in the second scene as in the first. The point is not that Jesus' mother here becomes the spiritual mother of all Christians, or even that a true disciple of Jesus becomes his spiritual brother or sister (cf. Mark 3:33–35). The point is simply that Jesus, before he died, arranged for his mother and his closest disciple to care for each other and provide for one another's needs. If there is symbolism here, it is a symbolism akin to that of the washing of the disciples' feet (cf. 13:14, 34). Those whom Jesus has loved must fulfill that love by becoming servants to one another in mutual ministry—in this instance, the ministry of a mother and a son respectively.

In the third scene (vv. 28–30), Jesus voluntarily gives up life itself. The scene begins with the connective phrase "after this" (Gr.: *meta touto*, left untranslated in GNB), suggesting that Jesus' provision for the needs of his mother and his disciple was his final responsibility on earth. Jesus was said earlier to have "loved those in the world who were his own . . . to the very end" (Gr.: *eis telos*, 13:1), and this last expression of his love now becomes the sign that **everything had been completed** (or "finished"; Gr.: *tetelestai*, v. 28). Jesus therefore **knew** (Gr.: *eidōs*; cf. 13:1–3; 18:4) that the end had come, and just before his death he put that knowledge into words: **It is finished** (Gr.: *tetelestai*, v. 30). Bereft of both possessions and loved ones, he was now ready to let go of life itself.

Death's certainty and immediacy are seen in close connection with Jesus' experience of thirst (vv. 28–29). But was his thirst literal or metaphorical? Was he thirsting for water?

My throat is as dry as dust,
   and my tongue sticks to the roof of my mouth.
You have left me for dead in the dust.
(Ps. 22:15)

or for God?

O God, you are my God,
   and I long for you,
My whole being desires you;
   like a dry, worn-out, and
      waterless land,
   my soul is thirsty for you.
(Ps. 63:1)

First of all, there is surely an irony in the fact that he who claimed to satisfy all thirst (4:13–14) himself became thirsty for the sake of those in need (cf. 4:6–7). Yet however great Jesus' physical experience of thirst may have been, his last, and deeper, personal need was the need to rejoin the Father (cf. 13:1, 3). It was his death, not merely his thirst, that would **make the scripture come true**, and it was not a particular passage of scripture that would come true, but the whole biblical testimony that "the Messiah must suffer and must rise from death three days later" (Luke 24:46; cf. John 2:17, 22; 20:9).

Ironically, Jesus' physical thirst was momentarily quenched by a sponge soaked in cheap wine proffered to him by the Roman soldiers (v. 29), but no sooner was it quenched than **he bowed his head and died** (v. 30). In the end, every attempt of the religious authorities to kill him had failed. No one took his life, but of his own free will he gave it back to the Father who had sent him (10:18; cf. also Luke 23:46).

The clear reference to Jesus' death in verse 30 means that, in one sense, all that is described in verses 31–33 is beside the point as far as Jesus is concerned. The purpose of breaking the victim's legs was to hasten death so that the bodies could be removed before sunset (v. 31), but in Jesus' case the procedure merely demonstrated to Jew and Roman alike that his death was outside their control.

315

The narrator, however, concludes once again that what he describes **was done to make the scripture come true**. In this case, two specific passages are cited (vv. 36–37): **Not one of his bones will be broken**, probably a citation of Psalm 34:20, and **People will look at him whom they pierced**, a citation of Zechariah 12:10. The first summarizes verses 31–33, the second, verses 34–35. The purpose of verses 31–33, therefore, is to explain why none of Jesus' bones were broken and why it is significant that they were not. The narrator had carefully prepared for this account by introducing as early as verse 18 the **two other men** whose legs, in contrast, *were* broken in order to hasten their death. The purpose of verses 34–35 is to call attention to another remarkable occurrence after Jesus' death that fulfilled scripture: the piercing of his body with a spear. When the soldiers discovered that he was dead, and as they were waiting for the two other victims to die, one of the soldiers idly plunged his spear into Jesus' side to make absolutely sure of death in his case. The narrator states that **at once blood and water poured out** (v. 34b), and refers explicitly to the testimony of a particular eyewitness (v. 35). Who is this anonymous eyewitness, and why is the appeal to eyewitness testimony found in the Gospel only here? Certain similarities in language between this statement and summaries placed at the end of chapters 20 and 21, respectively, suggest that the eyewitness may be the narrator himself, for example:

The one who saw this happen *has spoken of it, so that you also may believe* (19:35a).	**But these have been written** *in order that you may believe* . . . (20:31).
What he said is true, and he knows that he speaks the truth (19:35b).	**He is the disciple** *who spoke of these things,* **the one who also wrote them down;** *and we know that what he said is true* (21:24).

The similarities are generally taken as evidence that the anonymous eyewitness of verse 35 is none other than the "beloved disciple" (21:20–23), himself the author and narrator of the whole Gospel. Yet the parallels prove little, for they rest simply on common characteristics of the author's style. Jesus had spoken of John the Baptist, for example, in similar terms:

But there is someone else who testifies on my behalf, *and I know that what he says about me is true. . . . he spoke on behalf of the truth*. It is not that I must have a man's witness; I say this only *in order that you may be saved* (5:32–34).

316

And another Johannine writing, 3 John, written from "the Elder" to "my dear Gaius," draws to a close with a commendation of a certain Demetrius:

And we add our testimony, *and you know that what we say is true* (3 John 12).

These wider parallels suggest that verse 35 reflects merely the author's normal way of speaking about valid testimony. The anonymous witness remains anonymous. Verse 37, with its apparent identification of those who **look at** Jesus with those who **pierced** him, could suggest that the eyewitness was one of the Roman soldiers, perhaps the very one who plunged the spear into Jesus' side (cf. the officer who in Mark 15:38 confessed that Jesus "was really the Son of God!"). But again, there is no proof, only conjecture.

The most that can be said is that, if the anonymous witness is *not* the narrator himself (i.e., the beloved disciple), he is at any rate someone close to the narrator and well known to him, for the narrator says of this witness without hesitation or qualification, **he knows that he speaks the truth** (v. 35b). Like the anonymous disciple of 18:15–16, he is an important source for one small part of the story, and he *may* (as most commentators suppose) be the author of the whole story.

But what exactly did he see that was decisive? The entire crucifixion scene? The twofold fulfillments of scripture in verses 31–37? The spear thrust? Or the consequent flow of blood and water from the wound in Jesus' side? The accent is clearly on the latter two (v. 34). It is likely that the rest of Jesus' disciples first learned of the spear wound—a key to their identification of the risen Jesus in 20:20a, 25, 27—through the testimony of the eyewitness mentioned here. His "seeing" not only fulfills scripture (v. 37) but lays the basis for their testimony, "We have seen the Lord" (20:25; cf. 20b).

Also of significance is the **blood and water** he saw pouring from the wound (v. 34). Jesus' blood has been mentioned before in this Gospel only in 6:53–56, but neither the metaphor of drinking blood nor the association found there between blood and flesh plays any part whatever in the present scene. The references to blood in First John provide much closer parallels. The basic early Christian conviction that "the blood of Jesus . . . purifies us from every sin" is stated almost at the outset (1 John 1:7), whereas near the end of the book, blood and water (along with the Spirit) are seen together: Jesus "came not only with the water, but with both the water and the blood" (5:6); "There are three witnesses: the Spirit, the water, and the blood, and all three give the same testimony" (5:7–8). The testimony they bear is summed up in the words "God has given us eternal life, and this life has its source in his Son" (5:11). The notion of water as a metaphor for eternal life is well developed in John's Gospel (e.g., 3:5; 4:10–14; 6:35; 7:37–39; 9:7), and the purpose of the eyewitness testimony to **blood and water** from Jesus' side is simply to emphasize that this eternal life is only possible because of Jesus' *death*. Just as he quenches thirst by becoming thirsty, so he provides "life-giving water" (4:14; 7:38) in no other way than by shedding his blood.

The account of Jesus' burial (vv. 38–42) is a natural continuation of the events associated with the removal of his body from the cross (vv. 31–37). As far as Pilate was concerned, the granting of permission to Joseph of Arimathea to take charge of Jesus' body was simply an extension of the permission he had already given to the **Jewish authorities** to remove the three bodies from Golgotha (v. 31). Joseph of Arimathea is a new character in the story but is mentioned in every Gospel and identified in Mark and Luke as a member of the Jewish ruling Council. It is not surprising that he appears here in the company of Nicodemus (v. 39), introduced in chapter 3 as "a Jewish leader" (3:1) and "a great teacher in Israel" (3:10). The description of Joseph as **a follower of Jesus, but in secret, because he was afraid of the Jewish authorities** (v. 38) corresponds to what the Gospel's fragmentary information about Nicodemus suggests was true of him as well (cf. 2:23–3:2; 7:50–52). The narrator's reminder that Nicodemus **at first had gone to see Jesus at night** (v. 39; cf. 3:1) seems intended to confirm this impression. At least two who had "loved the approval of men rather than the approval of God" (12:43) were now, at last, coming out of the darkness of fear into the light of open identification with Jesus and those who mourned him (cf. 3:21).

The embalming of Jesus' body was extraordinary. Nicodemus brought seventy-five pounds (see note) of **spices, a mixture of myrrh and aloes** (v. 39), and the two of them wrapped up the body, with the spices, in linen cloths. The procedure and the use of spices may have been **according to the Jewish custom** (v. 40), but the sheer *quantity* of spices was not. Such extravagance recalls the wedding at Cana, where Jesus changed well over a hundred gallons of water into wine (2:6), and especially the whole pint of "very expensive perfume made of pure nard" that Mary poured on Jesus' feet at Bethany (12:3), to prepare him, as he said, "for the day of my burial" (12:7). Mary's symbolic "embalming" of Jesus in advance is here matched by Joseph and Nicodemus in their preparation of his body now that the actual time of burial has come. Whether the extravagance is intended as a final testimony to Jesus' kingship or simply as the expression of a love comparable to Mary's, its effect is to place Joseph and Nicodemus once and for all in the circle of Jesus' true disciples. Because of them, Jesus' body was not taken to a common grave for criminals but was given its own tomb, **a new tomb where no one had ever been buried** (v. 41), close to the place of execution and easily identifiable (vv. 41–42). The stage was set for the decisive events of Sunday morning.

Additional Notes

19:17 / **The Place of the Skull, Golgotha**: **Golgotha** appears to be a transliteration of an Aramaic word meaning **skull**. The name was probably given to the place both because of its appearance and because of its association with executions and death.

19:25 / **His mother, his mother's sister, Mary the wife of Clopas, and Mary Magdalene**: It is virtually certain that four women (rather than three) are being mentioned here. Grammatically, **Mary the wife of Clopas** could be understood in apposition to **his mother's sister**, but it is very unlikely that two sisters would both be named Mary. Of the four women, only Jesus' **mother** (vv. 26–27) and **Mary Magdalene** (20:1–2, 11–18) have any real part in the narrative, but the four are listed for the sake of completeness, probably on the basis of eyewitness testimony (cf. v. 35). **Mary Magdalene** is also mentioned in Mark and Matthew, but whether any of the other three can be identified with women mentioned in Mark 15:40 or Matt. 27:56 is problematical.

19:27 / **To live in his home** (Gr.: *eis ta idia*): The same expression is used in 16:32, where Jesus predicts that his disciples "will be scattered, each one to his own home." The presence of the beloved disciple at the cross suggests that he was not dispersed with the others (cf. 18:8–9) but only now makes his departure. Neither their dispersion nor his is seen as a disgrace, and in particular his departure for home is viewed here as an act of obedience to Jesus' command (cf. also 20:10).

19:29 / The **cheap wine** (Gr.: *oxos*) was a sour diluted wine vinegar used as a beverage among the poor. It was thirst-quenching and was offered to Jesus (probably by the soldiers) as an act of mercy. Though the incident is recorded with Ps. 69:21 in mind, the similarity is only formal because in the psalm "vinegar" (LXX: *oxos*) is given with hostile rather than merciful intent: "When I was hungry, they gave me poison [lit., "gall"]; when I was thirsty, they offered me vinegar." In any case, the purpose of the account in John's Gospel is not to describe a touching act of love toward Jesus but to emphasize that his real thirst was quenched, not by the pitiful momentary refreshment a Roman soldier was able to supply, but by what immediately followed, his return to the Father.

A stalk of hyssop: lit., just "hyssop." The plant that usually went by this name was a small bush with blue flowers used in the purification of sacrifices by sprinkling. It had no **stalk** capable of bearing the weight of a sponge. Because the plant described here obviously does have a firm stalk or reed (cf. Mark 15:36/Matt. 27:48), the term **hyssop** is being used loosely (as plant names often were in the ancient world) to refer to a taller plant with a real stalk. Though the term could have been chosen because of its symbolic associations with the Passover (cf. Exod. 12:22) and with ceremonial purification (e.g., Lev. 14:6–7; Ps. 51:7, RSV; Heb. 9:19), the use of it in connection with offering Jesus a last drink of cheap wine has no discernible ritual significance. This is more likely a case of narrative imprecision than a conscious attempt to make a theological statment (What would the statement be?). The famous conjecture that it was a "javelin" (Gr.: *hūssos* instead of *hussōpos*), supported by one very late manuscript, is more ingenious than convincing.

19:30 / **Then he bowed his head and died**: lit., "handed over the spirit." Some have seen in this expression a conferring of the Holy Spirit on the church (represented by the beloved disciple and the women who were present), but this is unlikely. The Holy Spirit is conferred in 20:22, when Jesus breathes on the assembled disciples and says explicitly, "Receive the Holy Spirit." What he hands over in the present passage is his own spirit (i.e., his life) and the One to whom he gives it is the Father; cf. Luke 23:46, "Father! In your hands I place my spirit!" and Matt. 27:50, Jesus "breathed his last" (lit., "let the spirit go"). In the same way that when the text says, "he bowed the head," it means "his head," so when it says, "he handed over the spirit," it means "his spirit" (cf. the expression, "to lay down [or "give up"] one's life" [see note on 10:11], which places a similar emphasis on the deliberate and voluntary nature of Jesus' death).

19:31 / **To allow them**: If the impression is given that the Jewish authorities were themselves going to break the victim's legs and remove the bodies, it is soon clarified by v. 32, which makes clear that the grim task was performed by the Roman soldiers (cf. the ambiguity in v. 16 about who was going to crucify Jesus and the clarification supplied in v. 23).

Friday: lit., "preparation." The word does double duty, because it was both the preparation of the Sabbath (i.e., **Friday**) and the preparation of the Passover (see note on 19:14).

Since the coming Sabbath was especially holy: lit., "for great was the day of that Sabbath." The following day was both a Sabbath and the fifteenth day of the month Nisan, the first day of the Passover Festival. The Jewish law that the corpse of an executed criminal should not remain hanging on a tree overnight (Deut. 21:22–23) must have conflicted frequently with the Roman custom of leaving bodies on crosses as a warning to other criminals. At festival times, however, the Romans made concessions to Jewish sensitivities, (cf. Philo, *In Flaccum* 83), and this year the fact that the following day was a Sabbath provided an additional reason for the Romans to be generous.

19:35 / **Believe**: The reading in the margin, **continue to believe**, represented by a few ancient manuscripts, is based on a Greek present subjunctive (*pisteuēte*) rather than the aorist subjunctive (*pisteusēte*) found in the text. The same variation is found in 20:31. It is doubtful that the difference in meaning is substantial enough to warrant an alternate translation and a marginal note in English. *Either* reading may properly be translated simply **believe**. There is abundant evidence that the Gospel is written for Christian believers, but the author wants his readers to grasp anew the reality of Jesus' person and work.

19:38 / **Arimathea**: The exact location of this place is disputed, but the most widely accepted site is that given by Eusebius in his fourth-century *Onomasticon*: west and slightly north of Jerusalem, not far from Lydda. Others have placed it well eastward, near Shiloh; in any event, Joseph was not a Galilean, but a Judean, disciple.

19:39 / **One hundred pounds of spices**: The Roman pound (Gr.: *litra*) was twelve ounces rather than sixteen, so that, in today's measurements, the equivalent amount would be approximately seventy-five pounds.

Myrrh and aloes were fragrant dried saps or resins sometimes used by the Egyptians in embalming. Though **aloes** appears to be plural, it is singular in Greek.

19:41 / **In the place where Jesus had been put to death**: This verse and the following one ("the tomb was close by," v. 42) furnish the biblical basis for the notion that Jesus' crucifixion and burial happened at the same **place** (Gr.: *topos*; cf. v. 17), though it is not specified exactly how far the tomb was from Golgotha. According to tradition, the two sites are so close that one building, the Constantinian Church of the Holy Sepulchre, contains them both, with much room to spare. Even the so-called Garden Tomb, venerated by many Protestants, is just a short walk from Gordon's Calvary, a rocky promontory overlooking the East Jerusalem bus station outside the walls of the present Old City. Whether the church's veneration of the two sites together provides independent attestation of the statements made here or whether it is based on those very statements is difficult to determine.

47

The Empty Tomb and
the First Appearance

JOHN 20:1–18

Early on Sunday morning, while it was still dark, Mary Magdalene went to the tomb and saw that the stone had been taken away from the entrance. ²She went running to Simon Peter and the other disciple, whom Jesus loved, and told them, "They have taken the Lord from the tomb, and we don't know where they have put him!"

³Then Peter and the other disciple went to the tomb. ⁴The two of them were running, but the other disciple ran faster than Peter and reached the tomb first. ⁵He bent over and saw the linen cloths, but he did not go in. ⁶Behind him came Simon Peter, and he went straight into the tomb. He saw the linen cloths lying there ⁷and the cloth which had been around Jesus' head. It was not lying with the linen cloths but was rolled up by itself. ⁸Then the other disciple, who had reached the tomb first, also went in; he saw and believed. (⁹They still did not understand the scripture which said that he must rise from death.) ¹⁰Then the disciples went back home.

¹¹Mary stood crying outside the tomb. While she was still crying, she bent over and looked in the tomb ¹²and saw two angels there dressed in white, sitting where the body of Jesus had been, one at the head and the other at the feet. ¹³"Woman, why are you crying?" they asked her.

She answered, "They have taken my Lord away, and I do not know where they have put him!"

¹⁴Then she turned around and saw Jesus standing there; but she did not know that it was Jesus. ¹⁵"Woman, why are you crying?" Jesus asked her. "Who is it that you are looking for?"

She thought he was the gardener, so she said to him, "If you took him away, sir, tell me where you have put him, and I will go and get him."

¹⁶Jesus said to her, "Mary!"

She turned toward him and said in Hebrew, "Rabboni!" (This means "Teacher.")

¹⁷"Do not hold on to me," Jesus told her, "because I have not yet gone back up to the Father. But go to my brothers and tell them that I am returning to him who is my Father and their Father, my God and their God."

¹⁸So Mary Magdalene went and told the disciples that she had seen the Lord and related to them what he had told her.

The story of the empty tomb is Mary Magdalene's story. To this point in the Gospel, Mary has been mentioned only once, with no further identification (19:25), probably because she is presumed to be well known to the Gospel's readers. In Mark, Matthew, and Luke she is mentioned first among the women who came to the tomb on Sunday morning, but here she seems to come alone. Only her statement that **we** [plural] **don't know** the whereabouts of Jesus' body (v. 2) betrays a consciousness of others present with her at the tomb (contrast **I do not know** in v. 13).

From the fact that the stone in front of the tomb had been moved, Mary inferred that Jesus' body had also been moved. Without looking into the tomb she ran to tell **Simon Peter and the other disciple, whom Jesus loved** that someone had stolen the body (v. 2). The account of the two disciples' race to the tomb and of what they saw is given neither for theological reasons nor to enhance the apostolic authority of either man but simply as the historical recollection of an eyewitness. The beloved disciple reached the tomb first and looked in at the **linen cloths** (cf. 19:40) but did not enter the tomb (vv. 4–5). When Peter arrived, he entered the tomb at once; what he saw is carefully described (vv. 6–7), but his reaction is not. Finally the beloved disciple went into the tomb, and his reaction is described: **He saw and believed** (v. 8). The implication is not that Peter saw but did *not* believe; it is only that the narrator tells Peter's story as an external observer but the beloved disciple's story as his own. He can say with confidence that the beloved disciple **saw and believed** either because he himself *is* the beloved disciple or because his account rests on the beloved disciple's testimony (cf. the anonymous eyewitness testimony mentioned in 19:35). It is likely that even the description of the placement of the **linen cloths** and the **cloth which had been around Jesus' head**, though introduced in connection with Peter (vv. 6–7), actually rests on the beloved disciple's report. He and Peter both saw it, but he is the one "who speaks of these things, the one who also wrote them down" (21:24). He is the storyteller, and the entire scene is viewed through his eyes.

But what exactly did the beloved disciple believe? And was his belief based simply on the fact that Jesus' body was gone, or on the precise arrangement of the linen wrappings and headcloth described so carefully in verses 6–7? The most plausible answer to the first question is that he believed Jesus had returned to the Father, just as he said he would (cf. 14:29: "I have told you this now before it all happens, so that when it does happen, you will believe"). The basis of his belief was the simple fact that Jesus' body had disappeared. The presence of the wrappings and the headcloth served to rule out the possibility that someone had stolen the body, for what thief would carefully unwrap a corpse before carrying it off? They ruled out even a miraculous resuscitation like that of Lazarus, whom Jesus had called from his tomb with "his hands and feet wrapped in grave clothes, and with a cloth about his face" (11:44). The mention of the headcloth in particular may be intended to recall the Lazarus story, but it is doubtful that the exact position of the headcloth in relation to the linen wrappings has any significance beyond an eyewitness's attention to detail.

Though the faith of the beloved disciple is valid faith and his testimony is a valid testimony, it is not quite the fully developed resurrection faith of the Christian church—for two reasons. First, it is based solely on a word of Jesus, not on the prophecies of scripture that Jesus **must rise from death** (v. 9; contrast the disciples' postresurrection faith, based according to 2:22 on "the scripture and what Jesus had said"); in Luke's terms, the beloved disciple's mind had not yet been opened to understand from scripture that "the Messiah must suffer and must rise from death three days later" (Luke 24:45–46; cf. 24:25–27). Second, the beloved disciple, unlike Mary and unlike the disciples as a group (cf. vv. 18, 25), had not yet **seen the Lord**. The risen Jesus was for him an absent Jesus, for what he **saw** was that Jesus was *not* in the tomb. Though formally he **saw and believed**, his actual experience matches the experience of "those who believe without seeing" Jesus (cf. v. 29).

Mary's story resumes after Peter and the beloved disciple went back to their respective lodgings in Jerusalem (cf. 16:32; 19:27). The narrative presupposes that she had followed them from where they had been staying to the tomb, and now she was alone again, **crying outside the tomb** (v. 11). Finally she looked into the tomb as the beloved disciple had done (cf. v. 5) and saw something that he, as far as we are told, did not see: **two angels there dressed in white, sitting where the body of Jesus had been, one at the head and the other at the feet** (v. 12). This second experience of Mary, even more than her initial discovery of the open tomb, corresponds to that of the women as a group in the synoptic Gospels (cf. Mark 16:5, "they saw a young man sitting on the right"; Matt. 28:2, "an angel of the Lord came down from heaven"; Luke 24:4, "suddenly two men in bright shining clothes stood by them"). The mention of **two angels** recalls Luke in particular, but what happens next is closest in structure to Matthew. Mary Magdalene is addressed first by the two angels and then by the risen Jesus:

Angels	Jesus
Woman, why are you crying? (v. 13a).	**Woman, why are you crying? . . . Who is it that you are looking for?** (v. 15a).
Mary	Mary
They have taken my Lord away, and I do not know where they have put him! (v. 13b).	**If you took him away, sir, tell me where you have put him, and I will go and get him** (v. 15b).

Structurally, the exchange recalls Matthew 28:5–10, where Mary Magdalene and Mary the mother of James and Joseph were addressed first by an angel at the tomb and then by Jesus himself. The angel said, "Do not be afraid . . . I know you are looking for Jesus, who was crucified. He is not here; he has been raised, just as he said. Come here and see the place where he was lying. Go quickly now, and tell his disciples, 'He has been raised from death, and now he is going to Galilee ahead of you; there you will see him!' Remember what I have told you" (Matt. 28:5–8). On their way from the tomb, the women met the risen Jesus, who echoed the angel's words: "Do not be afraid. . . . Go and tell my brothers to go to Galilee, and there they will see me" (Matt. 28:10). Both in Matthew and in John, an encounter with an angel (or angels) at the tomb is reinforced by an encounter with Jesus himself. The main difference is that in Matthew the angel bears testimony to Jesus' resurrection, whereas the two angels in John merely ask Mary why she is crying. Yet in John's Gospel the very positioning of the angels **one at the head and the other at the feet** in the place where Jesus' body had been (v. 12) dramatizes the testimony in Matthew, "Come here and see the place where he was lying" (Matt. 28:6).

Another difference between the two accounts is that Mary Magdalene did not immediately recognize Jesus when he appeared to her (cf. Luke 24:15). She fulfilled the role that Jesus had envisioned for his disciples in 13:33 ("You will look for me; but I tell you now what I told the Jewish authorities, 'You cannot go where I am going' ") and in 16:16 ("In a little while you will not see me any more, and then a little while later you will see me'). He had told them that "you will cry and weep, but the world will be glad; you will be sad, but your sadness will turn into gladness" (16:20). Now Mary was crying because she was looking for her Lord and could not find him. When he first spoke to her (v. 15), she thought it was the gardener (cf. 19:41), and when he made his identity known to her by speaking her name, her sadness was indeed turned to gladness (v. 16).

Mary Magdalene, no less than the beloved disciple, here typifies the experience of all Jesus' followers. As the "Good Shepherd," Jesus "calls his own sheep by name," and when he does, they "know his voice" and respond (10:3–4).

Mary responded at once with a term of recognition (**Rabboni**, or **Teacher**, v. 16), and Jesus' immediate warning, **Do not hold on to me** (v. 17), presumes that at the moment of recognition she embraced him (or possibly that she "took hold of his feet and worshiped him," as in Matt. 28:9). The prohibition serves to remind her that the time for reunion has not yet come. Even though she has seen Jesus and recognized him, it is still true that "you cannot go where I am going" (13:33). He is the departing one, and not yet the returning one. Her experience is like that of the two disciples at Emmaus who finally recognized the risen Jesus only to have him disappear immediately from their sight (Luke 24:31). Before he departs, Jesus leaves a message for his **brothers** (i.e., the rest of the disciples) just as he does in Matthew, but instead of summoning them to Galilee (cf. Matt. 28:10), he explains (to Mary and to them) why he now calls them his **brothers** (contrast 2:12 and 7:3–5, where his "brothers" are his natural brothers): **I am returning** [lit., "ascending"] **to him who is my Father and their Father, my God and their God** (v. 17). For the first time in the entire Gospel, God is seen as the Father of believers as well as of Jesus. He is in fact their Father *because* he is Jesus' Father. By rejoining the Father who sent him, Jesus will now establish a new and more intimate relationship with his disciples as well. From now on they will be his "brothers" and "sisters" (cf. Mark 3:35), united to him by faith and privileged, with him, to call God **Father**.

Mary Magdalene was to bring this good news because she was the first to have **seen the Lord** (v. 18; cf. v. 25). Step by step, Jesus has disclosed himself to his disciples in a series of incidents arranged to form a *chiasm* (i.e., a pattern that can be represented *a b c b a*):

a. Mary Magdalene looked at the tomb from the outside and saw that the stone had been moved (v. 1).

b. The beloved disciple looked inside the tomb and saw the linen wrappings (v. 5).

c. Peter entered the tomb and saw the linen wrappings and the headcloth arranged in a particular way (vv. 6–7).

b. The beloved disciple entered the tomb, saw what Peter saw, *and believed* (v. 8).

a. Mary Magdalene looked outside the tomb, saw two angels, and finally *saw the Lord himself* (vv. 11–18).

The effect of the arrangement is to emphasize the role of Mary Magdalene (and, to a lesser extent, the beloved disciple) in the story of Jesus' resurrection. She, not Peter (cf. 1 Cor. 15:5; Luke 24:34), was the first to see the risen Jesus. The disciples are never called "the apostles" in John's Gospel. The word "apostle" (Gr.: *apostolos*) occurs only in 13:16, in the sense of "messenger." But Mary was a kind of "apostle to the apostles," a messenger sent to Jesus' gathered disciples with the good news that he was rejoining his Father—and theirs (vv. 17–18). The Lord himself was close behind his messenger and would shortly confirm the good news in person (vv. 19–23).

Additional Notes

20:1 / **Mary Magdalene**: The name **Magdalene** (cf. 19:25) indicates that this woman's home was the village of Magdala, near Capernaum in Galilee. She was evidently among the "women who had followed Jesus from Galilee" to Jerusalem (Luke 23:49, 55).

20:2 / **The other disciple, whom Jesus loved**: The "disciple whom Jesus loved" (cf. 13:23; 19:26) is consistently referred to in the present narrative as the **other disciple** (vv. 3, 4, 8), possibly to link him with the "other disciple" who brought Peter into the High Priest's courtyard according to 18:15–16. In every case but the present one in which the expression "the disciple whom Jesus loved" occurs, the Greek verb for "love" is *agapan*, while in the present instance the verb is *philein*. The latter difference is probably only stylistic (cf. the alternation of the same two verbs in 21:15–17) and affords no basis for arguing that two beloved disciples are in view! The variations in terminology could be attributable to written sources being used by the Gospel writer here or elsewhere.

20:5 / **Peter and the other disciple went to the tomb**: In Luke 24:12 (at least according to most of the ancient manuscripts), Peter alone "got up and ran to the tomb; he bent down and saw the linen wrappings but nothing else. Then he went back home amazed at what had happened." This account could have come either from Peter's personal report or from the beloved disciple's external observation (without reference to his own involvement). In contrast to either, the Johannine narrative appears to rest on the beloved disciple's personal testimony as a participant in the action.

20:16 / **Rabboni** (Gr.: *rabbouni*): The meaning is the same as "Rabbi" in 1:38 except that the ending personalizes it (lit., "my Teacher" or "my Master") and makes it less formal. It is used in the New Testament only here and in Mark 10:51 (in a plea for healing). Mary may have chosen this word instead of the more common "Rabbi" (eight occurrences in John's Gospel) because she was using it, not as a form of address preliminary to saying something else, but as a cry of recognition in itself.

20:17 / **Do not hold on to me**. The present imperative suggests that Jesus is telling Mary either to stop doing something she is already doing, or to stop trying to do something she is attempting to do (some ancient manuscripts add, at the end of the preceding verse, the actual words "and she ran toward him to touch him"). The point of the words **Do not hold on to me** is not that Jesus' body is intangible (in contrast to later, when he invites Thomas to touch his hands and side, v. 27) but simply that because he is on his way to the Father, he cannot stay and talk with Mary. There is time only to give her the message she must deliver to the other disciples.

20:18 / **Told the disciples**: Though the term "disciple" is reserved for Jesus' male followers in John's Gospel, the interweaving of Mary's story with that of Peter and the beloved disciple, the use of her experience to typify the experience of all the disciples (cf. 13:33; 16:16, 20–22), and especially the statement that **she had seen the Lord** suggest that Mary too is implicitly regarded in the narrative as one of the **disciples** (and therefore, in the sense of v. 17, as Jesus' "sister"; cf. Mark 3:35).

  That she had seen the Lord: lit., "I have seen the Lord." It is better to keep the direct discourse here, with RSV, in order not to weaken the parallel between Mary's announcement and that of the disciples in v. 25. GNB and NIV have changed it to indirect discourse because the following clause is indirect discourse in Greek, but the very incongruity heightens the accent on the direct quotation of Mary's confessional words.

48

The Second Appearance and Its Sequel

JOHN 20:19–31

It was late that Sunday evening, and the disciples were gathered together behind locked doors, because they were afraid of the Jewish authorities. Then Jesus came and stood among them. "Peace be with you," he said. [20]After saying this, he showed them his hands and his side. The disciples were filled with joy at seeing the Lord. [21]Jesus said to them again, "Peace be with you. As the Father sent me, so I send you." [22]Then he breathed on them and said, "Receive the Holy Spirit. [23]If you forgive people's sins, they are forgiven; if you do not forgive them, they are not forgiven."

[24]One of the twelve disciples, Thomas (called the Twin), was not with them when Jesus came. [25]So the other disciples told him, "We have seen the Lord!"

Thomas said to them, "Unless I see the scars of the nails in his hands and put my finger on those scars and my hand in his side, I will not believe."

[26]A week later the disciples were together again indoors, and Thomas was with them. The doors were locked, but Jesus came and stood among them and said, "Peace be with you." [27]Then he said to Thomas, "Put your finger here, and look at my hands; then reach out your hand and put it in my side. Stop your doubting, and believe!"

[28]Thomas answered him, "My Lord and my God!"

[29]Jesus said to him, "Do you believe because you see me? How happy are those who believe without seeing me!"

[30]In his disciples' presence Jesus performed many other miracles which are not written down in this book. [31]But these have been written in order that you may believe[j] that Jesus is the Messiah, the Son of God, and that through your faith in him you may have life.

j. believe; *some manuscripts have* continue to believe.

T he scene shifts from the tomb in the garden to a locked room somewhere in Jerusalem, and from "early on Sunday morning" (v. 1) to **late that Sunday evening** (v. 19). Despite the faith of the beloved disciple (v. 8) and despite the message brought by Mary Magdalene (v. 18), the disciples as a group are still afraid. Their reaction to her message is not recorded in John's Gospel, but another tradition appended to Mark by later scribes states that after Mary had seen Jesus she "went and told his companions" and found them "mourning and crying;

and when they heard her say that Jesus was alive and that she had seen him, they did not believe her" (Mark 16:10; cf. the apostles' reaction to the report of the women who had seen the angels at the tomb according to Luke 24:11).

In John, the unbelief of the disciples as a group is not mentioned explicitly, only their fear of the Jewish authorities. The unbelief is attributed instead to one disciple, Thomas, in particular (vv. 24–25). The appearance to him in verses 26–29 is really an extension of the appearance to the gathered disciples in verses 19–23, even though it takes place a week later. Verses 24–25 link the two incidents together, so that in effect what is said to the disciples in verses 19–23 is said to Thomas as well, and what is said to him in verses 26–29 is said to them all. If this is so, it is incorrect to single out Thomas as the lone skeptic among the disciples. He is, rather, the disciples' representative and spokesman *both* in his skepticism (v. 25b) *and* in his faith (v. 28). The rest of the disciples, except for their report to Thomas in verse 25a, **We have seen the Lord!** are silent throughout the story, but Thomas' confession, **My Lord and my God!** (v. 28) is finally theirs as well.

The disciples' fear and helplessness before seeing Jesus and receiving the Holy Spirit is shown by the fact that on Sunday evening they **were gathered together behind locked doors, because they were afraid of the Jewish authorities** (v. 19). They were essentially no better off than those who earlier had "believed in Jesus" but who "because of the Pharisees . . . did not talk about it openly, so as not to be expelled from the synagogue" (12:42). Of those, the narrator had said, "They loved the approval of men rather than the approval of God" (12:43). The disciples had fled at Jesus' arrest (16:32; 18:8) and returned to their quarters in Jerusalem (cf. 19:27; 20:10); now (despite what two of them had seen in vv. 3–9) they were living in fear as fugitives. Only the presence of Jesus and the Spirit could transform them again into a missionary community ready to carry on their Lord's work (cf. 17:9–19). Yet **a week later**, *after* receiving the Spirit, they were still in hiding, gathered probably in the same place, with the doors locked (v. 26)! The only possible explanation is that their reunion with Jesus and their reception of the Spirit did not take effect—in some sense were not complete—until their skepticism (personified by Thomas) was overcome and their faith in Jesus found its voice in the decisive confession **My Lord and my God** (v. 28). This means that verses 19–29 present essentially one resurrection appearance of Jesus in two stages, a week apart. Together, they illustrate the same ambiguity about the disciples' faith that has been present in the narrative all along (cf., e.g., 16:29–33) and dramatize the terse statement of Matthew's Gospel that when Jesus appeared to the disciples on a mountain in Galilee, "they worshiped him, even though some of them doubted" (Matt. 28:17). The command **Stop your doubting, and believe!** (v. 27), though addressed to Thomas in particular, is an appropriate command for every disciple and every reader (cf. the cry of the father of a demon-possessed boy in Mark 9:24: "I do believe; help me overcome my unbelief!" [NIV]).

Jesus' self-disclosure to his disciples on Easter Sunday evening and a week later is most appropriately understood as the fulfillment of virtually all he had promised them in his farewell discourses:

The Promise	The Fulfillment
I will come back to you (14:18, 28). My Father and I will come to him (14:23).	**Jesus came and stood among them** (20:19, 26).
Peace is what I leave with you; it is my own peace that I give you (14:27). I have told you this so that you will have peace by being united to me (16:33).	**Peace be with you** (20:19, 21, 26).
In a little while you will not see me any more, and then a little while later you will see me (16:16). I will see you again, and your hearts will be filled with gladness, the kind of gladness that no one can take away from you (16:22).	**The disciples were filled with joy at seeing the Lord** (20:20).
I will ask the Father, and he will give you another Helper. . . . the Spirit who reveals the truth about God (14:16–17). The Helper, the Holy Spirit, whom the Father will send in my name, will teach you everything (14:26; cf. also 15:26, 16:7–15).	**Then he breathed on them and said, "Receive the Holy Spirit"** (20:22).

If the empty tomb signified to the beloved disciple Jesus' departure to the Father, his appearance to the disciples gathered behind locked doors signifies his return. He has come back, not to pay them a brief visit and go away again, but to stay. His return is not a momentary incident but the beginning of a new relationship. "In a little while," he had said, "the world will see me no more, but you will see me; and because I live, you also will live. When that day comes, you will know that I am in my Father and that you are in me, just as I am in you" (14:19–20). The new relationship is made possible by the Spirit, who, Jesus had said, "remains with you and is in you" (14:17). The disciples' gladness at this reunion is "the kind of gladness that no one can take away from you" (16:22).

Three times the risen Jesus revealed himself to the disciples with the salutation **Peace be with you** (vv. 19, 21, 26). The first time he verified his presence and identity by showing them his pierced hands and wounded side (v. 20). The second time he commissioned them (**As the Father sent me, so I send you**, cf. 17:18) and breathed on them as a sign of the impartation of the Holy Spirit. The act of breathing proves that Jesus is once more alive (contrast 19:30) and, what is more, able to give life. The verb **breathed** (Gr.: *enephusēsen*) corresponds to the Greek translation of Genesis 2:7, when God "breathed life-giving breath" into Adam at the creation (cf. 6:63: "What gives life is God's Spirit"). The Spirit, depicted in the farewell discourses as a person ("the Helper," 14:16, 26; 15:26; 16:7) is here seen as the divine power by which the disciples will be enabled to complete their mission, that is, to continue the work of Jesus himself (cf. Paul's allusion to Gen. 2:7: "Thus it is written: 'The first man Adam became a living being,' " to which he adds, "the last Adam [i.e., Jesus] became a life-giving spirit," 1 Cor. 15:45, RSV). Specifically, the work of Jesus that the Spirit continues is the work of forgiving (or not forgiving) people's sins, the two-sided work of giving life on the one hand, and bringing judgment or condemnation on the other (cf. 5:19–29). The same Jesus who told the royal official, "Your son will live" (4:50, 53), and called Lazarus out of his tomb (11:43) also told the Pharisees, "You are still guilty" (9:41; cf. 15:22–24). He came "so that the blind should see and those who see should become blind" (9:39). In this respect, his disciples' mission in the power of the Spirit would be no different from his own.

The third greeting of **Peace**, like the first, was accompanied by verification of Jesus' identity by the wounds in his hands and side (v. 27). In this case, even the manner of verification corresponded exactly to the sign that Thomas, in the meantime, had demanded of his fellow disciples (v. 25).

The resulting confession, **My Lord and my God** (v. 28) was Thomas's acknowledgment, first, that the man standing before him was Jesus, his beloved teacher (cf. "my Lord" on the lips of Mary Magdalene in v. 13), and second, that he now understood his beloved teacher to be none other than God himself (cf. Jesus' prophetic words in 8:28, "When you lift up the Son of Man, you will know that 'I Am Who I Am' ").

Jesus' response to this last great confession of John's Gospel is much like his response to all the other confessions. He accepts it, but with no special words of commendation (cf., e.g., 1:50; 6:70; 16:31–32). Instead of pronouncing a beatitude on Thomas as he does in Matthew's Gospel on Simon Peter ("Blessed are you, Simon son of Jonah," Matt. 16:17, NIV), Jesus reserves his beatitude for others who are not even present: "Because you have seen me, you have believed; blessed are those who have not seen and yet have believed" (v. 29, NIV). The purpose of the distinction is not so much to rebuke Thomas and the assembled disciples for their skepticism as to emphasize that Jesus' memorable words and tangible signs were not just for the immediate participants in the drama of his resurrection but for other believers and later generations as well. The pronouncement lays the basis for a significant comment by the Gospel writer to some who had **not seen** the nail marks in Jesus' hands and the gaping wound in his side—specifically the Gospel's readers (vv. 30–31).

At some stage in the growth of this Gospel's traditions, the last two verses of the chapter probably functioned as a summary statement of purpose for the Gospel as a whole. Jesus' ministry in its entirety is characterized as a series of **miracles** (lit., "signs") written down in order to foster belief in him as **the Messiah, the Son of God** (in contrast to those who saw his miracles but refused to believe, cf. 12:37). Such an understanding has much to commend it *if* the end of this chapter is also the end of the book, but in John's Gospel as it stands, this is not the case. Another chapter follows, with its own appropriate postscript to the book as a whole (21:25). To what **miracles** or "signs," then, do verses 30–31 refer? Some have argued that the summary once stood at the end of a collection of miracle stories (the seven "signs" of Jesus' public ministry, perhaps: the Cana wedding, the healing of the nobleman's son, the sick man at Bethzatha, the feeding of the five thousand, the walking on the water, the blind man at Siloam, the raising of Lazarus), but such a theory, even if valid, offers no help in explaining how the statement functions in its present position in the Gospel as we have it today. It is more likely that the term **miracles** or "signs" is here used to denote resurrection signs, like the "many convincing proofs" of Acts 1:3 (NIV). They are words or actions of the risen Lord that either made him known to his disciples or reinforced the instructions and commands he gave them (e.g., vv. 16, 17, 22, 27; cf. Luke 24:30, 39–42). The narrator implies that he knows—and could have included—many more of these, and that what he has provided is only a small sampling. The purpose of the sampling is **in order that you** [i.e., the readers of the Gospel] **may believe that Jesus is the Messiah, the Son of God, and that through your faith in him you may have life** (v. 31). The narrator's intent is that through his writing (especially his account of the resurrection appearances), his readers should enter into the once-and-for-all experience of Jesus' original disciples (cf. the invitation of the original disciples to do exactly that in 1 John 1:1–3). He wants them to claim for themselves Jesus' last beatitude, **How happy are those who believe without seeing me!** (v. 29). Their confession **that Jesus is the Messiah, the Son of God** echoes Thomas' exclamation, **My Lord and my God!** (v. 28), while the accompanying promise of life **in him** recalls the life that Jesus breathed into his disciples when he conferred on them the Holy Spirit (v. 22).

Much has been written on the question of whether verses 30–31 could have been addressed to those who were already "believers" or whether the phrase **in order that you may believe** implies that the recipients were unbelievers. The answer probably hinges less on whether the verb is **believe** (GNB text) or **continue to believe** (GNB margin) than on the analogy between the Gospel's readers and the disciples who literally saw the risen Jesus. The disciples were "believers" in Jesus almost from the start (cf. 2:11), yet in this resurrection encounter the group (represented by Thomas) "believed" once more (vv. 28–29), just as they had done on certain other occasions after their first expression of faith (cf. 6:69; 16:30). The narrator intends that this should happen to his readers as well. To him, faith is no static thing that comes once to a person, only to lie dormant, but a response to God that comes to expression again and again as one is confronted afresh with the story of Jesus (cf. 4:50, 53). It is therefore likely that the resurrection narrative—like the rest of John's Gospel—is directed at those who already **believe**, so as to engage them anew with the events on which their faith is built, events that may have seemed to be receding too quickly into a less defined and less insistent past.

Additional Notes

20:19 / **Late that Sunday evening**: lit., "late that day, the first of the week" (cf. v. 1). It is possible that the phrase "on that day" has eschatological significance because the events to be recorded are fulfillments of Jesus' words of promise in his farewell discourses (cf. 14:20: "When that day comes [lit., "on that day"], you will know that I am in my Father and that you are in me, just as I am in you"). More likely, however, the phrase looks *back* from the narrator's standpoint on "that [memorable] day," the Sunday when Jesus rose from the dead (cf. "that year" in 11:49 and 18:13). If so, the language reflects an early stage in a process that culminated in the formal observance of Easter.

20:22 / **Receive the Holy Spirit**: The most natural way of understanding these words is that the disciples were intended to receive (and did receive) the Holy Spirit at that very moment. Because the book of Acts records the coming of the Spirit fifty days later, at Pentecost (Acts 2:1–4), some have regarded the statement here as proleptic (i.e., as a promise that the disciples would *later* receive the Spirit). Appeal could be made to 2:19, where Jesus uses an aorist imperative ("Tear down this temple") to refer to something that did not happen until he was crucified. But the cases are not alike, for the imperative in 2:19 is conditional (i.e., "If you tear down this temple, I will raise it up"), whereas the imperative here is an actual command. This is the only recorded fulfillment of Jesus' promises of the Spirit in his farewell discourses (cf. also 7:39), and it is clear that the Gospel writer intends it as *the* fulfillment. In that sense it is the Johannine equivalent of Pentecost, not a mere foretaste of Pentecost.

Historically, there are hints in Luke and Acts that *even before Pentecost* the Spirit indeed played a role in the ministry of the risen Jesus to his disciples. The preface to the book of Acts states: "Before he was taken up, he gave instructions by the power of the Holy Spirit to the men he had chosen as his apostles" (Acts 1:2). In Luke 24, when Jesus revealed himself to his gathered disciples, he is said to have "opened their minds to understand the Scriptures" (i.e., by the power of the Spirit? 24:45); in this connection he said, "And I myself will send upon you what my Father has promised" (24:49a). The latter statement is more literally translated in the present tense: "And I myself am [now] sending upon you what my Father promised." Such an interpretation makes better sense of what immediately follows: "*But you must wait* in the city *until* the power from above comes down upon you" (24:49b). Clearly, something is given and something is still expected. Luke's emphasis is largely on what is still expected, whereas John's emphasis is exclusively on what is already given.

20:23 / **If you forgive people's sins, they are forgiven; if you do not forgive them, they are not forgiven**. The metaphorical equivalent of this pronouncement is the promise of Jesus to Peter in Matt. 16:19 and to all the disciples in Matt. 18:18 (as translated in NIV with the verbs "bind" and "loose"; GNB, with its renderings "prohibit" and "permit," has dissolved the metaphors differently from the interpretation presupposed here in John's Gospel). To "bind" is understood as "not forgive"; to "loose" is understood as "forgive."

The first part of Jesus' statement has a parallel in a similar resurrection context in Luke's Gospel: "And in his name the message about repentance and the forgiveness of sins must be preached to all nations, beginning in Jerusalem" (Luke 24:47).

20:24 / **One of the twelve disciples, Thomas (called the Twin)**: See note on 11:16. Thomas was actually introduced more abruptly in his first appearance in the Gospel than he is here. The designation of him as **one of the twelve** is supplied here to emphasize the point that he normally would have been present for the incident recorded in vv. 19–23 but was not. The **twelve** (though now only eleven because of Judas' departure) are still being viewed as a fixed group representing the whole church (cf. 6:70). Even though Judas has departed, Thomas must be present in order for the revelation to be complete.

20:26 / **A week later**: lit., "after eight days." A common ancient custom was to count both the first and the last days in a series, so that "eight" would be the equivalent of a week. The meaning is that the appearance took place on the next Sunday after Easter (cf. v. 19).

20:29 / **Do you believe because you see me?** The question is better understood as a statement: "You believe because you have seen me." There is no question either about Thomas' belief or about the basis of it. Jesus does not say that Thomas touched him, and there is no evidence in the text that his skepticism went so far as actually to accept the challenge laid down in v. 27. He believed because he *saw*, just as the rest of the disciples did (vv. 20, 25; cf. v. 8).

20:31 / **That through your faith in him you may have life**: More accurately, "that through your faith you may have life in him." The phrase **in him** (lit., "in his name") goes with the possession of eternal life, not with the act of believing (cf. note on 3:15; what seems to be true there is even more clearly the case in the present passage).

49

The Third Appearance

JOHN 21:1–14

After this, Jesus appeared once more to his disciples at Lake Tiberias. This is how it happened. ²Simon Peter, Thomas (called the Twin), Nathanael (the one from Cana in Galilee), the sons of Zebedee, and two other disciples of Jesus were all together. ³Simon Peter said to the others, "I am going fishing."

"We will come with you," they told him. So they went out in a boat, but all that night they did not catch a thing. ⁴As the sun was rising, Jesus stood at the water's edge, but the disciples did not know that it was Jesus. ⁵Then he asked them, "Young men, haven't you caught anything?"

"Not a thing," they answered.

⁶He said to them, "Throw your net out on the right side of the boat, and you will catch some." So they threw the net out and could not pull it back in, because they had caught so many fish.

⁷The disciple whom Jesus loved said to Peter, "It is the Lord!" When Peter heard that it was the Lord, he wrapped his outer garment around him (for he had taken his clothes off and jumped into the water. ⁸The other disciples came to shore in the boat, pulling the net full of fish. They were not very far from land, about a hundred yards away. ⁹When they stepped ashore, they saw a charcoal fire there with fish on it and some bread. ¹⁰Then Jesus said to them, "Bring some of the fish you have just caught."

¹¹Simon Peter went aboard and dragged the net ashore full of big fish, a hundred and fifty-three in all; even though there were so many, still the net did not tear. ¹²Jesus said to them, "Come and eat." None of the disciples dared ask him, "Who are you?" because they knew it was the Lord. ¹³So Jesus went over, took the bread, and gave it to them; he did the same with the fish.

¹⁴This, then, was the third time Jesus appeared to the disciples after he was raised from death.

In contrast to a series of careful time designations reaching back at least to 19:14 ("almost noon of the day before the Passover") and continuing through 19:31, 42; 20:1, 19, 26 ("Friday," "the day before the Sabbath," "early on Sunday morning," "late that Sunday evening," "a week later"), the account of Jesus' last resurrection appearance begins with the vague expression **after this** (v. 1; cf. 5:1; 6:1; 7:1). How long after, we are not told; nor are we told the circumstances of the disciples' journey from Jerusalem to Galilee.

The angelic message of Mark 16:7 intended for "his disciples, including Peter," was that "he is going to Galilee ahead of you; there you will see him, just as he told you." It may be that Jesus' appearance in verses 1–14 to seven of his disciples at **Lake Tiberias** (i.e., "Lake Galilee," cf. 6:1), with its accompanying dialogue with Peter (vv. 15–22) was remembered by Jesus' followers as the fulfillment of that specific promise. The narrator does not say so, but he does seem to have decided at some point that at least one of the "many other miracles which are not written down in this book" (20:30) *must* be written down in order for the book to be truly complete.

There is wide agreement that chapter 21 forms some kind of an appendix to the Gospel. Yet it is closely linked to what immediately precedes it, not only by the connective **after this** in verse 1, but by the more detailed notice in verse 14 that it **was the third time Jesus appeared to the disciples after he was raised from death.** Most commentators assume that it is **third** in relation to 20:19–23 and 20:26–29 as the first and second, respectively. Some argue ingeniously that at earlier stages of the tradition it was the the **third** of Jesus' *Galilean* miracles in relation to 2:1–11 and 4:43–54 as the first and second (cf. 2:11; 4:54). But in the Gospel text as it stands, verses 1–14 are most plausibly understood as the **third** resurrection appearance of Jesus in relation to 20:11–18 and 20:19–29, respectively. If the narrator is the same here as in chapter 20 (i.e., if the writer of the Gospel is also responsible for the appendix), then the reference in verse 14 to the **third** appearance presupposes the story line of both preceding appearance narratives. The beloved disciple's announcement, **It is the Lord!** in verse 7 thus corresponds to Mary's "I have seen the Lord" (RSV) in 20:18 and to the group's "We have seen the Lord" in 20:25.

Though it is true that the two appearances to **disciples** *as a group* are, rather, 20:19–23 and 20:26–29, yet the **disciples** in chapter 21 are, in any case, not the *same* group to whom Jesus appeared in chapter 20. They are not "the twelve"; nor are they eleven or ten; they are seven in number, and it is not certain that the two anonymous disciples of verse 2 were even included among "the twelve" mentioned in 20:24. The appearance being described is the **third** appearance to disciples of Jesus, not to one group of disciples in particular. The appearance to Mary Magdalene was a distinct and unique disclosure to one who functioned throughout as a disciple (even though the term was not used), whereas the appearance to Thomas simply verified and completed the decisive appearance to the so-called Twelve.

Why were the disciples fishing instead of fulfilling the task for which

Jesus had sent them (20:21–23)? The Gospel of John does not preserve
the tradition found, for example, in Mark 1:16–20 that Jesus called several of his disciples from the occupation of fishing to the task of being
"fishers of men" (Mark 1:17, NIV). Yet the resurrection appearance described in verses 1–14 builds on that very tradition. The activity of fishing
serves the narrator in two ways: first, as a literal description of what the
disciples were doing, and second, as a metaphor. This means that the story
must be read on two levels.

First, the story purports to be a literal account of a miraculous catch of
fish made possible by an appearance of the risen Lord in Galilee. It is not
so strange that the disciples are back in Galilee and engaged in the secular
task of fishing if one remembers Jesus' warning to them that "all of you
will be scattered, each one to his own home, and I will be left all alone"
(16:32). The beloved disciple had taken Jesus' mother "to live in his
home" (19:27), and even after he and Peter had seen the empty tomb of
Jesus they "went back home" (20:10). Temporarily, their "homes" were
in Jerusalem, but the same principle can be assumed to apply to their
permanent homes in Galilee. Nathanael is specifically said to be "from
Cana in Galilee" in verse 2, and Peter, at least, was explicitly identified as
a Galilean in 1:44 (for Thomas and the sons of Zebedee, cf. Mark 1:19;
3:17–18). No blame is attached to Peter's announcement that he is going
fishing or to the other disciples' decision to join him (v. 3). Fishing as a
livelihood is simply one expression of what it means to be "scattered" in
the world, and the disciples were indeed scattered, not only by Jesus'
predictive word (16:32), but by his sovereign action as well (18:8–9).
Their dispersion in the world was to be the occasion for their mission to
the world (17:9–19) and for the gathering of "all the scattered people of
God" into one (11:52; 17:20–23).

This background in the sayings of Jesus highlights the metaphorical
character of verses 1–14. Two things are being described simultaneously:
the efforts of the disciples to fill their net with fish and their efforts to
complete their mission of making God known in the world by proclaiming
the message Jesus gave them. In the first stage of their encounter with
Jesus (vv. 4–6), his identity was hidden from them just as it was hidden
from Mary Magdalene in 20:14–15 (or from the two disciples on the way
to Emmaus in Luke 24:15–30). They saw him only as a stranger standing
on the lakeshore early in the morning, after a whole night of unsuccessful
fishing (v. 4). The stranger's passing suggestion that they try **the right
side of the boat** precipitates the miracle (a net loaded with fish) and so

dramatizes Jesus' earlier statement that "you can do nothing without me" (15:5). It also makes his identity known, first to the beloved disciple, then to Peter, and finally to the others.

The form of the stranger's words may have been the first clue: **Throw your net out . . . and you will catch some** (lit., "and you will find") perhaps reminded the beloved disciple of the familiar saying of Jesus, "seek, and you will find" (Matt. 7:7/Luke 11:9). But it was undoubtedly the immediate, miraculous catch of fish that prompted his recognition of the stranger as Jesus. He had seen the empty tomb and believed that Jesus had gone to the Father (20:8), and he had shared with the other disciples in their decisive meeting with the risen Lord in Jerusalem, but now, like Mary, he had his own encounter with Jesus and the opportunity to share it with Peter and the rest. His testimony, **It is the Lord,** revealed the stranger's identity to Peter (v. 7a), though the other disciples may have conclusively known **it was the Lord** only in verse 12, after Jesus had invited them to his meal of fish and bread.

Peter's immediate response was to swim for shore, while the other disciples followed in the boat (vv. 7b–8). Normally a person would discard his or her outer garment in order to swim unhindered, but because Peter was wearing *only* the outer garment, with nothing under it, he instead tucked it or tied it around himself so as to allow maximum freedom of movement without having to come out of the water naked. Peter did not want to greet his Lord unclothed (contrast the young man who "ran away naked" from Jesus and the scene of his arrest according to Mark 14:51). Such vivid detail evidences once more the observation of an eyewitness (presumably the beloved disciple), not primarily the symbolic interests of a theologian.

There *are* symbolic aspects to the narrative, however. When the disciples came ashore, Peter swimming and the others in the boat, the first thing they saw was a **charcoal fire** (v. 9) burning as a reminder (to the reader of the Gospel if not the disciples) of another "charcoal fire" in the High Priest's courtyard (18:18) when Peter had denied his Lord three times. Peter had made his home for a time with Jesus' enemies, but now he and his scattered companions were back with the Lord at their true home, free to enjoy its fire and share in what Jesus had provided. The story of a miraculous catch of fish merges here into a story of a meal at which the disciples are the guests and the risen Jesus is the host. The stories overlap: The account of the meal is given in verses 9–13, yet woven into this account is the decisive ending of the story about the great catch of fish (vv. 10–11). It is the overlapping that most pointedly raises the question of the symbolic intent of the narrative as a whole. The conclusion to the story of the miraculous catch has suggested to many the theme of mission or evangelization. Fishing, it is urged, is used here as a symbol of being "fishers of men" (Mark 1:17, NIV), that is, of winning converts to Christianity by proclaiming the message of Jesus. The full net (153 fish is a lot of fish when they are all large) indicates the successful completion of that mission, while the unbroken net (contrast Luke 5:6) illustrates the principle, voiced by Jesus several times, that "I have not lost even one of these [the Father] gave me" (18:9; cf. 6:39; 10:28; 17:12).

Yet when the metaphor is pressed too far, confusion is the result. If the 153 **big fish** represent "those who believe in me because of [the disciples'] message" (17:20), how is it that Jesus immediately invites his disciples to a breakfast of—bread and fish (vv. 12–13)? The metaphor threatens to become one of cannibalism! It is true that Jesus has fish of his own prepared for the meal (v. 9), but he also tells the disciples to **bring some of the fish you have just caught** (v. 10). An easy way to clear up the confusion would be to drop the notion of symbolism altogether, but a better way is to recognize that **fish** are used by the narrator in two distinct ways: first, as a metaphor for the new community brought into being as a result of the disciples' mission (cf. the "one flock" of 10:16), and second, as one element in a fellowship meal by means of which Jesus and his disciples were reunited.

This distinction does not help very much until it is recognized that **bread** functioned on occasion in the same two senses. In the second-century church manual known as the *Didache*, "bread" is *both* an element in the Lord's Supper (*Didache* 9.3) *and* a metaphor for the church (9.4): "As this broken bread was scattered upon the mountains, but was brought together and became one, so let your church be gathered together from the ends of the earth into your kingdom." Such imagery is based on the Gospel accounts of the feeding of the five thousand (perhaps esp. John 6:1–13. It appears that the narrative of the miraculous catch on Lake Tiberias does for **fish** what the narrative of the feeding of the five thousand (beside that very same lake, cf. 6:1) did for "bread." And just as fish were incidental to the "bread" narrative (6:9), so bread is incidental to the **fish** narrative (21:9, 13). Even the statistical exactness of "five loaves of barley bread and two fish" (6:9) and "twelve baskets . . . left over" (6:11), with the concern "that nothing may be lost" (6:12, RSV), finds its parallel in **a hundred and fifty-three** fish and a net that **did not tear** (21:11). It is likely that if the feeding of the five thousand in John's Gospel had not been followed by a discourse on Jesus the Bread of life (6:26–59), it would have been interpreted symbolically with reference to the unity and corporate life of the church, particularly meal fellowship. In chapter 21, there is, of course, no comparable discourse on Jesus as the life-giving Fish—even though Tertullian, more than a century later, could write, "But we, being little fishes, as Jesus Christ is our great Fish, begin our life in the water" (*On Baptism* 1.3). (Even the letters of the Greek word for fish [*ichthus*] came to be widely used as an abbreviation for "Jesus Christ, Son of God, Savior.") Consequently, the story of the miraculous catch and of the breakfast by the lake is to be understood in connection with the mission and unity of the church (cf. e.g., chapter 17), and in particular with the expression of this unity in meal fellowship.

Even the terminology for Jesus' distribution of the food is broadly similar in the two passages (the italics indicate verbal parallels):

Jesus *took the bread,* gave thanks to God, and distributed it to the people who were sitting there. *He did the same with the fish,* and they all had much as they wanted (6:11).

So Jesus went over, *took the bread,* and gave it to them; *he did the same with the fish* (21:13).

The ceremonious, almost liturgical-sounding, descriptions of Jesus' procedure, as well as the fixed order (first bread and then fish, regardless of which has played the more prominent role in the narrative), suggest that the narrator may have in mind the fellowship meals of the churches he is familiar with as well as the specific historical incidents being described.

The third appearance of the risen Jesus thus brings the disciples from being scattered to their homes in Galilee into full involvement in the mission to which they were called, and so back into table fellowship with Jesus and each other (cf. 13:1–20). John's Gospel, unlike Luke's, is not the first half of a two-part work, yet chapter 21 functions as a small Acts of the Apostles, told in the form of one more symbolic narrative or sign rather than a continuous account of the establishment and expansion of the church in history. After the sign, it remains only to compare briefly the acts of two apostles in particular as models of what it means to follow Jesus.

Additional Notes

21:2 / (**The one from Cana in Galilee**): The notice is given as if the readers already knew that Nathanael came from Cana, but (despite the conjunction of 1:43–51 with 2:1–11) there has been no explicit statement to that effect in the

Gospel. That he came from Galilee, however, and from a town that was (like Cana) close to Nazareth, the readers could have inferred from 1:46.

21:5 / **Young men, haven't you caught anything?** Because Jesus is incognito, the address **young men** (Gr.: *paidia*; lit., "servants" or "children") should not be used to infer anything about Jesus' close personal relationship to his disciples. He is merely using a common way of addressing strangers in friendly or familiar terms (like "my friends," or the British expression, "my lads"). **Haven't you caught anything?** is a good idiomatic translation for the question "Haven't you anything to eat [i.e., with your bread]?" (Gr.: *prosphagion*; the word could refer to almost anything eaten with bread, the staple, but most often it came to mean fish in particular. A different word for "fish" is used in the rest of the story).

21:7 / **The disciple whom Jesus loved**: lit., "that disciple whom Jesus loved." The demonstrative pronoun "that" (Gr.: *ekeinos*) has not been used in this phrase before, but appears here perhaps to anticipate v. 23 ("a report spread . . . that this [lit., "that"] disciple would not die"), and the decisive introduction of "that disciple" as the Gospel's author in v. 24. Cf. possibly 19:35: "he [Gr.: *ekeinos*] knows that he speaks the truth" (though it is not certain that the same person is meant; see note on 19:35).

21:8 / **About a hundred yards away**: lit., "about two hundred cubits." A cubit was the length of a man's forearm, or about eighteen inches.

21:11 / **Dragged the net ashore**: Peter has more success handling the net full of fish than all the disciples together had in v. 6. But it is doubtful that the verb "to drag" or "draw" (Gr.: *elkuein*) is chosen intentionally with 6:44 or 12:32 in mind, as some have suggested. The account is first of all a literal story of fishing, not an allegory of God or Jesus (or Peter!) "drawing" men and women to salvation.

Big fish, a hundred and fifty-three in all: The best explanation for such a precise number is that the catch was counted and that an eyewitness (the beloved disciple) remembered the total (i.e., 153 in all, not 153 **big fish** plus more little ones: **all** the fish were remembered as being large). Many symbolic interpretations have been suggested, several of them based on the fact that 153 is a "triangular" number, the sum of every integer from one to seventeen. All such theories are highly speculative, and none is at all convincing. The most intriguing observation is that of Jerome, who in the fourth century claimed that Greek zoologists listed 153 different kinds of fish (*Commentary on Ezekiel* 47.6–12; cf. Jesus' parable in Matt. 13:47, in which the net gathers in "all kinds of fish"). One must take Jerome's word for it, however; the surviving texts of the Greek zoologists contain no such statement, and the tradition may have arisen among Christians after the fact as an effort to explain the reference in John.

21:13 / **Took the bread and gave it . . . did the same**: The use of the verbs **took** and **gave** and the phrase **did the same** (lit., "likewise") are reminiscent not only

343

of the feeding of the five thousand but of the institution of the Lord's Supper (e.g., Mark 14:22–23; Luke 22:19–20; 1 Cor. 11:23–25). It is doubtful, however, that the Lord's Supper is specifically in view in a passage that does not mention the cup at all. Probably an *agapē* or fellowship meal in a more general sense is intended (cf., e.g., 13:1–5, 21–30).

50

Jesus, Peter, and
the Beloved Disciple

JOHN 21:15–25

After they had eaten, Jesus said to Simon Peter, "Simon son of John, do you love me more than these others do?"

"Yes, Lord," he answered, "you know that I love you."

Jesus said to him, "Take care of my lambs." [16]A second time Jesus said to him, "Simon son of John, do you love me?"

"Yes, Lord," he answered, "you know that I love you."

Jesus said to him, "Take care of my sheep." [17]A third time Jesus said, "Simon son of John, do you love me?"

Peter became sad because Jesus asked him the third time, "Do you love me?" and so he said to him, "Lord, you know everything; you know that I love you!"

Jesus said to him, "Take care of my sheep. [18]I am telling you the truth: when you were young, you used to get ready and go anywhere you wanted to; but when you are old, you will stretch out your hands and someone else will tie you up and take you where you don't want to go." [19](In saying this, Jesus was indicating the way in which Peter would die and bring glory to God.) Then Jesus said to him, "Follow me!"

[20]Peter turned around and saw behind him that other disciple, whom Jesus loved—the one who had leaned close to Jesus at the meal and had asked, "Lord, who is going to betray you?" [21]When Peter saw him, he asked Jesus, "Lord, what about this man?"

[22]Jesus answered him, "If I want him to live until I come, what is that to you? Follow me!"

[23]So a report spread among the followers of Jesus that this disciple would not die. But Jesus did not say he would not die; he said, "If I want him to live until I come, what is that to you?"

[24]He is the disciple who spoke of these things, the one who also wrote them down; and we know that what he said is true.

[25]Now, there are many other things that Jesus did. If they were all written down one by one, I suppose that the whole world could not hold the books that would be written.

There is unfinished business with Peter. The scattered disciples have been brought into unity, but Peter's threefold denial of Jesus (13:36–38; 18:15–18, 25–27) is a special case that must now be dealt with. The three denials must be canceled by three affirmations. In addressing Peter each time as **Simon son of John** (vv. 15, 16, 17), Jesus speaks to him as if he were no longer (or not yet!) a disciple, for he goes back to the name Peter had when he and Jesus first met (cf. 1:42).

The framework for the set of questions is the principle, "If you love me, you will obey my commandments" (14:15). Jesus had said: "Whoever accepts my commandments and obeys them is the one who loves me. . . . I too will love him and reveal myself to him" (14:21; cf. 14:23). The form of the first question to Peter, **Do you love me more than these others do?** (v. 15) presupposes that all seven disciples love Jesus—as evidenced by the fact that Jesus has just revealed himself to them (v. 14). The purpose of the question is not to set Peter in competition with the other disciples (cf. Mark 14:29) but simply to single him out from the rest and examine his love in particular. The question marks a transition from the appearance narrative to the last half of the chapter, a transition that Peter's impetuous actions in verses 7 and 11 might have led the reader to expect.

The thrice-repeated pattern of question, answer, and commandment can be shown as follows:

Jesus' Question	Peter's Answer	Jesus' Command
1. **Simon son of John, do you love me more than these others do?**	1. **Yes, Lord . . . you know that I love you.**	1. **Take care of my lambs.**
2. **Simon son of John, do you love me?**	2. **Yes, Lord . . . you know that I love you.**	2. **Take care of my sheep.**
3. **Simon son of John, do you love me?**	3. **Lord, you know everything; you know that I love you!**	3. **Take care of my sheep.**

There is a fondness for synonyms in this exchange—two different Greek words for **love**, two words for **take care of**, and different words for **lambs** and **sheep**—yet the narrator's interest is in the repetition of the same thought, not in subtle differences in meaning of particular words. Peter is saddened (v. 17) by the persistent repeating of a question he has already answered, but the purpose of the repetition is to match his earlier triple denial and to elicit from him a firm commitment to continue the Shepherd's work during the time of the Shepherd's absence. If he truly loves Jesus, he must obey Jesus' commandments, and for him the single command is **Take care of my sheep** (cf. 10:7–16). Peter is here given a pastoral responsibility among Jesus' followers, to help see to it that what the unbroken net represents will come true in fact—that is, that none who belong to Jesus will be lost.

A good shepherd, Jesus had said, "is willing to die for the sheep" (10:11, 15), and it is not surprising that the mention of Peter's pastoral responsibility leads into a reflection on his eventual death (vv. 18–19; cf. 13:36, "later you will follow me"). Peter himself had adopted the terminology of the shepherd discourse in 13:37 ("I am ready to die for you!"), yet without any specific awareness of his responsibilities to his fellow disciples. Now Jesus returns to the subject of Peter's death in its proper context and against the appropriate background of his ministry as faithful shepherd to Jesus' flock. Jesus speaks solemnly to Peter, using the same formula ("I am telling you the truth"; Gr.: *amēn amēn*) with which he had earlier predicted Peter's denial (13:38; see note on 1:51). The saying that the formula introduces is based on a kind of proverb about youth and old age, but to Peter it must have seemed more like a riddle. Two conditions of humanity are being contrasted (v. 18, NIV):

when you were younger	when you are old
you dressed yourself	you will stretch out your hands, and someone else will dress you
and went where you wanted	and lead you where you do not want to go

The contrast seems perfect except for the expression **you will stretch out your hands**, which has no precise equivalent in the "youth" column. It appears to be an old man's gesture of helplessness or resignation preliminary to receiving assistance from others—at the cost, inevitably, of personal freedom. But the narrator, conscious of being inspired by the Spirit, has taken it as a sign of death, probably by crucifixion. Jesus was **indicating**, he says, **the way in which Peter would die and bring glory to God** (v. 19; the word **indicating** in Greek is *sēmainōn*, lit., "giving a sign"). But in contrast to 12:33, where the same terminology is used of Jesus' crucifixion (Jesus "indicated [Gr.: *sēmainōn*] the kind of death he was going to suffer"), Peter's death does not consist in being "lifted up" (cf. 12:32). Jesus' crucifixion is unique because it accomplishes and proclaims God's once-and-for-all victory over death. Peter's crucifixion (*if* that is the mode of death indicated) is simply the result of a disciple being faithful to his master, yet like the death of anyone loyal to Jesus, it brings **glory to God** (v. 19). In words drawn from other passages in the Gospel, it could be said that Peter would "eat the flesh of the Son of Man and drink his blood" (6:53) or that, as Jesus' servant, he would follow Jesus "so that my servant will be with me where I am" (12:26; cf. 13:38). But Jesus says simply, **Follow me!** (v. 19b), and leaves Peter to infer what the reader of the Gospel already knows, that he will follow Jesus to a violent death. Once again a good shepherd will die taking care of his sheep (10:11, 15; cf. 15:20, 16:2–4).

The final interplay between Peter and the beloved disciple (vv. 20–22) sets the stage for the Gospel's conclusion. The presence of the beloved disciple dramatizes the fact that there is more than one model for true discipleship, for he too was "following" Jesus (v. 20, NIV). Whether Peter heard the riddle of verse 18 as an outright prediction of death or not, he could hardly have missed the implication that something unpleasant was in store for him, and he wanted to know if the beloved disciple was to share the same fate (v. 21). Because this exchange is preliminary to the most significant information to be given about this disciple—that is, that he is the Gospel's author (v. 24)—he is identified (v. 20b) once again in terms of the scene in which he was first introduced (or introduced himself) to the Gospel's readers, 13:23–25. The thrust of Jesus' blunt answer to Peter is that the beloved disciple's fate is none of Peter's business: **If I want him to live until I come, what is that to you?** (v. 22). Discipleship implies a specific level of commitment but not a specific outcome to one's life. Everyone who would be a disciple must yield total obedience to the call and command of God, but the call and command is not the same for every person. For Peter, "following" meant an "imitation of Jesus" as shepherd, ending in a death that would be analogous (though not identical) to his. For the beloved disciple it meant something quite different. Jesus does not tell Peter what that something is, but he implies that the beloved disciple will **live** (Gr.: *menein*, lit., "remain") rather than die, at least that he will outlive Peter. It is in any case not Peter's concern. Jesus brings the brief exchange to an end by reiterating the command that triggered it: **Follow me!** (lit., "As for you, follow me!").

The narrative ends by looking back on the last words of the risen Jesus from the Gospel's later time perspective. Over the years the report had gone out among Christians (on the basis of Jesus' final statement to Peter) **that this disciple would not die** (v. 23). A clarification is given: Jesus did not promise that the beloved disciple would not die (i.e., that he would live until Jesus' Second Coming) but merely said that *if* this should happen, it was Jesus' choice (and implicitly the Father's), not Peter's. The clarification could have become necessary either because the beloved disciple had died by the time these words were written, or because there was a distinct possibility that he might die. If Jesus' statement in verse 22 were taken as a firm promise, and if the beloved disciple then died, the certainty of the Second Coming itself would be called into question. Although Jesus' Second Coming has not been a major theme in this Gospel (cf. only 14:3), the hope of it must not be made to depend on the survival of a single individual. Though Jesus had promised that "whoever obeys my teaching will never die" (8:51; cf. 11:26), he knew that *physical* death, at least, would be a continuing reality in the world and that none of his followers could be presumed to be exempt from it. His enduring promise was not that any particular person could be certain of living until his return, but that "whoever believes in me will live, even though he dies" (11:25) and "I will raise him to life on the last day" (6:44, 54).

It is not altogether evident who is making the clarification expressed in verse 23. Is it the beloved disciple himself, or someone else? Another voice makes itself heard in verse 24: **He is the disciple who spoke of these things, the one who also wrote them down; and we know that what he said is true**. The beloved disciple is here identified, not only as the source of the material to be found in the Gospel of John as a whole, but as the one who actually wrote it. The claim is that he is the Gospel's author, and therefore, one would assume, its narrator as well. Yet he is not the narrator in verse 24 itself. Someone else is vouching for his authority: **we know that what he said is true**. It is likely that the same person or group that appended verse 24 is responsible for verse 23 as well, and indeed for all the references to the beloved disciple throughout the last part of the Gospel. Since each of these is integral to the narrative in which it is found, a distinction should be observed in some places between the *author*, who first put the Gospel into writing, and the *narrator*(s) who edited what was written in such a way as to do justice to the author's own participation in the story while at the same time respecting his anonymity. Though the Gospel in its essentials was first compiled by "the disciple whom Jesus loved," its final form is probably the work of those who identify themselves as **we** in verse 24. Their actual identity can only be conjectured; their link with the beloved disciple is apparently close, and the most plausible theory is that they are the leaders of the church to which he belongs and which he perhaps founded, writing either shortly before or shortly after his death.

One of them adds a final word on behalf of the group in verse 25, a postscript modeled to some extent on 20:30. Its apparent purpose is to defend the Gospel against charges of incompleteness, or criticisms that this or that favorite or familiar story about Jesus (perhaps especially from the synoptic traditions) has been omitted. The **I suppose** with which the scribe brings the Gospel to an end allows him to stand out momentarily from the **we** of verse 24, and even indulge himself in a bit of literary imagination: Jesus' deeds could fill enough books to fill the whole world, and more!

Additional Notes

21:17 / **The third time**: This **third time** Jesus uses a different verb for **love** (Gr.: *philein*, the verb Peter has been using, rather than *agapan*, the verb Jesus used in vv. 15 and 16). But Peter is sad because of the repetition of the question, not because Jesus has changed verbs.

21:18 / **Stretch out your hands**: Applications of this idiom to crucifixion are found in early Christian citations of Isa. 65:2 ("I spread out my hands all the day to a rebellious people," RSV) and in early Christian reflections on the extended arms of Moses in Exod. 17:12 (see, e.g., *Barnabas* 12.2, 4).

Tie you up: This translation conceals the fact that the same word previously translated "get ready" is being used again. The emphasis is not on being tied up, but simply on being dressed (lit., "girded") in order to be taken somewhere. The contrast is between acting on one's own initiative in v. 18a, and being entirely subject to the initiative of others in v. 18b. Contrast Jesus' death on his own initiative according to 10:17–18 and 19:30.

21:23 / **The followers of Jesus**: lit., "the brothers." The use of this term for the Christian community (whether in one congregation or over a wide geographical area) is more characteristic of the Epistles of John than of the Gospel (e.g., 1 John 3:14, 16; 3 John 5), though it may be regarded as a natural extension of Jesus' designation for his disciples in 20:17.

But Jesus did not say: The Greek adds the words, "to him," at this point. GNB probably left the phrase untranslated because its antecedent is unclear. It could refer to Peter—as v. 22 and the direct quotation of what was said to Peter might suggest—or it could refer to the beloved disciple himself (note in the immediate context the phrases **this disciple** and **he would not die**). The former is probably intended.

21:25 / **The books that would be written**: The statement implies that the Gospel here being concluded is also regarded as a **book** or "scroll" (Gr.: *biblion*). The term offers no clue to the Gospel's literary genre, however, for it means simply a book or scroll regarded as a physical object that fills up space, not a distinct literary type.

Abbreviations

AB	Anchor Bible
ANF	Ante-Nicene Fathers
AV	*See* KJV
BDF	F. Blass and A. Debrunner, *A Greek Grammar of the New Testament and Other Early Christian Literature.* Translated and revised by R. W. Funk (Chicago: University of Chicago Press, 1961)
GNB	Good News Bible
HNTC	Harper New Testament Commentary
ICC	International Critical Commentary
JBL	*Journal of Biblical Literature*
KJV	Authorized King James Version
LCL	Loeb Classical Library
LXX	Septuagint (Greek translation of the Old Testament)
NAB	New American Bible
NCB	New Century Bible
NEB	New English Bible
NICNT	New International Commentary on the New Testament
NIV	New International Version
NT	New Testament
OT	Old Testament
Ps. Sol	Psalms of Solomon
1QH	the Qumran *Hymns*
1QS	the Qumran *Manual of Discipline*
RSV	Revised Standard Version

For Further Reading

Commentaries

Barrett, C. K. *The Gospel According to St. John*. 2d ed. Philadelphia: Westminster, 1978.

Bernard, J.H. *A Critical and Exegetical Commentary on the Gospel According to St. John*. Edited by A. H. McNeile. ICC. 2 vols. Edinburgh: T & T Clark, 1928.

Brown, R. E. *The Gospel According to John*. AB. 2 vols. (New York: Doubleday, 1966 and 1970).

Bultmann, R. *The Gospel of John: A Commentary*. Translated by G. R. Beasley-Murray, R. W. N. Hoare, and J. K. Riches. Philadelphia: Westminster, 1971.

Hendriksen, W. *New Testament Commentary. Exposition of the Gospel According to John*. Grand Rapids: Baker, 1967.

Hoskyns, E. C. *The Fourth Gospel*. 2d ed. Edited by F. N. Davey. London: Faber & Faber, 1947.

Kent, H. A. *Light in the Darkness, Studies in the Gospel of John*. Winona Lake: BMH, 1974.

Lightfoot, R. H. *St. John's Gospel: A Commentary*. Edited by C. F. Evans. Oxford: Oxford University Press, 1960.

Lindars, B. *The Gospel of John*. NCB. London: Oliphants, 1972.

MacRae, G. W. *Invitation to John*. New York: Doubleday/Image, 1978.

Morris, L. *The Gospel According to John*. NICNT. Grand Rapids: Eerdmans, 1971.

Newbigin, L. *The Light Has Come: An Exposition of the Fourth Gospel*. Grand Rapids: Eerdmans, 1982.

Perkins, P. *The Gospel According to St. John: A Theological Commentary*. Chicago: Franciscan Herald, 1978.

Sanders, J. N. *A Commentary on the Gospel According to St. John*. Edited by B. A. Mastin. HNTC. New York: Harper & Row, 1969.

Schnackenburg, R. *The Gospel According to St. John*. Vol. 1, translated by K. Smyth; vol. 2, translated by C. Hastings, F. McDonagh, D. Smith, and R. Foley. New York: Seabury, 1980.

Smith, D. M. *John*. Proclamation Commentaries. Philadelphia: Fortress, 1976.

Strachan, R. H. *The Fourth Gospel: Its Significance and Environment*. 3d ed. London: SCM, 1941.

Tasker, R. V. G. *The Gospel According to St. John*. Tyndale Commentary. Grand Rapids: Eerdmans, 1972.

Temple, W. *Readings in St. John's Gospel.* London: Macmillan, 1961.

Tenney, M. C. *John: the Gospel of Belief.* Grand Rapids: Eerdmans, 1953.

Westcott, B. F. *The Gospel According to St. John.* Grand Rapids: Eerdmans, 1950; reprint of 1881 edition.

Other Works: Background, Style, Theology

Abbott, E. A. *Johannine Grammar.* London: Adam & Charles Black, 1906.

———. *Johannine Vocabulary.* London: Adam & Charles Black, 1905.

Boice, J. M. *Witness and Revelation in the Gospel of John.* Grand Rapids: Zondervan, 1970.

Brown, R. E. *The Community of the Beloved Disciple.* New York: Paulist, 1979.

Corell, A. *Consummatum Est. Eschatology and Church in the Gospel of St. John.* London: S.P.C.K., 1958.

Cullman, O. *Early Christian Worship.* London: SCM, 1959.

———. *The Johannine Circle.* Translated by J. Bowden. London: SCM, 1976.

Dodd, C. H. *Historical Tradition in the Fourth Gospel.* Cambridge: Cambridge University Press, 1963.

———. *The Interpretation of the Fourth Gospel.* Cambridge: Cambridge University Press, 1958.

Fortna, R. T. *The Gospel of Signs.* Cambridge: Cambridge University Press, 1970.

Harner, P. B. *The "I Am" of the Fourth Gospel: A Study in Johannine Usage and Thought.* Philadelphia: Fortress, 1970.

Harvey, A. E. *Jesus on Trial: A Study in the Fourth Gospel.* Atlanta: John Knox, 1976.

Howard, W. F. *Christianity According to John.* London: Duckworth, 1958.

Käsemann, E. *The Testament of Jesus.* Translated by G. Krodel. Philadelphia: Fortress, 1968.

Kysar, R. *John the Maverick Gospel.* Atlanta: John Knox, 1976.

Lindars, B. *Behind the Fourth Gospel.* London: SPCK, 1971.

MacRae, G. W. *Faith in the Word: The Fourth Gospel.* Chicago: Franciscan Herald, 1973.

Martyn, J. L. *History and Theology in the Fourth Gospel.* 2d ed. Nashville: Abingdon, 1979.

Moloney, F. J. *The Johannine Son of Man*. Rome: LAS, 1976.

Mussner, F. *The Historical Jesus in the Gospel of John*. New York: Herder & Herder, 1967.

Nicol, W. *The Sēmeia in the Fourth Gospel*. Leiden: Brill, 1972.

Odeberg, H. *The Fourth Gospel*. Amsterdam: Grüner, 1968; reprint of 1929 edition.

Painter, J. *Reading John's Gospel Today*. Atlanta: John Knox, 1980.

Schein, B. E. *Following the Way: The Setting of John's Gospel*. Minneapolis: Augsburg, 1980.

Segovia, F. F. *Love Relationships in the Johannine Tradition*. Chico, Cal.: Scholars Press, 1982.

Smalley, S. S. *John: Evangelist and Interpreter*. Exeter: Paternoster, 1978.

Smith, D. M. *The Composition and Order of the Fourth Gospel*. New Haven: Yale University Press, 1965.

Whitacre, R. A. *Johannine Polemic: The Role of Tradition and Theology*. Chico, Cal.: Scholars Press, 1982.

History of Interpretation and Further Bibliography

Howard, W. F. *The Fourth Gospel in Recent Criticism and Interpretation*. 4th ed. Revised by C. K. Barrett. London: Epworth, 1955.

Kysar, R. *The Fourth Evangelist and His Gospel*. Minneapolis: Augsburg, 1975.

Malatesta, E. *St. John's Gospel 1920–1965: A Cumulative and Classified Bibliography*. Rome: Pontifical Biblical Institute, 1967.

Subject Index

Scripture Index

APOCRYPHA

NONCANONICAL BOOKS